Trawler

Trawler

A Journey through the North Atlantic

REDMOND O'HANLON

HAMISH HAMILTON
an imprint of
PENGUIN BOOKS

HAMISH HAMILTON

Published by the Penguin Group
Penguin Books Ltd, 80 Strand, London WC2R ORL, England
Penguin Putnam Inc., 375 Hudson Street, New York, New York 10014, USA
Penguin Books Australia Ltd, 250 Camberwell Road, Camberwell, Victoria 3124, Australia
Penguin Books Canada Ltd, 10 Alcorn Avenue, Toronto, Ontario, Canada M4V 3B2
Penguin Books India (P) Ltd, 11 Community Centre, Panchsheel Park, New Delhi – 110 017, India
Penguin Books (NZ) Ltd, Cnr Rosedale and Airborne Roads, Albany, Auckland, New Zealand
Penguin Books (South Africa) (Pty) Ltd, 24 Sturdee Avenue, Rosebank 2196, South Africa

Penguin Books Ltd, Registered Offices: 80 Strand, London WC2R ORL, England

www.penguin.com

First published 2003
5

Set in 12/14.75 pt Monotype Bembo
Typeset by Rowland Phototypesetting Ltd, Bury St Edmunds, Suffolk
Printed in Great Britain by Clays Ltd, St Ives plc

A CIP catalogue record for this book is available from the British Library

HB ISBN 0 – 241 – 14014 – 5
TPB ISBN 0 – 241 – 14015 – 3

To my wife Belinda

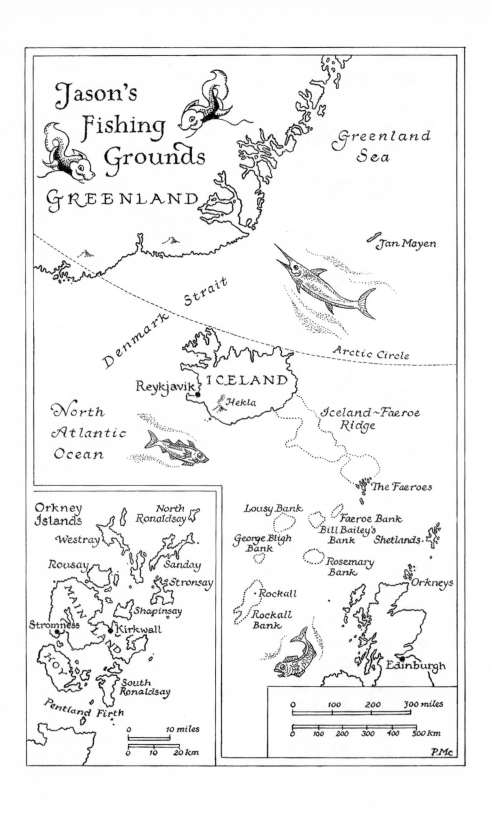

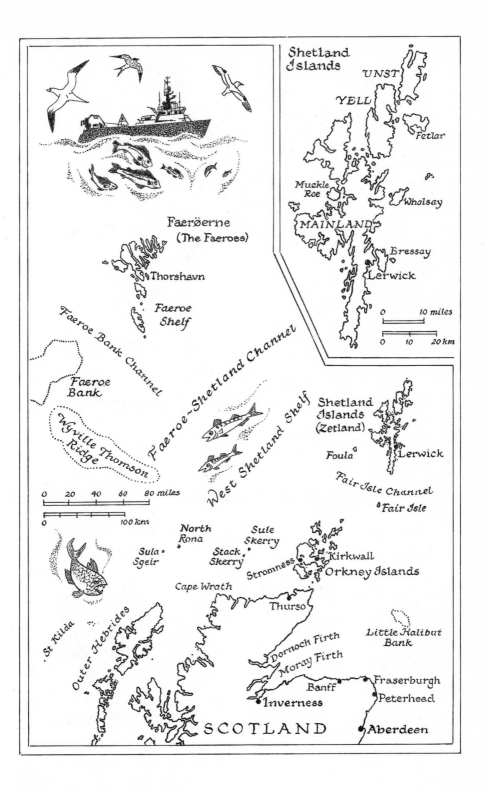

Shetland Islands

UNST

YELL

Fetlar

Muckle Roe

Wholsay

MAINLAND

Bressay

Lerwick

0   10 miles

0   10   20 km

Faeröerne
(The Faeroes)

Thorshavn

Faeroe
Shelf

Faeroe Bank Channel

Faeroe
Bank

Wyville Thomson Ridge

Faeroe-Shetland Channel

West Shetland Shelf

Shetland
Islands
(Zetland)

Foula

Lerwick

Fair Isle Channel

Fair Isle

0   20   40   60   80 miles

0   100 km

North
Rona

Sule
Skerry

Sula
Sgeir

Stack
Skerry

Stromness

Kirkwall

Orkney Islands

Cape Wrath

Thurso

St Kilda

Little Halibut
Bank

Outer Hebrides

Dornoch Firth

Moray Firth

Banff

Fraserburgh

Peterhead

Inverness

SCOTLAND

Aberdeen

'Redmond, you've got to get up here, fast. There's a storm coming in, big style! I have the satellite maps. Force 11, maybe more. Straight for Orkney. And Jason, the *Norlantean* skipper – he's called on Cellnet. He's north-west of Shetland. He says the weather's horrendous. And getting worse. Perfect! Just what you wanted! He says we sign on at Scrabster, Saturday, two days' time, 7 a.m., no later. OK? Good. So pick me up at home – 19 Pilot Square, Fittie. Be there! And remember – *nothing green.*'

The speaker was Luke Bullough, probably the toughest (and certainly the most modest) young man I'd ever met. A biologist at the Marine Laboratory, Aberdeen, a member of the Aberdeen lifeboat crew, he was a man with a vast experience of the real sea: as a research diver in Antarctica; as a Fisheries Patrol officer in the Falklands; on trawlers and research ships in the North Atlantic. Whereas me? Well, I've crewed very small sailing dinghies in races round plastic buoys in sheltered bays; and, oh yes, I almost forgot, I've taken passage on those cross channel car-ferries.

So this is it, I told myself, as I sat heavily down on the chair beside the telephone, by the front door of the small, snug, safe, warm house; by the door that let on to the ancient, stable, peaceful, comforting landscape of Oxfordshire. Yes, here's the defining moment – the one telephone call you've spent nine months trying to persuade to come your way.

Five hundred miles and one day later, in Aberdeen, on the dockside, I turned up a sidestreet in my little dark-green Renault Clio and parked beside one of my favourite hotels: the St Magnus Court. A four-storey block built of grey Aberdonian granite, its front embellished with three outflung projecting turrets, a large one at each corner, a little one off-centre above the drainpipe, it distrusts all who enter. The ground floor is occupied by a betting shop to the left, a bar to the right; a sticker on the hotel front-door proclaims: THIS IS A DRUG FREE ZONE. An electronic beam sets off a single stroke of an alarm bell as you step inside: *Ping!* ('a wandering psychopathic serial killer has just forced his way into this hotel'); there's another half-way up the stairs: *Ping!* ('he's on his way up!'); and, in front of the reception desk, there's a third – but this one you can annoy by walking in a tight circle: *Ping! Ping! Ping!* ('My god, he wants to *stay*. We have a madman on the premises!')

I checked into my large, tall, cheap, airy room, dumped my bags on the bed, and *ping*ed my way back out to the street. The very next building to the left, low-slung, with a roof pitched like canvas on a tent, is the *Lucky Boat Chinese Restaurant and Takeaway*. So, in the empty restaurant, I pot-bellied-pigged myself on McEwan's Export and crispy wan ton, on Lucky Boat Special prawns-with-everything, on lychees and McEwan's Export. I asked the young Chinese waitress, 'Is it always this quiet?'

'No, no,' she said, insulted. 'Last week we have knives! We have *murdah*!'

At three-thirty in the morning I drove east along the harbour: to my left stretched a long granite frontage of dockside pubs, ship's chandlers, marine insurance agencies, the office of the Port Authority; to my right the oil industry ships were berthed, sometimes three abreast: oil-rig supply-vessels, oil-field exploration ships, lit by their security lights, their orange-and-white shapes a confusion of radar pods, scanners, helicopter pads, derricks, cranes, Eiffel towers of scaffolding. The road swung left by the entrance to the lifeboat sheds, and past (I thought) the massive blue-and-white bow of an ice-breaker, past derelict ship-building yards, past the high darkness of nineteenth-century warehouses and on to a wide, cobble-and-tarmac-patch street. I turned right, over a narrow granite bridge, and into an earlier world, Fittie.

Fittie is a village at the harbour-mouth, set against the sea. Arranged in a series of quadrangles like an Oxford college, its attached rows of small granite houses (three rooms up, three down) face into their squares, opening only on to their tiny, compressed reminders of safe, farm-labouring cottage Britain: each with its own central patch of grass, flowers, a garden shed. Yes, I know, I thought – these garden sheds were once fishermen's bothies, huts built for the storage of nets and floats and lobster pots, but that's the point: the men who lived here, the fishermen, the whalers (the men who gave Aberdeen its first oil-boom, whose hunting voyages lit these same lamps, the city, the country with oil) – and, especially, the pilots who, in their open boats, in all weathers, had to race each other to win the work on an incoming ship: why did they want to live like this? Were their small fortresses designed, like an Oxford college, sensibly enough, to keep quiet work in and political chaos, lawlessness, out? No, of course not, I thought, as I knocked softly on the door of 19 Pilot Square: this is far more interesting because it's plainly psychological: no one who earns his living from the real chaos of the sea would want to look at it as he goes to sleep – no, these squares are defensive only in the mind; in here, it's peace, the female, sex, the wife, domesticity, children, the deep rewards of life. Out there it's . . .

'Shush! Quiet!' hissed Luke, index finger against his lips, easing the door ajar. 'Quiet! It's Ally – my new girlfriend. She's special. She's asleep. *Don't wake her.* Quiet!'

Dressed in his usual blue-denim shirt and jeans, Luke yet seemed even more athletic, compact, intense (and, somehow, more apologetic) than I'd remembered him. I followed him down a short passage, a closed door to either side, and into the kitchen. 'It's Alison,' he said, making me a coffee. 'You know – I told you. It's so difficult, to choose, all that. And I *hate* hurting people. I really do. But maybe you can help me – you see, it's like this: I think I'm in love.'

'I'm sure you are,' I said, collapsing on to a chair at the small wooden table. 'That's great. Well done.' (I know, I thought, *come on*, you could try a little harder: but then it *is* four in the morning, the hour when all body systems take a dip, when the body clock gives up, and when, statistically speaking, old people like you decide to roll over and die in their sleep.)

'No, no, *I told you*,' said Luke, placing a mug in front of me, taking the seat to my left. 'It's difficult for me. It always has been.' He put his elbows on the table and ran both hands up over his young but weathered face, his black curly hair. 'I can't make up my mind. I want to stop all this. I want to settle down. I want to have children. You know, all that. But I can't *choose*. It's my fault,

4

I've hurt so many people, but I don't know why – that's the problem – I can't help it. Ally: she's different, Redmond, she really is. I didn't know it was possible to have such, well, good sex. You know. *She cares.* She's a top accountant with an oil company. And here she is with me: nothing but a mature student working for his Ph.D. on £7,000 a year. Marine biology. It's not her thing. And she hates my life, she really does – the call-outs for the lifeboat, the risk, I suppose, even the trawlers, I don't know.'

Luke lifted his head. He looked straight at me. He brightened. He smiled. 'And she hates you, too, come to that. You see, you must understand, I know you do – for my own research into the deep-sea fisheries, the correlations between temperature and depth and current for these newly commercial species, 1,000 to 1,500 metres down or more – I can go out whenever I want: it does not have to be at the most dangerous time of year. It's very little to do with surface conditions. *It does not have to be in January.*'

'Uh.'

'Anyway – Ally. She's different. All this is new for me. I told you, on the *Scotia* – you won't remember – but I've joined a nightclub, a rock-and-roll dance-club. And now I get in for free: because I'm an instructor. It's *full* of girls. That's where I met her.'

'Luke – of course I can help you! I have a plan. If we survive this trip – if we're not swept overboard – then we'll be pleased, right? So you propose to this Ally of yours – and I'll give you a party at your favourite pub. An engagement party!'

Luke fell silent. He faced away. He felt in his pocket and, producing his plastic pouch of Golden Virginia and Rizla papers, he rolled himself, with mind-absent speed, a spindly toothpick of a cigarette. 'Redmond, you're so very . . .' he said, slowly, concentrating hard, inhaling, '*old-fashioned*. And as for being swept overboard – well, I don't quite know how to tell you this – but Dick, at the lab, the guy you met on the *Scotia*, he got emotional, he really did, he said he felt responsible. And he did something he's *never* done before. You see, he has a thing about his survival suit.

5

He's teased about it. He's very particular. It's a joke. He won't let *anyone* borrow it. He's superstitious. But he brought it to me at my desk in our office. Right there. Eleven o'clock. The coffee break. In front of everyone. He said, "Look, if you bring this back, and *it smells of fish* – I'll kill you. But I'm trusting you, Luke, it's your job. And if anything happens, it's your fault. Because that Redmond, unlike most people I've met, he's not a shit. Or, at least, he's not a complete shit. But it's obvious," he said – and excuse me, but *he* said it, not me, "that Redmond," he said, "it's obvious, when it comes to life at sea, he doesn't know *his arse from his tit*. And for Chrissake, Luke, in this department we can all see it on the fucking satellite pictures – you're planning to take this idiot straight into a hurricane."'

'I see,' I said, feeling, despite an instant effort, emptied of all confidence in anything whatever. I looked away myself: at the surrounds of student Bohemian life, at haphazard posters and post-cards on the wall, at the mess of unwashed everything by the sink, at the many-coloured beer cans in blossom above the bin, and, as I watched, all its young attraction drained away. If that's what Dick said, I thought, then this is serious, because Dick Adams is no ordinary academic physical oceanographer. No: he's an ex-Royal Marine diver, an ex-member of the élite SBS, the Special Boat Service, a man who's seen action in Suez, in the Borneo campaign and, no doubt, in many other impossible places known only to his unit. And if a mere trawler, a commercial trawler, for heaven's sake – if he thinks that's not a good idea, then maybe I'm not just lazy-afraid ('why get out of your bed for this?') but straight-afraid ('will I ever see my delicious stinking pit again?') . . .

'Hey Redmond!' said Luke, getting to his feet with excessive energy, throwing the bug-proboscis stub of his cigarette into the sink. 'You can't just sit there dreaming! We must go. A trawler skipper – he can't afford to wait. Not for anyone.'

Under the dull street-lamp, a cold wind from the sea, a stinging slanted rain, revived me. We filled the hatchback with Luke's equipment from Her Majesty's Government's Marine Laboratory, Aberdeen: boxes of specimen jars, bottles, labels, preservative fluids; a large electronic fish-weighing machine in an aluminium case; deep-sea-net temperature-loggers boxed with two small computers; a large plastic basket of oilskins, survival suits, sea-boots with steel toe-caps; and a mysterious stack of blue and red plastic biscuit-boxes.

To the north-west of Aberdeen, as the little car, struggling with its load, climbed, very slowly, the eastern foothills of the Grampian mountains, it began to snow: big, unhurried flakes, soft in the headlights, fluffy on the windscreen. In the small town of Nairn, on the Moray Firth, we found an early lighted café and a Scottish breakfast (mugs of tea, buttered toast, two fried eggs, sausages, black pudding, a half-pig pile of bacon – and all for £1.50 each).

'Luke, I have a question.' In the fug of fry and steam and comfort, there loomed and disappeared an elemental mother of a waitress. (Why can't we just settle down and *live* in such places? Why does breakfast ever have to end?) 'Luke – what made you say no green, nothing green? For me – that's a new one. I've never heard of it. I know you must never mention pigs or rabbits or foxes or cows or even salmon if you're at sea, if you're a trawlerman. Because – I suppose – it's disabling, it reminds you of life ashore. But green? What's that? Grass?'

'Search me,' said Luke, soaking up a leakage of egg yolk with a piece of toast. 'It makes no sense. After all – with a phytoplankton bloom the sea itself turns green; and nowadays the nets are green. All I know is this – there was a Fisheries officer, in some temporary post, from Singapore or somewhere, and they sent him out on a trawler from one of the Northern Isles. Well, he was a man who liked his clothes, you know, his shore clothes. And one evening he went up to the wheelhouse in a green suit. No one said a word. They *stopped fishing*.'

'Ah.'

'Yes. They went way off course. They took him to Norway. To

7

Bergen. They put him ashore with his bags of kit. They left him there.'

'They did?' I said feebly, wondering if a green sleeping-bag would be OK. And, 'I know about priests, ministers,' I said, trying not to be so ignorant, as we returned to the car. 'You must always turn back if you see a minister on your way to the boat. And no woman must set foot on your deck – or even touch the guard rails.'

'Yes, that's right – and you can't leave harbour on a Friday. But nowadays, Redmond, it's more complicated, not less. Your wife, for instance, whatever happens, she must *never* use the washing machine on the weekend before you go. Because it's like the sea, the whirlpool – she'll be washing your soul away.'

'Sympathetic magic!' I said, edging the car into the empty street, peering through the still ice-misty screen. 'Now I *do* know about that. It's like the Congo. Except, of course, that they have no washing machines. At least, not where I was . . .'

'Washout!' said Luke, as I mounted the central reservation, and, very cleverly, missed a bollard. 'Redmond!'

'Yes – that really is interesting. It's exciting – don't you see? It really *is* the same as life in the upper Congo. You tell me that trawlermen have the highest death-rate of any workers in Britain.'

'Yeah,' said Luke, frantically wiping the windscreen with his handkerchief. 'Yesterday – we got the official figures for 1998. Bang up to date. From the Marine Accident Investigation Branch of the Department of the Environment, Transport and Regions. There were 388 accidents involving United Kingdom fishing vessels. There were twenty-six fatalities. There were twenty-six vessels lost.'

We drove north over the bridge at Inverness, north across the Black Isle, north into the Highlands proper, in silence. The snowflakes no longer seemed so benign: they were smaller, manic, and they flew at us horizontally. 'This,' said Luke, 'is a blizzard. I think we may now, officially, call this a blizzard.' Up the long, twisting slopes of road, the little car's wheels spun, but, to my surprise, gained a constant purchase: because, I supposed, it was carrying the heaviest load of its life. There were no tracks of any kind in front of us, and no tracks to our right. Everyone was staying at home.

'So that's it!' I said, as a weak dawn filtered down to us, and the blizzard became less personal. 'Trawlermen protect themselves – mentally – because they must; they need it. So it *is* like the animism of the Congo. And for the same reason – the *immediate* press of death. So you surround yourself with a hundred little irrational fears, because you have to, because that's all there is to protect you against the big one. Your friend drowns? Sure. But someone was wearing a green sweater, or someone said pig or rabbit or salmon. So, in large thought, that's OK. Because it means there really *is* a force out there that cares about you – it even cares about your speech, your dress-sense! So why worry? We did the wrong thing, we offended, that's all. So please, don't even *mention* the real fear – the ocean that covers two-thirds of the earth and couldn't possibly give a damn about anyone.'

'Redmond! *Please* – try and drive straight. Calm down. We're in good time. We're nearly there. We'll make it.'

(Drive straight? Well you can't, can you? Not in a car with an engine no bigger than a decent motorbike, not on fresh snow. And especially not when full dawn has arrived, when there's so much to look at, when the air is suddenly clear of snow – and those really huge, black-and-purple clouds to the north, with their eerie white underbellies: have I ever seen anything like it? No, excuse me, certainly not. Is that just reflected light from the snow-white landscape? Or a warning that every sailor would recognize? And besides, the fields here are bounded not with hedges or barbed wire, but with wide, thin, upright, interleaved slabs of sandstone. We are now passing through a world of irregular rectangles, of cemetery headstones that mark no grave, of monoliths that stretch away for ever to all the far horizons . . .)

9

'Hey Redmond!' said Luke, doing a quarter-roll in the passenger-seat, pulling out his tobacco pouch. 'Hello? Are you there? Look – if you have offended, if you've said any of the words that may kill everybody – you simply touch cold iron, pronto. And there's plenty of cold iron on deck.'

'But that's great, too! Late prehistory,' I said, as we drove gently through Thurso, the most northerly resort on the mainland (a town that is part hotels-and-pleasure, part wind-raked desperation). 'The early iron age – I'll have to check – 3,000 years ago? And Luke, I know, I really do, it's not the same – our own history in these islands is so short term, so *parochial*. That's what you were going to say, isn't it? Ten thousand years of settlement, no more than that; we've only been here from the end of the last ice age. Whereas in central or east Africa we first mutated into *Homo sapiens sapiens* – when? OK – it depends on which timing on the molecular clock you believe – certainly 200,000, maybe 250,000 years ago. But you see, I have a mad hunch: I'm sure that some of us were here *right through the last ice age*: on St Kilda. Because if an animal as absurdly fragile as the St Kilda wren could survive, then so could an isolated group of our robust hunter-gatherer forefathers.'

'Redmond?'

'Yes?'

'What the hell are you trying to say?'

'Eh? Well – it's obvious. Your trawlermen with their 1990s belief in the magical curative power of iron – that idea *must* go back at least 3,000 years. Imagine it – preserved in oral memory, the astonishment, the admiration for the successful experiments of the early scientists, for a handful of intellectuals: for the undeniable, the magic production of iron – the enabler!'

'Look, I'm sorry,' said Luke, as we left Thurso behind us. 'I know you love all that – magic, superstition, whatever. But, unlike you, I'm a *genuine* atheist. I'm a scientist. A marine biologist. If I thought in those terms, in that world – even for ten minutes a day, Redmond – I'd never be able to answer a lifeboat call-out on time;

I wouldn't join a trawler; I couldn't function; I couldn't do my job. I am *not* a social anthropologist. You see – I like the *external world*. The deep-sea octopus, for instance, the sea-bat. I've never seen one . . .' And then, 'Oh *Jesus*,' he said, as we turned to the right off the main road and topped the rise down to Scrabster harbour.

Luke took a hard suck on his catheter tube of a cigarette. 'Look, Redmond, OK – it won't mean anything to you – that's OK: but, you see, I've come here every month for years, I have to – I have to weigh and measure a random sample of set species from all the landings. But hey! Look at them! This is big style! *I've never seen anything like it.* Every single trawler is in. Everyone has run to shelter. It must be bad. It must be *very* bad out there!'

'So why – so why are we going out?' I said (or, rather, I sang, like a castrato, as my gubernacula retracted and my testes shot back to their safe, pre-pubescent hiding-places). 'Who *is* Jason Schofield? Luke – is this normal?'

'Normal?' said Luke, as he directed me, right (RESTRICTED ACCESS) away from the scag of cliffs, the desultory row of houses, and into the small working-area of the harbour proper. 'Normal?' he said, affronted. 'Normal? Certainly not!' ('Turn left – no, here!') 'You don't understand, Redmond, I can see that – it took me *months* to find this guy!' ('Up that ramp, for Chrissake! No, here!') 'And look – I only did all this because you made such a fuss on the *Scotia*. The worst time of year – all that bullshit.' ('Stop! Over there – *slow down*. Park – over there; there! Against the market shed!') 'Well, Redmond, here we are – and get this: I have never met Jason Schofield; I have never set eyes on the *Norlantean*. I did this for you – I asked around, I read the *Fishing News*, and everyone agreed: Jason would be perfect. He was a brilliant student at the Nautical College, in Stromness – Captain Sutherland's place; Jason really was and is exceptional, apparently; but, Redmond, the real point is this: he married into a big tough Orkney trawler dynasty and his father-in-law gave him a post-marriage test: he gave him a second-hand trawler right enough, but Jason had no white-fish quota – so he had to convert his trawler for the new deep-sea fishery. And the conversion cost him upwards of two *million* pounds. Jason, at thirty, has a *two million* pound overdraft. Imagine that! (As you would say.) So it goes like this: simple mathematics: he must bring in around £50,000 every ten days. And the bank? Do you think they know or care about the weather? Does a Force 11, or a Force 12, a junior hurricane – does that appear on your statement? Of course not! And that's the point – that's why he's perfect for you! He *has* to go out in the January storms. But he's exceptional, he's very successful, he's driven – he can *think* his way towards the fish. He's opened new fishing-grounds: and that's not surprising, so they say, because when he came into the world, when he was a baby, his cot – it was a regular plastic fish-box!'

'Well, Luke, er – *thank you*,' I said, as we got out of the warm protective cot of the car. And into the shock of a cold that was almost painful.

'Another layer,' said Luke, opening the hatchback. 'And oilskins.' So we pulled on our second sweaters (naval blue), took off our shoes in the slush, clambered into our oilskin trousers (his: yellow; mine: bright orange; and Luke showed me that it was possible not to strangle yourself in the curl of rubberized braces), put on our yellow sea-boots. To our left, the sixteen-wheeler articulated trucks, the giant refrigerated transports, waited in their loading bays. To our right, on the edge of the quay, a line of Herring gulls stood, at strict gull-personal-space intervals, between the big mooring-bollards, disconsolate, not in talking mode, staring out to sea, their feathers puffed up against the cold. Along to our left one of those derelict trawlers was berthed: her upper hull had once been painted orange, her wheelhouse and decking white; but she was now so streaked and stained and patterned with rust, her steel plates so bobbled with layers of paint and rust, that she seemed alive, to be herself and no one else, to have grown old and used and wrinkled, and was now, where she lay, close to death. To my surprise, I saw

12

that the diesel-tanker truck parked on the quay beside her actually had its fuel hose extended over her stern; that men in the back of a container lorry were lobbing empty white plastic fish-boxes on to her deck . . .

'The *Norlantean*!' said Luke, quickening his pace. 'Isn't she beautiful? What a conversion! Look at that! Wow! Redmond! You'd *never* guess she was the old *Dorothy Gray*!'

A young man with short dark hair and a prematurely ragged face, dressed in a red oilskin jacket, yellow oilskin trousers and blue rubber gloves, was chucking the white plastic boxes down through a hatch.

'Hi,' said Luke, and introduced us. 'We're from the Marine Lab. Can we stow our kit somewhere?'

'Aye,' said the young man, with a lopsided grin. 'I'm Sean, like the film-star. Dump it up on the bow.' He had a strong harsh Caithness accent. 'When you're ready I'll show you the cabin. And boys!' he called after us. 'Welcome aboard! And the forecast – it's for a Force 12!' He gave an explosive little laugh.

We transferred the luggage; I moved the car to a bleak little car-park over by the ship's chandlers – and when I returned Luke and Sean were standing chatting and smoking in the bow. Sean, with both hands, turned each of the four big locking-handles on the steel door to the shelter-deck; and we carried the metal boxes and plastic baskets and kit-bags inside, stacking them next to a line of lashed oil-drums, paint-cans, piles of coiled rope. The shelter-deck was U-shaped, built around the base of the bridge, a protective steel cowling, enclosed against the weather from the bow, open at both ends aft to the working deck. Round on the starboard side was a narrow steel door, roped open, leading to the wheelhouse and the lower decks.

'No workclothes inside, boys,' said Sean, tugging his jacket over his head, dropping it on the deck and stepping neatly out of his trousers and boots. 'The skipper won't have it.'

In domestic dress, we followed him over the high steel sill of the door; in front of us steps led up to the wheelhouse; to our immediate right a steep stairwell led down to the lower decks. Sean grasped the rails, raised his thighs at right angles to his body, and, in a blur of blue sweater and blue jeans, slid down into the depths and disappeared. Luke, facing forward, sprang down the stairs after him; and I followed, slowly, one foot per step, facing backwards.

'Three crew cabins,' said Sean standing in the dimly lit passage, jerking his thumb at the doors. There was a full wraparound smell of rotten fish and, after the sharp wind on deck, no air to breathe. More or less intact imitation-wood brown panels covered the steel walls and ceiling; cut-out sides of cardboard boxes formed a sensible, easy-to-clean, bung-overboard carpet: it was obvious that no woman had ever entered this place.

'The galley's down there.' Sean's face broke into an emphatic, grotesque, infectious grin; his bloodshot eyes lit up with pleasure; it was clear that there was no guile in him; it was clear that he was everybody's friend.

'And I'm the Second Cook!' He nodded towards two closed doors opposite the galley, to starboard. 'The skipper's cabin! The engineer's cabin! They've got tellies in there! OK, boys – there's yer berths!' (A door right forward, to port.) 'Must go! See ya!' And he went back up the stairwell like a springbok.

'Smashing,' said Luke, opening the door. 'He's a smashing guy. But he'll poison us.'

Four bunks, in two tiers, filled the dark, airless cabin. Luke said, as one practised in such matters: 'Lights? Lockers? Toilet? Shower?' He threw a heavy metal switch by the door and a lamp (in industrial, protective casing) came on: by its small glow we could see that the mattresses on the two lower bunks had been cleared, and that the two upper bunks were piled high with discarded clothes, sleeping-bags, rammed-in cardboard boxes and the ship's supply of lavatory rolls.

'A shower!' said Luke, stepping between the beds towards a cubby-hole in the bows. The door of the makeshift shower-room, crumpled in the middle as if it had taken a heavy blow to the stomach, had come off its bottom hinge and was tied back with string. In the left-hand corner of the room was a lavatory; Luke pushed down the flush-lever. 'It works!' he said, delighted. And then, looking round, 'Christ!' he said. And we stared at a huge, inward bulge on the outward-slanting plates of the bow. 'Big style!' said Luke. 'Sean told me that Charlie Simpson, the second skipper, had had a ding. He hit something. But no one seems bothered . . . And anyway, Redmond, we'll be fine. She's double-hulled.'

So we decided to forget about it, and to try out the mattresses: Luke in the bunk to the left, me to the right, against the wall. 'Not too good,' said Luke, stretching out full length, wiggling his toes in his blue socks. 'But again – never mind. Because we certainly won't be spending much time in here.'

'Why not?'

'Because you and me and the boys will get an average of three hours' sleep in thirty-six.'

'You're joking!'

'Not at all. This way of life, Redmond – it's not easy. In fact I can't think of anything remotely like it. Your friends in the Special Forces, for instance – even in battle they don't have to go without sleep like that for *twenty or thirty days at a time*. Or do they?'

'Of course not. Even the youngest SAS trooper can't do it – he cracks up. In fact that's exactly the warning the Major in the training wing gave me: the very best guys can withstand almost any mental pressure; but *no one* can hack sleep-deprivation.'

'And besides – the three hours of sleep don't even come as a three-hour sleep. There's no time to complete even one normal ninety-minute sleep-cycle. It's broken up into separate periods of an hour, at most. You have to take your chance in between hauls, when the net's been shot. But only when you've gutted and sorted and packed and stowed the catch from the previous haul. And Redmond – the size and frequency of the catch depends on the skill of the skipper. The more incompetent the skipper – or, maybe, if you're lucky, if he's an older man who owns his boat, who's paid off his debts, who can afford to take it easier – the more sleep you'll get. But Jason: he's already famous among trawlermen: they say he's the best there is. *And he owes two million pounds.*'

'But Luke – I love my sleep. That's the very best time of life – sleep, dreams! I need at least ten hours . . .'

'And anyway,' said Luke, not listening, staring up at the low plywood ceiling of his bunk. 'They *do* crack.'

Apparently absorbed by some new thought, or perhaps some familiar inner problem, with his right index finger he began to trace an imaginary diagram on the low plywood ceiling of his bunk. 'You'll see. They crack up. When they come ashore. They get violent.' The diagram gathered pace. 'And you, Redmond, you, too – you'll crack up . . .' He paused. 'And so will I. I'll crack up. I always do. You'll see. You don't know who you are. You drink. You go berserk.'

'But Luke – at least you've got your work, your research; you have real interests outside yourself.'

'Yes . . . Maybe . . . I suppose so . . . But sometimes that doesn't help. Sometimes you're too far gone.' He turned his head to look at me, across the three-foot gap between our bunks, the diagram abandoned, if not concluded. 'But I'm forgetting. I'm sorry. You – you don't have to join in. You're not expected to help.'

'Of course I must join in! How else will I know what it's like?'

'No. You really don't have to – and anyway you probably can't. The boys – they're manic. They're very highly motivated.'

'I'm highly motivated!' I said, huffy. 'Well, sometimes . . .' I added, suddenly struck by an unaccustomed moment of self-knowledge. 'Now and then, in short bursts . . . at least . . . I can *remember* being . . .'

'You don't understand. They're *young*. The moment someone's not up to the job, he's voted out. It's a cooperative. Only the engineer has a regular salary. That's how it works. They're all self-employed. You'd be *amazed* how hard people can work when they know they're in it together – and yet they also know that each moment of communal effort increases their own pay, directly.'

'Yeah. It's a hunting group. I've seen it in jungles.'

'Not quite. Because here the hunting never stops. Ten days. You must fill the hold. And that's not possible – because the hold's so big it might as well be infinite.'

'Ah,' I said, pressing myself flat down into the comfort of my thin, sour mattress.

'Half the gross goes on the boat, so called. To pay off the bank. Eleven grand of the remaining half goes on expenses. The diesel, the engine oil, provisions, that kind of thing – right down to the cost of the fish-boxes. You have to pay 25p a week for every last one of those boxes! And then the fish market hits you with a landing due – from one to four pounds for each full box you bring ashore! The remainder of the gross – it's split into shares. The skipper gets two shares. A crewman gets one share – or three-quarters if he's a trainee. A crewman ashore on his time off – around one week in three – gets a half-share. And then, of course, Jason has to cope with all the incidentals, the unexpected – he had to have the engine redone in PD, in Peterhead, last month: it cost *seventy grand* to have it fixed and it should be like new, but it isn't, or so Sean says.'

Luke swung his legs off the bunk and stood up. 'Come on – we'll be leaving for Stromness any minute now! And out there in the Pentland Firth, with some of the most powerful conflicting currents in the world. And in this weather! Redmond – we may not be able to keep our balance, at least not to begin with – and we certainly won't be able to stick our stuff into lockers . . .

'Er, Redmond,' he said, turning round half-way up the stairwell, 'you don't mind me asking, do you? But, well – do you get seasick?'

'I've never been seasick.'

(And I at once felt queasy. And this, I said to myself, is only the movement of the boat against the quay; but come on, you'll get

17

over it; don't be such a wimp: it's only that stench of dead fish down there, and the lack of portholes in the cabin, and the smell of deep fry saturated into everything, and your bed made up with chip-shop curtains . . .)

'Good. That's all right then,' said Luke, with an odd little smile.

On the shelter-deck where we'd left our oilskins, a fresh-faced young man was unzipping himself from a red survival suit. He had a severe crew-cut, a silver ring through the upper shell of his left ear and a white Nicorette-inhaler tube held between his teeth. 'Hi!' he said, taking out the tube. 'I'm Jerry. I'm the cook. You've met Sean? Us two – we're the new boys here. See ya!' And he disappeared up to the bridge.

Our kit and Luke's lab equipment safely stowed, wedged and roped in the cabin, we put on our oilskins and walked on to the trawl-deck. How, I thought, am I ever going to decipher the precise working of this crowded chaos of winches, derricks, blocks-and-tackle? of pipes and tubes and levers and rubber feeds? of hawsers and yellow floats and green nets?

'I love all this!' said Luke. 'I really do. Can't help it. I love the machinery itself, you know – the inventiveness of it, the way it all differs from boat to boat. *So much more fun than writing.*'

'Yeah,' I said, lamely.

'Hey, I'm sorry,' said Luke, touching my arm, misinterpreting the look of despair I could feel on my face. 'I didn't mean it like *that*. I meant *my* writing – you know, that real ghastly torture, stuck at a desk, all stuffed up in the head, trying to write up my results, my thesis – when it's a beautiful day outside, *when you could be at sea.*'

'Sure, that's OK. But Luke – where do we start here? You've got to help me. What's that, for instance?' And I pointed at the biggest feature on the deck: four long parallel cattle troughs, filled not with water but with green net and car tyres – or at least they appeared to be car tyres – slotted in the troughs side by side . . .

'That?' said Luke. He had indeed become a different person: he stood straighter; his movements had quickened; he was confident; and, for the first time, his eyes were bright, alert, full of happiness. 'That? Why – it's a twin-rig system, of course. Two bobbin-track coamings. Three trawl winches. Norlau units. Jason's gone for two deep-water trawls. They're from Seaway Nets of Macduff, I'll bet you. Ten to one I'll bet you. Bolshed design. Sixty to eighty feet of rock-hoppers.'

'Oh, of course,' I said, none the wiser. 'So what the hell are all those old tyres doing? In the cattle troughs? He caught them in the nets, or what?'

'Car tyres!' yelled Luke. 'And what was that you said? Cattle troughs!' He bent forward, holding his stomach, tried to restrain himself, failed, and howled with laughter. 'Car tyres!'

'Good morning, gents,' came a soft, lilting voice behind us; a gentle, musical accent which I couldn't place. 'Car tyres?'

'Ah!' said Luke, spinning round twice where he stood. 'Redmond here – he thinks those are tyres, old car tyres you've trawled up!' Luke put both hands to the back of his neck, as if such merriment might take his head right off.

'They're rock-hoppers,' said our new acquaintance, who was obviously older than Sean and Jerry, a veteran in his late twenties, a short, spare, lithe man with sharp eyes and a long straight nose. 'Robbie Mowat,' he said, shaking hands. He wore red-and-black oilskins, and a red tartan cap tight on his head. I thought: he's a Pict, he's an Iron Age Pict. He's one of the mysterious people. He's one of those pre-Scots settlers whose origins and culture and script so baffle archaeologists and historians. He looks *exactly* like those Pictish warriors on their Symbol Stones.

Luke began to introduce us, to explain this tyre business, how such a thing could come about . . .

'Aye, we know all about you,' said Robbie Mowat, cutting him short. 'Jason told us. And Redmond – they are tyres, right enough, in a way. Only they keep the net, not a car, off the ground – they

19

roll over rocks on the bottom, they keep the net from snagging. At least, they do some of the time. Aye – you'll enjoy it. The trip. I can see – you've a lot to learn. But now we're away to Stromness. And then I'm ashore! So the other Robbie – Robbie Stanger. Redmond – I'll ask *him* to look after you. He joins in Stromness. You'll be fine with him!'

With a backward wave, he jumped a hawser, swung himself over the side of the ship, and dropped to the quay.

Two medieval limb-stretching torture-racks, complete with chains, hung port and starboard of the stern, ready to enforce discipline on board.

'Luke,' I asked, with 98 per cent reduced *sang-froid*, 'so what are those? Those medieval joint-dislocator torture things?'

There was an earthquake blast of deep noise. The *Norlantean* came to overwhelming life. The deck, seized by fever, was hit by rigors; we shook as if some maniac had us by the collar. The top of the funnel appeared to blow up; it erupted and was obscured, in a smoke as black as squid ink, a plume so thick it looked solid.

'Otter-boards!' Luke shouted in my ear. 'They're otter-boards! They power along at an angle in front of the net. They keep the mouth of the net open. Hey, Redmond! Big style! We're going to have a grand time, you and I!'

'Luke!' bellowed Robbie Mowat from the quay.

Luke, responding like one of Galvani's frogs' legs, shot to port and caught the heavy curl of mooring rope. Robbie Mowat hauled himself back over the side. We were off.

The *Norlantean* moved gently out into the harbour. No one on the quay, no one on board the other trawlers – on the high-bowed, squat-sterned, rounded Scottish inshore boats that hugged the sea, their shapes pleasing as a buttock – no one, anywhere, took the slightest notice of this great event. And neither did a group of twenty or so eiders – big sea-going ducks with forward-sloping heads and heavy bills, the females brown, the males in winter plumage, all-over black but for the white blazes on their folded wings: they sat snug on the water by the harbour wall, out of the wind, resting, half-asleep.

'Luke, shouldn't we go and see Jason? Say hello? Wouldn't that be polite?'

'Now? No. It's one of the rules – you never distract a Captain when he's manoeuvring out of harbour.'

So we stood against the side and watched as the white lighthouse-tower and attendant buildings, half-camouflaged against the snow-covered hills, passed to port; and only when we were parallel with the last cliffs of Dunnet Head to starboard, the most northerly point of the mainland, did we take off our boots and oilskins and climb up the stairs to the bridge, in our socks.

Jason was sitting in the right-hand one of two black swivel-chairs, behind a large U-shaped spread of a wood-panelled console, packed with instruments. He rose to greet us.

Jason was tall and dark; he had a slight stoop; he was lean, loose-limbed, quick; he was full of restless energy. (Of course, I thought, he's a direct descendant of those virile young Spanish officers who swam ashore from the ships of the Armada wrecked on the Orkney rocks . . .) 'Redmond, it's perfect for you!' he said, shaking hands, speaking very fast. 'Perfect! Exactly as you specified – the worst weather at the worst time of year. There's a Force 11 up there now and the forecast – it's a 12. And that's a *hurricane*! Perfect!'

'Smashing!' said Luke, with a manic laugh.

'And Luke – did you bring your minilog for the net? The depth and temperature recorder?' Luke nodded. 'Yes? Good. Well done. Because I really would like to know the optimum depth for redfish.' He turned towards a big-chested, powerfully built man of about his own age (all of thirty) who was bending over the chart-table, a table tucked away to the right and facing, through the all-round thick-glass windows, the stern of the trawler.

'Bryan Robertson,' said Jason. 'First Mate.' And they both laughed. 'Redmond O'Hanlon, unhinged writer,' announced Jason, as if he was the host of some television chat-show. (Well, yes, he could be, I thought; with those Spanish looks, the dark brown eyes, the high thick black eyebrows, the long black eyelashes, and so articulate . . . he'd pull ratings of 8 million plus, entirely female.) 'Luke Bullough, sensible scientist. A man of reason from the taxpaying trawlerman's own Marine Laboratory, Aberdeen.'

We all laughed.

'Welcome aboard, boys,' said Bryan, in a slow, deep, lilting bass. 'You've picked one hell of a time to come. And that's the truth.' (And you, I thought, should be an opera singer.)

At that moment we emerged from the sheltering headlands into the Pentland Firth. The waves seemed, to me, to be excessively long; the edges of their crests broke into the spindrift; the streaked foam blew in thin trails from left to right, spattering on the wheelhouse windows. The ship rolled in the cross-sea and, just in time, I managed to grab the edge of the console and save myself from pitching backwards down the unprotected stairs.

'So Redmond,' said Jason, flinging himself with graceful ease into his high-backed seat (which, I was appalled to see, had a belt-harness. Did things ever get *that* bad?). 'You'll be wanting to know about the instruments? Yes?'

'Of course. Yes please,' I said, both hands clamped on the wooden lip of the console-top, beside the fax machine. My legs, I realized, were having a breakdown; they were sending absurd signals to the brain; they'd lost their moral fibre; just when I actually needed them – they'd ceased to function. 'So what's this, Jason? A storm?'

'This? A storm!' When Jason laughed, his entire lanky body joined in: all the visible outlying bits twitched, for fun, in different directions. 'Bryan! What do you think? Force 7? 8?' Bryan shrugged. 'Yes – you see, Redmond, we have *almost* everything here. More or less all we need. But there's nothing to measure wind-speed. Because that's a waste of money. We don't need it. Pointless. Either you fish or you don't.'

'And when do you don't?' I said, vaguely conscious that I had lost not only the power of standing-on-two-legs, but also of speech.

'You only stop fishing when the wind ahead is more powerful than the engines below. Simple. You stop when you can't keep the net open. But Redmond – always remember: you make no money when you're hove-to. And you make no money when you're asleep!'

Jason waved his right arm, so flexible it seemed double-jointed, towards his far left of the console (to which I was attached, like a limpet) and swept back round to the right, coming to rest again on a small black lever at his side, from which, I assumed, he was somehow directing the ship. (A conventional wood-and-polished-brass spoked wheel waited unused, like an ornament in a pub, in

23

the centre of the U.) Various screens, side by side, faced threateningly out of the backward-angled, maroon-coloured surround of wood. On the broad ledge directly beneath them were ordered papers, incomprehensible-looking manuals, detached flexible controls – and something that I recognized from my previous life: a perfectly ordinary comforting yellow mug full of coffee; but even this yellow mug seemed exotic because it sat six inches out from the ledge, in its own projecting wooden nest . . .

'Most of this comes from Woodsons in Aberdeen,' said Jason. 'As you would expect. *That's* a JRC model 2254 4Kw 48-mile radar. I'm taking a course with them next month, when I get ashore.' He spoke, and the hand moved, so very fast that all the screens blurred into one. (And anyway, I reminded myself, you can't even use a computer. You've never tried but you can't, and that's that, everyone's allowed a phobia or two, or five . . .)

'That's the original JRC R73 radar,' he said, keeping his brown eyes forward, on the sea ahead. 'And I've got two DGPS receivers – marvellous! There, see? A Valsat 2008 Mk2 and a Trimble NT 200D. Now – *look* – these interface with the plotters *here*. And *there*. That's a Raccal Decca CVP 3500 unit. And that's a brand-new Quodfish plotter from Woodsons. And these are for back-up. It's worth it –'

(Almost all my conscious effort began to go on suppressing the upwelling thought of the morning's breakfast – so long ago but now so very present. That earth-mother in the cauldron of a café; if only we'd known; she was obviously a most distinguished poisoner: a woman of experience, one of the élite. She had made me *eat* that stuff. But it's OK, I said to myself, all you have to do is boa-constrict, python your oesophagus, keep it all down. And I could see the ooze on the black pudding, the grease-sweat beneath the bacon, the globular wobble and glisten of eggs . . .)

'You've used these, Luke?' I heard Jason say. 'Of course you have! But Redmond needs to know. See? Redmond? This is a Magnavox MX 200 GPS; and that's a new Furunco LC90.'

'Hey Redmond!' said Luke, *à propos* of nothing in particular. (Or had he picked up something subliminal? An early ancestral-mammal tree-shrew shriek of distress . . .) 'Bev's Kitchen,' he said, wandering about the room. He is unconcerned, I thought; Luke is pecking at grains of information like a young cockerel in a chickenhouse and yet he is *so* unobservant: he is apparently unaware that this hutch has somehow got itself airborne, that it is strung up in place on a big dipper . . . 'A mistake, don't you think?'

'Bev's Kitchen?'

'Yeah. You know. That place in Nairn.'

'OK, Redmond,' said Jason. 'Now look at these. The fish-finders. You *must* get the hang of these, and fast. Here's the main one – an Atlas Electronic model 382 colour-sounder . . .'

(Fish fingers? Please, no. In any case, I whispered to myself: *I must not be sick in here.* That really is obvious. This is not the place to throw up. Really, really not . . . Not at all . . .)

'That's original, reliable. But this is better – a new 28/200 KHz model JFV 250 3Kw –'

'You know,' said Luke, preoccupied, punching up some diagram on a screen or a laying box in the centre of the airborne henhouse, which was full of feather-dust, and mites, as you might expect, and the air was super-saturated with droplets of Bev's eggs, and you couldn't breathe . . . 'That place where we had the best breakfast on earth. And all for £1.50 – and now you're going to waste your money!'

'Ugh,' I said, from somewhere in the large intestine, yawning for air, mouth open, like a hippo.

'And the JFV 250 complements this,' said Jason, raising his quick, lilting, intelligent voice, warning off all further interruptions. 'The JFV 120 50 KHz – so there you are, Redmond! But you also need these receivers, of course – if you're going to compete, if you're going to give yourself a chance. So this is from Scanmar in Aberdeen – an RX 400 with a colour monitor for data from the actual trawl and the doors, the otter-boards. And I think, on balance, that you'll find this is the most interesting piece of kit for you, for you as a writer – so go and have a look!' The hand waved towards the stern, at a short collection of screens positioned almost flat on a waist-high ledge at the aft-end of the wheelhouse: five impossible paces away. 'That's from Smith Maritime at PD – with that you can shoot and haul on automatic or manual. But the really clever thing is this, Redmond – go on! Go and look! It works with the data from the Scanmar sensors. *It adjusts the trim of the net during towing.* So what do you think of that? Eh? Is that clever? Or what? It can haul in or pay out one of the warps – until you've got optimum alignment!'

'Aye,' said Bryan, unexpectedly, full of admiration, from the far corner.

'Well, go on!' said Jason, looking round, swift as a falcon. 'It's interesting. Take a note. Do something. Do whatever you writers do.'

'Can't.'

'What?'

'Can't move.'

'Redmond,' said Jason, in a flat voice, not bothering to look round again. 'You'd better go below.'

'Can't.'

'That bad?'

'Ik.'

'What?'

'Nutting.'

'Jesus!' said Jason, closing his eyes, throwing his head back, pulling his right hand across the top of his face. And then, 'Bryan!' he said, recovering. 'Could you clear that chair?'

Bryan, despite his muscles, nimble as an otter, piled the papers and books neatly in a trough on the console, took me by the arm and, kindly, without a laugh or even a smile, inserted me in the second helmsman's chair.

'Sit down!' said Jason. 'Hang on! Look at the horizon. They say that helps – concentrate on it. A stable line. The only thing that doesn't move.'

(Except that this one did – the far-too-close horizon was not a line at all, but a series of chaotic serrations, the bright edge of an upturned saw that, against the whirl of grey sky, cut without plan or rhythm . . .)

'Oh well,' said Jason. 'Cheer up! It won't last. It'll soon be over – won't it, Luke?' (Luke, absorbed in some task of his own, rearranging wires or computer feeds or detonators on the far side of the console, faced away.) 'Or maybe it will – because of course some people *never* adjust. They can't. People like that – they just keep throwing up, they get dehydrated, and if you don't put them ashore in a week or so they damn well die on you! People like that – *they really wreck your fishing.*' He looked straight ahead. 'But you're not like that, are you?'

'Ugh. Nik.'

'It's called marasmus, I think,' he said, picking up and replacing the Cellnet phone at his side. 'Death from seasickness, some silly fancy word like that. Anyway, you'd know . . .'

'Uck.'

'And of course we've got the usual boring things.' He took a fast gulp of cold coffee. 'Mini-M Boatfone Units for voice, e-mail and fax by satellite. A Motorola 7400 X mobile. And there's Philips CCTV all over the vessel . . .'

I closed my eyes. The three of them talked and talked, Bryan and Jason in their Orkney lilt, and Luke, now, in his spare, unemotional, flat trawlerman-and-lifeboat-crew English. And I held on to the arms of the safe enclosing chair as the *Norlantean* moved back and forth and sideways, and up and down – through (in words I'd read somewhere, and cherished): 'The six degrees of freedom – pitch, roll, sway, heave, surge and yaw.' This mantra was, somehow, a deep comfort. So the *Norlantean*'s response to that indivisible chaos out there, which Jason said was a mere Force 8, nothing at all – it could be broken into parts? It could be named? Which meant that someone else had felt like this – and maybe even in a lousy nothing, a Force 8. Which meant that I was not alone. So I felt better. And I repeated the mantra to myself, sometimes with eyes open and sometimes with eyes shut – and every time I got to yaw I went ahead and yawned, gasping like a fish.

In between periods of inner (eyes fist-tight shut) and outer darkness the coloured cliffs of Hoy passed to starboard, and so did the vertical stack, the Old Man of Hoy. Except that this particular pinnacle of rock would not keep still. It took off every few seconds: the Old Man of Hoy would blast straight up like a rocket from Cape Canaveral, think better of it, and return to its launch-pad. It took me a while to realize that there was nothing wrong with the Old Man of Hoy; he was fine; he'd retired; he was firmly attached to his bedrock. No; it was *us*; we were the ones not attached to bed, or rock, or anything half-way pleasant at all.

We rounded the north end of the island of Hoy; we entered the shelter of Scapa Flow; the *Norlantean* responded to security, at once; she calmed herself. And wasn't it about here, I thought, that an earlier *Dorothy Gray*, in 1914, at the beginning of the First World War, deliberately pursued and rammed a German submarine – even though two Royal Navy destroyers were only 3 miles off? Now what kind of crazy skipper would decide to risk his boat, his earning power, his family, his life and his crew like that? The answer came at once: Jason! And with it came a rising surge of rancid liquid: a solution of double eggs, bacon, sausage, fried bread, black pudding and beans suspended in duodenal hydrochloric acid which, just, I managed to dispatch back down my throat.

I closed my eyes, and perhaps I fell asleep, because when I opened them again Luke and Bryan had gone; Jason had slowed his ship: he was manoeuvring her through the navigation buoys and in towards Stromness. The wheelhouse clock said ten past three in the afternoon; and yet it was almost dark. The *Norlantean*'s lights were on; the navigation buoys flashed red to port, green to starboard; Stromness, like some Arctic frontier-town, glowed a feeble speckled orange against the blackness.

And, at last, Jason said something which I fully understood. His voice was slow and soft, quite unlike his normal over-energetic speech. 'This is the best harbour in the world,' he said, gazing at its lights. 'Every time I come in here – I feel good. I went to college here. I married here. I live here. I love this place. You know, Redmond, it's true – when I was four or five, a little child growing up on Sanday, I drew all the time. Pictures. Thousands of them. And every one was a trawler.'

So that's it, I thought, as the sickness began to pass away out into the calm of the harbour, that's why he lives as he does, why he could never do otherwise. That's why Jason is in debt, at the age of thirty or thereabouts, for two million pounds; and that is also why Jason is one of the happiest men I've ever met.

'And besides,' he said, recovering his normal fast precision of speech as we approached the quay and a three-storey-high narrow grey shed, 'the ice-maker here – he never cheats you. If he says he's given you twenty-two tonnes of ice, he's given you twenty-two tonnes of ice. That's Orkney for you. Redmond, I'm *sure* you'd never find anywhere like it – not if you searched the world for a hundred years.'

Standing at another set of knobs and levers close against the port-side windows, using the bow-thrusters, Jason nudged the *Norlantean*, a 38.5-metre-long deep draught mass of iron, up to the quay. By the light of her big square spotlights, which threw bursts of white reflection up from the wet grey stones, the puddled tarmac, I watched a fresh-faced young man in sweater and jeans and trainers catch the bow-ropes (thrown by Bryan and Robbie Mowat) and the stern-ropes (thrown, less accurately, by Sean and Jerry). He was obviously a trawlerman – even I was beginning to be able to identify one, generically: big shoulders, a flat stomach and, most apparent of all, massive leg-muscles: muscles so absurdly well developed that trawlermen seemed to have to buy their trousers many waist-sizes too big: their broad leather belts hold the extra cloth puckered tight.

'Allan Besant,' said Jason. 'He's a good worker. He's on for this trip. And so is Robbie Stanger. They're both good. In fact, Redmond, *this crew is the very best I've ever had.*' Jason was silent for a moment, apparently concentrating hard, looking sharp down through the window. 'And now I've got a genuine trawlerman's scientist aboard, which is good. Interesting. Good for everyone. Good for the boys to see!' (I got that warm feeling. I no longer felt seasick – well, we were roped to dry land; I felt useful, by association; I was here to help.)

Jason shut down the engines, or thrusters, or whatever it is you shut down at that moment; he turned to me with a sudden super-signal grin, with a spotlight-dazzle of young teeth white in his dark face. 'And now I also have a problem. I have a dangerous liability. I have one mad, seasick writer who's no use to anyone!' He gave a half-laugh, which was almost convincing; he put his arm briefly across my shoulders and said: 'Let's go! We must get the ice loaded!'

And at the bottom of the wheelhouse stairs, quick as Houdini, Jason was in his blue overalls and his yellow sea-boots.

The men in the grey ice-shed tower swung their large-diameter augur over the open hatch to the *Norlantean*'s fish hold, amidships. Luke and I, standing on the hatch-rim, peered down at Bryan (First Mate), Robbie Mowat (due for shore-leave: midday tomorrow) and Allan Besant (the athlete – a wrestler? a shot-putter? one of those Scotsmen who takes a malt or two and then bungs up-ended trees about? – we'd no idea, because as yet we'd only exchanged nods at a distance). Staggering in and out of view, they positioned a wide-mouthed, reinforced-plastic, steel-ring-ribbed tube beneath the spew-end of the augur. Almost at once it filled with a violent cascade of jagged ice-pebbles. Down below us we heard the sound of frantic shovelling. 'That,' said Luke, reflectively rolling a cigarette, 'is a really *rotten* job.'

A red Toyota truck pulled up on the quay. Emerging from the

shadows, Sean pushed past us. He gave a happy shout into the increasingly powerful wind, a wind from the west, already broken by the cliffs and hills of the main island's peninsula, which yet held the *Norlantean* out from the quay, taut on her ropes. 'Stores!' yelled Sean, his wide nostrils flared, as if he had just caught their scent. 'Stores!'

Luke called after him, 'Want help?'

'Aye! Down by the galley!' And Sean appeared to vault right over the side.

Down by the galley, we looked about us. The walls were clad with the same brown imitation-wood panels as the passage and cabins; at right-angles to the left and right of the entrance were two fixed brown tables, each with benches for four; a video-recorder sat on a bracket high in the corner to the left; also to the left, a refrigerated milk-dispenser waited half-way down the galley; there was a sink with dish-racks, and the mugs were stacked in wall-fixed wooden tubes with a slit for the handles. Off to the left, a heavy metal door led to a store room containing ranked shelves and a big fridge. And, in the galley, above the sink, there was a genuine porthole.

'Hey boys!' Sean's voice, disembodied, appeared to be shouting at us from the empty passageway. 'Where the fuck you gone?'

Sean's head grinned down from an open hatch above the galley entrance. It was an escape-hatch: small rungs led up to it: it was your last chance to save yourself from a chip-pan fire in the galley. Sean's head disappeared: 'Haggis, pork chops, fifty beef sausages, six dozen eggs,' it intoned up there, with excessive pomp, obviously checking some list. A lowered box dangled in front of us. 'The boxes, boys – pile them in the galley! And I'll sort them myself!'

The invisible Sean shouted: 'Fancies, bridies, Arctic rolls, shell pies, bere bannocks!' as if he was taking parade, and expected each one to answer to its name.

I said, 'Bridies? Bere bannocks?'

'Search me,' said Luke, passing me a box. 'But you can be sure of one thing – we won't be eating any fish. And after a bit you won't want to, either. Beef, haggis, pork chops. Grand!'

The galley and passage full of cardboard boxes, Sean released us. 'Opening time! See ya in the Flattie – down the pier, left, across the street. You can't miss it!'

So Luke and I had a pint of Guinness each in the Flattie – a small bar named after a type of flat-bottomed Orkney rowing-boat which was good for fishing on the lochs, so the barmaid told us. And, just as we were about to leave, Sean and Jerry arrived, so I bought another round and, when that was gone, Allan Besant and Robbie Mowat walked in. So I bought another; and Allan and Robbie and Jerry and Sean decided that they were off to a party in the capital, Kirkwall, a few miles down the road. So, as instructed, Luke and I walked up the gently curving stone-paved street to the Royal Hotel, where you could get good things to eat. And, so very pleased to be ashore, and forgetting that I was not going to stay that way, I decided to celebrate.

In the lounge bar, hung with pictures of the Hudson Bay Company's ships which had put into Stromness from the seventeenth to the nineteenth centuries to get their crews, to sign on the toughest, least-complaining sailors in the country, we took a table, and two more pints of Guinness, beneath a portrait of Sir John Franklin's vessels *Erebus* and *Terror*, which, as we were to do, I remembered, had sailed out of Stromness – never to be seen again.

So, to counter such thoughts, we ordered Scotch broth, and the most expensive food on the menu, halibut, and ice-cream, and Guinness. When we could eat no more I left a tip; at which point Bryan and Sean (who had somehow failed to leave for Kirkwall), pushed through the swing door, so I bought another round at the bar; and I told Bryan, straight, that he should join the nearest opera company, without delay; and Bryan said that was the most stupid thing anyone had told him in all his life; and so Luke and I set off home, towards the *Norlantean*. But before we reached her, there in the hotel lobby, Luke held my arm and took me aside, as if he was my father. 'It's all right, Redmond,' he said in my ear. 'You don't have to buy *everyone* a drink. The boys – you can't buy their friendship, you know. In our terms, they're rich. And in any case, they'll decide for themselves. Later. They'll judge what you *do*. How you are when things get bad. That's when they'll decide.'

The jump from the quay to the distant rungs of the high, short, inbuilt steel ladder, flush with the gentle upward concave curve of the hull of the *Norlantean*, looked impossible. I peered straight down into the gap between the wall of the quay and the deep black side of the *Norlantean*: a mistake. Floating way down below on the narrow oily slop of water were two empty plastic coke bottles, several tins, a broken fish-box, assorted potato-crisp wrappings – and one white face of a dead fisherman – which resolved itself, eventually, into one drowned water-logged Herring gull, breast-up.

'Jump!' said Luke, giving me a shove.

Up on deck he said, 'You know – one or two trawlermen die like that every year. They get back blind drunk; they miss their footing; they fall down the gap. The ship moves in. Their skulls are crushed.'

'Redmond! Redmond!' It was Bryan's voice, a big bass boom behind us. 'You're a crook!'

'You did a runner!' yelled Sean, following him on board.

'You're a crook,' said Bryan, coming up to me, waving a small piece of paper. 'A crook!'

'Eh?'

'And a pig!' He waved the small piece of paper before my eyes. It was a bill. '£28 for two!'

'A runner!' said Sean, much excited, punching my upper arm, for emphasis. 'You did a runner!'

'And from the Royal,' said Bryan. 'Now that really does take balls! No one – but no one – does a runner from the Royal!'

'Oh God,' I said, mortified, reaching in my pocket, paying up. 'I've *never* done that before. God, I'm sorry. I forgot . . .'

'He forgot!' chanted Bryan, on the bass line, going below. 'He forgot!'

'He forgot!' sang Sean, tenor, following him.

And they kept up the duet, all the way down the stairs.

'It's OK,' said Luke, with a tremendous grin. '*I* know you forgot. You were distracted. But they love all that – and it is remarkable. You have to admit. Because, well, look at it this way: you've only been here ten minutes, and *already* you're banned from every hotel and pub in Stromness!'

For the second time in our friendship, Luke held his stomach with both hands, bent forward, and, obviously trying not to do it (which made things worse), he laughed like a hyena. Luke's ears went bright red. Luke, I thought, comforting myself, Luke has sticky-out ears.

Safe in our sleeping-bags, the cabin lights off, Luke, sounding sleepy, said: 'Yes, word gets round, you know.' There was a snuffle of laughter. 'In fact, you'd better hole up here – on board. Might be wiser.' There came a small series of nasal plosives, like the sounds that hedgehogs make, after dark, in the mating season. 'But that was great. Well done! Now the boys won't think you're a phoney stuck-up southerner with hands like a girl. You're a *crook*!'

'Hands like a girl?' I said, instantly awake, outraged.

'Yes . . .' said Luke, drifting off. 'Don't you even dig your garden?'

'No,' I said, resolving instantly that if I ever saw that little garden again I'd dig it all over, every day. 'Certainly not. I told you – I sleep.'

And I fell asleep.

At first light, at nine in the morning, when Luke and I were putting on our oilskins on the shelter-deck, Jerry, Robbie Mowat and Allan Besant joined us, fresh from their Kirkwall party.

Robbie Mowat had kept his tartan cap, but not his looks. There was a red bump growing on half his forehead; his lips were swollen;

his right hand was bandaged, his arm in a sling. Allan Besant, still young and powerful and red-cheeked, was no longer quite so fresh. His right index-finger was heavily dressed and bandaged, as if it had turned septic in the night, the white cloth secured with a double wrap around his wrist and the base of his thumb.

Bryan, First Mate, stepped out of the companionway. 'Hey – you're late! What happened?' He was interested, but only just enough to be polite. It was obvious that if you wished to claim his whole attention, you must, at least, climb over the rail with your head in a fish-box.

Allan said, 'Robbie started a bloody stupid fight. So we had to join in. And the bastard bit my finger!'

'Which bastard?' said Bryan, pulling on his yellow oilskin trousers, as if, as far as he was concerned, the entire population of Kirkwall were bastards.

'Gillespie. The Big Fellah,' said Robbie, still aggrieved. 'I come out of the toilet. I go to pick up my pint from the table and Gillespie says, "Robbie Mowat," he says. "You've had enough. I forbid you to touch that pint." So – *bang!* I smack him in the mouth!'

'Oh aye,' said Bryan, pulling on his boots.

'No!' said Allan, also aggrieved. 'That wasn't it at all – it started long before that! They had this bloody stupid argument. Robbie had a go at Gillespie. And all because the Big Fellah never picked him for the football team – *when they were six years old!*'

Robbie, sullen, said, 'It was worth the wait. But there again,' he said, brightening, lifting the hair off his forehead to show us the bump to better effect: 'one more kick in the head – and I'm dead! And my teeth, Redmond . . .' With his right hand he pushed up his top lip (no front teeth); and with his left hand he pulled a dental plate from his pocket (buckled to bits, a write-off).

'Aye,' said Bryan, now in his yellow jacket, ready to start work. 'There's precious few trawlermen with their own front teeth!'

Jerry said, 'I sat on him too!'

'Who?' said Bryan.

35

'Gillespie. I sat on his legs.'

'Well done,' said Bryan. 'But Allan, your finger – what were *you* doing when the bastard bit your finger?'

'Nothing,' said Allan, who, with his good hand, was attempting to gather up a coil of rope from a side-lashed red plastic basket. 'I was sitting on his chest. I was poking his eyes out.'

Bryan laughed, and walked off to work. Allan followed, the rope round his left shoulder.

Robbie Mowat stood where he was, needing to talk; or perhaps he was just concussed, sandbagged by the events of the night. 'Redmond, the police came, and they took us and Gillespie to the hospital. In the van. Aye. But this is what I want you to know – Gillespie, he refused to bring charges.'

'He did?'

'Aye. And he said *sorry*. *He apologized*. For not picking me. For leaving me out of the team. So now it's OK. We're friends!'

'Good. I'm glad to hear it.'

'So when I get out of hospital I go straight back to the pub and I hold my glass in both hands to get the beer in – because my mouth is damaged. And then I go straight to the club. Because – here's a tip for you – you'll *always* get a woman if you look beaten up, if you've been in a fight. They love it. The men fighting. They can't help themselves.'

'And you did?'

'I did, too.'

Looking at me hard (his brown eyes appeared to be undamaged), as if, understandably, he had no idea why I was standing in front of him, no idea why this stranger was here at all, or, perhaps, re-membering that he was not officially on shore-leave until midday, Robbie walked away, with the odd slight stumble, out on to the trawl-deck, and into the ferocious wind.

Luke, unnoticed, had slipped below. Jerry, sucking on his stubby white Nicorette tube, was sitting on a rope-fast oil-drum.

I said, 'So what happened to you?'

36

'Redmond,' said Jerry, like an old professor in his after-dinner chair. 'Let me give you a word of advice about all this. Because you're new here. Listen – if a fight breaks out ashore – as it surely will – *wait*. That's the most important thing. And when someone's flat out on the ground, preferably unconscious – you go and sit on him, just to help out. OK?'

The next day, in the full, black, northern winter night of four o'clock in the afternoon, in a constant, unvarying wind of such violence that I found it almost impossible to stand on deck, the *Norlantean*, spotlights blazing, left Stromness.

From the starboard open-end of the shelter-deck, protected from the wind, Luke and I watched the separate white and orange lights of Stromness coalesce, grow lonely, and disappear.

Luke was dressed in dark-blue overalls, like Jason's, but they were even more impressively lived-in, action-stained with memories. Luke dressed precisely and without effort for every occasion here – I could see that – he was plainly at home in his own world, the only one that really mattered to him.

I said, 'So what happens now?'

'Nothing or everything,' he said, with a snort of happy laughter. 'It depends how you look at it! To reach his secret fishing-grounds Jason is going to steam north-west, flat out, straight into the weather. Right into a Force 8 or 9. Most young skippers *say* they like to behave like that, or they have to, because once you've mortgaged your life to a boat you can't afford to waste a day or a night: but I've never heard of anyone actually *doing* it. Except Jason

38

Schofield. And as you saw for yourself – we're the only boat out! Redmond – this has never happened to me before. Not even in the Falklands.' Luke absent-mindedly pulled a furl of blue woolly hat from his right-hand pocket and unrolled it, like a condom, down over his head: it sat tight across his forehead; beneath its rim a band of thick curly hair bushed out like a muff. 'Yes, Redmond, maybe (just between us) it's true, what they say: maybe Jason *is* a little crazy . . . And it's sad, isn't it?'

'What is?'

'Well, really exceptional guys like that – they die young.'

'Ah.'

'Yes. And Jason – do you realize he doesn't even have a standard fish-detector? A reasonable one costs £6,000. But he told me he didn't need it! He said he had to save money somewhere – and it was obvious: skippers who were good ten years ago go out now and, in his words, not mine: "they never catch a fucking thing!" Whereas he, Jason, so far, has never failed. He has the gift. But all the same, when you remember that just to replace those warps' – Luke nodded his head, his blue woolly hat, towards the winches – 'those steel ropes that tow the net, they're so simple, and yet they cost £17,000 . . . So really, despite the net monitors and sounders and so on – it's old-time fishing here!'

He stared into the darkness astern. 'On the other hand, Redmond, cheer up! Because we're off into that two-thirds of the earth which is covered by the sea – and the real point, the really exciting thing is this: *90 per cent* of that two-thirds lies beyond the shallow margins of the continents, as Gage and Tyler put it, and most of that lies below 2 kilometres of water – or even more! And 99 per cent of *that* is unexplored!'

Luke went to the line of pegs in the shelter-deck, to hang up his overalls.

'Look, Redmond – you know – I don't want to be offensive, but compared to your rainforests which, forgive me, you really do seem to think are the ultimate biological mystery, the deep sea is *totally* unknown! It's another planet! Why — hydrothermal vents were only discovered in 1977. Imagine! What an extraordinary shock that was — big style! We had to scrap the most basic concepts in biology! There are *plenty* of animals, big animals, megafauna, which live entirely without oxygen — in disparate but very large populations at the bottom of the deep sea. They don't give a damn about photosynthesis! *So what else is down there?* Look, Redmond, I was thinking, before you came — why not forget your rainforests? Because what depth are we talking about here? One hundred, two hundred feet? Pathetic! And anyway — even if we confine ourselves to the plants themselves — if you compare it, the plant biomass, cubic metre by cubic metre, down from the jungle canopy to the jungle floor, against an equivalent section down from the surface of the sea, almost *anywhere* in the oceans, you'll find that the microscopic plants in the plankton at the surface of the sea outweigh the vegetation in your rainforest. They bulk larger than all your huge trees and creepers! So how's that?'

'Great!'

'And imagine! In a day or two — *a day or two from now* — I'll be able to start showing you most of the deep-sea megafauna north of the Wyville Thomson Ridge! And, you know, speaking as me, from the heart, whatever, but not as a scientist, this is what I think about it — if you sat down with a pencil and paper to draw the most bizarre animals you could imagine, if you took every mad drug there is you still wouldn't come close to reality. You'll see! You really will! Wait till I show you a rabbit-fish! Or even' (he lowered his voice, seemingly transfixed, his right hand still holding the scruff of his overall, which was already safely in position on its peg), 'just maybe . . . we'll get a sea-bat . . . Now that *would* be something. I've never seen one, of course, but maybe . . . Who knows? It's great, isn't it? Hunting!'

'Yes!' I said, carried away. 'A sea-bat!' (having no idea what such a thing might be). 'Let's catch a sea-bat!'

'Hey Redmond,' said Luke, breaking up the fantasy. 'Why are

you hanging about? It's brass-monkey cold out here! And when we hit the open ocean, there'll be lumps! Big style! So what's wrong with you? Now is the time to go below. It's our last chance. Our last chance to get some sleep!'

'Luke,' I said, as we got into our sleeping-bags, 'what did you mean – *lumps?*'

'Lumps? Waves! To a trawlerman a big wave is never a wave, it's a lump. Cuts it down to size, I suppose. *Wave* is too serious. You don't want the sea to know you're frightened, do you?' He was silent for a moment. And it seemed to me that the *Norlantean* began to buck and kick, and, probably, I thought, froth at the mouth out there, and roll her eyes. 'Listen Redmond, it's obvious you know sod all about all this. Don't worry – no probs. Why should you? That's OK. But, yes, I now think I *should* warn you. Because it must be better to be prepared, mustn't it? Even though it catches you by surprise – and it always does catch you by surprise – and there's nothing you can do about it. After all, how could you shoot the nets and work the haul and do all the hundred other things you have to do if you were wearing a lifeline? Most of them don't even have a survival suit! And as for hard hats – Marine Lab Government Civil Service safety regulations! I've *never* seen a trawlerman in a hard hat – so if the rush of water knocks you over and whacks you head-first into a winch, well, bad luck.'

'Luke – hang on, wait a minute. What are you saying? What is *it?*'

'Uh? It? Why – the lump! The lump! Redmond, I forget the exact numbers – but it's the one thing I really don't like about life on a trawler. In a Force 9 or 10 and up – with every 100,000 waves, or was it 250,000? I can't remember, and of course it damn well doesn't matter when it's happening – you are, statistically speaking, 100 per cent certain to meet a lump. A giant wave. Which is in fact just two or more waves rolled into one – for whatever reason, in the chaos, a big wave behind has captured the waves in front. And

I hate that – because when it comes at you: *you can't see it coming.* You have to understand, Redmond – in a Force 10, with gusts up to 61 knots or over – you have no horizons. You're closed in by normal Force 10 waves and their white-out, the spray from their crests, and you've got to do something difficult – because it's always difficult in a 9 or 10 – so you're concentrating as hard as you can, and you're trying to stay on your feet, but somehow you feel it, I can't tell you how – and suddenly there's this monster, and I hate it, those five or ten seconds as you look up at it, as it looms over you, the terror . . .'

'Jesus!'

'Yes. Well. Can we be quiet now? Get some sleep? Because this is our last chance . . . Before the fishing-grounds . . .'

And despite the increasingly violent pitch and toss and yaw and surge of the bows, and despite a new sound which every few seconds overwhelmed even the eardrum-pounding, intestine-shaking vibrations from the engine-room beneath us – the great weighted thump of a wave on the hull, level with our heads: blows, surely, whose kinetic energy would have to be measured in many tons-per-square-inch – Luke fell asleep.

I lay on my back in the dark, my head on my pillow of pants wrapped in a shirt, my arms stretched down my sides, my left hand clamped to the edge of the mattress, to hold myself in the bunk. There was no oxygen left in the deep-fry, fat-saturated air. I could not stop gasping and yawning and swearing. All was confusion, and smelt bad. I pulled my right hand downwards over my face. My forehead was wet, slime-wet, and surprisingly cold. My chin was covered with spittle. I was dribbling like a baby. So yes, I said to myself, this is a cold sweat; and you are hypersalivating; and that's it, you can't stop it now, it's called sea-sickness: how *embarrassing,* how *shaming.* 'So let's get this over,' I said out loud, and, concentrating (the smallest movement was an effort), with my right hand I scrabbled along the outer gap between the mattress and the side of the bunk, found my head-torch, strapped the elastic band over my slippery forehead and turned on the lamp. Exhausted, I lay back on my pillow and stared at my lit-up ceiling, at the plywood board two and a half feet above me, the base of the upper bunk.

A leering trawlerman stared back. He wore a tartan cap with a bobble; his eyes were enormous, their pupils a pair of ventilation-holes in the plywood; a ring hung from the lobe of his left ear; the scar of a knife-slash, freshly stitched, disfigured his right cheek; the tough shoots of his beard were perhaps ten days old. Drawn in thick black felt-tip pen, his portrait was signed, 'CHUKKA from DY JANUARY '95' in the top right-hand corner, and 'Blakey FAEBCK MAY '95' in the left.

My gullet and stomach rose out of my body: up above the trawlerman they flapped right and left, like fish-tails; still rising, they jinked and dipped and surged; they broke surface and, like dolphins, leapt undulating forward on the mass of bow-wave. They played, they plunged, they drove down in one irregular turbulent fall – down through me, the engine-room, the hull, and into the deep circular rotating waves below us. With a double sideways lash, a violent flip-flap, they rose . . .

'Out!' I managed to say aloud. 'Out!' Go on, said the sequence of disjointed, feverish images, get this slimy head, get this long fat nematode worm of a body out of this burrow of a sleeping-bag and extrude the whole lot into the lavatory . . .

Smacked left, hard, against the steel plates of the inward-bulging port-bow and right, hard, against the steel partition of the rusty shower, I pitched to my knees in front of the seatless bowl and held on to the rim with both hands, hard. On the floor to either side were two big circular iron valves, each stamped SCUPPER DISCHARGE O/BOARD. I lowered my face into the bowl. The head-torch lit up every ancient and modern shit-splatter: one, particularly old and black, in front of my nostrils, was shaped like a heart. And then I said goodbye to all that Guinness, to the pig's supper at the Royal Hotel (£28 for two) and even, perhaps, to a day-old bolus of breakfast at Bev's Kitchen, Nairn.

Congratulating myself, assuming it was all over, I pushed down the lever and, hoping that I had not woken Luke, I wiped up the splash-zone with my face-flannel and managed, tottering, to squeeze out the goo in the basin.

I crawled on all fours back to the edge of my pitching bunk, hauled myself up, and slithered back inside the safe, army-green, Arctic-warfare, nylon-silky, sweat-soaked, tapering tube of a sleeping-bag. I wiggled my toes, I flexed my ankles. And this, I decided, is here and now the highest available of physical pleasures. A shiver of anus-tightening happiness spread up from the base of my spinal cord to the back of my skull. So that's it, I whispered to myself, now you'll be fine. *And no one will know.*

And in half an hour my intestines ejected me again, to repeat the process. And then once more. And again, until there was nothing left to throw up. Not even bile. And still I crawled out to retch into the bowl, my new, my only, my porcelain world. But it's obvious, I tried to tell myself, it's OK – we have *not* evolved to do this thing. Tens of thousands of years of minor fishing and gathering mussels and cockles along the shorelines: yes; our ancestral flat-worms wriggling along the seabed in search of food for several million years: yes; even our life as jawed fishes, an adventure which began 425 million years ago: certainly; but *at no stage* were we stupid enough to allow ourselves to be bunged about on the *surface* of the open ocean. No – to do that you have to be mad like Jason or Bryan or Sean or a Robbie, or even (and this thought was oddly worrying) Luke. Because Luke, why, he's doing this not for money, but for an interest, for *scholarship*. Luke is bonkers, Luke is barking. And, with this resolving thought, gasping for air like a lungfish, I fell asleep.

In my dream a giant flatworm, one of the *Platyhelminthes*, each of its mucus-slimy segments as big as a mattress, fastened on my shoulder. It had a bill like a duck. It was a Duck-billed-platypus

44

platyhelminthes, and shaking me. Luke's young weather-beaten face, a foot away, filled my entire field of vision. 'Wake up!' it said, manic.

'Luke – the *platyhelminthes*, the flatworms, do they have segments?'

'Eh? No. Of course not . . . Wake up! Come on! Wake up! We're at the fishing-grounds. It's first light up there. There's a lull in the storm. It's Force 8. It's OK. There's a heavy swell, but it's OK. Jason's about to haul! Your first haul! Up! Now!'

'Ugh. Please . . .'

'Look – I know, I know, we've all been through it – seasickness, terrible, but so what? It's not like your malaria or hepatitis or TB or whatever – it won't *kill* you, so who cares? You've been asleep. You slept for *eight hours*. Up! Up you get! Yeah, yeah, everyone knows – it begins with you thinking you're going to die, and eight hours later it ends, just as you're wishing you could. But you can't and you won't! Redmond, look, remember, they made you an Honorary Member of the lab, my lab, the Marine Laboratory, Aberdeen. One of the very best there is! So you're *my* guest. And these boys – the crew – we're here to serve them, not just with better nets and fish-finders and gadgets, but to make sure they have a future, that their fishery is *sustainable* – and that, that's *difficult*. For that we need their respect, if you like, their good will. So, I'm sorry, but *you can't just lie here*. You've been out for eight hours. Eight hours! So up you get – and you've got to be quick. The alarm's about to go. Here. Drink this. All of it.' Luke jerked my right arm out of its warm, sweaty, tubular-snuggle of a home in the sleeping-bag – and in my comatose hand he stuck a bottle of Lucozade. 'The trawlerman's secret weapon! Plus one day of ship's biscuits, dry biscuits. That's all you need! Quick! I've got a minilog on the net. I must go. See ya!'

'Luko's Aid,' I said (absurdly pleased).

'Well done!' said Luke, springing to the door like a sand-hopper. 'Lousy jokes! You're back to normal!'

And he went.

Slowly as a hermit crab, reluctantly as a caddis-fly larva, I worked my way out of my safely enclosing exoskeleton of a sleeping-bag and, lying back again on the bunk, I pulled on my pants, my trousers. I found my black socks (three to each foot, against the cold) and, bundling forward like a curled foetus, I lodged into my woolly carapace of a sweater. The effort of it: there was no rest anywhere, nothing would stay still ... The mind-emptying noise of the engines faltered, throttled back, dipped like a Lancaster bomber coming in to land, and at that moment the siren sounded, a piercingly high BEEP-BEEP-BEEP. Other, smaller, straining engines came into life directly beneath me, and the sound lifted my body, as though I lay helpless on a tray in a morgue, gently, very slowly, prone, through the hanging curtains of Luke's bunk, over his flat blue sleeping-bag, out the other side – and it tipped me off and down on to his linear collection of red, blue and yellow plastic biscuit-boxes. My buttocks, I'm sorry to say, must have landed on his favourite box, his red Jacobs biscuit-box, because under me its top and sides blew up, releasing a tight stash of small, empty, plastic screw-lid Marine Lab specimen-bottles all over the floor.

Too surprised to think, or even mutter, let alone swear, I held on to everything that offered a moving handhold and waited, until the tilting floor projected me out of the cabin to the base of the stairwell. Hunched, half-spreadeagled, I pressed myself up the narrow steps and, sitting on the floor of the shelter-deck, an elbow clamped over the steel sill of the door, I thrust my legs into my oilskin trousers and, eventually, my feet into my sea-boots. Standing up, I was thrown against the lashed oil-drums to starboard, but in one or three moves I slotted into my oilskin jacket. Rolling aft, I thought, like a seaman, I emerged from the cowl of the shelter-deck – and was at once thrown face-first into the circular steel side of a 7-foot-high winch. I held on to a pair of protruding bolts, my fingers as committed as the suckers on a squid. A rush of sea guttered

46

in and out of a scupper to my left – and that's a generous scupper, I thought, because if you fell on this slippery deck that scupper would wave you through with no questions asked – so maybe not, maybe you can't roll like a seaman if your thighs are merely average for the species and its relatives: round here you need thighs not like a chimpanzee or even a gorilla, round here you need thighs of another order altogether, like *Tyrannosaurus rex*.

At the starboard side of the stern I could see Bryan, the breaking spray blown across his yellow oilskins, one gloved hand on a lever at the base of the crane, waiting. To his right stood the other Robbie, Robbie Stanger, I assumed (because, apart from the unseen, the subterranean engineer, Dougie Twatt, he was the only man I didn't recognize, that I hadn't met). Robbie, my appointed protector, balanced himself on the absurdly rolling deck as if he lived there, which, I supposed, for at least two-thirds of his life, he did. And he looked as if he'd grown where he stood – and that too, I thought, is partly true, because in these conditions, unbeknown to him, his muscles must be growing even as I watch. And no matter how extreme the swell, his head, I noticed, stayed level, as if he'd developed a gyroscope in the rear of his upper neck. Just waiting there (for what?), he seemed alert, quick, as energetic as a stoat. His worn, stained red-and-black survival suit, head up over a navy-blue peaked cap, fitted him tight and easy as the cuticle on a shellfish. He was smiling at me. Beside big Bryan (a Viking) he looked tiny; he had dark eyes, a peaky face, a long thin straight nose (he was a Pict . . .). He's not *that* far away, I thought, as the deck rolled through 45 degrees. It's just that beyond this drum of coiled-steel cable and its two friendly bolts, in the middle of that 8-foot stretch of oily sea-frothed deck before the next handhold (the edge of a cattle trough or a net-coaming or whatever you call it), there might as well be a 1,000-foot crevasse. Robbie waved. He beckoned me astern. (No, *I'm not moving.* I'm staying here. For a fortnight, if necessary. And, if I could feel my hands in this cold, which I no longer can, I'd hang on even harder.) Robbie gave me

47

a double thumbs-up, a super-signal. (No, I'm not lifting a hand and as for shouting – you'd need a siren-in-the-throat to be heard in a wind like this.) Robbie gave me an emphatic V-sign. I could not respond. So he sent me a vigorous, an obscene, a graphically pumping one-finger up-yours. So we were *friends* . . . So at once one-twentieth of the mad, indifferent, violent, uncaring external world ceased to matter . . .

Luke – he was laughing – appeared beside me. (From where? Search me. I'd given up.) 'Well done!' he yelled. 'Redmond, you got out of bed! And look here, I know, we're all different, and for you, getting out of bed – that's very difficult!'

'Yes, yes. Always has been.'

'We're hauling. It's great! Your first haul! Now watch – this is *really something*. Every time. Because you never know – what's coming up? Eh? You never know! It's magic. Smashing! Look about!' Luke, again, shook my shoulder with a manic, a bound-less enthusiasm. I peeled my right cheek off the surface of my cold protective saviour, the warp-drum. And I looked about, or abeam, at the huge swell – but there were *gannets* out there, yes, gannets, our largest, most beautiful, most spectacular seabirds, hundreds of them, hanging in the wind, the purest of brilliant white, reflecting the early morning sun, their long thin wings iridescent in the low white light, their black wing-tips setting off their shining white, waiting. And there were kittiwakes, my favourite, my spirit-lifting brave little gull, a gull of the open ocean, rising and dipping, sheering into the high wind. And they were so close, so unconcerned, so close I felt I could touch them; tilting, they were suspended right there beside me, their bellies so white and strokable, their black legs and furled-up black-webbed feet dangling unconcerned, their little black eyes so friendly – and hello, they said, you look odd but even you must be a trawlerman, or you wouldn't be here, on our patch of distant sea, so far from land, so we trust you, we're in symbiosis, we live together. It's a partnership, you see: we give you comfort, we – we're very small works of art, we save you from depression: and in return you feed us, you give us all those bits of fish you can't bear to eat yourself . . .

'Hey Redmond.' Luke shook me again, not quite so hard. 'Don't go *off* like that, it's unnerving, it really is.' He transferred his grip, taking me by the left arm. 'This may be a Force 8, gusting 9. But so what? Who cares? We're in for a Force 11, maybe 12. But look, Redmond, at this time of year, for Jason, that's *normal*. He does it every year. So leave the worry to him – that's what skippers are for – it's much more important to learn things – so in a moment I'm going to guide you, we're going to go and stand by the hopper. Because I want you to see *everything*, every chance we get. And you have to try and *understand* what's going on, not just moon around and cling on – initial seasickness, fine, that's OK – *lots* of trawlermen suffer like you, on their first day back at sea. But that's it. You chose this life, remember? So more than one day sick – forget it! Go away. Stay ashore.'

'Yep. Ugh. Absolutely. Stay ashore . . .'

'Now – any minute, you'll see the doors, the trawl-doors, the otter-boards (what did you call them? torture-racks?), they'll break surface – and Bryan and Robbie will winch them up, bang to their gallows port and starboard. They'll disconnect them, stow them up there. Got that? Then the sweeps pull in the net itself. It's different, it varies on almost every boat. Weird. But there you go. The British fleet is so individual, haphazard, we never got standardized – and here it's the 'tween-deck net-drum that pulls in the sweeps, one deck below us, aft of the fish-room (and that, the fish-room, Redmond, as you'll learn, is the best place, it's *our place*). Jerry and Sean and Allan are down there now, right at sea level, no protection, no lifelines – and they have to pull in the net, they ride it, side to side. No grip, no nothing, and Redmond, that's *dangerous*. I'll show you – you'll see for yourself. With a following sea . . .'

'Luke. Listen . . .'

'Yeh?'

'Look Luke, I'm sorry, but I don't think I'm ready for that. You know. Not just yet . . .'

'Aye!' said Luke, with a yap of laughter which the wind snapped short and spat away to port. 'Of course not! Maybe I couldn't do it myself . . . at least . . . not now . . . not any more.' With a convulsive spasm, as if this particular hypothetical inability represented some deep personal failure, Luke's hand gripped me above the elbow, tight as a tourniquet. 'But – you'll see – we'll have other things to do. So much to do. So exciting . . .'

'Yeah. Great. Luke, I . . .'

'So the net's gathered in. Then Bryan lowers the power-block, and the boys heave the last section of net on to it, on to the three-quarters circle of rubberized hook – and then Bryan swings it right round from the stern to starboard, to the hopper there.' (An outsized tubular climbing-frame with a central suspended hook, above a closed hatch.) 'And then it's a ritual – *it really matters* – the skipper himself throws a grapnel on a rope into the sea to grab the lazy-deckie as they call it, the rope they need to attach to the lifting-beckett, the block above the hopper. To lift the fore-cod-end on to the block above the hatch. It's the Scottish system – other boats take the whole lot straight up the stern-ramp. And that's simpler, but far more dangerous. Because for that interval – with your stern-ramp down, and everyone's tired, and one-third of the ship open and vulnerable: well, one lump, one following lump, and that's it, you can't launch a liferaft, ridiculous, there's no time, you're all gone, you're finished. So this system, Redmond – I know what you're thinking: it's Scottish, it's a real drag, it's complicated, it's fussy, and it's expensive, because you need extra crew. But remember this – on average, ten fishermen a month die in UK waters. So we couldn't be out here at all, not expecting a Force 12, not unless we were in a boat like this . . . But hey – Redmond! *Don't look like that!*'

'Like what?' (Blank, I supposed. The spray in the eyes, and the cold, so very cold . . .)

'OK. So you don't understand? Huh? Well, you have to imagine the main warps way astern plunging down to the doors, the otter-boards. And the doors are bouncing and banging along the bottom, a kilometre or so down. Imagine *that* – it's pitch darkness down there, *really* black, because sunlight penetrates no more than 30 feet below the surface of the sea, and the pressure! One atmosphere per 10 metres. One mile down it's a ton, plus, to every square inch, and that – that's where Edward Forbes in your century, the nineteenth century, thought no life could exist. He called it the azoic zone. Azoic zone! And he was wrong, so very wrong. It's full of animals – and Redmond, *what animals*. You'll see – in less than half an hour you'll see, right here and now, down there' (he jerked an emphatic forefinger at the slimy deck), 'right below us, in the fish-room. I promise, just wait – it'll change your life!'

'Yeah?'

'Aye. For sure. But those doors – they're on the way up now – but just think of them still on the bottom. OK? So they're frighten-ing the fish towards the back of the triangle, the following net. And they keep the mouth of the net open – because they're so designed they want to sheer off port and starboard, but they can't, because the warps are pulling them forward, and astern they're attached to the sweeps, the two cables towing the net. Now, half-way along the sweeps, either side, the headline is attached – the rope which becomes the upper lip of the net. It's buoyed up with floats. And a length behind it the sweeps themselves curve inwards to become the groundrope – and that's rolling along the bottom on your car tyres, the rock-hoppers, the lower lip of the net. Sweet as a nut! Because the fish – before they even realize it, the net is above them! They're funnelled towards the cod-end. And there you go. A catch!'

'At last!'

'So you got it? You understood? You can picture all that?'

'No. I can't.'

'Look – I know it *sounds* complicated, but we're not talking

51

gluons and quarks and string theory and the origin of the universe here – it's ropes! It's cables! So let's start the other end, shall we? Here – on deck, right here. So – those main towing warps' (Luke released my arm, to point aft with his right hand), 'they're being hauled by the main winches. And at the moment they're controlled by the auto-trawl. The computer system. As they are throughout the tow. But Jason will take over from it before the doors arrive. And, as I said, the doors are made fast to the gallows – or sheaves, if you prefer. The warps are slackened and attached to the single sweep aft of the door by the pennant. This is hauled until the tension is taken off the doors. The doors are then disconnected from the system – at the back strops.'

My mouth lockjawed by the cold, I said, or thought I said, 'Wassa pennant? Wassa back strop?'

Luke ignored me, his eyes set on the appalling swell astern. 'Here they come!'

The massive rusted rectangles of iron, the doors, hoisted, clattered tight against their derricks, the gallows, to port and starboard. Bryan and Robbie to starboard, Allan and Jerry and Sean to port, crowded round the derricks, obviously engaged in intricate tasks which yet required great strength (oilskins taut across the shoulders).

'So now the single sweeps are hauled on to the main winch,' said Luke. (And you're a natural teacher, I thought, but manic. Or maybe it's just all this excitement, the being at sea, the hunting . . . but please, I haven't eaten a thing in years, and I'm fizzed up with Lucozade, and dizzy . . .) 'And when the double sweeps, the doubles or spreaders, arrive at the block, the boys will attach a messenger chain from the net drum to each one. They'll slacken the singles until the messengers take the strain. The doubles – they're hauled on to the net drum, on the deck below, and that takes tension off the main winch, so you can disconnect the single sweep. Simple! Alan and Jerry and Sean – there they go, down the port stairway – they'll be doing that any minute now. The net and the rest of the bridle system – the double-sweeps section – they'll attach that by the short messenger chains to the net drum. Then the rest of the sweeps – now you call them bridles – are wound on to the net drum. First the two wing-ends appear – they go on to the drum – then the headline with the floats and the footrope with the rock-hoppers. And most of that lot stays on the deck . . .'

Fortified by a brainful of bewilderment, I released my grip on the bolts of the winch and took a step towards the hopper. Luke grabbed me. 'Careful!' he said, guiding me gently but firmly by the arm, as if I was blind. 'We had a real lump just now. Awesome! Forty feet, fifty, maybe even sixty. I don't know. Everyone just stopped and stared up at it. You know, like I was telling you, a real monkey-bollock frightener of a lump! But she rode it OK – up and up. She's a great boat! We all took a tumble. Even Bryan fell. We all did. I fetched up against the gunwhale!'

'You did? Hey Luke. That explains it . . . something *really odd* happened to me down there. Down in the cabin . . .'

'Look! Redmond! The net!'

And there it was, streaming astern, snaking in the swell, one long green translucent line of mesh, seemingly far too small and narrow and fragile for all this effort, for the work of this whole ship.

'That's the bellies, nearest us, then the extension – the tunnel – and there's the cod-end!' (A big green mesh bag, bloated with fish, bobbing on the swell, white and silver, way astern.)

We lurched against the frame of the hopper and I held on, with both hands.

Jason, in blue overalls and yellow sea-boots, a grapnel in his right hand, bounded past us.

The kittiwakes and the gannets rose into the wind, banking round towards the cod-end. The kittiwakes alighted alongside the line of net (and they seemed so light, so delicate, so out of place in all this unremitting violence); they rode the small waves on the big swell with ease; they flicked up their wings as they pecked at the mesh. The gannets, 60 or 70 feet above the surface-hills of the sea, would flip over to one side, half close their 6-foot expanse of wing and, elbows out, streak down towards the cod-end in one long low oblique-angled dive, folding their wings tight against their bodies, a second before impact, to become a white underwater trace of bird and bubbles.

Bryan, back at his levers at the base of the crane, swung the big semicircular power block astern, amidships, and down. 'He's got to manoeuvre that under the net,' said Luke, adjusting his blue woolly hat under his oilskin hood, pulling it further down over his forehead and ears. 'Sometimes there's a rope they call a joker attached to the net – the boys use it to bunch the net and hoist it on to the block – it's easier that way. The winch hauls the bellies and extension and the boys flake them inboard – until the cod-end comes alongside. And as you can see . . . *Hang on, Redmond, try and roll with the boat . . . stand with your legs across the roll, for Chrissake, that's better, at 90 degrees to the roll . . .* we're beam-on to all this weather, and that's because the prop's stopped. Too bad – you can't risk fouling the net. If that happens you're powerless, you're in real trouble, big time . . .'

The power-block swung back round towards us, towards the hopper. 'That's right. He must keep the block high. To drop the fish in the extension down to the cod-end. Ach well, Redmond, I'm sure you've got it now. Got it sorted. My minilog – it's still on the headline. Hang on. I'll be back.' And Luke, as the *Norlantean* wallowed beam-on to the swell, stepped calmly away over the net-troughs, from rim to rim.

Allan, Sean and Jerry, appearing from the port stairwell, joined Robbie and Jason along the gunwhale where the extension hung from the power-block; the cod-end, bulbous, floated in the swell below, small fish hanging trapped and silver from its green mesh. From the gunwhale Robbie and Allan plucked out the fish they could reach in the extension, dropping them into a big plastic openwork basket at their feet. Sean, in front of me, climbed into the A-frame and lifted back the hatch of the hopper.

Jason threw the grapnel – and everyone seemed to move at once, a confusion of ropes, net, red and yellow oilskins, a swinging power-block. Somehow the cod-end pursued a rope up towards me over the side – and it came to rest, rounded and swinging and full, in the middle of the A-frame, right above the hopper. 'The jilson winch,' said Luke, from behind, in my right ear.

No one else spoke. They stared in silence – that meat-stare from the cave-mouth round the fire; except that this, I thought, as I tried to rub a little feeling back into my face, this is a fish-stare; and here and now it's so cold it hurts, right through, and there's no fire anywhere . . .

Robbie, without a word, took off his blue rubber gloves, laid them beside him on the deck, reached in under the big mesh bag and pulled a knot undone. Fish cascaded, out of sight, down into the hopper.

'Come on, Redmond!' yelled Luke, already several yards away. 'To the fish-room!'

I followed him at once without a thought, and I fetched up against the roped-back door to the bridge (stairs up) and the cabins (down). 'Better take off your boots and jacket,' said Luke, with an expert shake and twist. 'Carry them down with you.' Surprised that I no longer felt sick, that I seemed to be able to balance well enough to get where I wanted to go, within a couple of yards, or even less, and that, on the very small scale, the micro-scale, personally, life suddenly seemed to have a future back in its familiar place, I followed Luke down the companionway.

'Did you see that business with the cod-end knot?' he said, over his shoulder, as we slid on the cardboard squares of discardable carpet, along the passage past the galley. 'Did you see that?'

'Yes, I did. I'd no idea what happened, exactly . . . But yes, I did.'

'Good, because that's *important*.' He dropped his jacket and sea-boots to the floor, and paused to pull down the levers on a white-painted bulkhead-door. 'There are several types of cod-end knot. The boys here use a chain knot. Usually only one man in a crew ties it – I suppose it will have come about somehow' (he swung open the door) 'that if there was a big shot once, whoever tied the knot that time always ties it from then on.'

'A big shot?'

'Aye,' said Luke, picking up his yellow boots and red jacket, stepping over the high steel sill in his blue socks. 'Come on – you know. I don't have to repeat *everything*, do I? A shot. To shoot the net. A big shot, a *really* successful catch.'

'Ah, yes, I'm sorry,' I said, pitching awkwardly over the shin-high steel plate, barking my shin. 'Shit.'

'No. No shit,' said Luke, sitting down on a small bench to the immediate left, pulling on his boots, 'if that time he tied thirteen loops, then from then on there must always be thirteen and so on . . .'

'Yes, of course. Great!' I sat down beside him and tried to get my own boots on – in short bursts, because it was obvious that you must not lean forward, as the bare washed shiny dark wooden floorboards sloped down and away and your buttocks lifted clear off the tilt of bench . . . Wait. Here we go. Backwards. Lift a foot. *Pull.*

'Some say you shouldn't go out to the fishing-grounds with the knot tied, only at the last minute should you tie the knot . . . others the opposite . . . and so on.' Luke stood up and swung himself round into a small room to our left.

I stood up too, holding on to the steel door-jamb, and looked in: it was a changing-room of sorts, full of shelves and hooks, and in the left-hand corner was a perfectly normal, an absolutely ordinary white domestic washing-machine.

'Some boats I've been on – the man who ties the cod-end knot won't show you how it's tied: because there's a risk the magic will be lost if the secret is told. Nuts!' Luke was bending down beneath a shelf to the right, several coils of black electric cable over his right shoulder, trying to force a plug into a socket. 'One skipper collecting data for me wouldn't have thirteen anything. He was keeping records for me – and the haul-numbering took a bit of figuring out to start with – he'd write a series: eleven, twelve, fourteen, fifteen; or sometimes eleven, twelve, twelve plus, fourteen. Nuts!' Luke handed me a battered brown clipboard. The top sheet of graph paper, clamped beneath the rusted clip, was stained with engine oil. 'Take that please . . . Now let's see . . .' He reached up and pulled a 3-foot-long rectangular black metal box from the shelf level with his chin. 'Scales – the latest! For weighing fish. They lent me these in the lab. But I don't think they've been tried on *trawlers.* Or at least, not in January, not in a storm like this . . . It's

57

OK. Don't worry. I've got an old-fashioned one too, as a back-up. Let's see . . . we've got ten minutes or more, while the boys shoot the net for the next haul.'

And as he spoke the main engines started up, vibrating the ship, vibrating my spine.

'Come on, we'll set it up here.' He stepped across to a flat steel shelf beside a conveyor belt which divided the cavernous fish-room into two: a steel-sided, steel-grilled trackway that led from a tall, round, stainless-steel table (down to our left) to a closed hatch at my feet. A slosh of seawater, shin-high, washed across the dark brown swollen slippery wooden floorboards with each roll and, as the ship bent shuddering over to port, a part of the wave of slush and foam ladled itself out via the half-open drop-gate of the port scupper. As she rolled further over and down, fresh white seawater powered in, to toss and curl, as the ship righted herself, straight across to starboard, to repeat the process. 'Grand!' said Luke, switching on his scales (a red light appeared to the left of the long calibrated dial). 'Magic! It works – even in seas like this!' The steel ceiling of the fish-room was a confusion of pipes and cables (some encased in steel tubes, some simply slung and looped); strip lights; fuse boxes. The stainless-steel sides of the hopper occupied about one-fifth of the space, down in the left-hand corner, and from it another shorter conveyor belt led up to the circular rimmed table. To our right, to the right of the bulkhead door to the galley, lay a wide-diameter ribbed tube, an augur of sorts, a length of giant gut. Directly aft, at the end of the rectangular cavern, another open bulkhead door let dimly through to the net-deck, where the big winches for the bridle stood back-lit by the early morning light streaming in from the stern-ramp, from the bright surface of the heaped-up, following sea.

'Now, I'll need three or four baskets,' said Luke, 'for random samples, a selection of every species we catch. That's good – those three over there' (he nodded towards two red and one black plastic dustbin-sized baskets, roped to a pipe against the sides of the hopper). 'We'll pinch those. And that one.' (A red basket, to the other side of the main conveyor, against the far wall.)

'I'll get it,' I said, handing him the clipboard.

Intending to clamber over the 3-foot sides of the conveyor, I began to try to hitch up the civilian trousers beneath my oilskin trousers (there seemed to be so many belts and braces and rubber straps; and the whole outfit was so uncomfortable; and it was so difficult to keep everything up around a moving flop of stomach when the world would not stay still; and besides, my boxer shorts, long ago half-shredded by jungle mould, had now decided to give up altogether and to drop, dying, around my knees). And then, for the second time – and once again, so gently, without warning, so slowly – I was weightless, I was airborne. The conveyor belt passed beneath me; someone shot me in the left shin; the travelling wave of froth and foam came curling up to wash over me and to leave me, splayed out full length, against the rusty plates of the port side of the inner hull.

'Wow!' said Luke, as, half getting to my feet, I was slung back across the floor to the side of the conveyor. 'You flew!' he said, helping me over it. 'You flew! I told you – *stand at right angles to a roll. Never* face right into it.' And then, as I held on to the side of the circular table, he said, marginally more sympathetic, 'Are you hurt?' He stood to my left, a basket in either hand, just as if he was about to go off and do something sensible, like, say, picking up potatoes, in some thoroughly stable, reliable, muddy field.

'I'm not sure,' I said, confused, fumbling with my boot and socks, rolling up my two pairs of trousers. 'I nearly broke a leg.'

Luke laughed. It was a kindly laugh – the merriment, I reflected ruefully, of a lifeboatman who'd seen it all, real injuries, who'd probably pulled sailors from the sea with no legs left at all.

'It's nothing,' I said, inspecting a three-inch gash, horrified by the volume of blood running down into my socks. 'It's a scratch.'

'It's a 3-inch surface cut,' said Luke. 'No problem. Not worth dressing. You caught your leg on the edge of the conveyor. I saw it all. You flew! But you'll be amazed – cuts like that, even proper cuts, they heal so fast. It's the salt, I suppose. It's not like your jungle. There's no infection. No land bacteria can survive. Out here – everything heals.'

Luke took my arm. 'Stand here,' he said, positioning me on the starboard side of the circular table, a few feet from the wall of the hull. 'Stand on this box' (an upside-down fish-box) 'and wedge yourself in against this' (one of the stanchions supporting the deck above us) 'and then not even *you* can fly, whatever you do. This'll be *your* place. Your workplace!'

'Thanks,' I said, trying to balance.

Luke dropped the baskets beside me; and with a double kicked-up flash of yellow sea-boots in the fluorescent overhead lights, he vaulted right over the conveyor. Sure-footed, even as the mucus-slimy floorboards up-ended themselves and tilted away to port, he reached the impossible prize of the red plastic basket, released its lashing and, as the floorboards and their cargo of seawater heaved themselves up and over and down towards me, he vaulted back over the conveyor, the basket flying horizontally out from his left hand – and he slung it down beside the others.

'So here we are!' he said, stooping over a drop-gate at the base of the hopper, just above the bottom step of the small conveyor which led up to our table. 'At last! We're about to add to our knowledge, our knowledge of the new fisheries! The deep-sea fisheries! And believe me, Redmond, they're new, they really are! As yet – we know *nothing*.' He yanked up the stainless-steel gate. A flap of big, dead, dark flatfish fell out on to the belt. Carried away by his excitement, I caught myself thinking: I don't recognize any of them, but of course that figures, because we know *nothing*.

'Greenland halibut,' said Luke, straightening up. 'The boys call them Black butts. Because they're blackish both sides. And Greenland halibut, they're really interesting – it's their *evolution* – because it seems they don't want to be flatfish any more. They're camouflaged both sides. Their left eye has moved up to the edge of the head. So we think they swim on the ventral edge, like normal fishes – and not like a flatfish, blind side down. But surely, you're thinking, aren't you, their eyes are still wonky, they must be ill-adapted as hunters. But east of the Wyville Thomson Ridge they and the various species of redfish are the main commercial catch. So in biological terms they're *very* successful. But how? Well – most of the time they live one or two kilometres down, and the answer is, Redmond, we don't know. They're right here, a big fish *in UK waters*, common as blades of grass, and we don't know a damn thing! Isn't that great?'

'Yes!' I shouted, genuinely swept away, for a moment, by the intricate private life of the Greenland halibut.

Luke disappeared around to his right, to the port side of the hopper. There was a clatter and a scraping, the sound, I thought, of a corrugated-iron sheet being pulled aside, and Luke's voice, his shout, became hollow, a bounce of echoes. 'The French started it all!' he shouted, from inside the hopper. The boom of the declamation reached me in triplicate, stolen, around the edge, by the thud of the engines and the blows of the sea, but still, at the centre, laden with extra authority, amplified. 'The west coast of Scotland . . . Landings at Lochinver . . . Pioneered this whole thing . . . 1989 . . . *that* recent . . . Orange roughy . . . Roundnose grenadier . . .'

'At the time,' he said, reappearing in front of me, hopping up on a box the opposite side of the table, restored to his normal volume, shape and size, 'no one took much notice. But then they landed 50,000 tonnes of Orange roughy. 1991. *Fifty thousand tonnes.* That really did it. Because they'd also made themselves a market. They changed the name, Orange roughy, to *beryx* at first, but that didn't work, so they thought of Napoleon, as they do, and they called it the *Emperor fish*. And sales took off. The housewife – she loved it. All over France. Same in Spain.'

Luke, fired up by the inner sight of all those Orange roughy, all those deep-sea fish flying off the fishmongers' slabs, stared up at an innocent roundel of small levers directly above his head. He yanked

61

one down. (Nothing happened.) 'They did the same thing,' he shouted, still staring at the control box, 'even with deep-sea sharks like the Black scabbard fish. The French trawlermen call it the *siki*. Now – the Black scabbard fish – and we won't see it here, because you only find them to the west of the Wyville Thomson Ridge, they're all about a metre long. And we know almost nothing about them, about their life cycle.' He pulled down the second lever. (Nothing happened.) 'Where are the larvae? Where are the juveniles?' Luke, much moved, looked straight at me. (But I felt unqualified to make a substantive reply.) 'Here in the UK people wouldn't feed it to the cat! But in Portugal and Spain, I think, they call it Espada. In France it's the Sabre. And it sells well!'

Luke returned his gaze to the control box of small levers above his head. 'Redmond,' he said, as if it was all my fault, 'why the hell won't this work?'

'No idea,' I ventured, which was an understatement.

'Oh come on, I told you, all these trawlers are different.' He hopped off his box. 'You know perfectly well. There must be a master switch. A main power source way above the spray-level.' He stepped across the wet slide of shining floorboards, as if the soles of his boots were suction-pads, and inspected the chaos of wiring and junction boxes above the lip of the stern bulkhead door. 'Aye!' he said, jumping up, flicking down a switch.

The conveyor belt to my left came to life. The circular table, my safe handhold, began to rotate, remorselessly, clockwise – the big, round, trustworthy steel pail of a table began to move; it took its 18-inch-deep sides, its two-and-a-half-foot-wide inner sections, its central steel tube of a tower (double-layered with white plastic subsidiary pails), and my hands, with it.

'Let go!' shouted Luke, as I fell off my box. 'Och aye,' he said with an Uncle Luke laugh, as I swayed back up and on again. 'Stay where you are,' he said, back in control under the overhead levers. 'Balance *with your legs*.' Left arm above his head, he pushed up the right-hand lever, stopping the table with one of its receiving sections directly beneath the end of the conveyor – a cascade of big, dark, dead flatfish slid over the lip and slithered across the waiting steel tray, filling it. Luke pulled the lever down, rotating the table one section, repeating the process.

'So – these new deep-sea fisheries,' I said, trying to sound intelligent, wanting to learn, gripping the stanchion to my right with one hand (and this teacher of mine, I thought, with an uneasy meld of imagined pride and real dismay that I was growing so old so fast – he could be my legitimate son). 'These new fisheries – it's all the fault of the British housewife.'

'What is?' said Luke, turning another section.

'Their cooking habits. No French fish-soup. No Spanish paella. Nothing but cod and haddock and pretty flatfish – sole and plaice. So our own fisheries collapse.' And then, impressed by the amount of blood I still seemed to be losing (both feet, inside their sea-boots, felt soaking wet, but my left foot was *warm*), I had a dying, paternal thought. 'Luke, you should be a teacher. You should teach this stuff. Become a lecturer somewhere.'

Luke, across the table, looked straight at me. He stopped the table, he stopped the conveyor. 'You think so?' He straightened his shoulders. He pulled off his blue woolly hat. He held it out in his right hand for a moment, towards me, above the table, like an offering (and I almost took it). He thrust his hat awkwardly into his right trouser pocket. 'You really think so?'

'Yes, I do. It's obvious – you're made for it.'

Luke's face seemed to grow larger, his eyes brightened, his forehead lost its two deep crosswise furrows. 'Redmond, to tell the truth – I *had* thought of it. You know – becoming a lecturer. In a fisheries college somewhere. The one in Stromness. The place that produced Jason! Or the new North Atlantic fisheries college. In Shetland. At Scalloway. Smashing! A smashing way to live! But then . . . I have a problem. Big style . . .' He looked down at the full steel section of tray in front of him. 'I don't know, I don't think

63

'. . . you know, I just *don't think I've got the balls for lecturing.*' Luke ran his right forefinger along the outer steel rim, round to the left, round to the right. His hand was calloused and scarred and heavy with muscle. It seemed to belong to a man twice his size. He said: 'The thought of it . . . *standing up in front of people . . .*'

'Listen, Luke,' I said, in one of those moments of sudden, transitory exhaustion when the world goes dead for a second or two, when you feel hypnotized by whatever object happens to fall within your line of sight – in this case his disembodied hand, as it shuttled, left to right, right to left. 'You've got the balls for anything.'

'No!' he said, decisively, breaking the spell. 'Not for going up on stage. No. I've done it once. I was shit scared. I really was.'

'You were?' I said, reassured, over-eager. 'So when was that? What happened?'

'Not now,' he said, restarting both machines, raising his voice. 'I'll tell you later. Maybe. Yes. I promise I will.' And then, with no pause or warning, he gave me a grin that lit his whole face, a smile that came from somewhere else, the lop-sided, caught-in-the-act smile of a little boy. 'And anyway, Redmond, this dream of mine, this teaching business, you see, the fact is – *I thought I'd start with you!*'

'You did? But Luke . . . that's great. The lecturing, I mean. It's so good to know that even you – even you're afraid of *something.*'

'Me? Redmond, look, I'm afraid of *everything.* I really am.' He stopped a fresh section of table under the conveyor. 'And there again, ach well, teaching . . . Research, the deep sea, the oceans, papers, books – money and time for everything I live for! But forget it. Because there's no way I'll ever be able to stand up in front of hundreds of people and *talk.* It can't be done. Simple. So if I ever get my Ph.D. sorted I'll just take off somewhere. Work my passage. Go back to the Falklands.' He moved the table on one section. 'Because the fact is, Redmond – no one, but no one, is going to be as easy to teach as you.'

64

'Of course not,' I said, pleased.

'Because absolutely no one – zilch – no one that I have to teach will be as completely monkey-bollock clueless as you are.'

'Ah.'

'Imagine it! Teaching in Orkney or Shetland . . . Every last one of them will be a trawlerman's son. Or they'll know everything already, like Jason. Redmond – imagine it! – imagine trying to tell Jason what to do . . .'

'But you *won't* be telling a young Jason what to do! You'll be talking about marine biology, the possible distribution of fish, I don't know, life cycles, animals in the deep sea.'

'Forget it!' he said, jerking down the overhead lever, rotating the three full trays in the circular pail right the way round to where I stood. He shut off both machines. 'Forget it! It's just a dream or a nightmare or whatever. It's OK. I'm resigned to it. I know what'll happen. I'll have to get my old job back. Fisheries Inspector, the Falklands. With a Ph.D. So please, let's not talk about it any more. And anyway, I wouldn't get a post at Scalloway. I'm not good enough. And besides, you must concentrate, Redmond. Focus. The Greenland halibut, the Black butt. Because I must teach you to gut them – and gut them fast.' From fish-box to fish-box he came round to stand beside me, collecting, on the way, from their lodging place in the crack between a rusted pipe and the rusted ceiling, two 6-inch-long knives with red plastic handles and stained steel blades. He handed one to me. 'Because it's not just one or two Black butts you'll have to clean – it's one or two *tonnes* of Black butt.'

Luke pulled two pairs of new blue rubber gloves from his trouser pocket. 'Sean gave me these. They're for us. Direct from Jason. But he said – or at least, Redmond, I *think* he said, because he speaks *real* Caithness, and even I find that difficult to catch, you know, but we'll be OK eventually, you'll be amazed how your understanding increases as you work with someone – it can go from one word in ten to as much as one in two; anyway, Sean said,

"You're lucky, boys," he said, "you really are. New gloves! Now donna even *think* of asking for another pair. Och no. Because the skipper will na have it. Boys – he keeps them in the wheelhouse, in their plastic wrappings. And he *counts* them every watch, like a pile o'gold!"'

'But that's great, Jason's got it!' I said. 'Two million pounds in debt – and he's managed to fetish all his anxieties down to the rubber gloves!'

'Ach,' said Luke, giving me my sacred pair. 'Leave me out of this. This spooky stuff. I hate it. I really do. Life should be *rational*. Sean told me – if you *do* ask Jason for a fresh pair, he goes wild-eyed. For the boys, it's a joke. But not really. Because they understand. Every time you ask – even if you show him your old pair, ripped to bits on redfish spines – he'll say, "Don't you realize? Have you any idea? Every other skipper charges his crew full retail price! And these – they're the *very* best! Eight pounds and thirty pence a pair!" And then he gives you this terrible piercing look, and he's shaking all over, and believe me, you dream about it – it comes up in your bad dreams, for weeks afterwards, you dream about it, you panic, it's Jason's head . . .'

'And then? What happens then?'

'Then? Ach well. Then, of course, *Jason gives you the gloves.*'

'So he's a good skipper?'

'Ach. I can see. You don't understand. How could you? But the boys do. Jason – he's not just a good skipper, for Chrissake – *they love him.*'

'Yes, of course.'

'Please, Redmond, stop saying *of course.* Because it's like make-up on a woman's face. It doesn't *mean* anything, does it?'

'No, no, of course not . . . I mean . . .'

'Well, here. Look.' He picked up a yard-long Greenland halibut. 'You're privileged. You really are. Because all these deep-sea fish you're going to see will be big mature adults – and I often think this, because this is a new fishery, and in years to come people will say, about my measurements – that Luke Bullough, how he exaggerated! The whoppers he told! But here, come on, hold this –' (my gloves only just got a grip on its smooth slimy skin) '– you take a Greenland halibut. You open it from its green side, its black side, its blind side. You slit the knife through the gill arch between the ventral fin-pair. *Here.* Then up to the end of the gut. *Here* . . .' (The gut seemed far too short to sustain such a big fish, the soft organs far too compact; the whole lot contained in a small pouch, a tucked-away wallet . . .) 'Then you take it all out, this little handful, a little handful of liver and gunge. Then you slit the oesophagus, see? *Here.* And you scrape out the little heart. It's tiny – but it's important. The merchants really hate it if you leave the heart in. You *must* scrape out the little heart.'

'Hi, boys!' – and even as the floor dipped away through, it seemed to me, 45 degrees, Sean, appearing through the stern bulkhead door, managed to impart a swagger to his rolling gait. He shouted, 'Hi, boys – that's it, work your asses off.'

Big Bryan, First Mate, and Allan (equally broad-shouldered, athletic, but not quite so big) pushed past Sean without a word. To the left of the door to the cabins and galley they pulled up an outsize iron hatch (as if it was a sheet of aluminium); they unroped the large ribbed tube, the giant gut, from its place against the port wall, retied one end to the lip of the main conveyor, worked the other down through the hatch and, climbing on to the top rungs of a ladder, or so I assumed, they disappeared down into the fish-hold.

Sean was standing on a box to Luke's right. Robbie (who'd materialized so fast and silently I'd no idea where he'd come from) stepped up under the levers, in control.

I said to Sean, 'Where's Jerry?' And, looking at Sean, imagining Jerry (the friendly young jovial punk with the crew-cut, the Nicorette-inhaler, the earring), I lost concentration, and my third Greenland halibut, half-gutted, slithered back into my section, the full steel tray in front of me.

'Fock it!' said Sean, with his squashed-up grin. 'You nearly took yer thumb off! Jerry? He's the *cook*. So he's gone to the *galley*. In one hour – *breakfast*. Two meals a day. Breakfast, dinner. Meals you'll never forget!'

'Grand!' said Luke, dropping ungutted Greenland halibut into his red plastic basket. 'Breakfast. Redmond, you remember? Bev's Kitchen, Nairn? How you never wanted to leave? How you wanted to *stay there for ever*? Well, this is something else. It always is. It's five, six times as big! I meant to tell you then – "Redmond, if you think *this* is a breakfast. Just you wait. Redmond – try it on a trawler!"'

A memory trace, a sharp wave of nausea, swept up my gullet and dissolved my next anodyne ignorant question in a back-of-the-throat pool of bile and acid.

'Hey Luke!' said Sean, elbowing him, with excessive force, in the ribs. 'What you doing? Redfish, no. But Black butts – you're meant to *gut* them!'

'This,' said Luke, one blue-gloved hand, despite himself, rubbing the point of impact, 'this,' he said, in automatic, serious (some things in life *really do matter*) scientific mode, 'is a *random sample*. Sean – I'm taking five. That'll do for now. There'll be many more, later, at different stations, places, *hauls* to you. Right? I'm going to sex, measure, weigh and age them. And the same applies to all the other significant species we catch. It's OK. I'll gut them later.'

'Age them!' said Sean, with a laugh.

'Aye – I'll cut out their otoliths, and pop them in a specimen bottle, and label each one, and then we'll age them in the lab.'

'Otoliths?' said Sean, interested, his knife poised in mid-air. 'Their balls? Tits? What's that?'

'Their ears,' said Luke. He laughed. He liked Sean. 'Ears!'

'They don't have ears!'

'They do, they do!'

'Well, aye, suppose they do,' said Sean, wary, plainly thinking that he, the new boy, was being teased yet again. 'Far out, man. I mean, *freaky*. Like, their ears? Who the fock would want their *ears?*'

'They're inside!' said Luke, entranced by this unexpected, this whole new take on fish and their ears. 'They're hidden away. It's grand, Sean, it really is. Because their little ear-bone, the otolith, it lays down growth-rings every season, like a tree. You put it under the microscope. You count the rings. And there you are! Sweet as a nut!'

'Nuts!' said Sean, not to be fooled, just in case. 'Nuts yourself.'

'It's true!' shouted Luke over the thump of the engines, bearing his prize off to his new weighing machine.

'Otoliths!' said Sean, moving up a box, standing beside me. 'O-to-liths! He should tell that to his nan!'

Robbie, opposite us, the boss of the Greenland-halibut-gutting unit, had, somewhere along the jagged pitching line from the open deck to the sheltered fish-room, changed out of his survival suit (which was obviously, as Dicko thought, something special, expensive, an investment for life to save your life – a flotation suit – and, above all, not a piece of clothing that should smell of fish). He now wore standard oilskin trousers-and-apron (his were red in front, yellow at the back), the Jason-regulation blue rubber gloves, a fish-filthy dark blue tracksuit-top, and a peaked black hat that hugged his head and curved down to cover his ears – and he was gutting fish with unnerving speed, somehow performing the task in one unbroken movement: you pick up a Black butt, your knife in your right hand, you slit it – in goes your left thumb, you runnel the guts on to the table, you sling the fish up and over and down the central tube.

Sean was half as fast; and I was still on my third big slithering corpse that refused to let me grip it at all, that seemed to be still alive.

'So, Sean,' I said, 'how did you get started, as a trawlerman?'

'Trouble.' He tossed a gutted fish up in the air and down the tube. 'Big trouble. So Jason's family took me on. They like us! I've got fifteen brothers and sisters. So it's not easy, you know? Aye.

69

Drink driving. The court – they fined me! Three thousand pounds! And it wasn't even my car. Well, I told them straight, I don't *have* any money. "Find it!" they said. "You've got six months!" So Jason's father-in-law, he took me on. And that was the making of me! The *Viking*. Aye! You should see her. She used to be the biggest trawler in all the British fleet. *Beautiful*. And I had eight days off in six months. But I made it! I did it! I paid the fine!'

'Well done!'

'Aye!' He flipped another fish, with extra energy and skill, way up in the air and straight down the rolling, pitching, yawing tube. 'And then Jason's father-in-law said to Jason (know what I mean?), "That Sean," he said. "He's good. He's *trained* now – so you take him."'

'And what's it like?' (As the ship levelled between rolls I finally managed to snick in the knife and scrape out the little damson-red heart: Black butt number three.) 'The work?'

'The work? It's no hard, the work. It's the being away. Eight days off in six months! I never saw my nan. I never saw my mates. So this is much better! But it's no very warm. Now's the worst – January's the worst. But even in summer, it's the mending the nets up there, you canna go any faster and it's no very warm. And there again, right enough, you never know the hours you'll have to work – maybe it's twenty at a stretch, maybe only twelve. And you're away all the time. It's worse than the mining. The miners – they go home! One shift and they're home! And there again – here it's more dangerous, much worse. Sometimes, well sometimes, you're so scared you *shit yourself*. It scares the shit out of you!' Sean gave one of his happy laughs – an all-in laugh on his squashed-in face, an energetic, infectious, sweaty, biological laugh. 'But *you* won't, Redmond. Not even when we get this Force 12! You'll be OK!'

'I will?' I said, squaring my shoulders. 'Why's that?'

'Because you've chucked it all up! You've nothing left!'

Robbie, concentrating, shut off the belt from the hopper; he rotated the table: every second tray or so, with a sharp metallic clang, he dropped open a trap-door in front of him – the guts fell through into a steel chute, a high-sided trough that emptied itself through the starboard scupper.

(So why hadn't I noticed that? Why hadn't I even registered that steel slide – big enough to stand in – leading to the steel gate of the scupper, where the light from the sea outside shone so white, where, I supposed, the gannets and the kittiwakes waited, and whence, as the *Norlantean* took those violent rolls to starboard, the cold fresh manic sea powered in and swept across the deck? It's OK, I said to myself, stop this nonsense, you're in another world – you don't need these self-imposed anxieties; you can't expect to understand everything at once – relax; because there's so much time ahead of you, so much genuine, external, comforting *real* fear – and it's all coming your way . . .)

Robbie switched on the main conveyor: a narrow shoal of gutted Greenland halibut juddered up the incline from the base of the circular gutting table towards the hatch, the inserted open mouth of the tube down to the hold. Luke returned, stepping up on a fish-box to my right, to Sean's left. He tipped his measured and gutted fish into an empty tray, wedging his red plastic specimen-basket on the floor beside him. Robbie began to start-stop the table again, refilling every section.

'Hey, Sean,' said Luke, 'I've been watching. That Robbie – he's *quick*. About the fastest gutter I've ever seen!'

'Aye, right enough,' said Sean, leaning confidentially towards us, in a three-man privacy in an outer world of speech-absorbing, body-shaking noise. 'He's a Jack Russell of a fighter. Luke – mind this, whatever you do – if Robbie's bin drinking, keep out of his way. Leave the bar. Because he's fast, he's so fast you wouldna believe it. In fact, Luke, do what I do – leave town. You say goodbye, Stromness, or up yours, Kirkwall – or even forget it, Thurso! Because it's no safe. He's so fast you'll no see it coming. And that's the truth!'

'Thanks,' said Luke.

'Ach,' said Sean, with an apologetic grin as the now-full table came to a halt. 'I'm forgetting. I didna mind. Robbie – our Robbie Stanger – he's na touched a drop in ten months. And what's more, boys, he says he's no missed it! And he doesna smoke, if you know what I mean. But there you go, he doesna fool me, because he's old, mebbe even thirty – and his girlfriend, she's lovely, she's *sixteen*. So he's clean, *he has to be* . . .'

'Aye,' said Luke, as if he, of all people, would never understand a problem like that, looking away, as it happened, at the lip of the conveyor from the hopper. 'Redmond!' he shouted, full volume, pointing with his gutting knife: 'A Rabbit fish!'

Luke grinned, a crackly grin on his lined and weathered face, a face that seemed twenty years older than its owner. 'A Rabbit fish! *Chimaera monstrosa*,' he said, as if he'd conjured it up all by himself. 'How's that?'

Well of course I'd seen no fish like it. I said, 'Woof!'

The monstrous chimera, the mythical freak, two or three feet long, was on its back, its creamy underside shiny with slime, its pectoral fins like wings, and where its neck should have been was a small oval of a mouth set with teeth like a rabbit's. It slid down, flop, on to the tray. Its foot-long rat-tail whiplashed after it.

Luke shouted at Robbie, signed, with a circular sweep of his right hand, to send that table-tray all the way round to us: and there was the Rabbit fish in front of me, entire. Luke turned it over; he held it up, for inspection. The back and sides were mottled grey-brown on a blueish sheen of slime; the eyes were bulbous, huge – and it was looking at me, smiling. The lateral-line canal (as if someone had cut into its flesh with a Stanley knife) swept up in a happy curve from the base of its thick conical snout to the top of its cheek: a false mouth set in a permanent, emphatic grin. 'How's that?' said Luke, proud of his Rabbit fish. 'Weird, or what?'

'Weird! . . . And what are these?' I said, running a gloved finger over a line of spaced-apart pits (as if someone had drilled into the flesh with an awl), small holes, five above and six below the lateral-line grin.

'Electroreceptors! They can detect the tiny DC fields set up by the muscles of their prey. The high-frequency waves of mechanical energy, Redmond, the waves that travel *really* well in water – the fish clocks these with its inner ear. For low-frequency waves, short-range disturbances, you use your lateral-line system, a series of perforated tubes under the skin. That's how you detect something odd and near you in the current – different waves, different pressures: so is that a presence you can eat? Or will it eat you? Or is it a rock? But you knew that, of course.'

'No, I didn't! I really didn't!' I shouted, exasperated by my own ignorance, and conscious, too, that some system, some inner, land-based, sleep-fed system necessary for emotional control was beginning to desert me. 'I did *not* know that!'

'OK!' said Luke, leaning away from me, towards Sean, holding the Rabbit fish (slack, bendy) in front of him, as if he was about to launch it across the fish-room. 'Electroreceptors! Their senses are far more complex than ours – as well as all the usual: smell, taste, sight, hearing, temperature, pressure – they live in a world of electrical stimuli: imagine it, you're a shark, there's a long piece of prey down there, a weak electric field, a static, wounded eel, so you attack. And guess what? It's an underwater electric cable!'

'Horrible!'

'But Redmond, *here it is*, the Rabbit fish. And I love it, I really do, because it's common, it lives off our own shores, and yet we know sod all about it! Isn't that exciting?'

'Yes! Yes!'

'The Rabbit fish! Sometimes known as a Rat-tail! But not here, Redmond, not *at sea*. Because I told you – you must never say *rabbit*, you must never say *rat*. So here we call it *King of the herrings*, because it so happens that it comes up from the depths, it moves into the shallow seas off our coasts to spawn at exactly the same time as the migrating herrings arrive . . .'

73

'Aye!' said Sean. He pressed his forehead, hard, for a fraction of a second, I noticed, against the rusted iron of the stanchion behind him. (Of course, I thought, he can't touch it with his hands because he's wearing Jason's blue rubber gloves . . .) He turned. He yelled into Luke's right ear: 'Fockin' stupid superstitions! I don't believe a word of it! Bullshit! Bullshit!'

Just in front of the first dorsal fin of the fish there was a spine, sticking up like a marlin spike. 'What's this?' I said, pulling it forward, releasing it: *ping*!

'Don't do that!' said Luke, at once dropping the Rabbit fish into his specimen basket. 'It's dead. Sure. So it's OK. *But don't do that.* That's poisonous. Really poisonous. There's a venom gland and a pump beneath that, like a hornet sting, only far worse. Some people say it can kill you. So, Redmond, calm down, go slow, whatever . . .'

'Ah. Sorry.'

'Look here, that's OK, don't worry . . .' Luke held my left arm a moment. 'Just don't *worry me*. It makes me *tense*. OK? Please – don't go falling all about the deck, and try not to *fly*, and don't go flicking spines about – you know, calm down, watch me, don't be so *active* . . .'

'No. Yes,' I said, flattered, as the trawler began one of its excessive long jarring epileptic rolls to port. (Active? I was now too afraid to move at all . . .)

'Look – lots of fish species have evolved a venom-delivery system, independently. Rabbit fish, stargazers, dragonets, catfish, toadfish, scorpionfish, weever fish, as you know . . .'

'No, *I don't*.'

'OK. But it's fascinating in itself, don't you think? How did they adapt their mucus glands like that? How did they do it?'

'No idea.'

'OK. That's OK too. Because no one else has any idea either. Not really, as far as I can see. But Rabbit fish – we think – they swim slowly over the bottom, down to 3,000 feet, and they crunch

74

up crustaceans and molluscs in that weird mouth of theirs, with its opposable bony plates. So they're a natural target for any passing deep-sea shark – but imagine it! You're a shark. You try and swallow this slimy nothing of a fish that can't swim fast – and the pain in the roof of your mouth! The pain! So you spit it out. And you feel ill, so very sick for days and days, and you wish you'd never been born, and from then on – one sight of a Rabbit fish and you throw up!'

'Yeah!'

'But Redmond, they're theoretically interesting – that's the main point.' Luke, as he talked, was gutting Greenland halibuts, almost as fast as Sean, a slit, a scrape, a back-handed upwards chuck, a flap of fish down the central tube. 'They evolved when? Two hundred million, three hundred million years ago? We'll have to check. We must get this right. Because the Rabbit fish is a real missing link, a living intermediate between the cartilaginous fishes – the sharks and rays – and the bony fishes. Its skeleton is made of cartilage, it lays its eggs in horny capsules, the male has paired claspers to hold the female and fertilize her internally, like a shark, and the heart and brain of a shark. Yet it has a gill-cover to protect its gills, like bony fish, and its upper jaw is fused to its skull instead of being joined by a ligament, as in sharks. Aye, and you'll like this – *the anus of the Rabbit fish is distinct from the urinogenital opening.*'

'I'm glad to hear it,' I said, which was a mistake, but most of my brain (or so it felt) was entirely absorbed by the attempt to instruct my blue rubber prongs of hands on the getting of a grip on my sixth Greenland halibut ('You'll have to gut *tonnes*'), and my personal mantra sang: 'You must *join in*! You must help! You must gut and gut. You're a fat slob. You're old. You're finished. And no, *you can't go to bed, you can't get to your bunk.* Here people are watching, so it's not possible: *you can't pretend you're somewhere else.*' And, holding the sharpest little knife I'd ever held, as the trawler rolled and surged and yawed and shook and dervished to starboard, to screams and drumbeats, to high trebles, to deep bass notes, from the wind, the storm, blasting through the open bulkhead door from the stern-ramp: I missed the tiny package of Greenland halibut guts and slit the blue rubber palm of my left-hand glove.

'Hey Redmond!' said Luke, six inches to my right, flipping yet another gutted fish up and over and down the tube. 'You're not listening, are you?'

'I am!'

'OK – but look, it matters, maybe I didn't explain it properly. The sharks and rays evolved around 400 million years ago – and Redmond, *that is 165 million years before the first dinosaurs appeared* – and yet they're still here, they're abundant, they're almost unchanged, they're everywhere, they got it right, they're successful. And then there's the break-out, the next stage, and that's the mystery, because why bother? Why bother when you got it so very right? Nuts! Nuts! But there you are, there's the evidence, the Rabbit fish' (with his knife he flicked at his specimen basket), 'and from that came – the bony fishes!'

'Yes! But Luke – is this it? Is this a Force 12? Conrad talks about it – you know, in *Narcissus*, in *Typhoon*: I remember, in a real storm, he says, you hear banshee wails, deep drumbeats . . .'

'Wails? Drumbeats?' Luke laughed. 'Redmond – that's Fleetwood Mac!

From the hold came a tremendous metallic banging, steel-on-steel, a hammer-gong from below.

Robbie leant right forward over his tray and yelled, full power, at Sean: 'Gut! You big girl's blouse you! Get gutting!' And then to Luke, by way of apology, 'They've nae fish. They're short below!'

And so we gutted Greenland halibut, and Luke showed me how to gut tusk ('Redmond, you spell it t-o-r-s-k'), which was more difficult than you might imagine, because the torsk were three to four feet long, and slimy, and their skin appeared to be made of rubber, and they were grossly distended: they had sicked up their stomachs: their stomachs hung out of their mouths. And that, said Luke, was because torsk had swimbladders. And swimbladders were interesting. Because the average fish is denser than water, so how, if you're a fish, do you stop yourself sinking? The sharks and tunas don't have swimbladders – so they have to keep swimming, angling their paired fins to act as hydrofoils; but they've also reduced their overall solidity by storing low-density lipids in their bodies ('Redmond, that's why you call them "oily fish"') – and shark-liver oil is five or six times as buoyant as an equal weight of water. And with fish like mackerel, of course, said Luke, it's obvious, isn't it? Fish like that, fish that make vertical migrations of many hundreds of feet every day – and as you know that applies to lots of oceanic mesopelagic species – a moment's thought will tell you that a swimbladder is a bad idea. It's just not possible to inflate or deflate it fast enough. As we could see from these torsk. There they'd been, maybe a kilometre down, cruising over coarse, rocky ground (the only kind of ground they like), when the net trapped them – and there'd been no time to secrete gas (oxygen, nitrogen and carbon dioxide – although carps only use nitrogen) back into the bloodstream. They're bony fishes, said Luke, related to the cod, and most bony fishes have evolved an internal gas float, a swimbladder – it's developed from a primitive lung ... (So, I thought, had their ancestors squirmed ashore like the lungfish, thought better of it, and gone back to sea? Had they gulped air at the surface, like newts in a pond? I decided to ask later, should life ever become peaceful again ...)

The slopped piles of fish making their way up the slatted belt towards us dwindled; the fish began to judder up in ones and twos. Luke, stepping off his box, jumped over the base of the conveyor and disappeared round the side of the hopper. With a scrape and clang of corrugated-iron-on-steel, we heard him pull the makeshift door aside. A wild, multiple echo reached us: 'Redmond! A sea-bat! A sea-bat! Quick!'

I fell off my box, I scrambled over the conveyor, I flayed around the hopper-wall – and found myself hanging on to the thigh-high sill of the entrance.

At the centre of my field of view, at the bottom of the steep, inward-angled, stainless-steel panels of the tall container, to the right of four Greenland halibut which lay where they'd slid (just below the lower lip of the open drop-gate to the conveyor), there spread across the slopes of floor, there swirled round Luke's yellow sea-boots, a semi-transparent globular mass of brown and purple, a gelatinous colourless shine which you could see right through, a something from another world, a dead creature which, as I stared, resolved itself into far too many long viscid arms studded with white boils, eruptions, suckers to hold you fast . . .

'*Haliphron atlanticus!*' yelled Luke. 'Redmond, this – this is only the second specimen recorded in Scottish waters!'

Between the jellied hump of the body and the base of the tentacles, two enormous brown eyes stared up at him.

'It's not *really* a sea-bat because' (he pushed his right boot between a pair of tentacles) 'there's no *web*. But it's your deep-sea octopus right enough – and we know that because we find their mandibles, *beaks* to you, in the stomachs of Sperm whales: and the Sperm whale story, I promise you, Redmond, it's smashing, it's extraordinary, I'll tell you later, I really will, remind me, OK? But for now . . .' He stepped over the octopus, flipped the four Greenland halibut through the drop-gate on to the conveyor and, grasping my arm as the rolling *Norlantean* pulled me backwards, helped me over the sill. 'For now you stay *here*. I'll get a basket. We'll keep this, if we can.'

And as if it was the simplest of matters, Luke returned with one of his red plastic baskets, laying it on the steep-angled steel floor in front of the tentacles – and we tried to gather up the octopus, the globular mass, which looked so ghost-like, so insubstantial, and which was yet so very heavy.

'Of course it's heavy,' he said, as we managed to slop the last thick tentacle into the basket. 'It's mostly water, and that's the trick, because water is almost incompressible, so you need that, you really do, if you want to live, if you want to make a living 1,500 fathoms down.

'Aye,' he said, as we slung the basket over the sill, '*at least 40 kilos.*' He jumped after the red basket on to the slimy planking and, as the *Norlantean* rolled to port, pushed it hard against the stern bulkhead, lashing its rim to a steel pipe. I clambered out, back round to my post. The gutting table and the conveyor were still; Robbie was uncurling an arm-thick hose from its brackets against the port wall. 'Breakfast!' said Sean, peeling off his gloves. Robbie flicked a switch that brought a hidden pump to life, pulled the end of the hose across to the table and sluiced the spatter of fish guts from Sean's oilskins, back and front. 'No idea,' he said to Sean, 'aye, that's your problem. *No idea of cleanliness.*' He turned the hose on me (and the pressure knocked me off my box). 'New oilskins, Redmond. The best. So look after them.' Robbie hosed Luke, Luke hosed Robbie. And Sean, the junior, was told to wash down the table and conveyor. 'Breakfast!' said Robbie. 'Jerry can do breakfast. Dinna touch his soup. But he can do breakfast. I'll give him that. Come on, boys!'

Luke followed Robbie to the bench by the forward door where they took off their boots and oilskins and where I arrived, a little later. 'Dinna worry, Redmond,' said Robbie with a tired smile. 'You wait. You'll get your sea-legs. Dinna worry. They'll come.'

After the cold and the air and the slosh of sea in the fish-room, the galley was stifling, a closed vat of fry and droplets of batter and heat. My glasses fogged over at once, so I sat down on the bench to the immediate right of the door, took them off and tried to wipe them clear with my handkerchief, a piece of cloth as salty and sodden as the rest of me. Jerry the cook came into blurry focus through the murk, red-faced and sweaty. He paused beside me and squeezed my shoulder, a friendly squeeze that stopped just short of snapping my collar-bone. 'Go help yourself. It's all ready in the pans. I'm away to relieve Jason. Eat as much as you can, you'll need it. When the weather comes – there'll be no cooking!'

Luke sat down opposite me. I looked at his plate, appalled. There was a pyramid of food on it. 'What did I tell you?' he said, inhaling at the apex. He leant back on his bench and with his fork tapped the base of the pyramid, a two-inch-high plate-across discus of batter. 'Aye – pizza for two, deep fried. Proper chips, made by Jerry' (the next layer up). 'Three fried eggs, three sausages, bacon – and Redmond, if you really want it, there's a battered Mars bar to stick on top! What did I tell you? Eh? Is this even better than the breakfast at Nairn? Or what?'

At the mention of Nairn the nature of the problem became clear. I was going to be sick.

'I'm going to be sick.'

'You can't.'

'Why not?'

'You've nothing left!'

'I don't care.'

Jason came in. 'What's wrong?'

'Redmond's going to be sick.'

Jason gave me a quick, kindly grin. 'Oh well,' he said, 'at least you're good for *something* – you're cheap to feed!'

I pushed myself to my feet and turned to the door. 'What's that?' said Jason. 'There – on the back of your shirt?'

'Eh?' I said, twisting round to look, imagining a sea-bat sucker, or worse.

'Oh I see,' said Jason with a sharp laugh, 'it's your mattress!'

'*Haliphron atlanticus* . . .' said Luke, dreamily, full of batter, rustling down into his sleeping-bag in the dark cabin, getting comfortable. 'That was *really* something. Almost as good as Signy Island. But we'll never manage to keep it. I don't like to ask the boys to pack it in ice and put it in the hold. Not all 40 kilos. I'll preserve the beak. That'll have to do . . .'

'Signy Island? What's that?'

'Signy Island? Haven't I told you? Aye, that was the very happiest time of my life! In the *South* Orkney Islands, as it happens, in the South Atlantic, the same latitude as here, but there's no warm North Atlantic Drift, so it's ice. Antarctica. Two and a half years. Straight. Without a break. I was there for two and a half years!'

'And that was *happy*?'

'Aye. Smashing! The best job in the world! I was marine assistant to the British Antarctic Survey. There's nothing like it.'

'I'll bet there isn't . . . The cold . . .'

'I never wanted to leave. I was counting Fur seals and Weddell seals – they pupped in the winter – and Leopard seals and penguins. *It was a magic place*. The base was on the site of an old Norwegian whaling station. I was the base diver.'

'You went *diving*? In those temperatures?'

'Humpback and Minke whales would turn up for your dives and they'd stay with you . . . I went diving with Fur seals – well, you couldn't avoid it – there you'd be, concentrating on your job, diving, diving for some specimen, a mollusc say, and Fur seals, they're playful, they really are, they can give you one hell of a fright, they'll rise up behind you and give you a knock on the head, a gentle head-butt when you're not expecting it! Or there again, when you stick out a hand to collect your mollusc or whatever, some Fur seal will appear out of nowhere and mouth your arm – take your arm in his mouth like a dog and give it a shake. They think that's funny! Or sometimes they'd rush straight at you with their mouths open. Boo! And then there were the most beautiful birds in the world – Snow petrels. Snowies. Perfect white. Perfect. And Giant petrels. GPs, Geeps. And Cape pigeons . . .'

'And the people? Two and a half *years* with the same people?'

'Honestly, Redmond, in all that time, I can honestly say, in all that time, in those first two years together – I *never* once heard anyone raise their voice. If there's an ideal society anywhere, that was it. And when you think that the winter night lasts from March to October or November and that the one ship came in November . . . That was great – great excitement all round. The ship brought your mail – you'd had no mail for eight months. And a year's worth of beer, cigs, food and books. Plus one video and one CD a year each. You were allowed two contacts a month towards the end of your contract. Two 150-word messages. So I'd send one to my mum and one to a girlfriend. But lots of messages came the other way – scientists all over the world would send us their requests, they needed two of that species and two of the other. Magic shopping lists! And then I'd go out and try and find whatever it was they wanted. Mostly by diving. There was a lot of interest then in the Icefish. Because it has no haemoglobin – it takes its oxygen directly, in solution. So it leads a *very* slow life, it's laid back, nuzzling about under the ice, right up against the glacier-face. Or maybe someone would want an animal from our lab – we kept Long worms in the aquarium, gigantic worms, a bit like hagfish, and like hagfish they'd knot themselves up together, disgusting. And they'd escape! They'd force up the lid of the tank somehow and get out across the floor, they'd slime right down the corridor! And we kept Glyptonotus, the giant isopod – they looked just like one of the trilobites, as if they'd come back from the dead, you know, from the great extinction 245 million years ago when a comet whacked into the earth, big time, and wiped out 96 per cent of all life in the sea. Talk about an ancient environment – tell me, what system of living things is older than the ocean's? Redmond, just think of the millions and millions of animals waiting to be discovered in the abyss, the hadal depths. And the trillions of different organisms that live in the abyssal ooze . . . Aye, I had lots of time to dwell on all that, lots and lots of time. And it never got too much. I never got anxious and ill like I do in Aberdeen, trying to write this doctorate . . . No. Not at all. Down there we had *dingle days*. We called them *dingle days*, I don't know why – bright sunny days when you could go skiing or mountain-climbing and *take a grip*, take a photograph. It was a day like that when I had to go and find a dead penguin for David Attenborough. He needed a dead penguin for one of his films. A dead penguin! And I went diving for him to collect sea-worms, Nemertean worms, Proboscis worms. He was the very nicest of guys to work for – he actually wrote and thanked me! And those worms you know, Nemertean worms, they come in all the different colours there are. You wouldn't believe it . . .'

'So how many of you? How many on the base?'

'Twelve, twelve of us – a doctor, an electrician, a diving officer, a cook, a radio operator, a diesel mechanic, a terrestrial scientist and his assistant, a marine scientist and his assistant (me), a limnologist – there were these extraordinary lakes under the ice that opened up in summer – and a chippie, my special mate, Steve Wheeler. He was thirty-six, a good bloke, and we gave him the title of boatman, too, because he built his own sailing boat, a beautiful little fourteen-footer. We were all so pleased we held a launch party – we broke a whole bottle of whisky across her bows. He would whistle up fish and sing to the seals and he even thought he could hypnotize girls – you know, just by looking at them. Aye, it was a paradise really, so peaceful and productive, until . . .'

'Until?'

'Well, Redmond, I know it sounds terrible to say this, but the fact is it was a paradise *until the women came* . . . Aye, three students – an English girl studying isopods and two Dutch girls working on algae. When they arrived they *screamed* at each other. You feel bad – you think why? And the answer is you haven't heard anyone shouting at someone else for two years. Poor Steve fell in love with one of them – but of course she wasn't going to fancy a chippie, no matter what he did or said. She went for one of the scientists. And I'm afraid it drove him mad. He appeared in the mess one day with a bottle of whisky in one hand and a knife in the other. The doctor calmed him down. But long term we had to radio for help. And at last the navy got to us. They took him off in a helicopter.'

'Luke?'

'Yes?'

'Do you ever sleep? Could we get some sleep?'

'Hey – I'm sorry. I really am. It's like I said – sleep deprivation: you'll find at first the boys talk their heads off, then they'll go silent, and after that they'll get red eyes and terrible skin and they'll hardly look human. It's like rats, there's a famous experiment when rats were deprived of sleep – eventually their skin split all over and their fur fell off.'

'Yeah. Well. I really don't want my fur to fall off.'

And in half an hour the siren sounded and woke us up and my body told me it was another day and my brain disagreed; and I realized I had already lost all sense of rational time.

84

Luke, without a pause, slid out of his sleeping-bag into his trousers, his sweater, his hat, his socks, in that order, and disappeared in silence as if he was sleep-walking.

I lay in my warm nylon-silky army-green cocoon. With my toes I stroked the end of the bag; I flexed my ankles, my calf muscles; yes, my entire body ached, every set of muscles had had enough, even in my neck. So how had that happened? Head down, tense, hunched over the table, gutting fish for ever . . . It's OK, said the inner voice, just a few more moments, in fact why not a few more days? After all, as Luke himself told you, you're not expected to join in, you're paying £50 a day for your keep, you're not a burden to anyone, in fact you'd probably help most by staying exactly where you are – you're in the way out there, they're doing serious work, it's all a bit desperate, in fact they're *manic*. And in general, now you're lying here thinking, so warm and relaxed, why don't we consider the bigger picture? How about a good long illness? And anyway, isn't it time you retired? One glance and anyone can see that all your best work is behind you. So why not just lie here and *enjoy* it? No one will blame you. It's OK. And anyway, and you know this always works – I have *very* bad news for you, you don't know it yet, you're in shock, in fact you've forgotten the entire battle, but the platoon is talking of nothing else: the way you charged that machine-gun nest with such exemplary bravery, such a sight to see, of course it goes without saying that you'll be mentioned in dispatches and the word is that you may well be recommended for a Victoria Cross . . . But look here, you must lie still, very still, because you took a bullet in the stomach from a General Purpose Heavy Machine-Gun. I'm sorry to have to tell you this. I know how desperate you are to go straight back into action, old boy, but even if it takes all your great instinctive courage, all your vast reserves of will power, I'm afraid that I must order you to lie *absolutely still*. The very slightest movement and you're a dead man . . .

From a yard or two beneath me the engines for the hydraulic

lifts opened up, shaking the bunk with a new pulse, just faster than the excess adrenalin beat of an impending heart-attack. I struggled out, careful to hang on to the edge of the bunk with one hand as I pulled on my trousers with the other. No, I thought, I really do not want to go flying again. I don't like flying, not one bit.

In the lighted companionway a man with dark shaggy hair, wearing a white singlet, blue overalls like a crofter, and with a pair of bright orange ear-protectors slung round his neck, stepped slowly, with deliberation, over the sill of the open door to my left. From the engine room. So he was Dougie, the engineer.

I introduced myself. 'Aye,' he said with a slow, gentle smile, removing his ear-protectors and hanging them on a hook to the left of the galley entrance. 'I know all about you. You've been ill. You've no eaten. So come in here a moment. We'll have a little chat.

'Dougie,' he said, shaking my hand. 'Dougie Twatt. So – sit here a while. I'll get you something. No hurry. You and I – we'll have a chat.' He ambled down the pitching galley to the storeroom off to the left. He was older than any of the crew, maybe even over forty. And calm. He's probably calm anyway, I thought, but it must help – to be on a fixed salary . . .

He returned, equally slowly, and in front of me he set a mug of water and six thick dry biscuits, on a white plate. 'Now,' he said, taking the place opposite, folding his arms on the table, staring straight into my eyes (I thought: hypnosis). 'This never fails. It never has. It never will. I'm going to watch you – until you've eaten every last crumb.'

I took a bite – a mouthful of gravel. And a gulp of water. 'You must love engines,' I spluttered, for something to say.

'Aye,' he said, not taking his eyes off my face. 'Aye, I was brought up on Eday. I worked on the croft till I was twenty-one. Fifty acres. All sheep. But there was no enough work for us all – so I went to sea. I knew all there was to know about tractors. You have to –

86

there's no a crofter in Orkney who's no his own mechanic. You mind the engines – they were good and simple then. You knew where you were. I still love tractors. I collect old tractors. That's what I live for, really. Don't get me wrong, I like the engines here, they're old, Blackstones. They're always interesting, always a surprise.'

'A surprise?' (Biscuit number two.)

'Aye, because you never know which bit will fail you next. I'm a nurse down there, I nurse them along. But the truth is – it's no very nice down there.'

'How did you learn?' (Only four biscuits to go.)

'Marine engines? I learnt the best way, I taught myself, I learnt at sea.'

'And what do you do at home? When you get home?'

'Aye, I love to be at home. At home I look after my tractors. You'll no find better. I've four tractors. A Ferguson . . .'

'A grey Fergy? The little grey Fergy? My father-in-law had one! My wife learnt to drive on it!'

'Aye. They made them from 1947 to 1956. And then I've three Fordsons. 1929. That's my best one. That's special, that was my father's. Made in Cork. The Ford Motor Company. And I've a 1939 and a 1940 model. They're all in working order. I could start them up for you . . .'

'And what about a car? Do you have an old car?'

'A car? No. No – *that's a real waste of money*. No. I've a motorbike. A Matchless. A 1953 Matchless 350 . . .'

When I regained my place at the gutting table the trays were already full – and in his arms Sean was holding a different kind of flatfish. It was around 4 feet long, thick-bodied, black on top, pearly white underneath. Sean, his eyes askew and shining, was shouting at Luke: 'So Jason says to me, "Look Sean," he says, "if it's for your nan, that's OK, that's OK by me – if it's for *her*," he says, "then nothing but the best *will do*." One time I took her a halibut like

this one – a real whole White halibut! Aye – mebbe eighty pounds'
worth! That's the kind of skipper he is . . .'

'Aye!' shouted Robbie, from across the table, at his senior position beside the waist-high entry and knee-low exit conveyors, in
front of the drop-gate lever for discards down the steel chute to the
starboard scupper, beneath the overhead stop-start table-controlling
levers. 'Luke! Fock all that. That's his nan in Caithness like. She
brought him up! But that halibut there, I'm telling you, that's for
the galley!'

Sean, with uncharacteristic gentleness, even reverence, lowered
the White halibut, the prize, the prince of North Atlantic fishes,
into Luke's red plastic specimen-basket.

Luke, over-excited, it seemed to me, even at the thought of this
best of fishy dinners, said (half-way to a shout), 'That's *rare* right
enough. It's rare to catch one in a trawl – they're fast, too fast for a
trawl, great predators, you get them on long lines, they hunt about
the bottom, they feed on fish, especially redfish – and I promise
you, Redmond, you and I will see *lots* of redfish with Jason as
skipper, because he knows, the boys say he never fails . . . Aye,' he
said, chucking yet another Greenland halibut up and over and
down the tube (nothing stops him working once he's started, I
thought, whereas here am I gawping about a mere White halibut,
doing sod all) 'the White halibut, they're the number-one fast
hunters down to a kilometre and a half – and in cold water, too,
around 2.5–8 degrees C. But if we ever get the chance in the UK
I'm *sure* we could breed them, farm them. In the far north –
Shetland. Magic! They're not like your average pussy-soft flatfish,
there's no lacy undulations of the fringing fins for them – no,
they're rock-and-rollers, they've got muscles, their whole bodies,
their zap-thrust tails. And they've a *great* trick, Redmond, because
when they're on the bottom on the upper slope where the light
penetrates, when they're young, their topside, the dorsal surface –
it's coloured like the seabed. If a White halibut's taking a rest on
mud its back'll be black. And if it whops over to a patch of sand –

88

it'll grow pale. And if (yes it's OK, I hear you, these are observations from an aquarium) – if it has its head on sand and its body on mud, it'll have a pale head and a black body!'

'Hey Redmond!' said Sean, focusing on me for the first time. 'Where you bin?'

'I've been talking,' I said, as I tried to concentrate, pronto, on the gutting of my first Greenland halibut of the day (if it *was* a new day). 'I've been talking – or rather listening, I've been listening to Dougie.'

'Dougie! Dougie?' Sean dropped his Greenland halibut back into the tray. 'Dougie? Dougie's a *grand* old guy. But talking? Talking's not his bag, man. Dougie's *no a talker*! Hey Robbie! Redmond here – he's been *listening* to Dougie!'

Robbie, his responsibilities forgotten, stopped work and leant across the table. 'Dougie? Talking? Look, Redmond, like: *Dougie doesna talk*. He's an engineer. He's different. Know what I mean? Engineers – it's difficult, all that. And fock it, I should know. You see Jason – and I want you to hear this – Jason has *paid*, twice, for me to take my engineer's exams in Aberdeen. Because it's the law – you canna go to sea in a trawler without a qualified engineer on board. Now I really want that ticket, dinna get me wrong, I tried, I really did, I owe it to Jason, because he has faith in me, he has the faith, and I want it for me, for Robbie – because if you're an engineer you have a *salary*. And if you have a salary you can go to a bank. You're respectable. People respect you. You can get a flat. You can marry! But in Aberdeen they're bastards, real bastards, they failed me *both times*. It's difficult, to be an engineer – and then when you are, it's difficult, your head's full of engines, systems. Like here – the *Norlantean*, she's packed with ancient metal. She's great, she's old, but if truth be told, Redmond – she's a focking death-trap. And Dougie? He's old too – and Jason asks himself, especially at this time of year, what the fock is Dougie doing putting up with all this? He does not have to face a Force 12 every year of his life! Why should he? He could get a safe job just like that'

89

(Robbie clicked his blue-gloved fingers with a report like a pistol-shot) 'in a garage, parts and services, farm machinery, an oil-rig, anything. That's why Jason needs me. And I keep failing him! Christ, fock it, Redmond, you know what I mean? If Dougie's *talking*, we're in real trouble . . .'

Sean, getting back to work, said softly, almost to himself, 'Robbie, Robbie, you did yer best. We all know that. You always do yer best. You didna let him down . . .'

Luke, a native in this world of high emotion which I didn't understand, said, 'Och aye, Redmond. But what did Dougie *say*?'

'Biscuits. He made me eat these biscuits . . . He said if I *looked him in the eye* and ate these biscuits, every crumb, I'd be cured. He said that on this trip I'd never feel seasick again, not for a moment. It was weird, odd, whatever, so what . . .' And then a different part of me said, or rather shouted, in a tone and volume devoid of the charm, the friendliness, the social control that I liked to imagine I possessed at all times (and particularly in times of stress, be they merely internal or obvious and real) *'And I fucking well don't want to talk about it!'*

'Aye!' said Robbie, relaxing at once, picking up a Greenland halibut. 'Dougie, the treatment. That's all it was. Aye, hypnosis. He must've decided he *liked* you. Dougie's treatment – that never fails.' He laughed. Sean laughed. 'Aye,' said Robbie, 'Dougie's got the gift. But there was a mate of mine once – he was seasick every time he went out. For the first two days like. He'd be gutting – right there where Sean is. He'd be talking to you, standing on his box, gutting away and bang! He'd lean over and throw up – into the scupper chute. Then carry on gutting and talking, talking and gutting – that's courage, that is. Dougie didna like him. He'd said something bad to Dougie, called him old or an oddball, something like that. So Dougie wouldna help. So my mate just carried on, working, chucking up, all over the place. Aye, that was a man, right enough.'

'So what happened to him?' I said, chastened.

'Och aye. He saved every penny. He was no a drinker like. He had a wife at home. And believe me, Redmond, *that really helps.* Up here that's the most important thing. Orkney, Shetland, darkness half the year. So when you meet someone at sea, when there's a new man in the crew, you ask yourself, does he have a wife at home? Because 90 per cent of the time, if he does, you'll know, that's OK – *you can trust him with your life.* He'll no let you down. Look at Bryan. Aye, if you dinna believe me – look at Bryan!'

To my right, Sean muttered, again almost to himself, 'Robbie, Robbie. Aye – you're a dirty old bastard. Jesus, you've done things.' (And this was said with an obvious and deep admiration, as he picked up a fish that was the weirdest fish I'd seen since the Rabbit fish, a week or so ago, was it? And he threw it up and over and down the central tube, ungutted.) 'But you've got a girl right enough.' (At this point I realized, flattered, that Sean, who never even glanced at me, to his left, close-cramped beside him on my adjacent box, was, *sotto voce, talking to me.*) 'Aye, and she's all of sixteen. She's at school, for Chrissake. And you've given up the drink for her. And you're no a smoker, if you know what I mean.' (Sean gave his current Greenland halibut, his Black butt, a squashy wink of his right eye.) 'Aye, you dirty old bastard you. You give her everything, focking everything. And if she doesn't focking well watch herself, you'll marry her!'

'Robbie!' I shouted across the table, 'What happened to him, your mate, the one who was sick?'

'Eh? What's that? My mate?' shouted Robbie, his thoughts already somewhere else. 'I told you! I just told you – the minute he got the price, he bought a shop, a grocer's shop. A peedie bit of local meat like. That too. His wife planned it. He gave her all the money he got, as he got it. She planned it all! And I tell you, they're happy. *Really happy.* They got a baby! No fish for the baby! No fish for him! No fish for her! If you want to upset him – give him a fish!'

'Aye!' shouted Sean, joining in. 'Sling a fish on his counter – he's well unchuffed!'

'Tell me, Sean,' I said in his ear, 'what did he mean, Robbie, what he did mean about Bryan? What's special about Bryan?'

'Aye,' said Sean, not looking at me. 'Bryan – you've no sussed him? *Everything*'s special about Bryan. You go overboard? You think you're going to die? Give it five minutes max, right? Who do you want to see at the rail? *Want like fock?* Bryan! And why? Because he's calm and he knows it all and he'll no panic and he'll do something. Aye. Robbie's right. You can trust your life to Bryan. He's a real man right enough. He got married – and he took on the woman *and* her two kids. Aye. Now he's one of his own. But he treats them all the same. The whole family. You'd never mind they weren't all his. Aye. Focking marvellous, really. Like my nan. A focking marvel. And no a drinker . . .'

'And he's no a smoker,' I said, getting into the roll and pitch and swing of things, beginning to think I was myself again.

'Aye! You're right! Bryan ashore? Forget it! Bryan ashore? Now that's a turn-off! He's no a *raver*. Know what I mean?'

The routine seemed interminable, the sudden absence of the human voice (or so it seemed to me) in the chaos of overwhelming inhuman sound began to be intolerable. ('Don't talk,' I told myself. 'You've no staying power. At least stick at it like Luke. Don't be a wimp. Please, be as silent and committed as Luke . . .') But I couldn't take it, stand it, hack it, and my extraneous thoughts came in threes of emphasis, like that, like the onset of a fever. So I picked up one of the increasingly common strange new species of fish in my tray (a tray which I managed, now, most times, to half-clear, before Robbie revolved the table, dealt with my leavings and everyone else's mere guts and discards, and turned on the hopper-conveyor for another delivery). And I held it up for Luke's inspection. 'So what's this?' I said.

By the tail, which was not a fish-tail as you might imagine it, but several inches of raw-hide whip, I hoisted the 2-foot-long, huge-headed, slender-bodied, grey-silver, big-scaled, armour-plated, snub-snouted, underslung-mouthed pre-human fish to eye-level – and eye-to-eye it was truly disturbing, because its eyeball was three times the size of mine.

'Eh? That?' said Luke, roused from his automaton working-trance. 'That? I've told you, haven't I?'

'No. You haven't!' I said, aggrieved at once, but also comforted that Luke, too, was obviously no longer entirely in control of his short-term memory. (But then this thought was also vaguely frightening, as if we were all about to become drunk, semi-clinically mad, angry-about-nothing.) I shouted, 'No! You haven't!'

'No? Well, I meant to,' he said, red-eyed, taking the fish and dropping it down the tube. 'We can sell that – in Germany. They like them in Germany. And I like them, too, personally, but not to eat.' (He carried on gutting.) 'I like them because they cruise over the bottom of the deep, as *you* might say, Redmond, or as *I* might say, that fish, a Roughhead grenadier, *Macrourus berglax*, is a Rat-tail, a member of the closely related family the *Macrouridae* – and they're deep-water fishes that live on the continental slopes *and across the abyssal plains of all the oceans on earth*. Their armoured heads, those heads of theirs, they're pitted with sense organs, and their *eyes*, I tell you, in 1908 a German biologist, August Brauer – he worked out that the retina of a Rat-tail had around 20 million long slender rods in an area of one-sixteenth of a square-inch. And that, Redmond, is around 225 times more than we have in our own eyes. Now, as you know, the rods are for night-vision, so in dim light a Rat-tail may be able to see over 200 times as well as we can! And that's not all, because on the underside of most Rat-tails, but not ours, not this particular one, the Roughhead grenadier, there's an open gland in which they play host to luminous bacteria. Most of the time they leave their bacteria alone, but when they need a torch, a flashlight, they've a special muscle waiting round the gland and they *squeeze* their bacteria, they annoy them – and

93

the bacteria light up! And they've other special muscles too, like haddock — they've got really big swimbladders, the Rat-tails, and in the males, only in the males, they have these bizarre muscles set round the swimbladder. So it's obvious, isn't it? Their function must be entirely sexual. So imagine that! The males *drum* in the abyss — in the black night, the perpetual darkness, they drum up their females! And Redmond, it must be noisy down there, and full of the *weirdest* flashing lights, reds and purples and blues, whatever — because I. G. Priede, Monty Priede, a hero of mine, at my own university, Aberdeen: he's estimated that for just two species of Rat-tails in the abyssal depths, *Coryphaenoides armatus* and *yaquinae*, at a population density of about 200 fish per square kilometre, you have a global biomass of around 150×10^6 tonnes. And that, Redmond, is just about the total world commercial fish catch!'

'Wow!'

Robbie shouted, 'Hey Luke! Will ye swap places? I've something to say to Redmond there! Will ye take charge?'

'Jeesus,' said Sean, as Luke and Robbie changed places. 'Jeesus, man, did you hear that?' he said, his brain obviously overloaded, like mine. 'You know what I mean? That Luke! His head! That's no right — it's no right to have a head like that. It's stuffed with fish. Fish!'

'Aye,' said Robbie, immediately gutting the Greenland halibut that Luke had left half-finished. 'It's just this — dinna get me wrong. They'll all tell you — my girl Kate, she's sixteen like, *but we're serious*, I've just taken my car for its MOT — and I did 22,000 last year, all on Orkney. Canya believe it? I drive her everywhere, everywhere she wants to go! And I've a peedie boat. For the lochs like. She loves that! And *I've fixed a fish-finder on it*. To get the monster trout. Everyone knows. There's a monster in one of the lochs. But I'll no tell you which one!'

'Quite right!'

'And another thing, my engineer's exams, dinna get me wrong,

I passed three papers and failed two. So I'm more nearly there than I'm not – so Kate says, no need to despair like. And anyway, I love her, I really do, so I'm saving up like, for a place of our own. So when Jason gives me leave to study, on a third share, I always do a bit extra – you know, in the roll-mop herring factory in Stromness, filleting and such (that's boring, believe me!), or roofing, specially in winter, there's always a demand for trawlermen to repair roofs in winter. You know why?'

Robbie gave me a nudge in the ribs that, again, very nearly knocked me off my box. Hanging on to the stanchion to my right, I said, 'No!'

'Because we dinna care about the weather, we're used to it, we've seen it all! Aye, we dinna stop for hail, let alone the rain, and we dinna care about heights – and a roof, Redmond, it stays still, it's piss-easy like, even in a Force 10! Aye, there's lots of money to be made in winter, in emergencies, when the slates of those new houses come right off – houses built by Scotsmen, southerners, Scotsmen who canna believe it when the Orkney wind comes in!'

'Robbie,' I said, suddenly feeling paternal, even towards Robbie, the toughest little wiry Pict you might ever expect to see (and he was sprouting, I noticed, a black start of a beard which grew well on his chin and upper throat but had not yet appeared any-where else). 'Robbie – maybe it's not a good idea to go out working all day when you're meant to be studying? Don't you think? Eh? Studying for exams is *serious*, it's a full-time business, something you're meant to devote all your energies to, you know, when . . .'

'Studying? Sitting indoors at a desk all alone all day – when there's real weather and people and money to be had outside? You're crazy! You really *are* mad! Just like they say! Studying! That's *reading*, Redmond, that's for when it's *dark*, when you canna do anything else!'

'Ah.'

We were silent.

Then, 'Robbie,' I said, my physical self, such as it was, thoroughly agreeing with him, with his sharp fast movements (the speed of his knife!), the tight abundant energy of a man who was super-fit, and happy. (And anyway, wasn't Orkney dark for half the year – and wasn't that why one of its main exports was scholars?) 'Robbie,' I said, for something to say, in an inner silence in all this noise that was beginning to make me inward-shaking anxious: the sea out there, the connected oceans that excited Luke, the mindless terrible explosions of those waves against the man-made hull, double or not, so fragile, the insane ferocity . . . 'Robbie, how did you get into this? This way of life, for Chrissake? You know – *being a trawlerman?*'

'Aye,' said Robbie, with an enormous smile (his teeth were all his own – no one had ever been quick or accurate enough to smack the fighting-terrier Robbie in the mouth). 'I left school fifteen years ago,' he said in a matter-of-fact, a calming tone of voice. (Robbie, I thought, paranoid, is being kind. He's seen all this before. He *knows* how greenhorns feel in a storm like this. He's probably *heard* my inner voice that won't stop talking, the one that says: 'I'm not sure I can hack this even for the one trip – that vast unshaped unrelenting violence that's out there, and out to get you, and that goes on for ever – so maybe I'll just wind myself up into a fat-ball; and I'll try and roost it out well away from everyone in some locker or other . . .')

Robbie said, 'I worked in a crab-factory in Stromness, and then in a smoked-salmon factory in Kirkwall, for a peedie bit more money. And after that, for a lot more money, even as a junior deckie, I went to sea in pelagic boats. Aye. I went to the herring. Just at the wrong time. *After* the gold rush, the herring rush. Aye, Redmond, it's no funny, what your politicians in England have done to us, at the fishing like. It's no all their fault, right enough, but most of it is. In the sixties and seventies there was a gold rush for the herring. At that time – think of it! – we had only a 3- or 6-mile territorial limit. It was a free-for-all, in Scottish, but much more important – in Orkney and Shetland waters. We let them all in, the bastards and bastards, taking our fish, taking our jobs! And down in London nobody cared. All they cared about is the farming. And why not, right enough? Because they're so far away, you know? So very far away. And anyway, the fact is, Redmond, we look to Norway, or even Denmark – forget Edinburgh, up here we dinna like Edinburgh and as for London: forget it. That's another country, that is – Shetland's as far away from London as Milan, and Milan's in Italy! Anyway, as every trawlerman will tell you, in the sixties the Norwegians moved in with purse seiners, deep circular nets like, which tightened when they finished the sweep. Now that was bad, but no so very bad, because we can't help it, we know them, we can't help it, we like the Norwegians. And the Icelanders were here, too, right up close, everyone forgets that – the Cod War later, you know? Brave little Icelanders! And then the Russians arrived, *6 miles* off. Cold War? What Cold War? No one put up a fight for us. Not for trawlermen. The Russians came with ninety purse seiners, ninety! And they offloaded on to these new factory ships of theirs. Bulgarians, Poles, East Germans, you name it, they all came. The factory ships processed the herring and dumped everything else they caught. Dead fish everywhere. No wonder your birds liked it – no wonder your fulmars spread all round the coasts! Christmas for them, every day! Aye – and then your English Prime Minister sold us out to the Common Market. 1973. It looked good to start with – a 200-mile territorial limit from Europe's coastline. But the coastline, the fish – *they're all up here.* So in come the Spaniards! Imagine it! What if it was farming? Hey, you poor Spaniards, you who've exhausted your own soils by lousy farming practices – come and have ours like, go ahead, take two-thirds of our land! Eh? I dinna think so. Nah – that Heath, we all signed up to pay, each of us, £5 for every man woman and child every week, to the farmers, for the Common Agricultural Policy. And the fishermen? Forget it. You see, it's like this – we can vote and vote till we drop down dead. But it doesna matter. Because compared to you, the south, Oxford, London, wherever – Orkney and Shetland, there's no a person here, our islands – they're uninhabited! Aye . . . I'm sorry,' he said, laying a blue-gloved hand on my oilskin arm. 'I'm carried away, I'm out of order like . . .'

'No you're not, really not. You see – I should know these things, I damn well should. But I don't. So then what happened? To you, I mean. To you, *Robbie*.'

'To me?' Robbie looked surprised. 'To me? Aye, well, it was a nightmare right enough, failing catches, terrible skippers, I worked for several skippers, you know, in different pelagic boats . . . They were a nightmare, all of them. Their tempers, failure I suppose, you couldna blame them, being in debt like, but all the same – it's not as if *we* were doing well, there was nothing left at the surface out there – and some of them, I'll no name names, some of them drank at sea, a nightmare, you wouldna believe the rages! Terrible, the swearing, the insults, your family, everything – hell, really. In some ways you never recover, aye, you wouldna believe it, but even now I sometimes dream I'm back on one particular boat and I wake up sweating, thrashing about, and Kate says: "What's up, Robbie? What's wrong?" And I say, "I dreamt I was back on the —" And she says: "Well, forget it, you're not. It's different now – because you're a skipper and I'm your first mate. And you and me, *we're going to be happy!*"'

'Oh shit, Robbie . . .'

'Aye, so like I said: Jason. He's not ordinary, you know. I want you to get that right. Because I've suffered more skippers than anyone else on this boat. And because I can see you know fock all – and so Jason, well, you'll think he's ordinary.'

'Aye,' said Sean. 'Right on, Robbie! Jason knows my nan. He likes us, the whole family!'

'You'll not know,' said Robbie, ignoring him. 'You'll think Jason's the norm. Because you canna know any different unless I tell you. Well – he's not. It's true, maybe he doesna shout at us as much as usual, because you're on board. But he's a focking miracle, really. That's what he is. The real exception. I know you, Redmond, your type, first-timers, people who want to be trawler-men, you know, straight out of college in Stromness, aye, and if not even their fathers were at the fishing, they're starry-eyed, they talk about *love-of-the-sea*. Jeesus! So I'm telling you, being on a trawler, Redmond, you probably think the only problem is the weather. The weather! Who cares? You either die or you don't – *and you die all together*. No, no – it's the skipper. Because most of them are madder than the weather. More violent, you could say, more unpredictable. Now dinna get me wrong. I'm sure I'd be the same. Millions of pounds in debt. Like Jason. And then Jason has a wife and child at home to look after, and another on the way, I shouldn't wonder. And there again, his father-in-law, the greatest Orkney trawlerman of the last generation – skipper of the *Viking*, the *Viking*, for Chrissake! And we all know what *he* says to himself every waking minute of every focking day – "my daughter, the *loveliest daughter in all the world*" (along with her sisters, of course, if she has any sisters) '– that Jason she married, is he a real man or just a no-good slack-arsed focking southerner?" Aye. The strain of it. Being a skipper – that's not for me. I'd go mad too, I know I would. But here's the thing, Redmond. Jason, he's quick as a focking ghost, one problem and he's out the brown door of that wheelhouse quick as a focking ghost – and I'm telling you now, he's *sane*.'

'And he doesna drink?' (Sean, to my right, snorted. I liked Sean.) 'But you, same as me, you had a problem?'

'Aye. Some problem! Redmond, you canna keep a secret on a boat. That's another thing for you. You should learn that. *And some more*' (Robbie was mildly annoyed, annoyed with Sean, he'd fingered Sean . . .) 'because if a bird taps on the wheelhouse window, it's a sign of death! And if the ship's bell tolls of its own accord, you're all goners like . . . Because the bell is the soul of the ship.' Robbie raised his voice. 'And if you forget and say R-A-T!

99

instead of Long-tail, or P-I-G! instead of shit-shifter, or R-A-M! instead of Hurdle-bunter, or E-G-G! instead of I've forgotten what the fock, you say COLD IRON! – just like that, at once, and everything'll be OK.' (Sean, I couldn't help noticing, in the rising tension, had his forehead pressed hard against the iron stanchion – as if he was taking a rest, cooling his aching head . . .)

'Aye!' Robbie shouted – for some reason at Luke: 'If your wife, your girl, Kate – if she wants to come and see you off at Stromness, you say, No. Never. You must NEVER do that. And Kate, there's to be no knitting on a Sunday – because that will mean the sharp needles will tear the net. And there's to be no washing on the day before we sail, and especially no washing-machine, because that's almost as violent as the sea, a Force 10! – and that'll be washing me down in a whirlpool to a watery grave. And as you know – sailors' graves have no headstone, no resting-place, no peace – unless they go down with their ship in Scapa Flow. Aye. No flowers grow on a sailor's grave, as they say – so dead trawlermen, they come back to *the places they loved, the people* they once loved, on land, at home. Aye . . .' said Robbie, the joke turned bitter and real. 'Aye,' he said, gutting furiously. 'Aye!' he shouted. 'And always turn your trawler with the sun!'

'That's right,' said Luke, taken aback, only just loudly enough to be heard above the onslaught from outside, above the inner, engine-pulsing, shaking, mind-emptying noise. 'I've just heard this one, Robbie. But I'm sure you'll know it. Although mebbe not – because it's from Shetland. Get this – if you've had an unlucky streak of fishing, you can sometimes cure it by *burning the witch*. You know? You take a fiery burning torch around the boat and smoke out or burn the bad luck. They still do that – or so I've heard. And I'm sure you know that some say that for a new net to be lucky, then a virgin must piss on the net . . .'

'Holy water!' I shouted, pleased, somehow restored to myself for a moment. 'Holy water! From the primal font!'

'Aye!' yelled Sean, putting an arm across my shoulders. 'You old freak! You're old enough to be my father, my focking grandad! *Cool!* Holy water! You hear that, Robbie? Robbie, Robbie, dinna get the horrors! Dinna get on a downer! You're great, and you beat it, that alcohol-drug shite, that whole scene, and you dinna even smoke! You did it, man! Tell him about it, tell Redmond here, and Luke – tell them about it!'

'Aye, well, it's no a great story,' said Robbie, gutting away, still upset, speaking far too quietly. 'It's like this – it's all to do with alcohol. You know – SAD. Seasonal something depression. That's it right enough. It's difficult, so they say, to live in the dark more-or-less for half the year, and then in weak sunlight in the summer – it's light, aye, but it's no enough even to ripen the focking barley, no even for our own malts, Highland Park, Scapa Flow. We have to import barley! Aye, anyway, mebbe it's no excuse, but it's the northern-belt drinking, so they call it – the way we all tend to drink till we canna stand up. And I dinna just mean here in Orkney or in Shetland. No – it's northern Canada, it's right across, the Norwegians, the Swedes, the Finns, northern Russia, Alaska, right across – even the Eskimo, the Inuit, you give him a bottle and he canna stop. So there you are. I tapped two policemen.'

'You what?'

'I *tapped* them, Redmond. I smacked them in the face. Right and left. I knocked them out. Unconscious. *Pompf!* They just went down. The one moment they were insulting me, right there, big fellas, you know? Really big. In the bar. And the next they'd gone. They left me alone. Just like that. They went. *Pompf!* I was surprised, I really was. No more hassle. Except there was. Because they hadn't really left at all. Turned out they were there all along lying on the floor. Right in front of me. So they won, really! They should have left . . .'

Sean, much excited, yelled, 'They didna know! They hadna chance! If they'd minded it was you, Robbie, Robbie Stanger – they'd've left right enough. Aye – no messing, man, they'd've bin out of there like the furry things that live in fields, right back to their burrows in Edinburgh or the Lowlands or wherever they focking well came from . . .'

'Redmond, I didna know them,' said Robbie, morose. 'They were Scottish, outsiders. I hadna been to school with them. I didna know their families.'

'So then what?'

'Then what?' Robbie turned to me. He brightened. He gave his shoulders an odd little power-waggle. He stretched back his neck. He laughed. 'I went to prison!'

'To prison?' I repeated stupidly, bemused.

'Aye! To prison!' he shouted, coming alive, as full of life as a stoat in spring. 'To prison! Inverness! Do you know? Have you any idea? Prison – I'm telling you, marvellous! A holiday! A hotel for trawlermen! I still canna believe it, Redmond – we had a *menu*, I promise you we had a *menu*, and you could *tick off* the food you wanted. You ticked these little boxes on a list, like a laird! Aye – and my mates in there, and the screws, you know, they were so respectful, it was Robbie this and Robbie that and so you're a boxer and a trawlerman, are you? "So what can we get you, Robbie, because you're ashore now, you know, and a trawlerman, that's no a life for an ordinary man who's right in the head. No, we dinna see many trawlermen in here, that's for sure, because all those fockers drown at sea, poor buggers, so you're a rare piece of scum you are, and are you comfortable, are you getting enough to eat?" And you willna believe it but there was *football*. All these wonderful things. And you were never cold. *No cold at all*. And trawlermen you know, the football, they've got the legs, they can't help it, they can kick the focking ball for miles!'

I said, 'I'm sure they can!'

'Goal!' yelled Sean.

'Goal!' yelled Luke.

'Aye!' yelled Robbie, encouraged. 'I didna tell them at first. They didna know. But I was running for Orkney in the Scottish

North District Championships in 1980. We came third in the league. Aye, but in 1984 I was running in the Cross Country League, the Open Championships in May. And I won. I focking won. I focking won the race!'

'Goodonya, Robbie!' yelled Sean.

'Magic!' yelled Luke. 'Magic!'

'Aye – so our team, the football, Inverness Prison, a great place, a great team, we beat the shite out of anyone they set against us!'

'Well done!' I shouted.

'And the kitchens!' shouted Robbie. 'You wouldna believe it! All the kit you needed – and then some, lots of stuff you'd never dream of! And guess what – they let me cook in those kitchens! Aye. Big time. Tatties and beef and all sorts, for hundreds of people at a time! You know – they let me do that every day, every day I wanted, a white coat and a hat and the steam and the warmth and the friends you make! Aye, that was grand . . .'

Robbie fell silent. His face lost its life. He began to slit and gut at twice his normal speed – a flick of the knife, a pluck of the hand, a scoop into the tray, an angry, upward throw.

'So then what?' I said, trying, and failing, even now, to get a grip on yet another slimy Greenland halibut, a Black butt. 'What happened then?'

'Och aye,' said Robbie, tense, furious. 'I shoulda known. They were bastards all along. Real *bastards*. The lot of them.'

'Eh?'

'Och aye, Redmond – dinna go making excuses for them. Real bastards. All of them. You know what? *It's meant to be the law.* The focking law, for Chrissake! The judge *promised* me. He made me a promise, right there in front of everyone. He said, plain as could be, though I couldna take it in at the time like, "Mister Stanger," he said, "I hereby sentence you to six months!" *Six months*, Redmond, so there I was, enjoying every minute of it, and I thought to myself like, Robbie, I thought, it's OK, you've nae worries, none at all, there's nothing you can do about it but you canna go to sea, you're safe and warm in here, you've nae a worry in the whole wide world and you've the three months owing to you yet, every day of it . . .'

'So?'

Robbie, affronted, mimicked my accent. '*So?* I'll tell you *so!* Redmond – they threw me out! Right there and then – they didna care! They didna mind – they owed me three full months! Aye, the bastards, they threw me out, just like that, with never a word to me, never a word. They threw me out for good behaviour! Jeesus! If I'd known they could punish you like that, if I'd known they could do that to you, Redmond, throw you out for good behaviour – I'd've tapped the Governor, that's for sure!'

Two trayfuls later, when my new section came to rest in front of me, I found myself staring at three fish that I certainly did recognize – right here in this cold foreign place, fish from childhood, the perfect, the ordinary mackerel, the same mackerel that I used to be sure were the most beautiful fish in the sea. They had the same bright-green, shining, glossy backs alive with patterns of inde-cipherable mystery-message inky writing; the same go-fast forked tails; the same five finlets over and under the wrist of the tail (to keep them on course at speeds you couldn't imagine); and they even had those small fins to each side of the tail, just like the silver fins, the stabilizers, on my Dinky Toy Gloster Meteor, our first jet-fighter – and for the same reason, as I think my father explained: to keep them level on their supersonic whizz-bang flight beneath the surface of the ocean. And the white of their tummies was still as bright as the light off the level sea at the height of a childhood summer . . .

'Luke! Luke!' I yelled with sudden eight-year-old excitement across the cold circle of steel sections. 'Whass mackerel doing here? In a deep trawl?'

'Robbie,' said Luke, his face thinner than ever, taut, black-stubbled, his ears sticking out, thrust forward beneath the rim of his blue woolly hat: 'Shall we swap? Redmond – he needs help. You finished with him?'

Robbie and Luke changed places.

'It's winter,' said Luke, with a grin. 'Redmond, you're like everyone else – you're a holiday fisherman! Look – last October these mackerel left the surface-waters. And then – well and then – look, Redmond, *I'm only human you know,* all your questions, question after question, the fact is, look, I need some sleep, I'm not in good shape right now, not for teaching, you know, even practice teaching, but I'll try, this one last time . . .'

'Christ, I'm sorry, forget it, I . . .'

'No, no. That's not it at all. It's just that we need sleep. You know, *we've had no sleep.* I get *confused . . .*'

'Yeah.'

'Yeah? Aye, well. And then, in November those mackerel – *they all met up together.* Weird, I know, but in November you'll find them in dense concentrations, in a number of very localized positions, as we say, in little hollows and troughs on the sea-bottom, near the shelf-edge. Around Christmas they start to move out from these tight aggregations, real packed crowds, call it what you will, they spread outwards over the surrounding areas of the seabed. And all this time they're feeding on bottom-living shrimps, amphipods, worms, small fish – but Redmond, they're not taking *nearly* as much food as they do later, in their pelagic phase. Towards the end of January, towards the end of this month, right now, or in early February, they form shoals swimming up towards the surface. They start on their migrations, as Alister Hardy describes it, they move towards their spawning areas – which we now know are in the Celtic Sea, south of Ireland, west of the English Channel. They spawn over deeper water towards the edge of the shelf. April to June or July. That's when they're pelagic – they feed like crazy on the animal plankton, especially on copepods, *snap, snap,* one at a time. And then in late July or so they change their behaviour yet again – they disperse into these small shoals and move into inshore waters. They change their *diet*, they go for small fish, *pow!* Young herring, sprat, sand-eels, the little fish swarming in the shallow bays round our coasts. And that's when you, Redmond – when people like you catch them from a rowing boat, with hooks baited with white cotton or even feathers on a length of string!'

'Hey Luke – that's all so *marvellous!*' (I gave him an awkward oilskin hug, side-on.) 'You know, that's really *special*, that it's all so intricate, if you know what I mean – so like the life of mammals on land! And there's real geography down there. Contour lines! And it's all got this extra dimension – animals apart from birds that can move thousands of feet, OK, sometimes miles and miles, straight up and down! And the temperature differences! – just vertically, it's like travelling from the tropics to the North or the South Pole, all at once, right? – And there's currents instead of wind, and filtered light at the top, and perpetual darkness below . . . You know . . .' And then my own manic-tired, vestigial but still functioning mental-censor cut in; an inhibition or two came to life and flashed a warning light. And I fell silent, and felt silly.

'Aye,' said Luke, 'and imagine! – If only we knew a tenth as much about this new deep-sea fishery, *right here* – about the lives of all these new fish you're seeing. For Chrissake, Redmond, we're not even sure how *old* those Grenadiers, those Rat-tails are – according to one or two tagging experiments, I forget details, you can't even trust their otoliths. The same rules, the seasonal growth-rings – they just don't apply! For all we know those fish may be a hundred years old!'

'Aye,' said Sean, coming alive. 'Ot-o-liths! Bullshit!'

'And as for mackerel even – it's all different in the North Sea . . .'

'Is it shit?' said Sean. 'Well, *fock the North Sea*. Horrible place. One big bad trip, the North Sea. Nasty little place, a screaming come-down, know what I mean? Lucy-in-the-shit-with-diamonds, that's the North Sea, boys! And these mackerel' (he gathered them up) 'they're going down the focking chute!' (He threw them down the focking chute.)

I said, 'Jesus, Sean! You threw them away? Why'd you *do* that?'

'Because Jason's no got a quota. And by the way, Redmond, Allan, Allan Besant – he says you, he says you focking well look like Worzel Gummidge!'

'*Worzel Gummidge*? You've read that? Great! I remember Worzel Gummidge! Rosie-bud! I had that read to me before I could read!'

'Read it? Read it! *He's on the telly.* Dumbo! Jesus wept!'

'Quotas, Redmond,' said Luke to me quickly, with a worried half-smile, a concerned, caring kind of look. 'Quotas – that's another thing you need to know. Here it's chaos, in the UK, in the EU, a disaster. But in Iceland, yes, they *deserved* to win the Cod War. They're brilliant, they've devised their very own system, brilliant. And as an ex-Falklands Fisheries inspection officer, I should know. That's something I really do know about. Get this – *they've no discards.* Anything you catch, you land. No waste. No waste at all. And then it gets clever – if you land too much haddock, for example, by law you can buy that extra quota from someone who's not fished enough haddock, who has quota to spare. So gradually the bad skippers are *bought* out – only the Jasons survive. So they have fewer, more efficient boats – and there's more money for those boats, and more money for government-funded patrol vessels. In their 200-mile territorial limit, within their very own exclusion zone, there's *real* control, benign regulation if you like, because it's strict but fair. Every skipper can see the sense of it. There's no *point* in a grab-it-now, ghastly, destructive EU free-for-all. The young stocks are monitored, *really* monitored. There are *lots* of inspectors like I used to be – enough to go aboard any trawler they want, whenever they want, and if more than a quarter of the fish in a random sample they measure on board are undersize, then that whole area, the current nursery area, is closed to fishing. And that is why, Redmond – that's why every night Iceland Air flies cargo planes into Heathrow packed with full-sized cod for the UK fish and chips!'

'Far out, man,' muttered Sean, just loud enough for me to hear. 'Get it on, baby, because right now I need a joint, know what I mean? A stiff joint, well inspected, full-size, 2 feet long!'

The long haul, or rather the long gutting of the absurdly productive short haul, was over – there was nothing coming up on the conveyor so Robbie switched it off; Luke went to hose out the hopper. 'Redmond! Take a look at this!' came his shout (but not with real excitement, not as if he was confronting an almost-sea-bat). 'You'll like this!'

Expecting some minor curiosity, I stepped into the stainless-steel hopper, right leg first, over the sill – and stopped. My left leg (despite its outer oilskin protection, its inner high yellow rubber sea-boot complete with steel toe-cap) refused to follow. From my brain it received the down-both-legs forked message before I did. It already knew that my right leg, at the level of the lower shin, was one engulfing snap away from a permanent goodbye to a length of oilskin, one half of a right yellow welly complete with its toe-cap of steel, one still flexible ankle and a perfectly usable right foot.

Because six inches from my right shin was a three-foot gape of mouth; and the inside of this mouth was black; the outer lips were black; the whole nightmare fish, if it was a fish, was slimy black. The rim of the projecting lower jaw was set with shiny black masonry nails, points up, all vertical, not one out of line – a mix of one-inch, half-inch and quarter-inch masonry nails, waiting. Above them, beneath the drawn-back curve of the upper lip, curling up to a snarl below the centre of the broad black snout, there was a complementary set of masonry nails, points down, waiting. And between the globular black eyes, wide apart, fixed on me, were a couple of long black whips, wireless aerials . . . And, very obviously, there was only one thing on the mind of this monstrous something – it wanted to *eat*. And it didn't look, to me, as if it was a picky eater. Discrimination, taste, *haute cuisine*, no, that was not its thing. Not at all . . .

'Aieee!' shouted Luke, creasing up, two blue-gloved hands across his ridiculously flat stomach. 'Aieee!' he shouted, straightening, trying to get a grip on himself, failing, creasing up again. 'It's dead!' he yelled. Luke was laughing, really laughing, which was unnecessary, you know; it was *stupid* of him. 'It's dead! Redmond! It's dead! Aye! Bad dreams? Eh?' And for some reason he snatched off his silly blue woolly hat and stuffed his face right into it. 'An anglerfish!' he shouted, muffled. 'Nothing but a common anglerfish!' His eyes, bright with laughter, appeared above the blue woolly stupid comforter of his hat. 'Aye! A whopper! I'll give you that – a real whopper!'

Once I'd got my left leg over the sill, and Luke had begun to behave like an adult again (sort of), between us we lugged the 5-foot length of pure horror out of the hopper (Luke lifted the massive head, the bulbous holding-sack of body, and I helped, holding the tail, right at the end). After all, I thought, my heart still thumping, it's all very well, but Christ, the damn thing nearly killed me – abject fright, OK, but so what? – Just stop laughing, will you? – After all, Luke, it's all your fault, it really is . . . We slopped the giant terror into a white plastic fish-box (one of the two boxes loose in the fish-room, boxes which rode the wash from the incoming, outgoing sea, port to starboard, starboard to port, all day, all night, forever). And Luke lashed it to his specimen basket.

'That was *great!*' he said, more or less in control. 'I *knew* we'd have fun, you and I!'

The monster was too big to fit in the box: even with its powerful tail bent into a semicircle, its broad head reared up above the rim; and its eyes, even though I now knew they belonged to a mere anglerfish, seemed not one whit less malign. Three or four inches behind its hypnosis-inducing globular pond of a right eye were two growths, one the size of a chicken's egg, the other, an inch to its left, an emergent bud no bigger than the egg of a blackbird. Both eggs were fertilized; and they'd shed their shells – they were a dull orange-yellow filigreed with the red traceries of blood vessels.

So *this* is an anglerfish, I said to myself, well, so what, it doesn't look in the least like its comforting little picture in my *Collins Pocket Guide, Fish of Britain and Europe* – not *emotionally*, that is, it doesn't prepare you for the shock of the real thing, not when it's about to take your ankle right off, and I'm fond of my ankle, it's mine, and besides . . .

'So Luke,' I said, huffy, asserting myself (I know things too, yes I do), 'these growths, that's the males, right?' I prodded the growths with my finger – they were both surprisingly hard. 'I know about anglerfish. The males are tiny, yeah? They're minute, free-swimming little fish until they find a big female, yes? Then *wow*, they get it right, it's not just a passing moment (OK, probably an hour and a half for *you*), it's not just penetration of the female with a mere penis, there's nothing casual about it, *no*: it's total, real commitment for life, not even a feminist could object, because you go right in, head first, it's *total penetration and you become completely absorbed in all her concerns*, yeah? You lose your mind, your will power, your own identity, your eyes, your lungs, your gut – you make no mess – you're no bother, *really not*, because you're not only prepared to do the housework, the washing-up, *you also agree you'll never go out again*. You're a sensitive new male, that's for sure, because whatever she decides to do, wherever she wants to go, you agree, because as it happens you've also lost your voice, and your legs. In fact all you've got left is the bit that she really cares about – and that's your balls. So now that's all you are, a gland for sperm. But from your point of view, I agree, from my point of view – it's not that bad, in fact there's a lot going for it, this new life. Because *you never have to go out to work again* . . .' (On the bench by the door to the galley we tugged off our boots, released ourselves from our oilskins.) 'Luke, look here,' I said, unable to stop. 'Luke, don't you see? You can forget the entire strain of sexual selection – the horrible sweat of so-called honest advertisement of your qualities to potential females: you know, the male–male competition she watches so carefully before she makes her choice. In other words, how do your male contemporaries rate you? Are you *really* a good farmer? Can you bring in the fish, like Jason? And let's wait and see – will your contributions in art, science, literature, music or football really amount to anything? Let's see, let's have a good hard look at your long white tail (if you're a Bird of Paradise) or the short purple underside of your tail (if you're a woodpigeon). Is there any shit on it? Are you diseased? No, Luke, you can forget all that pressure, you really can – all you have to do is lie in bed all day and feel warm and snuggly and *prepare*: you look at lots of porny mags – until your moment arrives. Because, remember, you're attached – the little that's left of you – and even now, when you're just your balls (the insult of it!), you're described as *parasitic*. There you are, stuck in somewhere around the area of her genital opening and – hey, here it comes – at last she's releasing her egg-veil, a diaphanous veil of eggs. And at one touch of those silky knickers you've had it, orgasm after orgasm!'

As we entered the fug of the galley, full of people (my glasses misted up again and I took them off, wiping the lenses on my sleeve), I heard Sean's voice from nearby, to the right. 'Come on, boys! What kept you? Jerry's done clapshot!'

'Crapshot?'

'*Clapshot*, Redmond. An Orkney dish! Neeps and tatties. And haggis! The best! And boys, as we were saying, it's true – you deserve it!'

My vision partially restored, I saw that everyone – except Jerry himself, who must now be in sole charge of the *Norlantean*, K 508, up there on the bridge – everyone was already seated: Dougie; Big Bryan, First Mate; Allan Besant, whom as yet I hardly knew; and Robbie, at the four places along the bench-table to the left. To our right sat Sean, opposite Jason – and a place each, a piled plate each, complete with knife and fork, awaited us. 'Watch it, Redmond,' I said to myself severely, 'get a grip, *be a man*,' as I sat down in the welcoming 3 foot of bench beside Jason, 'you've had no sleep, don't overreact to this simple kindness . . .'

'Aye!' said Sean, as Luke sat down beside him, opposite us. 'Boys! You deserve it! I set the places myself! There's *one of you*, dinna get me wrong – and he can *gut*, that's for sure! A *real* help – and we didna expect it!'

'Aye,' said Bryan, in his slow bass voice, not looking up from his food, a plate piled heroically, Homerically high. 'That's a fact. Twenty-one boxes of Black butts . . . And they came so fast. Down below we couldna believe it . . .'

Jason, as if he was making a considered announcement in front of some packed hall, a leader of the community, which, of course, I realized, he was, said: 'Luke, I can tell you, right now – *you really know what you're doing.*' And this too, I realized obscurely, was the very highest of praise, as high as it gets on a trawler at sea.

'Och aye,' said Luke, furiously forking his deep soil of haggis. 'Aye, it was a clean catch . . . the cleanest I've seen.' Luke's pale face, I noticed to my surprise, had turned red – it had suffused with blood in the heat; or was he blushing with pleasure? 'Redmond here,' he said over-quickly, too loud, 'you know what he said to me? Boys, there was a monk left in the hopper, a big one, with a couple of growths on its head, cancers probably, and Redmond – he decided they were parasitic males, you know? And he says to me, "Luke," he says, "*that's* the life, Luke, because once you're stuck head-first into a female, *you'll never have to work again!*"'

Everyone laughed.

'So those weren't a couple of males? *Cancers?* How do you know?'

'Because it's the wrong species! The wrong order! That's *Lophius piscatorius* out there! The monk, a monkfish to the trade. The biggest I've seen, but it's still a monkfish. You – you're thinking of the *Deepsea anglers*!'

'Far out!' said Sean, seeing my disappointment. 'But they're freaky, man. I'm sure they are!'

'Aye, Redmond, don't you worry,' said Bryan, being kind. 'And who knows? Maybe we *will* catch one of the Deepsea anglers. It's not impossible. And they're as weird a sight to see, right enough, as weird a sight to see as anything on earth – but the ordinary monkfish, you know, it's not *that* ordinary. The female lays eggs like frogspawn – except that the jelly can be 40 feet long and 2 foot across! And there's an Orkney story that people in a rowing boat off Scapa Flow saw one of those masses and thought it was a sea monster, a dark snaky patch in the water, you know, and they rowed for their lives! Well, it's a great *story*, but we dinna know their names. So there you go, it's bullshit.'

'If it's stories you're after,' said Robbie, helping out (I was still finding it impossible to look up from my plate – how could I have got a species, an *order* wrong? That was unforgivable, that was ignorance when there was no excuse, why hadn't I read more? Prepared better? Marine biology, yes, maybe there was nothing simple about it . . .), 'then you must meet Malky Moar! Orkney – there's no a better place for stories. We'll find Malky, he's always in the bar. And Malky'll say to me like – well, it's true, Redmond, we'd had a focker of a thunderstorm – and the next night in the bar Malky says to me, he says, "Robbie, you heard the thunder?" "Aye." "You saw the lightning?" "Aye." "Well then – there's my old man sitting in the kitchen at the farm. You mind the kitchen?" "Aye." "So that lighting, it comes down the chimney and into the stove. Now my old man – he's got his feet resting on the stove. You mind the stove?" "Aye." "So that lightning – it goes up his legs and out the back of his head and it kills two pigs in the yard!" So in the bar we all laugh like. And Malky Moar, he turns on us and he says, "Robbie Stanger," he says. "My old man – does he keep pigs or *does he not*?" And Malky, he looks really angry like, so

113

I say, "Aye, he does." Because he does. And Malky stops looking angry and he fixes each of us in the eye in turn, and he says, Malky says, *"I rest my case!"*'

We laughed.

And Sean said, 'Cold iron!'

And Jason said, 'Don't you worry, Redmond. No, it's true, we *can't* promise you a Deepsea angler. But don't you worry – the sea's *full* of strange things, and some of them are a lot stranger even than any of your Deepsea anglers, believe me . . . I've caught a few big deep-sea sharks in my time, Greenland sharks, and they're *odd* – not so much because of the way they look, or even because of the things the fisheries scientists like Luke tell us about their habits: no, they're odd, Redmond, because their flesh is *poisonous*. It's toxic! And who the hell could have expected *that*? Shark meat, great! But not this one, no – it can *kill* you! Now the real wonder is this: the Icelanders, pure Vikings really – and the Vikings are a people that I have a lot of time for, as a skipper, you know – the Icelanders use the Greenland shark for its oil and skin, and that's not all, because the flesh, they don't waste that either, they bury it until it's putrid, dig it up and dry it – and eat it! So how did they work that out?'

'From the Eskimo, I shouldna wonder,' said Bryan, at the table to our right. Bryan, Big Bryan, was big all right – dark-haired, black-stubbled, a Viking none the less, a Robertson; his deep-set dark eyes were now haggard with physical exhaustion, but they still looked like the eyes of a man who took his time, who wouldn't be hurried, who thought deeply about things that had not yet begun to trouble Sean, and which I had ceased to care about – such as the purpose of life. There was a small silver stud in the lobe of his left ear, perhaps a potential payment to Neptune, perhaps not. He wore a wedding ring. Bryan, I thought, he's a Viking that even the superstitious monks of Lindisfarne might be compelled to respect, despite themselves . . .

He was saying: 'They're also known as the *Sleeper shark* because they move so slowly – they'll no give you a nasty surprise' (in my

114

reverie I'd missed something, some vital information), 'and as the *Gurry shark*, from gurry, like slurry, except it's the offal, the mess you sluice overboard after fishing or whaling – and in Greenland, the Eskimo, the Inuit, they bung seal guts and blood or whatever's to hand down through a hole in the ice and bring the sleepers to the surface. And they're big, really big, they can be 20 feet long – Redmond, only the Whale shark, the biggest, up to 70 feet long, the Basking shark, around 40 feet, and the Great white, around the same length but chunky – those are the only sharks that weigh more. So it's worth the hunt!'

'Aye that's right,' said Luke, 'but they don't just feed on carrion. Because you often find them with a parasitic copepod *covering* each eye and we think these copepods are bioluminescent in deep water, six or seven thousand feet down – fish go for their little lights and the shark eats the fish head-first, *snap*, and that's why, mostly, you'll find the fish in their stomachs have no tails!'

Sean, directly opposite me, in comradely mode, said, *sotto voce*, 'So there you go, man, there's plenty that's freaky that's no a Deepsea angler. It's like they say, *a little knowledge really focks you up*, so it's cool to cut it out!' He gave his head a half-flick towards Luke (sitting right beside him) and, leaning forward across the table (its surface covered in sticky Velcro to hold your plate in a Force 7 or 8, but in this (a Force 9?) – you had to hang on to your plate with your left hand and fork your clapshot and haggis into your mouth with your right), he gave me an expressive, a knowing, squashy wink of his left eye.

I was beginning to feel better, a little less terminally, throat-cuttingly foolish and empty, and besides, the clapshot, the neeps and tatties, the buttered mash of turnips and potatoes (Orkney crops that, even that far north, you really could rely on) was warm in my stomach (Jerry was a *great* guy), and the haggis, it was special too, Orkney haggis, yet still familiar – I decided that I actually liked minced sheep's-oesophagus-and-stomach, both lengths of colon, the rectum, the entire alimentary canal, as long as it had that reassuringly acrid background taste of gunpowder . . . And the more I ate, the less apart, less cold, less alien, the outside world became.

So, 'Jason,' I managed to say, hoping that he'd realize I'd had it, surrendered, abandoned any claim to combative male status, 'What's the weirdest thing you've ever caught in your nets?'

'Ah, let me think —' said Jason, and gave me a friendly, knowing smile.

So maybe I wasn't the very first post-seasick greenhorn he'd had to suffer on board, which was a comfort, of sorts, and Robbie, I remembered, had told me that a surprising number — a percentage 'you wouldna believe' — of fully trained graduates from the Stromness Nautical School went to sea in earnest in winter for the first time and then, desperate to get back ashore, sought jobs in *anything* the fisheries had to offer: in the market as apprentice dealers, or simply as junior you-to-me fishmongers, or in filleting, processing, fish-farming, transport, or even as *lumpers* — casual labourers, summoned at short notice, sometimes at three in the morning, to get down sharpish to Scrabster harbour, to be ready, for £200 a time, to unload an incoming trawler whose crew were too knackered to do it themselves . . .

Jason now had an emergent all-over black beard (dark as his Armada ancestor's beard, the swashbuckling sailor who had swum ashore, still feisty, ready to go, escaping easily from the small setback of a mere shipwreck, the loss of everything he owned . . .). Jason was the man who had had the least sleep (according to Sean, who kept an internal log on everyone's sleep, measured in half-hours) and Jason was the only man who still looked fresh, in control, sane, easy with himself. 'The weirdest thing in the nets?' he said. 'It's got to be the Ocean sunfish. They're rare, really rare in the north, so it was frightening, that's the only word for it — it was frightening when we caught one, because we didn't know what it was. Huge. It weighed over a tonne. Deep body, fins straight up and down, tiny mouth, no rear end, no tail — what kind of a fish was that? We were surface-fishing at the time, and it just lay there in the net, half asleep . . . But all the same, the size of it . . .'

'Aye,' said Bryan, 'I've seen one too – they've these thick skins, you canna harpoon them, you canna shoot them with a .22, you'll be needing a .303!'

'That's why they've no need to worry,' said Luke, 'only a net can bother them. So they just eat plankton and seaweed and lie around and sleep like Redmond wants to do – but there's a penalty for that, boys, because their brains are tiny, and in a fish that can weigh one and a half tonnes, its spinal cord, guess what – it's only half an inch long!'

Everyone laughed. We're *bonding*, I thought, half delirious from lack of sleep and, it seemed to me, the increasingly violent movements of the *Norlantean*, K508 (lost at sea, no mystery, a hurricane, a baby hurricane; so there'd be a page, maybe, in the *Orcadian*, and three or four lines, maybe, in *The Times* in London). So, unlike the Ocean sunfish, massively happy, immune from predators, sleeping whenever it feels like it, we're OK, because we have *big brains* . . .

'And I've also caught an Opah, maybe 5 feet long, *beautiful*,' said Jason, getting up, going with long-limbed ease to refill his plate from the clamped saucepans on the stove. 'And that was interesting, Redmond, interesting in itself, so beautiful,' he said, sitting down again, 'a dark blue back, gold sides, pink belly – and these *deep red fins*.' He took a mouthful of haggis. Jason even *ate* fast. 'And they're also interesting because they're related to the oarfish – and that's weird enough even for you, and as far as I know, Luke'll put me right, we know sod all about the oarfish. You can't catch them in a trawl, they're far too fast, they swim, they undulate like a sea-snake' (with his right hand and arm he made a quick sinuous movement across the table), 'you only see them when they're sick at the surface or washed ashore dead – and that must be really something, because they can be a good 20 feet long and their bodies are flattened, really flattened, a foot or so deep and only two inches

117

across! But that's not all, it's bright silver all over, and along its entire length there's an unbroken dorsal fin that's the brightest scarlet – and right over its head this fin erects into a brilliant scarlet crest, a mane, a huge Indian headdress! So there you are, there's no bullshit about it – there's your sea monster, your genuine sea serpent!'

'So have you seen one?'

'No. No, I haven't,' said Jason, calming down. 'But I damn well know people who have, so don't you go getting the wrong idea!'

Sean laughed.

'Of course it exists!' said Luke. 'It's been filmed. We've got specimens in museums.'

'Oh aye,' said Sean. '*Museums*, is it?'

'And anyway,' said Allan Besant, still looking young, red-cheeked, his finger no longer bandaged, 'Redmond, Worzel here, old Worzel Gummidge – he didna ask about *monsters*!' He leant forward from his place in the far corner of the right-hand table, across Dougie. 'No, Worzel asked about *sex*. Worzel wants to know about sex!'

Even Dougie laughed.

'So tell him about the seabream!'

'You tell him,' said Jason. 'Tell him yourself!'

'Nah,' said Bryan, 'dinna go asking Allan. He'll get it all mixed up. The seabream, Redmond, they can be female one minute and male the next. And that's a fact!'

'Transsexuals!' I said.

'Aye,' said Allan, looking mean. 'It's *them* that's all mixed up!'

'Christ, boys,' said Sean, sitting right back in his place, back against the wall. 'And you let me *eat* them! I even took a couple to my nan!'

Luke laughed. Sean's views on biology, I could see, gave Luke a special, professional pleasure. 'It's OK,' he said, 'it's not like a disease. You can't *catch* it. In fact it's surprisingly common at sea.'

Sean said, flatly: 'Is focking not.'

'In the sea!' said Luke. And then with a sudden howl of laughter: 'The fish!'

'Dirty bastards,' said Sean, not particularly reassured.

'Aye, take the wrasses, for instance, lots of them are hermaphrodite, and females change into males. Our own Cuckoo wrasse, that's a lovely fish, a cleaner fish, a barber – I'll tell you about that too, sometime.'

Sean said, 'Keep it ter yerself.'

'It's like Tiresias,' I said. 'He'd been both a woman and a man, and he was able to report that women not just enjoyed sex more – they enjoyed it ten times more!'

There was a silence.

And then, 'The sneaky bastards,' said Sean. 'So how come they keep saying no?'

'You should wash more,' said Robbie. 'You should wash your hair.'

'Ach,' said Sean. 'Don't be such a sissy! What's a pillow for? Eh? It's a *pillow* that cleans your hair. You should see the state of mine!'

In the next haul there were several hundred blue-backed, white-bellied little fish, a by-catch which excited Luke: 'Blue whiting, Redmond! They may look like nothing to you – fair enough – but they *could* be very important. You see, they're vastly abundant, as we say, but as yet we know very little about their real life cycle, their true distribution. So that's part of my job too – maybe we could fish for Blue whiting, sustainably. But as yet no one knows. They're codlets, in the cod family, and here in our fisheries they're the main food for hake. So I wouldn't want to be a Blue whiting, not really, because imagine it – at night you go to sleep in mid-water, peaceful as could be, and that's when the big hake, who've been resting all day on the bottom, that's when they swim up from the depths and swallow you.'

After the haul I stayed behind with Luke in the fish-room, wedged on a box, hard against the side of the conveyor to the hold, beside the small steel ledge on which Luke had set up his weighing-machine. Sean, stepping out of his oilskin trousers and sea-boots, shouted: 'That's it, boys! Go for it! Go for the *science*, that's what I say! And boys, you've got plenty of time for now and that's the truth! Because Bryan told me – that focking Force 12 you wankers wanted is almost on us, and Jerry's made sandwiches. So it's gotta be bad. It's gonna be heavy, man. *Sandwiches*, for Chrissake. So there'll no be any cooking, that's for sure, and boys' (he held the steel door to the galley and cabins half open), 'if we're lucky, there'll no be any fishing. So you – you'll be doing *science*. And me – I'll be in ma focking bed! See ya!'

I held Luke's clipboard, and in the appropriate columns on the Marine Lab stencilled sheets (a dispiriting stack of them caught in the jaws of the rusted bulldog-clip) I pencilled in the letters and numbers he shouted against the rising chaos of sound outside: 'GHA!' (Greenland halibut). 'Length —!' and 'Weight: —!' (so *many* numbers). And, a quick slish of his short red-handled knife to its underside: 'Female!' or 'Male!' (a ♀ or a ♂ in the blodgy wet column that wouldn't stay in focus). And then a quick slit to the head of whatever species of fish it happened to be – and there'd be a tiny otolith in his rough ungloved hand. He'd pick the right size of plastic screw-top bottle from the red biscuit-box held in place against the conveyor-strut by his left boot – and then, most impressive of all, pull a stub of pencil from behind his left ear and, in the gathering violence of the trawler's movements (which to me now seemed frantic, terminal – how could this manmade thing withstand such an onslaught one moment more?), Luke would *write*, on the steel shelf, balancing himself without apparent effort, and he'd fill a label (so small) headed *DAFS Scientific Investigations* under: *Haul no. . . . Net . . . Depth . . . Duration . . . Area . . . Date . . .* He'd add *AT* ('Average temperature at that depth!'), and there was a system, I realized. There was a basket, red plastic, for each haul so far. 'MBE!' ('Grenadiers! *Macrourus berglax!*'), 'LIN!' (no explanation), 'BLI!' (ditto) . . . We were going to work through them all. I thought: 'BED!' and 'BED!' and: 'Someone should do something nasty to that Sean, pronto.'

And then a handful of small remarks from books I *had* read surfaced randomly from my subconscious, an inner turmoil that was beginning to be worrying, frightening even – and sleep, I thought, it's obvious, one of its purposes must be to keep a strong fine-mesh carbon-fibre filter hard down on that part of our mind which is as unrestrained as the sea out there – yes, Alister Hardy, I thought, the religious nutcase, the man who all his life had wanted to prove the existence of God, scientifically, once and for all, and who, in his last years, set up an institute for the study of the paranormal in Cambridge (from which, not surprisingly, we still await results), was none the less a truly great pioneer in the study of the natural history of the sea. Alister Hardy, as my mother might have said, was 'not the marrying kind'. (And yes, it's true, I thought, the unleashed or even one-eighth-unleashed subconscious throws up scum and euphemisms and clichés because it deals not in advanced words, but in the primitive power of images, cave-paintings, pictures, rituals, inner photographs clicked by emotions we want to forget.) 'Look Alister,' his perplexed tutor at Oxford had said to him. 'Of course you can solve the small matter of the existence of God one day, but that's for later in your career, dear boy, and you've done so well in your finals, and it's obvious to all of us that you love *fish* – so how about a doctorate study of plankton, instead? God's work and all that? OK?' And the result, eventually, had been his two classics in the New Naturalist series: *The Open Sea*, volume one (1956), *The World of Plankton*, and volume two (1959), *Fish and Fisheries*. But the image that presented itself was not of his research. No – somewhere in those two volumes, I remembered, he insists how essential it is to get on, to make friends with those tough trawlermen, those heroic fishermen. And his chosen method (as I'd learnt from the oral tradition): it was simple. After every voyage he stripped naked to the waist on the quay and he offered to *fight* or, rather (not at all the same thing), he offered to box (Queensberry rules), all his former companions, one by one.

'Hey Redmond!' I heard Luke shouting. 'Don't go off like that! Stay awake! Blue whiting! It's OK – we only need to measure and weigh and sex them!'

I thought: never, not even in my young student days of coffee and amphetamine, have I gone without sleep for so long.

'Just *stay awake*, Redmond, because all this is *very* important for you, for us, for all of us, in *evolutionary* terms, and you like that, I know you do. Because the most basic biochemistry of our brains' (the loudspeakers, Fleetwood Mac, the Corrs, they'd ceased their singing; Jason up there on the bridge had obviously switched them off, because as far as he was concerned the haul was in and gutted and stowed in ice, down in the hold – and yet a deeper mega-bass of wilder drumbeats continued, far louder, drumbeats whose rhythms didn't give a damn about artifice or restraint, and wails, yes, those really were inhuman banshee wails out there . . .), 'our chemical inheritance – it means we *must* have been eating fish fats, and you can't find those on the savannah . . . (Blue whiting! Here we go – just start a separate line, that's right, and label it BW) . . . Aye, it's obvious, the human brain could never have developed as it did if we hadn't moved out of Africa along the shorelines, eating seafood. DHA, one of the fish fats. It's part of the make-up of our nerve-cell membranes! And fish oils are vital for the health of the cardiovascular system – there's no argument about that – and so it stands to reason' (he began on the hundreds of Blue whiting), 'if you have a problem with your heart, your brain is the next to go. As Crawford says, "where cardiovascular disease leads, mental health follows". The UK consumption of fish, Redmond, it's dropped by half since the 1950s. And that's not all, because now we eat mostly white fish. Whereas it's herring, mackerel, sardines, pilchards, anchovies, salmon – the oily fish – that's what we really need. And Crawford thinks that's why there's so many depressives like you and me, so many schizophrenics, so many minor nutcases all about the place. And why not? It makes sense. In the developing foetus, 70 per cent of the energy that crosses the placenta is devoted to brain growth – and for that you need a really good blood supply. And the brain is 60 per cent fat and needs specific fats, especially the Omega-3 fats, the very long-chained, unsaturated fats, the three main fish oils. And if you don't believe me, *consider this*: to convert vegetable oil – from walnuts and soya, rape seed, pumpkin, hemp seeds, whatever – to those fish oils is a slow and costly business for the body. And when's the *only* time that *Homo sapiens* actually does that? Eh? Can you guess? No? Well, I'll tell you. It's in human breast-milk! So it's obvious, isn't it? If I ran the country I'd find a way to manage our herring and mackerel stocks exactly as the Icelanders husband their cod – and I'd stuff all our pregnant women with oily fish every moment of their waking days, and everyone else, too, and I'd single-handedly make this country the most intelligent place in the world! And I'd save our fisheries!'

Sean pushed open the steel door and, in his socks, stepped over the sill. In his right hand he held a couple of inch-thick ham sandwiches. 'Hey boys! Get these down you!' he said, handing one to me (which I started in on at once). Getting close up to Luke (Sean obviously had something he wanted to *say*), he gave him the other (which Luke dropped into the empty fish-slimy Greenland halibut basket, for safe-keeping). 'Aye Luke, I really rate you, man, know what I mean? I didna mind what science was. At school, you know? We bunked off that, in Caithness like. But Luke, you're *cool*, so why bother with all these measurements? Eh? Who cares? Who'll know? Luke – you look *terrible*. I've never seen anyone look so focking knackered. And I like you, you know. You're cool, man, you really are. So why not be sensible? Listen to me, to me – *Sean*. Chill out. *Make it up*. Later. Speed kills, know what I mean? No one, nae a soul, should work like you do. Even Bryan, for Chrissake, he does his grafting right enough – and then he says *fock it* and knocks off. But you, Luke, you're a cool guy, and you do all the gutting, same as us, *but then you do this shit*. You dinna sleep! So get this – Redmond here, Old Worzel, you give him half an hour and he's chilled right out, in his bunk, *like a dead man*. And look at him, so old, and he's finished his sandwich, and yet here he is with us, and he's still alive. See what I mean? For me, look – fock it all,

all of it, I dinna care, but to me and Jerry, that's what we said, Luke
– *you're a hero*. Know what I mean? You're no doing it for the
money. And that's great, man. That makes me feel good. *Far out*.
It's just, you know, I wish I'd tried harder at *school*. But I'm worried
about you, Luke. And it's no just me. It's Jerry, too. So get this,
Luke' (Sean grabbed Luke's right arm and shook it), 'you're a freak!
A real freak! For Chrissake, man, go to bed! Or you'll kill yourself!
You'll die! Get some sleep!'

And Sean, suddenly overcome by all this deep emotion, turned
without a backward glance, fumbled with the lever of the door,
and was gone.

'Hey Luke,' I said, and again I was ashamed even as I heard
myself saying it, 'do you know? Can you guess? What else does the
brain need to operate smoothly? Eh?'

'Aye,' said Luke, entirely in control of himself. 'Sleep! So that's
OK. Look, I'm almost finished here. So that's OK. So go on – go
get some sleep.'

'Aye,' I said for the very first time in my life. 'Maybe I will.'

Luke woke me, an hour later. 'Come on! Jason wants you in the
wheelhouse!' (The nylon-silky enclosing body-stocking bliss, the
stilled aches in every joint in my skeleton – *and I had to get out and
up*?) 'I told Jason you were asleep, I really did.' (I focused on Luke's
skin-flaky blotched red-eyed face – so, I thought, you, you bastard,
you haven't had any sleep at all.) 'And Jason said to me, "Luke,"
he said, "I don't care – for all I care, Redmond's dead. But even if
he is I want him up here *now*. I want him to see this. Because I had
to stop fishing. You understand?" So that's the skipper. So you've
no choice. And it's true, it's what you told me you wanted – a
hurricane. At least, Redmond, I'm sorry, but it's probably a Force 11
gusting 12. So it's the tail-end, I'm afraid. A Force 12, a Category
One Hurricane, you know, a baby, the lowest category – not as
bad as you hoped. I'm sorry. I really am. But Jason says it's the best
he can do. And you must see it, right? Because in six hours or so

it'll be gone, dispersed. It'll probably hit the far north of Norway as a mere storm. So up you get!'

As I climbed the stairs of the companionway to the bridge, the hurricane (why did Luke have to say *baby*?) took the use of my legs away, and it seemed it might also rip my arms right off (my hands clamped one after the other, left, right, hang on, up the rails).

I stared out of the curved-around stern-window of the bridge; Luke held me hard, steady, by the shoulders (how come little Luke has got so tall? I asked myself, and the answer, pronto, was vaguely shaming: *because you're almost on your knees . . .*). It was black night, but the *Norlantean*'s main stern searchlight was on, and the black night was a white-out of spray, a chaos of whirling streaks of foam – in patches so thick that at first the lines and spirals seemed almost stationary in the inverted cone of the fierce rays of light. And then, as I withdrew my mesmerized gaze from the furthest penetration of the beam (which was not far – just enough to give me a glimpse of the *Norlantean*'s starboard gunwhale, now rolling down, down, *digging in* to the waves I couldn't see, and would she come up? *How could she come up?* And why did she have to move her whole stern like that, a fast side-to-side rear-end waggle like a cat about to pounce, and then wallow deep down in, and slew obscenely left-to-right in a movement I'd certainly not felt before . . .), as I focused on the very brightest patch of spray and bunched foam a yard or two out from the searchlight, I realized that all this torn-up water was moving so very shockingly fast, and I felt sick, but it was not seasickness – no, it was far worse, it was entirely personal, hidden, the steely stomach-squeeze of genuine all-out fear, that sharp warning you get before you panic and disgrace yourself to yourself for ever . . .

I turned my head sharply away – and there was Jason behind me in his harness, in his skipper's chair, turning to us himself, and he said: 'Good evening, gentlemen.'

I thought: Jesus, how can he joke like that? When we're all about to die? What's funny about that?

'Here!' said Luke, changing his grip from my shoulders to the backs of my arms just above the elbows, pinioning me forward to the second chair, the First Mate's chair, buckling me into the harness and himself standing easily, at ease, beside me. And I thought: that's not right either, *how come this thin small Luke has gone and got himself such muscles*? Nothing, nothing at all is as it should be . . .

Jason said, 'Good evening, Redmond. Welcome to my bridge.'

Luke said, 'I'm sorry, Redmond, you know, don't get me wrong, thank you for all your help, the *companionship*, you know, I really appreciate it. I want you to know that. But I've got to go – you know, I want to sleep.'

Luke, I realized, as he disappeared from my immediate-left field of vision (I had my head thrust back rigid against the high curving rest of the chair, which seemed a comfort of sorts, and I was not going to move my neck for anyone), Luke (and this was, obscurely, an even greater reassurance), Luke, I thought: he is no longer in control of his own thoughts. And better still, I thought, Luke has lost his powers of speech – he keeps saying *you know*, doesn't he? Hundreds and hundreds of times, over and over. So it's obvious, he's had it, he's *finished*. Clapped out. So at once I forgave him for being such a hero, for being so alien-competent, for saving me, for fixing everything so that I could almost function in this world of his. Luke, after all, despite appearances, Luke was *human*. So that was OK, wasn't it?

'Jason,' I said, 'yeah, good evening. But is this it? Is this a Force 12?'

'Aye,' he said, not looking at me. 'Maybe. Maybe not. Who cares? Only you! But I'll tell you this, Redmond. In my opinion, and please, feel free to disagree, I'd say *it's a stormy, stormy night*.'

'Jeesus, Jason,' I said, turning on him, for some reason, with real aggression (and holding tight with both hands to the arms of the chair, despite my chest-harness), 'don't *you* sleep? How can you do this?'

'It's like I told you,' he said, speaking fast, clipped, articulate, staring straight ahead at the whited-out central bow-window, 'I sleep at home. Here I'm the skipper-owner, the *best* – and OK, so she's not really mine, she still belongs to the bank. But come on, how many bank managers have you seen at sea? Zero! So when I'm out here, she's *mine*. The responsibility – it's *all mine*. You know? The boys, their women, their homes, their health, their morale – if you like – *it all depends on me*. And I promise you, there's no greater kick than that. To know, for sure, no argument, that it's all up to me, as skipper. I decide where and when to fish – it's up to me and no one else at all, anywhere; it's up to me alone to decide where to shoot the net, to start the trawl. And if there's nothing in the cod-end – who do you think gets the blame? The EU fishing-policy tossers? God? The bank? The weather? No, Redmond: it's Jason Schofield – he's the only one who can fail!

And I tell you, Redmond, my dad, you know, he's younger than you, but I can see, you two, *you'd get on so well*. When you were young, your kicks, real kicks, what were they? Jeesus, you sad old fucks, you lot who thought you were going to change the world (save us!) – you beatniks, hippies, flower-power jerk-offs, gentle layabouts, whatever you called yourselves, what did you *really* do? Books, fine, I'll give you that, you loved books, and that was great. And you loved your music. But give me a break, look, so what? The fucking *sparrows* love their music. So you gave up and lay around and smoked dope or cannabis or hashish or gear or grass or hemp in spliffs or joints or whatever you chose to call it – all those words! Worse than winos! And that's right, *shit*, I remember, that's the word, you smoked *shit*, in a mental world of hippie *shite*, real shite, and in the least aggressive possible way you fucked up your own lives, and you took away the motivation for your children. And free love! Spare us! So it was all cool, man, to leave one chick and *hang out* with another. Except, fuck you, one of those *chicks* happened to be my mother. Yes, my mother! And to me, not to you, *a mother is a serious business*. And if you leave her, you ought to be shot!'

'Jason, hang on, what are you talking about? I thought you'd been here for ever. I thought your great-to-the-nth grandfather swam ashore from the Armada . . .'

'You know what I think? I think there's nothing bad in itself about dope. Not in itself. Of course it does less harm than alcohol. Of course it should be legal. It's a piss-nonsense. But you people, you, my dad, the old UK hippies – you invested that shite with wisdom. Just because it made you feel good. A herbal ga-ga tranquillizer. It's a *plant*, for Chrissake! Harmless. A couple of dreamy relax-me pills. No more, no less. And you made a fucking religion out of it!'

'Jason, hold on. Please – tell me about your dad, *tell me about your mother.*'

'My mother? She's a Costello. Spanish. She was a great beauty in her time. Still is. And one of her very first boyfriends was John Lennon.'

'Christ.'

'And my dad – he was *very* clever, Cambridge. He was a rocket engineer, a rocket scientist in your part of the world, right down in the far south – and then he decided he shouldn't be doing *anything* that might help people make weapons, so he came up here and bought a croft on Sanday. The house – it's called the Fish-House! It's right on the sea. And the sea came up and up and into the house once. Slim Schofield, that's him – and you two'd get on so well! The croft, it's basic – 30 acres and that's it. He keeps cows. He milks one by hand! You'd like him, Redmond. And his latest girlfriend, she's just moved out, she lives down the road. Yes, you should go and stay there, with my dad . . .'

'Yeah, I'd like that . . . I really would . . . but Jason, you know, what's happening now, at this moment, technically speaking?'

'To speak *technically*,' said Jason, obviously trying to control something stronger than amusement (which was good of him, but offensive all the same), 'to speak technically, Redmond, we are now *dodging*. All I have to do is keep her head into wind. And for that I trust Dougie . . .' (The incipient, the imminent burst of outright laughter receded from his face, from his lanky frame, from his taut body – which seemed over-active even when it was double-cross-strapped into a purpose-built withholding chair.) 'We all have to trust Dougie with our lives, Redmond, but it's only for three or four times a year, in January and February. So that's OK. This just happens to be one of them. That's all.'

'What do you mean?'

'Mean? What do I mean?' (Jason turned to me briefly; he looked concerned.) 'You're *tired*, aren't you? You've lost it! You'd better *sleep*. And here was I, thinking you'd be intelligent! *This* is what I mean, Redmond – if Dougie's done his job, and he always does, because I've picked the best engineer in Orkney, *but don't you go telling him that*, then the buggered old Blackstone engines in this boat, my boat, maybe they'll last *one more* stormy night. OK? But if he hasn't done his job, if he's not good enough, if I misjudged him, then it's my fault.'

'What?'

'If the engines fail! If we turn beam-on to this weather!'

'Then what?'

'Then what? Then what! Then, Redmond – *we drown*. It's so simple. There's no argument. I like that. I like that a lot. There's no uncertainty about it. No bullshit. There's no maybe this and maybe that, and on the other hand, and if you look at it from a different point of view, or perhaps percentage this and percentage that, and you could say it's his rotten childhood or his bent social fucking worker or his great-fucking-granny, or come on, that Hitler, he only had one ball, so *of course* he had to invade Poland. No! Here there's no bullshit! That's not what it's like here! You make a mistake? Simple. *You drown*.'

I was silent, mesmerized by the lines of foam streaking towards the bow window, lit by the bow searchlight, flying seawater whipped into white by winds gone berserk, like snow in a blizzard, except that the snowflakes had got together, coagulated, as if they were whole long lines of detached wave-crests, coming at me in a solid weighted mass – and yes, I thought dimly, hang on, that's right. Except that you can bunk off the simile. As Sean might say. Or perhaps not. But where was I? Yes, that's right, these *are* entire detached wave-crests coming at you horizontally, and each onslaught probably weighs half a tonne . . .

'Anyway,' said Jason, 'go on, Redmond! Next time we're up here alone, I'll show you something to cheer you up. On the main computer. Davy's tow! But for now – you're OK. You'll do, I suppose. But go on, show me! Because Redmond, I'm going to count to three – and on the count of *three*, no matter what, I don't care, you've no choice, no choice at all, *you are going to unbuckle yourself* and then, steady as a trawlerman, *you are going to go safely to your bunk below.* And sleep. And sleep. OK? So: one . . . two . . . three!'

I rose like a ghost. I went aft like a sleepwalker. And that's exactly what you are, I thought, except that you're walking *towards* your bed, falling towards a sleep that even you have never wanted so badly, never, not in fifty years – and yet I'm feeling so *peaceful*. Hypnosis, yes, they can all do it. They've seen too much, these people.

And, as I went (very slowly), half-way down the wheelhouse stairs I heard a spectral laugh that rose above the drumbeats, the banshee wails of the outside world (a world, it has to be said, that was almost half-stilled in the quiet, double-insulated, wholly enclosed braincase of the ship's bridge). But yes, there was no doubt about it, it was a *laugh*, the overwhelming, energy-packed, unrestrained laugh of a focused and happy young man at the height of his physical powers, a laugh to which there was no possible reply, the kind of laugh that, once heard, you know you will never be able to expunge from your head. And, as I pinned this sound to its source above me, I thought: could there possibly be a laugh that's worse, right now, you know, from a personal, from a selfish point of view?

'Armada!' it yelled, full-throated, into the storm. 'Fuck that for a laugh!' And, with a howl of appalling happiness: 'Save us!' And then, on a rising note of all-out hilarity: 'Armada-Dada! And he's a writer! Get that! The Armada-Dada!'

I fled.

I slotted myself into my sleeping-bag with no difficulty – and why? Because, I told myself, your conscious mind is now entirely occupied with that laugh and its implications, and so it's not particularly surprising that your involuntary, sympathetic autonomic nervous system can get on with its vital simple life unhindered. But that's not soothing in itself, is it? No, of course not. So what? So what's so funny? The Armada, the Picts, the Vikings, the genetic history of the Orkneys – why is that so funny? OK, so maybe this country, which is supposed to be your country politically – and Jesus, it's not as if it's *big* – maybe, just maybe (and this thought gave me a great rush of unexpected happiness), just maybe, despite the depressingly short time-span, the all-modern, the as-it-were-yesterday mere 12,000 years maximum since the end of the last Ice Age, maybe this place is not quite so very boring as compared to the 200,000-year-old mutation (which is, after all, still so very recent), the mutation or series of mutations that gave birth to *Homo sapiens sapiens* in Central or East Africa. *Because you have to*

think of this place differently. OK! So it wasn't the Armada! And yes, Jason's right, because this is a different kind of place altogether – this is not a place that belongs to origins, to the autonomic nervous system, to the preconscious lungfish coming ashore, to hominids, to our 5-or-3-million-years-ago pre-articulate immediate ancestors, or even to our 200,000-year-old forebears, the us-as-we-are-now-in-our-present-minds. No, this is a place, Orkney, a magical place if ever there was one, somewhere that belongs to Skara Brae, a village built so well, so recognizable, so snug and right with its stone furniture, its safe *beds*, its beds that are 5,400 years old; an intellectual place, too, somewhere that was so alive and thinking so hard – whose people built the Ring of Brodgar and made exquisite architecture at Midhowe long before Stonehenge or the Pyramids were even imagined . . . yes, that's right, Jason's right, this is a place, Orkney, to which people *wanted* to come. This place is *desirable*. This is *at the end* of the process to date. This is somewhere to which people *chose* to come. And still do. And that's great, I thought, that's OK, so I don't need to feel quite so catastrophically diminished by that laughter. But, all the same, the inner voice said, you'd better forget this, and you're not going to tell anyone, and personal dignity, you know, it needs a constant vigil to preserve it – so, above all, *you certainly will not tell Luke* . . .

'Luke,' I said, just short of a shout which, against the shockwaves that, second on second, hit the hull, was no more than a whisper. 'Are you awake?'

'Aye, of course I am,' came his oddly testy voice from the darkness to my right. 'Look, I told you Redmond, I warned you, I really did – I told you, plain as could be, upfront, I said: "Redmond, as yet you don't know your arse from your tit here," at least, that's what Dick said in the lab. I was honest with you, I said, "Look, Redmond, you'll get so tired you won't know what to do with yourself – and then you'll find you're so tired you can't sleep. Your brain – it's all fucked up, it's like a fever – and I know you've had plenty of those in your jungles, but in a way this is *worse*, because you're fully aware that you have *not* been invaded by a bacterium or a virus and yet there's nothing you can do to help yourself. Your body thinks there's a battle on, and so it's packed you full of adrenalin – and as you try to sleep you know your brain's all fucked up, because it feels like a fever, and all it does is give you short snatches of nonsense that keep changing, and *you can't stop it*. So you realize, don't you? Give it five or six days and nights of no more than half a sleep-cycle a time – forty-five minutes max every twelve hours – and you hit the manic phase of sleep deprivation. And the boys go through this every time they go out! It's something chemical in our brains, Redmond. No sleep. So the brain tries to order itself for survival, to sort its memories, to clear itself for action by *talking* instead of dreaming. You tell people things you shouldn't, your subconscious is out there for other people to see – but at least it's the same for all of us here, you know, everyone's the same, and perhaps that's why you make such *intense* friendships or hatreds on a trawler, at sea; and you know, Redmond, I can honestly say: I remember *every* man I've been to sea with, at the fishing. There's *nothing* like that on land is there? What do you think? One or two, maybe three close male friends – and one woman, max, at a time. And even then it's *messy*, isn't it? Really messy – all over the place, your emotions. *There's nothing clean on land.* Anyway, there you go, I'm drifting, like I said. All I meant to tell you is *this*: the next stage, you know, give it a day and a night, no more, it's *this*: the brain, memories, pictures, they shut down, they go all dead and dark, they don't care any more. You'll see! We'll be unable to speak. Zombies! But then of course you will be too – if you keep on like this, trying to join in . . . Gutting fish and gutting your own gloves! I've seen you! And flying – how you flew! It's dangerous, you know, I thought you'd sleep eight hours a night, like a sensible old fuck, and just be an *observer*. Isn't that what writers are meant to do? Eh? How can you possibly have a sensible thought when you're as fucked up as the rest of us? And besides, I can't look after you *all the time*. God knows what you'll do next – and as Dick said, you're *my* responsibility. If you disappear overboard it'll be *my* fault. Right? And the effort you put in just to get up the stairs to the bridge! I can't look after you all the time. Jeesus. I have a doctorate to do, to write, to finish. You know, I'm *desperate*. And there again, you think you ought to keep smiling. To show you're OK. And Redmond, that's when you have this smile like something out of a fuck-bad film. You know – some Hammer-Horror stake-in-the-heart fuck-bad Dracula-film! *Eeee*, grizzly, yuck, that OK smile of yours – you know, it makes the flesh creep! Horrible! Really horrible!'

'For Chrissake, Luke, just be quiet for a moment, will you? You talk so much, you're such a *talker*. Jeesus, Luke, I can't get a word in. So how's about we have a *conversation*? Could you handle that? No? Well, you *should*, because I've been thinking about you, Luke. And I've solved your problem.'

'You have?'

'*Of course I have*. I really have. You should be grateful. And instead of that you attack me! About Jason's gloves! Luke, I want you to know – I only put one or two slits in the palm of my left . . . OK, OK, I hear you, so yes, let's be really honest with each other because you're right, we're really not alive much longer than a dragonfly – yes? So OK, so may be it was seven slits, or eight. But that's not the point, Luke. Not at all! You remember? Your problem? Your real bar to happiness? And no, Luke – no, as it happens, I must tell you right now: I *don't* think it's funny. You know? Right? The way women waggle their rear ends at you and flutter their wings and fly off with that special lead-on flight of theirs and knock you off behind a bush?'

'Eh?'

'Yeah, yeah. But you don't fool me! Don't be so modest. I thought this was a no-bullshit zone! I thought we'd at least – absolute minimum – I thought we'd agreed to *be honest with each other*!'

'Eh? Aye! Big time!'

'So there you are, if you'd just stop interrupting, I could help you. I really could!'

'I'm sorry! Aye! Nuts! Nuts! Nuts!'

'Nuts? No, Luke. *This is science.* So let's calm down. Let's be rational. Right? Let's be *scientific.* Your problem – in biological terms, it's simple, *now that we know about it.* But of course that means that in your case and every other case it's deep and complex and there's fuck all you can do about it – and that's the great attraction of biology, of ethology, the study of animal behaviour, and the fact is, Luke, you told me yourself, and I've seen it in Aberdeen, in your own nest: you, Luke, are an alpha male. Yes! Nick Davies in Cambridge, I met him once, he did this great experiment. Yes, the Reverend Morris's bird books, you know, *A History of British Birds* by the Rev. F. O. Morris, BA, Member of the Ashmolean Society, 'Gloria in excelsis Deo', London: Groombridge and Sons, 5 Paternoster Row – *the very first books I bought myself*! And plate one, Luke – it was a GRIFFON VULTURE – the feathers, so beautiful, and the eyelashes round its big brown eye, and I watched the clouds whenever I could, because I did *not* want to miss it, the moment when a Griffon vulture would spiral down and land on the Vicarage lawn and eat Roger, for sure, my dad's fat old bad-tempered Cocker spaniel that kept trying to bite me . . . And I bought these books when I was eight years old. I saved up my pocket money and every three weeks I'd go with my dad to Salisbury and the two kind old ladies in Beach's Bookshop let me buy them, one by one. They kept them for me, under the desk to the left of the door. Magical, small red volumes with gold letters on their spines and hand-coloured plates inside – and in one term and two holidays of saving I had the lot! The complete set. All eight of them! Two whole *pounds* and ten whole pennies! And in each volume (magical word!) I wrote my name. And the address of our house, in case they got lost. Redmond Douglas O'Hanlon, The Vicarage, Calne, Wilts. Anyway, where was I? Yes, stop *sighing.* The Hedge sparrow! The Hedge accentor, not, in fact, related to the sparrows, as you know.

137

Well – Morris took the Dunnock, or Hedge sparrow or Hedge warbler or Winter fauvette – how I loved all the *names* he gave his birds! – he took the Hedge sparrow, as he wrote in February 1853, as an unobtrusive, quiet and retiring, humble, you know, *sober* exemplar of the Godly life 'which many of a higher grade might imitate, with advantage to themselves and benefit to others through an improved example,' or some such pre-*Origin of Species* natural theology: God's works, God's lessons to us in all his Creation! Lovely, so very *comforting* . . . Yeah, so every night in my little bedroom, lying in bed next to my collection of birds' eggs in a tray packed with cotton-wool – eggs which, I was sure, all the birds in the garden had agreed to give me (just the one each): a blackbird, a thrush, a chaffinch, a wren and even a bullfinch – eggs nestled in their wooden tray on top of the chest of drawers: I'd do as promised and read the set lines from my boring little green pamphlet of SPCK bible extracts. Yes! And then I'd read a golden passage or two from my Morris's *British Birds*. And my dad'd come up for a goodnight prayer and he'd say, "Lighten our darkness, O Lord," and I'd reach up and switch the bedside lamp off and on a few times. And then I'd go to sleep!'

'Magic! Nuts!'

'Yes! But Morris got it all so very wrong (not that we can really blame him, because the *Origin* wasn't published till 1859) and in particular he fucked up with the Hedge sparrow! Big time, as you'd say. Because Nick Davies in Cambridge, not so many years ago, he took a length of hedge and he DNA-fingerprinted every Hedge sparrow in it. (You know those nests, you must do – you must have sought them out as a kid – the dull brown little birds, Dunnocks, in the dull ordinary hedge: and then you find a nest – *pow*! The miracle of it! The perfect sky-blue eggs!) No? Well anyway, he got these extraordinary results – in the middle of the hedge, you know, the dominant male, the one with sex appeal as defined by Hedge sparrows, the famous guy, the great scientist, the President, the rock-star, he had his nest. And how do we know he was the alpha male? Simple! Because *all* the females for hundreds of yards to either side fancy him like crazy. And how do we know that? Is this a Just So Kipling story as jealous molecular biologists stuck in their airless labs like to say? Are they wrong? Is Dawkins right? You bet he is! Because all the females for hundreds of yards to either side fancy the top guy like crazy. And how do we know that? Because in *his* nest, every single one of those sky-blue eggs belongs to him – he's the undisputed dad. And in the nests immediately to either side of his down the hedgerow, half the eggs are his – and so it goes on, until in the far outer reaches of his line of influence only one of the eggs in the distant nests will be his. Now, at the time, the mathematics of all this in the current computer models made no sense at all – why was he so profligate with his energies? So much so that he died at the end of the breeding season? The mathematics made no sense – until two young female doctoral students arrived in the lab. They knew what was wrong! Pronto. They solved the mathematics in a couple of weeks. And how? Because they instinctively considered the problem from *a female point of view*. The alpha male, the Luke in the hedge, he had sex appeal. Right? He'd got it. Whatever it was. So every female wanted him. The mere thought of him made them weak about their tiny knees. Yeah? Got it? So they didn't give a damn about him *as a person*, you understand, and why should they? Only his regular mate could be expected to care if he died of clinical conkers at the end of the month. And Luke, you may have forgotten, terrestrial biology, you know, so boring for you, but in House sparrows the direct stimulus of spring sunshine – rays straight through the top of the skull – it tickles their dormant testicles, the hormone-release swells their internal balls to *fourteen times* their winter size. Now, I know, don't bother – Hedge sparrows are not related to sparrows at all – but I'll *bet* they get that very same feeling in their boxer shorts. Yes? Anyway, the *women* don't care what he's thinking – all they know is that they *have* to collect at least some of his sperm, even if it's only the one time. So they wait and watch –

and when their own low-ranking husband is out foraging for insects to feed the family, working his third-class arse off, and when the rock-star's high-ranking wife is off doing likewise (because an alpha male has *no time at all* to devote to domestic life), then this low-ranking female whips up the hedge, just ahead of her low-ranking rivals, and she flutters her wings like a begging fledgling; and she lowers her head and she raises her vent – and she lures him off, fast, behind a bush. And it *has* to be fast, because if her low-ranking terminal yawn of a jerk of a hard-working husband sees them together – he'll desert her, the nest – finish. And she can't afford that, not at all. But it's still worth the risk, because she's had this great excitement, this massive orgasm, and all her internal sexual cilia have been beating fit to bust – and she's got the alpha male sperm stored right up there in a special pouch, waiting for her next egg to slot down the tube. And so, however many times she couples with her low-ranking jerk of a shaming husband, she can rest easy – at least one of her eggs will meld her genes (deliciously) with those of the highest achieving, super-sexiest man in town. *As judged solely by her fellow females.* Because that's the point. You see, Luke, when I was young, *when I was alive*, biologists of my generation (not that I was a biologist) – they didn't bother to *read* Darwin, they didn't know that *The Descent of Man and Selection in Relation to Sex* was really a two-volume brilliant treatise on the importance of sexual selection *by female choice.* They thought that the study of animal behaviour had begun with Von Frisch and Konrad Lorenz and Niko Tinbergen!'

Luke, in a high voice I didn't know he possessed, as if he was being strangled, said: 'Redmond?'

'Yes?'

'I am *not* a Hedge sparrow . . .'

'Of course you are! That's exactly what you are! Look – I forget the precise figure, but let's say it's 30 per cent: 30 per cent of the eggs in that hedgerow were actually fertilized by the local alpha male. They were nothing to do with the lower-ranking husbands who'd been duped, who sweated away to bring up the resulting chicks. It's now called the *sexy-son-syndrome* (isn't that great?) – the female unconsciously wants, needs, to mesh her own genes with some guy that all the other females have decided is irresistible, pouting-gorgeous, centre-spread *fit*, because that's her one big chance to spread her own genes, the essential *her*, throughout the next generation. Via an alpha male like you. And if you don't believe me, consider this (as *you* might say): you up-end a hedgerow (and I *think*, Luke, that this is my very own contribution, entirely original, but consider this – I'm giving it to *you*, Luke, *gratis*) – and what do you get? A tower block! And guess what? A DNA study *was* mounted on a tower block in Leeds, under the guise of an HIV survey, and yes! Thirty per cent of the children in that tower block were entirely unrelated to the poor sods who thought they were the fathers! So it's not surprising, is it, that *every* mother-in-law, when face to face with her daughter's new baby, whose red globby crumpled features might very well belong to a Martian, for all she knows, turns to her son-in-law and she goo-goo croons: "He/she/it" (if it's a hermaphrodite) "*looks exactly like you!*" Because *she* can be sure, she knows her own wizened born-again genes *are* in there OK, and she knows damn well that those genes need feeding, supporting.'

'So what are you trying to say? Barking, Redmond! Nuts! Nuts! *So what's this to do with me?*'

'Everything! I've been thinking about it. And by the way, Luke, I *don't* think your problem's funny. It's *so* interesting! It's real. In contemporary society, it's as if you're a Yanomami warrior in the Amazons. Napoleon Chagnon lived with them off and on for years and his statistics are irrefutable. If you're manically brave, if you've killed people in the constant low-level group-to-group warfare in the jungle, even if you die at twenty-five, when your reactions aren't quite as fast as they used to be, when you're coming of age and losing your ruthless edge, when you'll probably be picked up by *someone else*'s 6-foot-long arrow and pinned back-to-trunk against a tree – even so you'll leave *six times* more offspring than an ordinary husband. Because the women in the shabono, the oval, communal, stockaded, open-centred dwelling place, like a theatre – they listen *very* carefully to the returning hunter-warriors' tales around the home fires. And then guess what? For the next warrior-resting week they whip the current alpha male off behind a bush and collect his sperm, fast, when no one's looking!'

'Nuts!'

'Nuts yourself! Of course it's not *nuts*! And anyway, stop saying *nuts*, and just a friendly word – you know – stop staying *you know* all the time, OK?'

'Oh come on, Redmond, let's sleep!'

'Certainly not! Luke – just you stay awake and *listen*! Because this will change your life! *All men should know this.* Biology – it's such a *wonderful*, relaxing study. And you, you're supposed to be a biologist. Jesus, *you're so privileged!*'

Luke groaned, an anxious kind of mid-pitched groan . . .

'So there you go – your top Yanomami warrior will reproduce like crazy, in his brave brief life he'll spread his genes. He'll pass on his alertness, his aggression. Whereas you – you *won't* – because I'm sure that all your many serial girlfriends in Aberdeen (and *each time* you think it's love, you poor sod), I'm sure that every last one of them is on the pill – so despite your great efforts, your real wish to settle down, your genes stay right there with you. In your bunk, as it happens.'

'Eh?'

'Yes! And you don't know why! Well I'll tell you! It's *really* sad – because in all the societies that are vivid to me, the Iban, the Kenyah, the Kayan, the Ukit in Borneo; the Curipaco and Yano-mami in the Amazons; the Bantu groups, the pygmies in the northern central Congo – in all those places, Luke, you'd be the Number One! By now you'd have twenty or thirty children . . .'

'But please, *please*, Redmond, I don't want twenty or thirty children . . .' (And this was said with such unexpected force, such

142

emphatic pleading, that it silenced me. I could almost *hear* him thinking. And then, into this pleasing, mental, thoroughly human world of a one-to-one exchange of ideas – a local, comforting, feel-good *conversation*, one of life's perpetual pleasures, a pleasure which, if you had a residue of health and energy, you could rely on, no matter what – into this world-for-two there came the sound which we had managed to outwit, *to exclude for at least half an hour*: the sickening onslaught of an outer world that intended to kill us. And I thought: Jesus, Redmond, it's *such* a luxury to have someone else here with you as you prepare to die, just before that rusted inward-bulging section of bow four yards from our heads finally bursts – if we can't sleep we must *talk*, we really must, because that sound out there is the source of all fear. The spur for all religions. Yeah, yeah, and I know, dickhead, how often have you said that external fear is *comforting*? That the *real* fear is nameless, internal, the panic, the generalized paranoia, the rocking-back-and-forth anxiety of (say) clinical depression? Yeah, yeah, but that particular outer fear was a human, personal one, *just for you*, the fear of an arrow in the guts, of a Kalashnikov burst, of a swipe from a machete! And how romantic it was! And how quickly it passed! And how pleased you were, how *proud* you were afterwards! Whereas *this*, this massively weighted indifferent murderous pounding all about us – there's no romance about it, nothing personal, it's such an easily forgotten, such a commonplace and truly foul way to die, and it doesn't stop, *it goes on and on . . .*)

I yelled: 'For Chrissake, Luke, *please*, say something! Shout at me!'

'No! Really not!' (A shout.) 'Twenty or thirty? How would I be a *good father* – and I mean *really* good – how would I be able to really really love twenty or thirty children? No! You're barking! Redmond – if I have children, just the one or two, and yes, you're right, as it happens I *really* want children, then I'll be their own dad, and no mistake, and to me they'll be the most special people in all the world! And I'll want to be with them *all the time*. You know?

143

But of course that'll be impossible. Because I'll have to work. Work my arse off. To support them. But when I get home they'll be the *whole point* of my entire life! The centre! The anchor! The chain that *never* gives way!'

'Of course they will! But don't be silly. *The point is this*: all those women are attracted to you like hover-flies to a sunflower. And Luke, you'd be a 16-foot sunflower! Because you're an alpha male! And why? Because you're prepared to leave the warm comfortable lab or the relaxing pub or the snuggly paradise of your bed in your little cottage – you're prepared to leave all that pronto, instantly, day or night, at the cold-call of your emergency bleeper! And you go straight out, half awake and, I suppose, at this time of year, as often as not you go straight out into a fucking hurricane like this! But in that ridiculously small boat, that lifeboat you showed me! A cockleshell! So *that's* why they want your sperm! But that's also why *they don't want you*. Or not for more than a month or three. Because from the female point of view, to live with someone, to settle down and breed long-term – for that, you want a good, quiet, ordinary, kind, reliable down-the-hedge male. And in your world, I suppose, that would be a university lecturer on a permanent contract . . .'

'But I *can't* lecture! I can't do it!'

'And yes, it's great, isn't it? The vast explanatory power of Darwin's second idea – evolution by sexual selection, by female choice!'

'Aye! Whatever! *But I can't do it!* I am *not* going to lecture . . . to stand up on a stage!'

'So Luke – have you even *tried* to imagine what it must be like to live with you? There you are, a young woman in love, in the prime of life, and you *know* you're beautiful, desirable in every way, and you've won this guy that all your friends fancy like crazy: and yet there you are, unable to sleep, so anxious, and the wind's coming in screaming from the sea a few hundred yards away – fit to take the roof off the whole fucking Fittie terrace! Yes, and your man, your lover – *such amazing sex* – and yet he's just abandoned you, right in the middle of such out-and-out happiness. And you run through it in your mind, over and over. Where did you go wrong? Why – *he just left you* – and why? For a *shout*, as he calls it, a call on that ghastly little bleeper that he keeps on his body, clipped to his belt, or on the floor by the bed, *at all times*. Yes, there's no doubt about it, *he abandoned you*, in the middle of *such* love-making; and in that *so well-trained* but still desperate and personal hurry! And why? Just to save the lives of *other people*, people that you don't know, people that *he* doesn't know, *strangers*, strangers that, once rescued, he'll never see again! That's right, he's abandoned you for foreign sailors, Russians probably, or Muslims, Laskars, whoever the hell they are, people who can't even speak English, people who've put to sea in those illegal rusting hulks you can see tied up in Aberdeen harbour every day of the week! And then you have to get up all alone and go to work, and the cottage is so *dead* and there's this *howling* wind and rain – and sometimes there's no word for sixteen hours! And of course you forget that that's *exactly* why you fell in love with this absurdly brave alpha male in the first place! The alpha male you and all your friends fancied like crazy! Because now you know – all that *wickedly* good love-making later – you know there'll *never* be a single evening, not *one* candle-lit just-the-two-of-you evening when he'll be entirely 100 per cent yours!'

'Aye! Aye! Maybe there *is* something in what you say! Maybe! Because it's true, Redmond, when I was doing part of my lifeboat training you know – sorry! – down in Poole, where the RNLI has its headquarters, when we were picking up a new Trent Class boat to take back up round the coast to Aberdeen – the RNLI museum curator took me and Julia, my girlfriend, round the museum, the archives. He took us, the real climax as far as he was concerned, to see the *Ornate Book of Remembrance*, some such title, and he took it out of its case for us to look at, for us to handle – as if it was the most precious thing in the world, which, I suppose, for him, it *was*.

You see, Redmond – it's the book where crewmen who've lost their lives in the service are recorded. Their names, in gold script, one to a page. And then there are their service dates and the dates of their main actions, all their major successful rescues at sea. And then there are secondary pages, you know – aye, the odd poem from friends, and the saddest brave remarks from their mothers and fathers and wives and children. All that – that was *terrible* to read, to look at – there'd even be a drawing or two, you know, *there was a drawing from someone's six-year-old daughter*; and drawings and words meant to capture their character, you know, from their *colleagues*, the ones who hadn't got to that particular shout on time. Aye, and *how guilty those guys feel*! For no reason, *but you can't help it*. Anyway, this museum curator, he turns to me and Julia, and he says, all emotional: "Mr Bullough, *Luke*," he says, "if you *really* dedicate yourself to the service, do you realize that you, *you yourself*, you could be in here one day?"'

'Jesus!'

'Aye!'

'So what happened to Julia?'

'*She left me that weekend.* I've not seen her since!'

We were silent. Surely, *surely* sleep would come? That unreachable deep healing state . . . way beneath the surface of all these terrors . . . and how I hate life on the surface of the sea – and why won't my brain take orders and abandon this bullshit? *Why?* Obvious! Because it's true, the things your children say, yeah, yeah, I know, they say it with a laugh, but it's true all the same, because nowadays they say, 'Daddy, it's terrible. You've become such a *sad old fuck.*' Please . . . so . . . . 'Luke!' I yelled. 'Are you awake?'

'Aye! But *steady*, Redmond. Go easy. Get a grip . . .'

'Well, that's *good*. Because there's one thing about evolution by sexual selection – or by natural selection, come to that – one thing that *really* worries me. And I'd like your opinion!'

'You would?'

'Yes, I really would. Because I've thought about this. So I'm *serious*.'

'Aye?'

'Yes, I really am. I've been thinking about two of the great classics in modern marine biology, you know, Alister Hardy's volumes in the New Naturalists series – your intellectual ancestor, in a way . . . And about W. D. Hamilton. You know about him? *Hamilton's Rule?* Kin selection, all that?'

'Aye! Well – no, not exactly. You know, the mathematics . . . Fact is, Redmond, you'd have to be a genius to understand the primary source, his actual papers!'

'Yes! Yes! He even *looked* like a genius! He came to supper with us once. He came to our house!'

'W. D. Hamilton? To *your* house?' Luke sounded fully awake. 'W. D. Hamilton? To supper? With *you?*'

'Yes! *He damn well did!*' I shouted, offended, sitting up with sharp indignation, banging the top of my head, hard, against the base of the upper bunk and lying down again, more offended than before. *'Why the hell shouldn't he come to supper with me?'*

Luke, shocked, aye-less, said: 'Well, you know. W. D. Hamilton – he was a genius!'

'Of course he was! I told you, didn't I? He even looked like a genius! Shaggy hair, leonine face, wonderful! Jesus, and so abstracted, distracted, whatever, you know – out of touch, so otherworldly. That story about Einstein, one of so many, but it stuck in my mind – Einstein went to a tea-party with some hostess (and so of course I imagine him in the Vicarage in Calne in which I grew up, the home of *all* tea-parties, *parish* tea-parties . . .): so he talked boring tea-party bullshit for about half an hour (all he could take), and then, sitting in his allotted tea-party chair, he fell into a trance of thought – and no! You're wrong! It was *not* about the wife he wanted to leave! Don't be vulgar, Luke – no: it was *certainly* a trance in which his spirit had deserted his body and gone on a journey, exactly as the sorcerers in the northern Congo describe it, except

that on this particular journey, and thousands like it, his spirit was *really* travelling into a space-time where no one had been before him (the courage of it! Yes?). Into a universe of his own imagining that also happened to be real, that was finite but unbounded – which Max Born said was one of the greatest ideas about the nature of the world which has ever been conceived. And the sole difference between his journeys and those of every sorcerer (more or less every night) in the Congo jungle? Well, *major*, really, Luke – because his thought experiments, as he called them, turned out to be true, and, eventually, *testable*: he brought back a new reality, things as they actually had been since the beginning of time!'

'Aye! But the tea–party, *what happened*?'

'Oh yes, well – the hostess came down the next morning. And he was still sitting there!'

'He *was*? Then what?'

'She clipped him round the ear, whatever, I don't know – but she brought him back from several squillion light-years away and gave the awkward bugger breakfast and kicked him out!'

'So what's the point?'

'Eh?'

'W. D. Hamilton!'

'Oh yes, I'm sorry, well – it was only when I met Bill Hamilton that I realized that all the freaky worship-Einstein stories might *not* be myths. Not at all. I'm sure that 90 per cent are true. As they are for Newton. Or for Beethoven. And for around one hundred people in written history – no more. Because it's *rare*, Luke. Obsession – that's commonplace, a real pain in the arse. But *successful obsession* – an apparently mad preoccupation with some laughable private reality that turns out to be the real thing, *actual reality*, a world that exists of itself and always has, yet a world that no one had even suspected might be all around them – Jesus! Fancy that!'

'Magic!'

'Yes! So Bill Hamilton came to supper! But all you had to do was ask him about the lives of the social insects he'd studied in the

Amazons – even about his first contact with killer bees – and he was *big*, you know, and he'd turn his great face on you: and *zap*! He'd light up the room!'

'*Pow!*'

'Yes – he came to supper! The greatest English theoretical biologist since Darwin! The guy who solved Darwin's *second last problem*! Because Darwin's first problem, Luke, as you know, was the one he stated himself: "our ignorance of the laws of variation is profound." Because in some matters, Luke, even a genius like Darwin had to think the thoughts of his time, about the mixing of bloods, Lamarckian inheritance, liquid genetics – all that was solved by Mendel and his intellectual descendants. Because of course, as we now know, the mechanism of inheritance is *hard*, particulate – it lasts! It's *not* a mix of liquids. It's not at all as it appears on your stained sheets . . .'

'Redmond! English? – you think you're *English*? Nuts! For starters – apart from your character, you know, your behaviour – you ever copped a look at your own name?'

'So this great genius comes to supper in a battered Ford Fiesta or some such – and once he's inside and talking I fall under his spell, of course, because I can't believe that anyone can talk with such intensity and knowledge and tenderness *about the lives of bees and wasps and hornets!*'

'Great!'

'Yeah, well, he's talking away, and the whole story of the evolution of the social insects is becoming so simple and unexpected and filled with light . . . And then his wife, who's been talking to *my* wife Belinda (and Luke, she's the best! You'd *really* like her! She can be bored stupid, you know, *even by me*, something you wouldn't understand, would you? And yet she still smiles this I-forgive-you, tolerant female smile!') –

'Aaaaah! Please . . .'

'So Hamilton's wife, as I say, she's around one hundred miles away down the table, or so it seems, until she says, in a sudden, loud, parade-ground voice: "Bill! I've fixed it all! I've got a job as a dental assistant, on Rousay" (I think it was Rousay), "and that's in Orkney."'

'Eh?'

'Yes! Well, Luke – I've asked a couple of psychiatrists, you know, and I now realize that this is a common strategy when you have something worrying, OK, *devastating* to say to your husband or wife or partner. You pick a safe, neutral place. And what could be safer than a supper for four in a cottage where there's a fat old guy who's been married for thirty-two years to the same woman who's right there and still alive? Two people you've never met before and who, *most certainly*, you do not intend to see again?'

'Aye, but Redmond, why the hell, excuse me, why did W. D. Hamilton want to go and see you in the first place?'

'Because Luke, I told you, I'm sure I did, it was only a hobby, but Jesus I was *passionate* about it, you know? I was running the natural history pages (yeah, yeah, *right*, with a great deal of professional help) at the *TLS*, the *Times Literary Supplement* – and it was only the one day a fortnight, for years, but Luke, what a privilege! And the *vast* amount I learnt – and you won't believe this, but they *paid me* for it, ninety whole pounds a fortnight (which seemed ridiculous in those days, an absurd amount of money for something you would have done for free, several times over!). And it was great, you know, the intellectual companionship, the intense sharing of interests – *Jesus*, Luke, I'd be driving home to Oxford mega-happy after a day at the *TLS*, and I'd *forget*, I'd forget, that I'd just spent a working day in this *very* highly selected manic hunting-group of people who *loved* books, who were constantly trying to stimulate old talent and *hunt the new and young*: and as I attempted to drive home (and unlike you, Luke, I'm a country boy, I'm afraid, and so *no*, I do *not* know my way round London), I'd be stuck in a traffic jam (but so much to look at! And the great buildings, you know, the architecture, it's all been cleaned, and it *shines* in the light! Even in midwinter, you know, fuck the weather

150

– *it shines!*) – anyway, so, I'd see some guy *running* from the Tube station, and I'd catch myself thinking, "Yeah, that's *great* – *he's running home to read his book!*"'

'Aye! But Jesus, Redmond! You're fucked! You've got it bad! W. D. Hamilton? You remember?'

'Of course I do! And Luke – stop interrupting! Because you confuse me, you really do – and I almost forgot the most interesting point, which is this: the *pleasure* of a literary editor is intense, but entirely without egotism: it's weird, it's pure and personal, because your own name appears nowhere, and only one or maybe two people in the office know what you've done: and yet you're so pleased with yourself (to yourself) that you're in danger: you could short-circuit! You could blow up! Eh? Jesus, please, Luke, stop *groaning* like that, stop *sighing* – because I find it offensive, I really do! So yes – Bill Hamilton, your hero and mine: at the *TLS* we *cleaned up* on Bill Hamilton, *we really did*, way way ahead of any other paper! And why? OK – sod it, I know, Luke, we've sworn to be 100 per cent *honest* with each other, haven't we? So yes, yeah! So you're right, yes, OK, I hear you, you're *right*, you tough sceptical scientific shit-bag you, it *all* came via my old friend Richard Dawkins (I knew him when we were alive and young) – and because of Handsome Dawk we *cleaned up* on Bill Hamilton! We really did!'

'Magic!'

'Yes! First of all I got his memoir – a really beautiful emotional piece that took us from the thirteen-year-old butterfly-collector, via a birthday present of E. B. Ford's *Butterflies*, to the great evolutionary theorist; to the way he wanted to die . . . But the main point was obvious, as he himself said, the most important thing of all for a scientist (if you want to be any good at all) was to preserve, conserve, *protect* that childhood passion, to carry the interest safe within you, the sense of freshness and excitement, as he called it, that astonishment, the rush of unwilled, unexpected pleasure at the extraordinary way the natural world really works . . .'

'Aye! But his *death*?'

'Yeah, Luke, that was really something, that was *special*, and forgive me, please, I'm sure you'll understand, but maybe my account right now will not be 100 per cent accurate, because I'm not 100 per cent sure of anything at the moment, you know, I'm not quite sure who I am, for example, I'm not at all sure any longer that I have *consistency*, that I have a past which informs my present, it's so strange, Luke, I don't like it, and *everything*'s slipping away from me . . .'

'Oh *come on*, W. D. Hamilton! Aye? The death he wanted?'

'OK, *yes*, he was studying these dramatic golf-ball-size scavenger beetles in the Amazon jungle. He'd staked out whole dead chickens in cages (to keep off the possums and vultures) – and as he watched by torchlight these beetle-monsters, their cuticles gold, yellow and green, with a huge *back-swept* horn, would bust-up around the corpses (their eruption-mounds as big as mole-hills) and they'd bite off a pink ball of chicken flesh *half their own size* and carry it in their arms – where? Yes! To the female of course! But Luke! Jesus! She's so scary. She's bigger than the male, her colours just as brilliant! And her *horn*, hang on! It's *bigger* than his! So what's going on? How can this be? How's that for sexual selection? (Do the *females* fight? And the males watch? And choose the victor? Of course they do, but Luke, that's my idea, and *you* can have it, *gratis*!)'

'Aye! Nuts! *Thanks!*' And then, inspired, Luke said: 'Stop this poncy *gratis* business, OK? And, by the way, stop saying I *hear you* because that's a *pain*, it really is.' And he laughed, he really did, like a hyena, *just* like the alpha-dominant leader of the night-time pack who is always, without exception, female. 'So then?' (hyena howls) 'His *death*?'

'His death? Jesus! In the *Congo*. My patch. As he told me – he thought it must be true: he'd been sent a paper by an epidemiologist in Australia who'd exactly correlated the spread of AIDS with the Salk II polio vaccine in Africa. Yes, a big League of Nations anti-polio effort. For us in the West the vaccine was cultured on

1. The *Norlantean* K.508

2. Stromness in January

3. Bryan Robertson, First Mate

4. Jason, the skipper. It's lonely being £2 million in debt.

5. Allan Besant

6. Sean and Jerry

7. Luke and Robbie in the Arctic calm. Robbie is about to start mending the net.

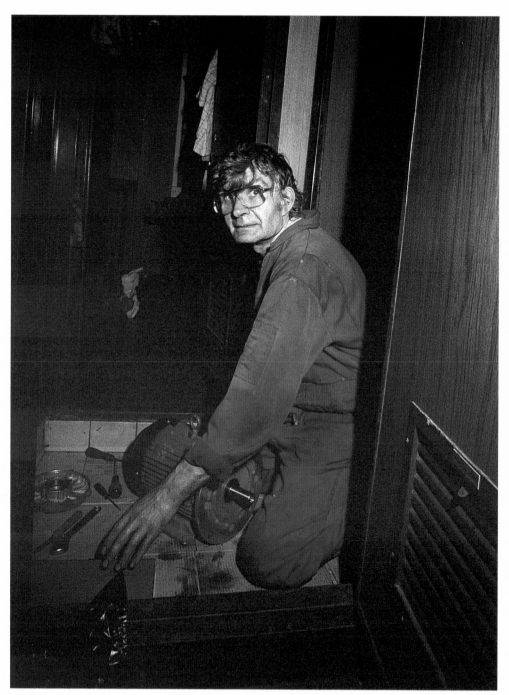

8. Dougie Twatt, engineer

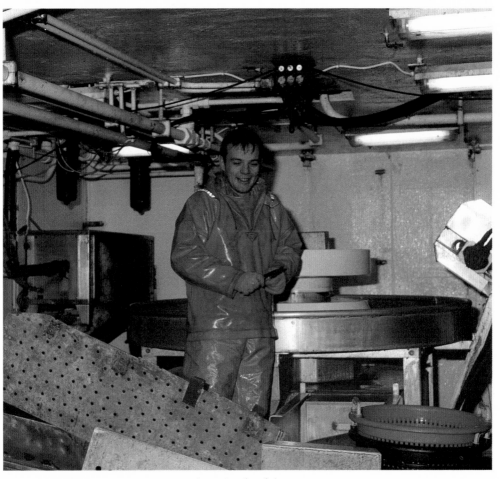

9. Sean in the fish room

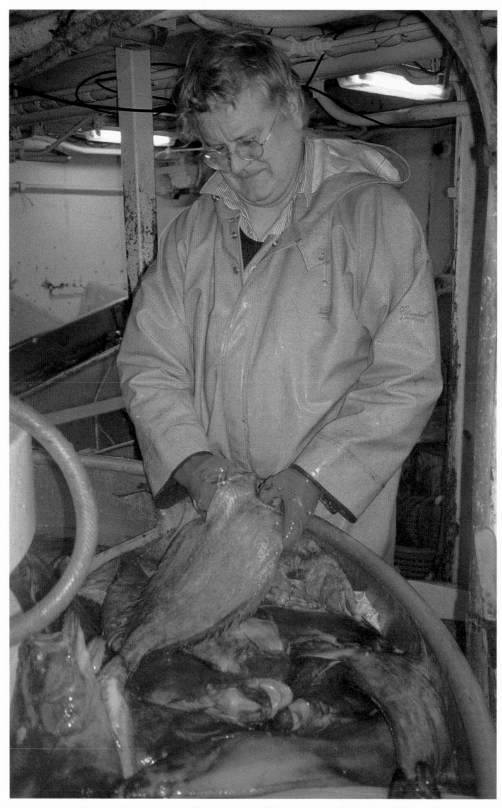

10. Gutting's not easy (photograph of the author, by Luke Bullough)

the livers of cows, but in central Africa, in the small savannahs and vast jungles along the equator, there *are* no cows – the tsetse fly carrying the sleeping-sickness trypanosome sees to that – so the polio vaccine, a huge developed-world aid-project, you understand, self-interested, yes, but self-interested for *Homo sapiens* as a whole, the entire *species*, to *zap* this parasite of ours – it was grown on the kidneys of Green monkeys apparently, and chimpanzees (and Green monkeys, certainly, they're carriers of Simian HIV virus, they've learnt to live with it, for millions of years, probably – so it no longer bothers them). Anyway – so Bill goes out to check this story, and all he needs is a chimpanzee turd from the area of jungle where the original chimps were killed, to check the DNA against the actual vaccine, samples of which are still stored in Sweden. So he equipped himself with a big umbrella to open, downside-up, at the right moment! Anyway, the story goes that he died of cerebral malaria, but when they got him back to Oxford, still in a coma, the Tropical Diseases Department couldn't find a single trypanosome in his body . . . so he was probably poisoned . . . No one knows. He never recovered . . .'

'Och aye! I heard about all *that*! No, no, tell me – his fantasy death? Eh? And I'm sorry, but you know, not *everyone* in Her Majesty's Marine Research Laboratory, Aberdeen, reads the *TLS* – at least, not every week, not all the way through . . .'

'*Oh yes they will* – because if I ever get out of this big doomed piece of complicated metal, Luke, I *can promise you*, we're going to move into marine biology in every way we can – because, guess what? Who do you remind me of, young as you are? W. D. Hamilton! That's who! Because *he* turned me on to dung-beetles – and that's easy, insects, *butterflies*, for Chrissake! Whereas you, you've made *fish* fascinating! Sean's right – fish! Why didn't you tell me years ago you – you *bastard*!'

'Bastard yourself! And get this, Redmond, you're forgetting, you're right, your grip on your own past is going – and I warned you, I really did, that's what happens when you have no sleep for a week or more: you're *misremembering*: it's obvious: I didn't know you years ago!'

'Well, *where were you* then? The whole thing – *it's all your fault*. But anyway, your hero – Bill Hamilton – I got him to review the whole of the Collins New Naturalist series to celebrate their fifty years of publishing and Alan Jenkins, he's a pro all right, like you, he's a poet – but in the office, literary journalism, his *job*, you should see him in action: intense concentration, ignoring newspaper-life all around him, reading some article – and then, with his poncy brown shoes, it's one-two, three-four, he'll scuff the carpet, *so hard*, his under-desk News International office carpet-tiles have to be changed each year, and *bang*! Every time! There's a heading – this particular one: "On first looking into a British treasure", and you may laugh, Luke, but that really summed it up, and I *promise* you, very, very few people can do that with ten minutes to go . . . And his heading for Bill's *Memoir*: "No stone unturned, A bug-hunter's life and death" – and if you don't think that's brilliant, *with ten minutes to go*, then let's give up! And the fantasy death Bill wanted? He wanted to be laid out like those chickens in his cages; he wanted to be buried, pink chunk by pink chunk, by those male monster dung-beetles, as food for their larvae, their children, and then, himself, his self-rearranged, he'd buzz from the soil, he said, like bees from a nest, only *much* louder than any of his own social insects, no, he'd buzz *louder than a swarm of motorbikes* (you see, Bill only ever owned a bicycle) – into the Brazilian wilderness, at night, beetle by flying beetle, so that *finally* he would "shine like a violet ground beetle under a stone".'

'Magic! Magic!'

'Yes! Yes! But that's not all – that's one half of one per cent of it! So how's this, say, for two stray ideas of his I happen to remember? One: when trees in autumn turn their leaves yellow and gold and red (and this chemical change *costs* them energy), they're *signalling*, like poisonous wasps and hornets and caterpillars. They're saying: "*hang on, baby*, you moths and butterflies that are even *thinking* of laying your disgusting little eggs on my skin, to hatch next spring and try and eat me: *get this* – I'm producing the latest toxins I can, and I reproduce sexually, you know, so my genetic ability to manufacture poisons that make your tits and your balls drop right off may well be ahead of your defences – so *go away*! Lay your worst on someone else!" So there's autumn for you! And isn't that as good as Keats? Of course, we want them both, Keats *and* Hamilton! But isn't that great? And Luke, number two is even *better*, freakier! *Clouds!* Yeah? Clouds – so obvious, but *why* do we have clouds? Water molecules only condense if they have a particle to condense around. *Dust* – that's the usual explanation. Dust! Yes, sure, but most of that dust, said Hamilton, will turn out to be *bacteria*: clouds are *biological*. Clouds are the servant-agents, sustained, created, if you like, by bacteria to distribute themselves – just as the Great apes are the distribution servant-agents of the hard seeds in the succulent fruits of rainforest trees. Yeah? And as far as I know, and you're right, I *don't* know very far – only one experiment has been done on this. And guess what? Clouds are *pullulating* with bacteria! Every time it rains, down they all come! Biology! *Life!* Winter bacterial pneumonia . . . TB . . . but good ones, too, bacteria from all over the world! *Poompf!* Down they come!'

'Magic!'

'Yes! Yes! *And so I went to Bill's memorial event* (*no* Christian nonsense) in New College – and I did this *Mirror*-journalist thing – straight afterwards I grabbed Richard Dawkins half-way round the quad, the quadrangle of beautiful buildings dedicated to scholarship (what a triumphant idea, uh? How special is *that*!) and I made him promise to give me his marvellous script . . .'

'Aye, well, I guess you got lucky!'

'Yes, I really did. You're right. You're always right! So then – remember? Bill's wife has just announced that she's off to Rousay? In Orkney? To be a *dental assistant*? So then we get out my copy of the *Times Atlas* and I turn the plates of the UK – and Bill says, mildly interested (she's the mother of his brilliant children, after all, and he loves his children, *so he remembers who she is*), Bill says, "But it's rather far away, isn't it? Will I see you at weekends?"

'And she says: "No, Bill, you won't – I'm leaving you."

'So the meal carries on, and he talks to me *brilliantly* – you know, the kind of man who makes you feel *intelligent as you never felt before* and, as he talks, you *understand* all the reality behind the predictive mathematics of kin-selection, of the new altruism, of the biological necessity of this altruism that has nothing to do with Wynne-Edwards!'

'Aye!'

'And in the morning,' I shouted, in triumph, 'you can't remember a thing!'

'Aye! Aye!' shouted Luke. 'That's right! You can't!'

'So get this!' I yelled. 'Keep calm! We got through the Tesco pavlova and cream, the cheese and coffee, and I'd been telling him about my pond – I love my pond – and in those days it was only a few years old and OK, Luke, I hear you, so let's be honest, perhaps it *is* just a few square yards of water in a big black sunken rubber condom – but to me, you understand, it's a *lake*! And I go out every night with this huge long non-compensatory black Maglite torch and I *stare* into it, and the things you see in there! So, just between us, I'll tell you the secret: you think yourself down to a pinhead in the water, Daphnia-size, OK, to you and me, *waterflea* size – and then you get the real terrors! Delicious! Here comes *Dytiscus*, the Great water beetle larva, two inches long, dislodged (by the end of my stick) from its ambush position – the Water Tiger, the most ravenous killer in the pond, flicking its rear end, its front-end injection-mandibles so obscene and long . . . Anyway, OK? So eventually Bill says, "Let's go and look at this pond of yours." So I hand him the mega-Maglite torch, and we step out the few yards from the back door across the little lawn, and we stare into the pond, *together*. And Bill says, "Redmond, you have two discrete populations of *Daphnia*, associating solely with their con-specifics."

'And meanwhile, his wife and my wife, Belinda, are walking to

156

the car in the drive (OK, the drive-in), so we amble over, and as we go Bill stops and turns to me and he says: "You know, Redmond, this is the first I've heard of it, but I think that *perhaps* my wife is leaving me because I don't earn enough money. I think that must be it. Yes! Because, you know – I only have an *ad hominem* Royal Society Research Professorship at Oxford. Nothing else!"

'And he drives off in his little car (nothing as *grand* as mine, Luke, you understand, not a *patch* on a Renault Clio 1.4 super-limo) and it backfires (OK, so it didn't backfire). I think: yes! Yes he's right! Those *Daphnia*, waterfleas to you and me, those *beautiful* little waterfleas that under the microscope hold their arms up and forward over their heads: I bought one watery plastic bag of them from the Burford Garden Company and the other from Waterperry!'

'Great! I love that! Christ, Redmond, you got lucky, *big time!*'

'Yes, yes! But I haven't finished! Get this! You know what? *At the end of the very next month*, when she'd left for good, when she'd gone to Rousay for ever, he won the Crafoord *and* the Kyoto Prize for biology! Worth *much* more than the Nobel!'

Luke yelled, 'Goal!'

I yelled, 'Goal!'

And then, together, we yelled: 'Go-aaaal!'

After a silence between us, from the darkness that threw itself about, Luke said: 'Redmond, your thought, you know, it's all broken up – it's fractured. What *is* this? Why do you want my opinion?'

'Fractured?' I shouted, stung (but I resisted the impulse to sit up with outrage, with instant aggression, because the top of my head still hurt from the last time, and how *civilized* you've become, I thought, as I lay there, rigid). 'Fractured! Come on – *it's obvious*: Bill Hamilton, like you, was an alpha male. But in his case he was mentally, not physically, absent. You see, Luke – *it comes to the same thing*. Because he was never 100 per cent available to the person he loved most in normal life. Because of the constant presence, the unremitting pressure of a possible *shout*, as you call it, from his very own personal pager, like yours, the essence of his life, the whole purpose – but in his case it wasn't from the lifeboat station, it was from the subconscious on-call of his own ideas. *Imagine it*: Quick! Drop everything! Get out to this one! Save it! Before it disappears for ever!'

'So no woman could stay with him?'

'Right! She decided, unconsciously, once she'd had her alpha-male children (and Luke – look here – I never met Bill's children but I'll *bet* they're brilliant), she thought – Jesus, if I want to be happy, if I want to feel *totally* noticed, if I want to be full-time no-distractions 100 per cent valued by a male whose life will be centred on *me*, then, while there's still time, I'd better go grab a decent, hard-working, useful, indispensable dentist! And who the hell could argue with that? Jesus, Luke, when you reach my age, *the toothaches*: our inherited fish-ancestor sensitive long-snout nerves all squashed-up in our pug-dog faces – and to our *teeth*, for Chrissake! And if there's a God, that's another big mistake he's got to answer for, you bet, and come to think of it, my dentist from always, Bob Farrant, it's a damn good thing he doesn't know how much I really value him!' (And Jesus, I thought, the whole left side of my face – it hurts, and has it gone puffy? Do I have an abscess? Yes, I think I do, but 'Bad luck, babies!' I said to them. 'You several billion parasitic bacteria breeding like Irish rabbits in my back upper-left dead molar's root-canals, where you and I know there's no blood supply, so no phagocytes of mine, no antibiotics of Bob Farrant can penetrate. Bad luck, babies! Bad choice! Because you and me, *all of you*, we're going to drown together!')

Luke snuffled into his pillow. He blew. I heard it. Distinctly. He surfaced, presumably, and he blew again: 'No!' And he re-snuffled. And Luke's hilarity, I thought, it is so unfunny. How can he possibly laugh at a time like this? *And laugh* fit to bust – just when things are so *very* serious.

'You're such a kink, Redmond! Such a screw-up! Jesus, how old are you? Fifty-plus! And to think I used to be sure that people like you, writers, whatever – I used to be certain that people like you, at least, as they grew older they became wiser! What a laugh! What a horrible joke! But then I knew, I knew we'd have fun, you and I! You're so bookish. And of course that's a compliment! Even though it *is* a bit kinky, as you'd say, because the content of those books, it's not the whole story, is it? Redmond, I'll bet you, ten to one, you're the kind of freak, I'll bet you – you're the kind of freak that opens a book you fancy, *when you think no one is looking*: you open it right in the middle, don't you? And you place your big nose – and hey! – you've got a nose just like Mister Punch! Anyone tell you that? It almost meets your chin! Aye! You place your nose right at the bottom of the gulley between the two pages and you push it up to the top, inhaling, taking a deep breath. Aye, you're the kind of kink that *smells* books!'

'Yes! You bastard! Yes. I do. I do!'

'And so do I!'

'You do? So we're friends, Luke! Eh? We're *real* friends! For life!'

'Aye. Jesus. *Spare us . . .*'

'Uh?'

'Well, aye, *it's not really funny*, because there's something else I'd really really like to do, as a *pure pleasure*, in my life, as you call it. Imagine! I get a job at this new outlier of the brand-new idea of the University of the Highlands and Islands (can you imagine anything more romantic?) and in this great new reborn country, Scotland!'

'You do?'

'Aye! At the North Atlantic Fisheries College at Scalloway, in Shetland. Wild, Redmond! Wild in every sense! And Scalloway – so beautiful! So that's *my* impossible fantasy. So listen! As you'd say (and by the way, Redmond, it's such a pain, the way you say that) – so listen! Here's the constant dream – I've already won a job at the college! Nuts! Right?'

'Right!'

'So somehow or other I'm already *teaching* (aye, I know, *imposs-ible!*) and I have my research (*anyone* can do that!) – and the Boss, the President, whatever he's called, he takes me aside in a corridor one day. And it's January, you know, and there's a Force 11 storm outside, and yet inside the college itself, it's so *warm*, and the lights are on, and my halibut-breeding programme is going so well and by now I have a little cottage *all of my own* down the road, one of those *beautiful* little cottages, aye? You know? Those cottages that look so *right* they might have *grown* where they stand?'

'Yes! Yes! But come on, Luke! I'm not the only one whose mind is fucked! You're *wandering*! Yes! Yes! You are! So what's your point? *Indeed, Luke*, it occurs to me, your thought is *so fractured*! Yes! Yes, it is! So perhaps you can't remember?'

'Aye! Well, Redmond! Know what I mean? Stop being so *aggressive*! Aye. Stop interrupting!'

'Och aye! Nuts!' I said, pleased with myself, and then, unbidden, the nuts tumbled out, and to me, they all seemed so *very* funny: 'Pea-nuts! Hazel-nuts! Brazil-nuts! Testicle-nuts!'

'Jeesus! Stop it, Redmond! *Be your age*, right? And listen! Because I've got a long-term mortgage on it, because I have a *regular, secure job*, right? Aye? So I have this *beautiful*, this really old Scalloway cottage . . .'

'The Vikings!'

'No! But yes – it's old this cottage, of course it is! And snug! And so good to look at, *from every angle*, and it's built long ago by real masters of the art: it's built to withstand a Category Five hurricane, winds at 200 mph-plus, and it has a little walled-in garden at the back – and there in the Highlands and Islands University, in this warm corridor of the *college*, the Boss, the President, he says to me, he says: "Dr Bullough" (because by then I've *got* my doctorate from Aberdeen), "Dr Bullough," he says, "I don't want to pressure you in any way, but as you know we're a *very* young institution and we're trying to build up a library in marine biology, *a library of international standing*, and it so happens that *every* member of the Committee decided – and so I think we may call it a *unanimous decision*, don't you? – we decided, every one of us, *without exception*, that you, Dr Bullough, you are the only man capable of building up our new collection. I'm sorry, I truly am – but there'll be no increase in your Lecturer Grade One salary to cover the extra work

161

– we have no provision for that – but it so happens that we've just received a *very* generous bequest for the buying of books. From the widow of a famous Whalsay trawler-captain! It's OK, Dr Bullough, nothing said and so on . . . and I fully expect you to refuse, and *no one* will think any the worse of you, but . . ."

'And I say, "Aye! Aye! I'm your man!"'

'Luke – you've begun to *swear*, I'm certain of it!'

'I do? I did? Well – I'm sorry. But who cares? Because it's just a silly fantasy, and I'm never going to be able to lecture. So that's it. *Finish* . . . When all this is done, Redmond, I'll have to be off back to the Falklands, as a fisheries inspector, and there's nothing wrong with that – because those guys do a great job: know what I mean? The fish stocks in the South Atlantic are still *so rich* – and without those inspectors you can say goodbye to the whole lot! The Japanese . . . But on the other hand of course I may as well slit my throat with a gutting knife!'

'Christ, Luke, you're right, it's like you said: this is far worse than any drug (but you didn't say that, did you? No, of course not! Because you were never a wreck like me – you never *took* drugs! But there again – *don't be so smug* – maybe it's just that you're *young*. So you never had the time! Anyway, this feeling, it's more than a bit frightening, actually, even for an old ex-soft-druggie like me: the sixties, Luke! Way before you were born! But you're right – no wonder the gentle sophisticated torture of choice for army interrogators is sleep deprivation! Because right now I'd say anything! Anything! I can't stop! I've *never* felt like this before: the boss, the organizer, you know, the internal *tough guy* that we sometimes resent but always obey, the Mister Big who directs our thoughts, Luke – he's gone! He's ceased to exist!'

'Aye, aye, *don't be a wanker*, I warned you! And this is *it*! The boys, Redmond, *Jesus* – they go through this *every time* on a two-week trip. *For their entire working life.* I told you! And you – you think you're *special.*'

'Luke! You're so wrong! How dare you say that *I* think I'm

special! Fuck you! If I thought that – *even for five minutes a day*, as you might say, then I wouldn't need to take my scrip of anti-suicide, *really* life-saving, thank-you, *thank-you* science: Prozac. And as it happens, real chance, long ago I met the genius, the guy who discovered or invented or created it: Fluoxetine. A wonder drug if ever there was one, a saver-of-lives, like you (and yes, I hear you, Luke – but it does that for you, too, eventually: it stops you even *considering* whether your own life is *worth* the saving). This genius – and Luke, he was *so* quiet and shy and retiring and modest that I can't even remember his name – he was sitting opposite me at a supper given by Mark Boxer for Anna Wintour, the editor of American *Vogue*. He was her attendant husband. So I asked him what he did. And he said, "Do you *really* want to know?" And I said, "Yes, I really do!" (because he had this sudden light in his eyes – and so I really *did*). "Well," he said, coming alive, like a bumble-bee that's finally managed to get itself sun-warmed enough to be able to fly – "I don't know how much science you have" (that's what they say! that's how they talk!), "or even interest in the subject, but I'll tell you. I've spent the past few years collecting the brains of young people in the United States who've committed suicide – and there are a lot of them, believe me, the danger period is from sixteen to twenty-five years old. Now, of course, some parents are far too short-thinking or imploding-distressed to let me help them (or rather all the others to come, long-term) by gathering the evidence I need – but even so I have a *huge* sample (because it's such a very common form of death amongst the otherwise disease-free young in the United States) . . . I have a sample *way beyond* the demands of significance in statistics. And that's a *joy* to me. Personally. Because my one-to-a-hundred hunch about this has turned out to be *entirely* correct. And generally, professionally. Because I think I can prevent many of these pointless stupid young deaths in the future . . . I think I really can! Because all these brains – you put them in a centrifuge and analyse the mush it produces – they had one thing in common: an absence, a complete lack of a mystery chemical, serotonin. Whereas in the controls – young men and women of the same age killed in car-crashes, other mishaps, the serotonin levels were almost always at a normal constant. So – this one chemical – I now call it the happiness substance! And I really think it may be possible to prevent its degrading and dispersal in the brain – to conserve it!"'

'Magic!'

'Yeah, so Luke – if you want to be happy in a different way, to settle down, as you say, then: you must give up the lifeboats! Because, come on, you're not that young any more, and you've done it all, you've been heroic for years! And if you keep going much longer, right up here in the north, you know better than I do, don't you? Statistically speaking, as you say. Two or three more years. And you're dead, Luke, you'll drown. Remember the *Longhope*? Not a single crewman came back! And, like you, all volunteers, saving other people's lives for free! And all dead.'

'Aye.'

'So now's the time. Go on! You're so *good* at it. And Luke, I should damn well know! Jeesus, Luke, I know about teaching and academic obsession (so rare!) and I've seen you in action, and look here – for Chrissake, Luke, I'm old enough to be your father, and yet, after all these days and nights of no-sleep, and what normal student could say that? – you still bring all these fish alive for me. Fish! And what, before *you* taught me otherwise, before *you* inducted me into their impossibly ancient biology, their *kinky* high-anxiety, their truly bizarre, gangster-brutal – and–then–some – unexpected and shocking personal lives: what could have been more *boring*, biologically speaking, or just general-ignorance-speaking? *Fish*, for Chrissake! Fish! But now I know otherwise – so Luke: become a teacher! Become a lecturer! Settle down! And I can tell you now, Luke, *right now*, if we survive this, if we ever get out of here alive – if I hear, on the academic gossip-line, as I surely will, that you've applied for a lecturing post in marine biology somewhere, anywhere, then I'll damn well ring up the boss personally, and I'll go right ahead and tell him or her how you couldn't even stop teaching a dumbo, a pre-first-year unqualified dumbo about your subject, because you love it all so much – and for Chrissake it was all on a *commercial trawler,* in a storm gusting Force 11 to a Category One Hurricane Force 12! So how's that?'

'Terrible! That's terrible! Because if you're my referee, they'll *know* it's all hopeless, because it's obvious, you – you're barking! But it doesn't matter. So I forgive you! Because it won't happen – because it can't happen. Because I can't, Redmond. I just *can't.* I can't lecture. *I can't go on stage!'*

'Hey Luke, tell me, what *is* this fear of yours? Luke, it's OK, take it easy. Let's do this thing. Let's do it together. Right? Let's face it *now* . . .'

Luke was silent.

And the sea out there, it was genuinely terrible, anyone would say so, and how easy it is, I thought, to sound decisive, even courageous on someone else's behalf (what a pleasure!), and the noise of that vast murderous, uncaring force out there, it's worse, it's getting worse . . .

'So Luke, tell me!' I yelled. And then, regaining a little self-control, adjusting the volume, 'So Luke,' I said, 'tell me – what *is* this fear of yours? Not being able to lecture? Eh? Sorry, but I'm interested. Because I've done it, lots of times. It's part of the job, sometimes, for a writer. So you do it all for a month or two. Or however long the stretch is. And this is the trick: you pretend you're someone else, your most confident self, the butch you. And you do it. And afterwards, you pay for it, as it were, you probably get ill, you pick up any passing infection – but in any case you take to your bed, you dream and you dream, for two days and nights, or more, you jabber, you whimper. But no one knows, if you're lucky, only your wife and your children know (but it's true – they never forget). And then you reappear; and you can work again. And so really you're the only one who's registered that delayed fear inside, the panic . . .'

'Ach. No. That's *normal*. It's not like that! *It's far worse.* It's the *stage*, you know, standing up on stage!'

'A stage? A stage? Oh *come on*, Luke, you know very well: even as a professor you're not always grand enough to have a *stage* . . .'

'I was! I really was! We had to raise money for the RNLI! You know! All the Aberdeen crewmen had to agree to take part! And, Redmond, for the RNLI this was an event that *really* mattered, because Aberdeen then – full of oil money – it was the richest city in the UK. So they gave us no choice! It was a Shell business dinner – for two whole departments of the company. You know, hundreds of people, and every man in a dinner jacket, evening dress. All very formal. Well-mannered. Official. Dignitaries, you know! And it was a big stage, with lights, like a theatre.'

'Well done! You did it!'

'No . . . Not at all . . . You don't understand a thing! You've no idea . . . So, as I say, the RNLI picked five lifeboatmen from the Aberdeen crew, and that was that, and I was one of them. And we rehearsed, over and over and over, in the locker-room of the new lifeboat-shed that cost the earth – and all that money was raised by local people, you know, and it *guts* you, the support from local people, and most of them can't afford the amounts they give, and they're not rich at all: *they just believe in us.* And although it's true we don't get paid a penny, that's not the point – the point is that all these local people *believe in us.* Imagine it! There's some van driver who works his arse off round Aberdeen every day – and yet he gives us part of that labour, cash that he ought to keep for himself . . . So it's not just us, you know: we're only the ones who get the adrenalin rush, the blame if we get there too late, the praise if we don't!'

'Hang on, Luke! You were talking about this *lecture* you gave . . . I really want to hear about that! The lecture on this big stage?'

'Aye. We rehearsed for so long. So many hours of our time. And when it came to the date itself – you know, the one I'd been dreading, like some terrible exam, all those days that pre-date, and those post-date days which you can't believe will ever exist, those far-off date-less days of unimaginable happiness . . .'

'Luke – the stage?'

'Aye. Well. When it came to the date itself we had to stay backstage – in full kit from eight in the evening to midnight. And no drinking allowed, of course. So you can imagine – you can imagine just how bad that was!'

'Eh?'

'Aye. I'd rather've been on a shout, strapped in my harness in the crew cabin in January, you know, monkey-bollock cold out there, and you sit inside like people in a mini-bus or something, except you're rolling – not just down to the rails, you know, but through 360 degrees if it's really bad, because the boat, she capsizes, turns turtle, whips over and rights herself, as she's designed to do, so you hardly lose power, and all the time she's tracking towards the GPS position, the May Day origin. And you're ready for action – everyone knows the job he'll have to do when he gets there. Aye, it's rocket lines, inflatables, anything and everything that a boat can do – and if it's really bad we'll have RAF helicopter back-up from Lossiemouth. So there's nothing like it! Nothing can match it! And then we strap the survivors into the seats in the crew cabin or on to the stretchers and give them first-aid – and it's sometimes *heavy* first-aid, you know, burns, the lot – and if they're well enough we give them soup, lots of soup. And you wouldn't believe how pleased they are! Aye! For those few hours back to Aberdeen harbour – these other human beings, strangers, people we don't know, they love us! Can you believe it?'

'Yes Luke, I can! I really can – but Luke, let's be brave and do this thing! Right? Yeah? The stage! The stage – remember?'

'Ach, Jesus, och aye, Redmond, the stage – so there we are, in full lifeboat gear including helmets: and then midnight comes. And Redmond, it was so horrible, so squirm-making. And I've never forgotten it . . .'

'Yeah?'

167

'Because under our *sensible*, brilliantly designed and thoroughly tested kit, you know, survival suits with many very special and expensive standard RNLI extras – stuff that works, every time, even in weather like this, and out there, right in the sea itself if you're unlucky – under this kit, Redmond under this kit that I really respect, we're wearing these truly horrible nasty little dishonest thongs, skimpy red thongs.'

'Thongs?'

'Aye. Porn-stuff. And they are so uncomfortable! They rub your bits off?'

'What?'

'Aye. So midnight comes and on we go. We troop on, in a line. And then the band strikes up and they play that terrible tune. I think of it even now – every time I strap on my helmet for a shout: "You can keep your hat on!" Aye. And we crewmen – we did the full monty . . .'

'But Luke!' And I really laughed – all the insane tension of the fear, the howitzer-blasts against the inward-bulging decrepit rusted plates of the hull a few yards in front of our heads: it all dissolved in a howling laugh. 'Luke! . . . Luke! . . . But Luke! . . . you won't have to strip off!'

'Aye! Well . . . maybe not. I don't know. Maybe not. But that's how it'll feel! Of course it will!'

'No Luke, it *won't*. In fact I think it's safe to say, I really do – look, Luke, if you strip off while engaged in an academic lecture . . . I think we can say . . . I think we can say with some conviction: *you'll get the sack*!'

'Aye. Well, maybe. I hadn't thought of it. Like you say, it's the subconscious, I suppose. And it's not funny! You said so yourself! *And I don't want to talk about it!* OK? And while we're at it – those *skates*, remember?'

'Yes?'

'Aye. There's one small thing on which I'd like your *opinion*.'

'*My* opinion? You would? You really would?'

'Aye. You remember you said you liked the way those skates *smiled* at you?'

'Yes, I do.'

'Good! Then perhaps you can tell me, *in your opinion*: why would a skate want two eyes, why would a skate want two eyes when *the only ones it's got* stare straight into the mud?'

'Uh?'

'Nuts! The eyes are where they should be – on top of the head! Nuts! Nuts! Nuts! Those holes you thought were eyes, dumbo, *they're nostrils!*'

Someone turned the light on; Sean had turned the light on: 'Up ye get, boys! Ye've had a whole eight hours! And the storm's gone – there's yer heavy swell up there right enough, but it's *bright*! Ye can see the sun! Sunlight! It's cool! It's great! We're *alive*! Ye can see the sun!'

Sean came up close between the bunks, level with our heads, confidential. Sean, it was obvious, had had no sleep: his wide red eyes, the peeling skin on his nose, his red-blotched face. He was the youngest, I remembered, so perhaps he had had to stay on watch in the wheelhouse – it was possible that Sean had had no sleep for forty hours or more . . .

Luke's frizzy, dark-haired head was turned away to port, faceless on its pillow, dead, or asleep – and Sean, intending to whisper, it seemed, in the strictest man-to-man privacy, bent down low over Luke's left ear; but, pressed by his immediate need or, perhaps, released from all inhibition by forty hours of no sleep, he shouted (loud enough for me to hear, loud enough for Jason on the bridge to hear): 'It's Bryan! He's a big eater! It canna be helped . . . He's blocked ours! He's blocked it again! It canna be helped! That's Bryan for yer! So . . . please! . . . Luke? Canna use yer toilet?'

In their blue sleeping-bag, Luke's legs thrashed. They propelled him – and the blue sleeping-bag – off the bunk and out of view to port.

Sean, permission sought, honour satisfied, scrabbled with the rope behind the open door, released the knot, slammed the bent sheet of metal as almost-shut as it would go, and, with unexpected modesty, tied it tight.

From somewhere on the floor to my right, Luke said, with clarity: 'Redmond, that's another thing . . . what happened to my red Jacobs biscuit-box? They're rare, red ones . . . they're a different size . . . *and that was my very best box!*'

But I was already dressed and half out of the cabin. And, yet again, I was thrown through the steel doorway. I took a sprawl to the right – along the passage to the galley; I recovered; I made a spider-climb up the stairs to the shelter-deck. Standing, for a moment, bemused, in front of the pegs to the left of the companion-way, I remembered that the day or the night before I had left my sea-boots and oilskins in the fish-room: yes, it was all coming back to me, how bad, how *shaming*: I had talked too much, I had talked, I had burbled more in one go than I had ever done before, anywhere. Perhaps I had gone mad? Or was that being kind to myself? What the hell had I said to Luke? I'd no idea – but it was bad, very bad, I was sure of that, and, losing concentration, I stood level with, rather than at right angles to, a slow, gigantic roll. I took a helpless running lurch aft – and there I was: in my socks, frightened, right back in my very own place of inner humiliation. I was there, once again, in the pre-death place, my right cheek pressed ice-glue-cold against the side of the first winch, my left hand and its fingers, rapidly losing all sensation, locked hard around my familiar saviour, the protruding steel bolt . . .

OK, I thought, so at least I'm *safe*, and I'm not going to fall down sliding out through that huge scupper, and my feet – they're knife-cold in this slosh of water but soon they won't hurt at all, I won't feel them, so that's OK too: and there are my gannets and kittiwakes, so close, so very beautiful and Sean is right, as always, because it's the early morning sub-Arctic sunlight . . . But hey, hang on, because that really is very odd, the cod-end out there, appearing and disappearing on that vast irregular swell – on those waves that look as if the rolling green downs of my Wiltshire childhood had detached themselves from their bedrock and were after me . . . And the cod-end, it's red, light and silver and blood-red . . . And I shouted into the wind, loud as Sean: 'Red fish! Those fish are red! Red fish!'

'Aye!' said Luke, right behind me (where'd he come from? why give me a fright like that?). 'Redfish. *Scorpaenidae*. Scorpion-fishes. And here they're a species of *Sebastes*. Aye! This is different. Exciting. We're in Redfish country! So come on!' And, with the strength of a man three times his size (but that's a false comparison, I reassured myself, that only applies to males *who live on the land*), little Luke forced me back to the safety of the shelter-deck, where his tone changed: 'So what the hell do you think you're doing?' Luke's English accent had surfaced; Luke was angry; Luke was very angry, maybe even furious (and so Luke was special: because Luke cared . . . He really cared . . .). 'Jesus!' he said. 'Do you realize what you did? You were out there *in your socks*! You think that's funny? Or what? You think frostbite's a joke? Is that what you think? Some poor surgeon in Aberdeen has to amputate your toes? It's so common! But that's only when it's *serious*, when there's a man overboard up here – and he has to kick off his boots to swim to the stern-ramp, if he can . . . And how do you think you'll walk with no toes? Eh? You think that's funny? To go paddling out there with nothing but your socks? You shit-stupid barking? Or what?'

'I'm sorry . . . I didn't mean . . . I got . . .'

'Oh *come on*,' said Luke, pushing me through the companionway. 'Go and dry and *rub* your feet, *and find some new socks* – and god knows you've got enough – *they're all over the cabin!* The mess – *the mess you make!*'

★

172

Down in the fish-room, the bulkhead-door to the net-deck was open; Luke and I (in full gutting-rig) watched as Robbie, to port, and Allan and Jerry, to starboard, rode the great pile of green net, clinging to the top, hauling more of it inboard from the following sea. As the *Norlantean* rolled to port the net would slide down the sea-washed steel incline and pin Robbie against the side wall; as she began to right herself, Robbie would throw a right-hand punch into the spray towards Allan and Jerry above him – and he and the net would rise up . . . and slip down to starboard, when, from below, Jerry would throw a punch at Robbie . . . I thought: they're heaving at the net with every muscle of their upper bodies and they're see-sawing a mere few feet away from the stern-ramp in this terrible swell – and yet they've still got the energy to *play* . . .

'Come on,' said Luke, 'I've got things to show you. And besides, it's dangerous with this door open. It's not a good idea.' (He forced it shut.) 'It's all going to be different now. Redfish country!' He reached up beside the control levers above the gutting table, pulled out a steel, a knife-sharpener, a tapering rod of roughened steel with a wooden handle, the kind of thoroughly domestic steel you might expect to see flicking lengthwise from side to side of a carving knife (as your salivary glands dribble like those of one of Pavlov's dogs) before that impossible, unreachable pleasure: a Sunday roast with your family in a house that doesn't bung you about the place . . . Luke plucked a couple of gutting knives from their lodgement above the pipes tight against the ceiling to his left. One knife had a red plastic handle which, I knew, would be stamped LOEWEN MESSER with accompanying lion *couchant*, to the left, as you held it in your blue-gloved right hand, and SOLINGEN GERMANY 825 to the right – whereas, I wanted, I realized, I *really* wanted, the other knife he held, the plain, unmarked, wooden-handled, double-steel-riveted genuine ordinary knife . . . If you can just use *that* knife, my subconscious said, or imaged, or however you think the powerful deep-controlling subconscious communicates – if you can just have that particular knife, the only gutting knife on board that has a wooden handle: *then nothing bad can possibly happen to you.* And *whoaa!* said my battered conscious mind, the rational me I still took some pride in: what's *this*? You think you're studying deep-sea fishermen's superstitions in some academic way? Hey! *Haven't* we caught you out? Who's now afraid of *everything*? Who's sensibly transferred it all to one poxy little wooden-handled knife? Eh? Any answer?

Luke passed me the plastic-handled knife, sharp and fresh and ready to go. He replaced the steel. He kept, in his right hand, the wooden-handled knife, which mesmerized me.

'OK,' said Luke, assuming the control position at the gutting table (and I wedged myself into my usual place against the stanchion, where I felt secure), 'in front of you – incised into each section of the table, yes? Two lines set apart? Yes? Good. So all you have to do with redfish – you measure them against that standard length set by MAFF. If they're too small – leave them in the discard tray. If not, chuck them down the tube . . .'

'Hey Luke . . .'

'Aye, and we'll get three different species, if we're lucky, the true redfish, *Sebastes*: *Sebastes mentella*, the Oceanic or deep-water redfish; and *Sebastes marinus*, the Golden redfish, my favourite, really big ones; and then Norway haddock, wee dumpy ones that produce live young. And they *all* have nail-sharp spines along the dorsal fin – and an extra set, to surprise you, on the gill covers. Your gloves, Redmond, whatever you do – you'll shred them! And your hands? Pin-cushions! But the wounds heal or, at least, most of them do – and that's not the best bit, no, it's their *parasites*. You wait! I *love* parasites . . . So many millions of years! And there they are: perfect, for now . . .'

'Hey, Luke, I'm sorry . . . but could we swap knives? You know, I've . . . well, I've developed this *thing* about that wooden-handled knife. You know, it's not exactly a superstition . . . well, yes, actually, of course it is . . . But there again,' I said, suddenly inspired, 'it's no worse than your thing about your red Jacobs biscuit box, is it? Well, maybe it is . . . but all the same, Luke, couldn't we swap? Please? And anyway, look, I'm sorry, I should have told you, but it seems so unlikely and, look here, it's not the kind of thing I'm used to – but that *lump* you talked about, well, I found myself in the air, suspended just above your bunk, and I landed on my right buttock on top of your box, and somehow it's all rather disgraceful . . .'

'Ah, so that was it? Then that's OK,' said Luke, as if it certainly wasn't. 'That's OK!'

We exchanged knives, lobbing them across the table.

'But that red Jacobs biscuit-box – you know – that was my *best* box, they're a different size, red ones, they're rare, they're difficult to find and they're just right for the larger specimen-bottles and anyway, I liked that box, and now it's shattered, destroyed. It's gone!'

Robbie, in control position, filled the gutting-table sections. Luke stood to my left, Jerry to my right. The redfish were about 16 inches long, covered in scales, firm to the touch, and looked exactly as a fish is supposed to look, except for their eyes, which were huge, bulbous, half-popped-out of their heads. The scales on their backs really were a delicate red, shading down to pinky-white on their bellies – and their fins were a darker orange-red. Their lower lips protruded and curved upwards, giving them a permanently hungry, a begging look – but don't you get superior, I heard an inner voice say to me, because we were *all* fish once, and if you don't believe me, take a look at the human embryo at – what is it? – six weeks? It has *gill slits* . . . and these fish are clean and free of slime and firm to the touch and altogether *beautiful*.

'Luke,' I said, 'you didn't tell me, they're . . . they're *beautiful!*'

'Eh?' said Luke, preoccupied with some altogether more sensible thought of his own, throwing redfish, one to each hand, down the central tube. 'Their eyes? That's right. They *are* slightly enlarged.

Because these *Sebastes mentella* have been trawled up from around a thousand metres down – but their eyes are naturally gigantic. As you can see for yourself, these fish' (he flapped one in front of my face) 'have gone for a strategy of all-round awareness, speed – feel their muscles! – and a semi-armoured defence. Scales, not slippery slime, and spines – lots of spines. Fifteen or so on the dorsal fin, three on the anal. But we're lucky – their speed, as it were, makes us lucky, because their spines are not poisonous. They just *hurt*, that's all. You'll find out!'

'Their speed?'

'Aye! It all costs, as you know, it all costs biologically, as I told you, it costs whatever you decide – so these fish are *almost* fast and *almost* armoured, a little bit of both strategies. Escape-generalists, you might say. Whereas – isn't this great? A close relative of theirs – aye! magic! dingle day! – but I've never seen one of course, the very same family, the scorpion-fishes, *Scorpaenidae*, guess what? The stonefish, genus *Synanceia horrida* – horrid! you bet! – *that* is the absolute number-one most poisonous fish in the world!' (Jerry, to my right, stopped sorting the fish in his tray. He leant across me, the better to catch this startling news, his mouth slightly open; the hair on his head was bristle-short; and a silver ring, clipped into the outer whorl of his left ear, just below the rear-top downwards curve, winked at me in the overhead lights.) 'As far as we know, of course. Because as I told you – and you must always remember – the deep ocean is 95 per cent unexplored. And that's great too, isn't it? So get this – if the stonefish is the most poisonous fish in the world, what else is special about it?'

'It's slow!' I yelled, caught out, as delighted as if I was back in the remembered simple days of primary excitement – the release and revelation of biology at school.

'That's right!' said Jerry, in front of me, fully attentive, not moving his head.

'Aye!' shouted Luke. 'It's so slow it stays still! It lies on the bottom like a monkfish, *but in very shallow seas*. Each spine has two

176

poison sacs near its tip – you tread on one – and a sheath slides back down the erect spine and the venom ejaculates into you along a couple of grooves. You scream with instant agony – terrible! – you scream and collapse and go mad and *rave*, you make a lot of noise – your legs swell up fit to burst and your fingers and toes turn black and drop off and in six hours you're dead!'

'Great!'

Jerry said: 'Shit!'

'Aye!' said Luke. 'But I'm sorry, you'll only find it from the Red Sea to East Africa – and across the Indian Ocean to the northern coasts of Western Australia. And that's another thing, Redmond – about marine biology, I mean, you know – the species reach, it can be *vast*. Not like your jungles!'

'Yes!'

'And another weird thing, these redfish' (two more down the tube), 'right here in the north-east Atlantic – guess what? Despite all these spines – they're one of the staple foods of Sperm whales. I like that, I like Sperm whales, they've got the biggest brains on earth, they're intensely social – the females defend and help each other and suckle each other's calves . . . And come to that, *their* range, that really is vast – every ocean in the world, the females around the equator, the immature males in groups to the north and south, the huge old males, up to 60 feet long, spending most of their year feeding around the north or south pole, taking two months off to visit the schools of females in the tropics . . . They're extraordinary animals, they really are – but hey! It's too good a story to waste . . . I can't concentrate. Not now. Not in here. But I'll tell you about it later. I promise I will . . .'

Simultaneously, Robbie, responsible, standing across from us, his own section empty – and unable, in the pounding noise, to share in the pleasure of Luke's deep knowledge – shouted at Jerry: 'You big girl's blouse you! Get gutting! Bryan and Allan! They're short below!'

★

177

No one spoke – for an interminable number of revolutions (it seemed to me) of the constantly reloaded gutting table: and Luke's two big specimen-baskets filled with fish and crustacea that I could not believe had evolved to be as they were, to look as they did – so improbable, such animals from another world; which they were, of course, but I'd lost the nerve to ask, and besides, out of the dead mouth (below and in front of the manic staring eyes) of around one in twenty of the redfish in my tray, a long white living string of a worm attempted to wind its way to safety, a new home . . . So I'd take the redfish in my left hand and the worm in my right, and pull. And no matter how hard I pulled, the worm never broke – you couldn't break the spirit of these worms – no, they just thanked you for your help and emerged intact, 8 inches or so of will-power, of a refusal to despair, and I slid them on to the cold steel lip of the tray, where they pulsed forward, full of hope, searching for a new life. And there again – on about one in a hundred of the redfish in my tray something obscene had attached itself . . . It was white, this thing, fleshy, intimate, shaming in a medical way, and it obviously hurt horribly, because where it had grown out (or perhaps it had driven itself in), the delicate pink scaly skin of the once-beautiful redfish was purple-black, and the fish itself was thin, wasted, haggard. And from the bruise a short stalk protruded, towing a flat semi-transparent disc with a dark centre, and at the rear of the disc were white frills, and from the white frills there trailed two long thin filaments . . . And how would you hide something personal and horrible like that, I asked myself, a rooted-in-you extension of you from your genitals or your side that was one-third your own length? What would you do? Because you can't cut it off. Because you have no hands. And you can't bite it off – because your neck is armour-plated scaly-rigid. So what do you do? Shove its slimy bulbous and tubular mass down a trouser-leg? Wind it living round your thigh so it doesn't drop down and spasm beneath your skirt? And at last Luke said, just loud enough for me to hear: 'They're extraordinary animals, Sperm whales.'

'Yes, yes,' I said, agitated. 'I'm sure they must be. But what *are* these things?' And I held up a redfish, its hanging obscenity attached.

Luke stuck his gutting knife, blade first, behind his right ear. And I thought: why do they all do that? Why that insane nonchalant gesture? Because each time I see it – and all their knives are slit-sharp and would take off an ear like the stalk on a lettuce – I get a weak and trembly feeling right across those creases of skin at the backs of the knees . . .

With his freed right hand Luke leant across and plucked the swinging length of twin tails and glob and filament out of the belly of the fish: it came away – *shiek* – as the purple wound split open and two white, linked lobes, covered in blood, slid into the palm of his blue glove.

'A copepod, a parasitic copepod,' he said, directly into my left ear, as softly as anyone could speak on a trawler and still be heard. 'The head, the holdfast, the anchor' (with his left index-finger he poked the hard white lobes in his right palm); 'the body, the gut' (the circular glob with the dark centre); 'the ovaries' (the frills); 'and the egg sacs' (the twin tails); 'and these copepods, they're so efficient, *big time*, if you like parasites, and it's one hell of a story, right enough, but now – now's not the time . . . Because it's tense here, Redmond, there's real pressure, you know, pressure to get this haul done, sometimes it happens like that . . . for no particular reason . . . so we'll talk later, OK?'

And eventually even this massive catch was sorted and sent along the conveyor to the chute down to the hold (or out on the discard chute to the starboard scupper for the kittiwakes), and Allan and Bryan had all the full-sized redfish packed in ice in the hold . . . and it was time to eat.

And this was no ordinary supper, or breakfast, or whatever it was – this was fish and chips as I'd never tasted it – Sean's chips were special (Sean was good on chips, even Jerry said so) and Sean's

179

batter had all come right ('At last!' said Jerry, next to me): and the fish? The fish was halibut, white halibut, as fresh as fish can be, and the steaks so big they overhung even the outsize trawler plates . . .

'Oh shit,' said Jason, stepping into the fug, looking very tired, red-eyed, his stubble, now almost a beard, jet-black, his movements less lanky, less loose-limbed, his shoulders almost stooped. 'Fish and chips is it? *Fish and chips?*'

Jerry, sitting beside me, dug me in the ribs. 'Good, eh? That Sean, he's learnt. At last! But don't forget – *I taught him!*'

Jason, his plate piled, sat down next to Luke, opposite me: 'And Redmond, I've been thinking about it. You remember, you asked me what was the *oddest* thing I'd caught in the nets? Aye, well, now I know you: I don't think that's what you meant. No. Not at all.' He looked straight at me, his eyes without expression, his face sour, ragged – and so close. (Jason, I thought, you're the skipper, for Chrissake, so why don't you sleep when you need to? Just an hour or two? And inside my head Luke's voice answered at once: this Jason is the only man in the whole trawler fleet who can *feel* his way towards the fish. He's got it. He's blessed. So of course he can't trust anyone else to shoot the net . . .)

Jason repeated, 'No,' aggressive, 'you meant to ask me: "Jason, what's the *worst* thing you've ever trawled up?" Well, it didn't happen to the *Norlantean*, not to us, it was the *River Dee*. They brought up forty bodies from a Chinook helicopter crash and the bodies – they were in a bad state, believe me. The amphipods and hagfish had had a go, but the clothes were still there, and the skeletons, bits and pieces. And the whole lot was hidden in the fish in the cod-end and fell into the hopper – and the horror of it, you know, call it what you like, but thank god they had some bright spark like Luke in the crew, always sticking his nose in the hopper, as he does, I've noticed, looking for rarities or fucking wonders of the deep . . . Search me . . . And that guy saved the crew, they're all still at the fishing, so they were lucky – because if those half-chewed heads and feet and bits had come up the band and on to

180

the gutting table, do you think those boys would ever have gone to sea again? Never! Of course not! Not one of them! And there again, the bodies were lucky too, a chance in a million – a real freak of a chance. Because I told you, *no flower grows on a sailor's grave* – but this one time they did, the flowers grew . . . Not that those bodies were sailors . . . but thanks to the *River Dee* those men had a place *in the land itself*, in dry land, and that's it, that's the point – so the people who loved them when they were alive, and I'm talking real love here, so that means their mothers and fathers and daughters and sons, and wives, if they're lucky, very lucky; and two or three friends, if they were exceptional men, good men, and those friends, three at most, you can't handle more than three real friendships, they'll be male friends – because no good man can have a really close female friend who's not his wife, it can't be done . . . Anyway . . . here's the point: because of that haul on the *River Dee* each one of those men – clothes, dental records, they got the pieces identified – each one of those men had a patch of real earth to himself. The people who loved them could go somewhere to think in quiet, and bring back all those memories one after another and sit down in a place set apart from ordinary life and bring it all back . . . So those men lived again for a time, in other people's heads, for a little while, and that's the only immortality there is . . . And each one of us needs it, deserves it, when we're dead . . . But trawlermen?' he said, faltering. The anger and dominance, the mastery left his face. 'Drowned at sea? Forget it . . . You're gone . . . Forgotten.' He appeared not to be able to raise his head; he stared at his still-full plate of halibut and chips, not sure, I thought, where he was, and he said, in a hollow voice, which seemed, by itself, to make a tunnel of cold emptiness right through the communal comforting fug, a something without weight or form that was waiting for us, between the two familiar tables, in the narrow passageway, in the otherwise thick, hot, fat-saturated, enveloping air. 'Because your people have no place,' he said, to his untouched golden-battered halibut and his pile of hand-cut, irregular genuine

181

potato-chips. 'Nowhere *visual* to go . . . And which one of us can set time aside in a day, real *time* – without that effort, a release, a physical journey, a *place* to visit . . . to really remember someone? It's not possible . . . Lost at sea . . . Aye! You bet! Too right! Lost at sea? Lost for ever!'

I looked away, anywhere, but, as it happened, at the top corner of the galley, to the left, at the big television on its bracket, which was playing some violent film on video as always, and the soundtrack, as always, hit by the thump of the engines, was inaudible. And besides, the cars and guns, the knives – it was all so safe and easy, it was all from a so desirable and previous life, it was all, all of it, set on dry and stable land, and concrete.

Robbie, brave little Robbie, terrier Robbie – he broke the silence. Sitting at the other table, in the corner, beneath the television, he leant forward across Dougie. He looked at me and raised a grin. 'Do you mind Malky Moar? Malky and the lightning?'

'I do!'

'Aye well, Malky's got a rabbit he's fond of like. An ordinary rabbit – but it flops about his place, you know. A wild rabbit, but a wild rabbit that no fears Malky. And Malky respects the rabbit. "Robbie," he says to me one night in the bar – and now I go to hear Malky, not to drink, you understand? I drink a coke or two, and that's it. And you know what? I've surprised myself, right enough. I've no missed it for a moment. And I'll no touch it again, ever. So Malky's rabbit, as I was telling you, "You mind my rabbit?" he says. "Aye," I say. And I'm forgetting, you should know that Malky has an old sheepdog. And Malky, he loves that old sheepdog. But he also loves his rabbit. Because the rabbit *chose* Malky, if you know what I mean, whereas Malky, for his dog, *he paid money*. His rabbit, I've seen it, you know, it eats Malky's cabbages and he doesna mind! It's just a fockin ordinary wild rabbit, it's just a *rabbit*, but it's big, of course, really big, a fockin great buck rabbit fed on Malky's cabbages! Anyway, as I say, Malky says to me, "Robbie, you mind my rabbit?" "Aye." "You mind I made

182

good that fence of mine? All those rotten posts?" "Aye." "Well, Robbie, you'll be wanting to hear this – I forgot myself one day and I left my hammer behind. You mind the one I used to knock in the staples?" "Aye." (And I did, because I'd helped him with the fencing.) "Well, there I am sitting by the stove and having a wee dram because it's dark – and in comes the dog. The dog, noo, he's *crying*. He's got blood on his nose. So I think no more about it and I'm away to ma bed. And when I wake up, the dog, he's got that size of a bump on his nose he canna see out. And I go to the fencing. And there's nae a hammer in sight! So I put two and two together like, and Malky, I say, there's no three ways aboot it. That rabbit, he picked up that hammer, and he stood up on his back legs and he brought that hammer down – *bong*! – right on my old dog's nose.

' "And from that day to this, when my dog sees my rabbit, there's nae bother, nae bother at all. And that rabbit, I just know that rabbit, he's got my hammer, right down his hole, just in case – and who'd be blaming him?" '

We laughed. We cheered. And Jerry, beside me, said, 'That's no much of a story. A right bubbly jock! And I've heard it all before!' and he clapped, and so did I, because perhaps, just perhaps, life was not so brutal or so pointless after all, and Robbie, triumphant, raised his voice and his right fist, punching the sweaty used-up fat-fried air: 'So that's why I go to the bar, even though I dinna touch a drop – I go to hear Malky, the stories of Malky Moar!'

Jason did a manic loose-wristed knife-and-fork drumroll on his cleaned-out plate. We cheered. It was true – we still had a few fully functional tomorrows owed to us. Somehow or other, we were in credit – maybe something, somewhere, owed us a tomorrow.

'Aye,' said Jerry, getting up, holding his plate, knife and fork in his right hand, and pushing me with his left thigh (which felt more like the trunk of an oak) out into the passageway, out into the emptiness that had almost, but not quite, vanished. 'So now, boys – it's sticky-treacle spongy-brain pudding! With absolutely safe artificial plastic cream! And I made it! I cut the clingfilm shite right off – all by myself!'

'Well done, Jerry! Good on ya!' said Allan Besant, without the trace of a smile.

Half happy that I still existed, even in this cold and receding emptiness, in the fug, I stood at a loss between the two bolted-down tables and their screwed-tight benches: with Dougie and Robbie, Allan and Bryan to my left; with Jason and Luke, at my own table, to my right. And then I remembered that I had a genuine dog-bouncy, an all-four-feet prancing throw-me-a-ball Labrador question to ask Robbie, so I sat down.

'Hey Robbie! You've said it twice now – and each time it gave me this moment of happiness, you know? But what does it mean? Exactly? What does it mean – when you're annoyed with someone – why do you shout: "You big girl's blouse you?"'

'Aye!' shouted Robbie. He looked interested, almost happy himself. He elbowed Dougie backwards into the bench-rest, he took possession of his side of the table. 'Aye – that's for us, on the *Norlantean*, so what d'ye call it, friendship? Ach! *Comradeship!* That's it, among the boys. Because we love it, it's our latest saying. So it's no an insult like. Except that mebbe it is – because it's no a compliment.'

'Ah come on,' said Jerry, reappearing through the wrap-around steam and stale fat-fried air, 'what you talking about?' And – full of enthusiasm for the mere thoughts of such an image, he forgot his manners, by-passed Jason, and brought Robbie the first giant castle of treacle sponge in a moat of cream. 'It's obvious!' he shouted. 'Tight round – stuck fast on the big nipples! There you are' (he set the big bowl down, decisively, in front of Robbie), 'you're clinging! You're clinging tight all over! You're clinging tight to the big breasts!'

Dougie, moving his upper body slightly forward away from the back-rest, down towards the table, said, slow and mournful, 'Aye, that's right enough . . .' (Jerry stood still for a moment, because

184

Dougie – Dougie was *talking* . . .) Dougie stared at the table-top. 'And it's no a bad idea . . . Not at all . . . No when you come to think of it . . .'

'But Redmond, Old Worzel,' said Jerry, returning with two more steaming gold-and-white castles of pleasure, 'take a tip from Jerry. If you want to pick up a *really* big girl – or any kind of girl for that matter – *never* say you work on a trawler! They dinna like it, they hate it, too wild, dangerous, whatever, I dunno, but they dinna like it – so say you're away at the oil-rigs. Steady money. A job for life. That works – every time!'

'Aye,' said Bryan, in his big bass voice, shifting in his seat, looking at his huge wack of treacle pudding as if he'd been short-changed, 'but suppose it's a Norwegian girl, or a Dutch girl – then tell them the truth. Because the only thing they canna stand is a lie. And that's obvious too, isn't it?' Big Bryan, First Mate, held his spoon poised in his right hand, but he'd yet to touch his treacle mountain; Big Bryan was becoming passionate, carried away: 'Because the Norwegians, they're our people, *seafarers*! No just sailors or seamen, they're *seafarers*. And the Dutch? Why do we like the Dutch? Up here in Orkney and Shetland?'

I said, my mouth full of treacle and sponge and fluffy cream, 'Nosh idea.'

Bryan raised his head and looked straight at me. 'Because they beat the shit out of you English! They sailed right up the Thames!'

Dougie, concerned, said, 'But he's Irish!'

'Irish? Of course he's not Irish! And even if he was, forgive me, Dougie, but all that *religion*. Ireland, it's almost as bad as Lewis and Harris – a *total* bullshit zone. No truth at all! Not anywhere!'

Jason, opposite me, said suddenly: 'Redmond, that's your eating done for now, you're fat enough already. Go on – it's your turn. Sean's on the bridge, and we don't want him doing a Davy . . . I've got a nasty feeling he's on to his second forty-hour stretch . . . And even if he *is* crazy, and the youngest, we shouldn't treat him like that, should we?'

185

'No of course not,' I said, chastened, dropping my spoon, jumping up. And I made my way to the bridge.

As I reached the floor of the wheelhouse, Sean scrabbled out of his harness, out of the skipper's chair. He looked manic, wide-eyed, certifiable from lack of sleep. He bolted past me, like a young rabbit breaking from cover, as if the dog of his own terrors was right behind him, all the way back down the stairs.

So I'm on watch, I thought, but for what? Enemy submarines? And what do I do if we hit one? And if there is something out there I won't see it until it's in the arc of the searchlight, and the swell, it seems gigantic . . . and the radar-screen with that wiper-thing that leaves dots and blobs behind it instead of scraping them off . . . But look here, I'm sure I could handle the wheel and keep her on a compass bearing, any fool can do that, but this brass-and-mahogany wheel, this ancient compass, I *think* they're decorations, because real life seems to happen only on all these alien screens, and with these little levers, squat gear-sticks . . . And anyway I don't know the compass-bearing, Jason says I can write anything I like, but if I give away the positions of his hauls he'll push my head in a bucket of water and drown me dead as a Black butt . . .

And hey, it's lonely, I'm really lonely; this is the only place you can find loneliness on the entire ship . . . And please, I don't like it . . .

I was thrown (but this time without undue aggression; the tail-end of the baby hurricane seemed to have lost its murderous one-on-one intent) – and I fetched up facing aft: in front of a comforting, a friendly machine. He introduced himself, in plain English, as I clung to the wood surround: 'Smith Maritime,' he said, at eye-level (well, perhaps my knees were bent a little). He was an Enlightenment, a reasonable machine, and he clearly expected me to participate in his interests in life: in five neat rectangles, outlined in white on his black fascia, he offered, to anyone who could read, two big buttons apiece, one below the other, in each section, headed, in series (and *such* an orderly series): MAIN CLUTCH; AUTO CLUTCH; WINCH SPEED; AUTO PUMP; CRANE. So how's about, just to please him, to honour this new friendship extended in words that even I can understand, how's about I press one or two? Or maybe all together?

There was a pounding of feet up the stairs, two lots of desperate feet, it seemed to me – and Jason appeared, moving almost as fast into the wheelhouse as Sean had gone out of it: and looking almost as crazed.

Close behind him – so that's all right! – there came the reassuring Robbie.

'Jesus!' said Jason, grabbing me, one hard hand to each shoulder, pushing me towards the Mate's chair. 'To think I sent *you* up here! On watch – Jesus! I forgot – I've grown used to it, having you around, and you're not much good, but it's true you gut your arse off, and you're getting better, and you haven't bunked off since the beginning, you haven't taken to your fucking bunk, not at all, so how was I to remember? How the fuck was I to remember that you're just an idiot?'

'Ah, thanks . . .'

'Jesus wept!' said Jason, thrusting me into the high-back chair, buckling me in with a decisive snap; and his own long limbs bent into the skipper's chair, easy as a curling snake, no harness needed.

'Aye!' said Robbie, standing lightly beside me (Robbie seemed to be able to perch anywhere with dignity, like a bird, a Pictish bird). 'Jason forgot!' He put his arm round the back of my child's high-chair, in which I was strapped, and brought his head forward, level with mine. 'Jason forgot!' he said, with a tremendous grin on his bird-alert and beaky face. 'We couldna believe it. Bryan was laughing inside like and he winked at me, you know, and he held up his right hand – five fingers up. So we waited, to see what would happen, five minutes like, and that's a long time – and then *boom*! We shouted, all together, and Allan joined in, "Worzel's on the bridge! Old Worzel – he's on watch!" And Allan shouted, "Go it,

Gummidge!" And Jerry shouted, "I'm away to ma bed! I'll die in ma bed!" And Dougie, you know, he just *stared* at Jason, and he looked *terrible* . . . And Jason here? He was out of his seat like a focking ghost!'

'I'm sorry,' said Jason, with an eerie change of voice, re-slotted back into his familiar place of calm, of command, of contemplation. 'So where, at this time of year, this week in fact – where on the continental slope, the great shelf-edge toward the abyss, where would I want to be if I were a redfish? Above which canyon? Hanging out, yes, but in which current?' He laid his right hand gently on one of the stubby gear-sticks. He glanced at the radar-screen on which the freed windscreen-wiper went round and round and, far from pitching into panic, he seemed to grow further into his alpha-male equilibrium. 'I'm sorry, Redmond, forgive me, but you must understand, it's a terrible thing at sea – it's *the* one big sin, it's a crime really, among sailors, it's not right, to leave your bridge unmanned. I know, I know, your poncy round-the-world yachtsmen and -women do it! But then that's who they are, what they're like, all alone, showing off, and if we run them down we get the blame! But the fact is they're not the only ones, because sodding great tankers do it too! Can you imagine that? You're registered in Liberia or whatever, there's no law out at sea, so you stick it on autopilot, just like a round-the-world-twice yachts-woman, and you go to sleep! Can you imagine that? Can you?'

'Yes, I can,' I said, despite myself. 'Sleep . . .'

'Oh come on,' said Jason, leaning forward, tapping computer keys. 'Stop it. Be a man. This'll cheer you up – like I promised, remember? – Davy's tow! Now don't get me wrong – Davy's a great guy, he really is, tall and blond and fit, you know, the girls love him, but the real point is – well, it's this: he's a lifeboatman. So there's no way round it, however you look at it, you can say they're mad maybe, but that won't do, not at all, because consider this: is a lifeboatman selfish? Thinking of himself, like everybody else? No, he's not! He's ready to die, week in, week out, for the rest of us! So yes, Redmond, let's be honest, that's one reason why I had to let *you* on board my *Norlantean*, because you came with Luke, a *lifeboatman*. And I'll tell you this for nothing, he's a damn fine trawlerman too, believe me, and I'd give him a job tomorrow, whereas you . . .'

'Davy – Davy's tow,' said Robbie. 'Eh? Jason? And you should be telling Redmond here – aye! Davy – Davy was pinged!'

I said: 'Pinged?'

'Aye,' said Robbie, excited. 'He was pinged right enough. He was knackered like, he didna mind it was there, he stood on a slack cable, flat on the deck, aye, one of the warps – and *ping*! they go as they tighten, *ping*! And Davy – he's shot 20 feet in the air, Bryan says 30, and *bosh*! Right over the side! Man overboard! But Davy kept his head, he's a lifeboatman, they're *trained* for it. And we all panicked, but Bryan yells: "To the ramp!" So we all run aft and fall down the ladders and Davy swims to the ramp and Bryan throws a rope and we haul him in – and he's alive!'

'Great!' I yelled. 'Well done!'

'He was sick right enough. Really sick. Sick with the shock of it. But then? Can you guess? What'd Davy do next?'

'No idea!'

'No? You can't? Well – he went straight back to work. Not a word said. Cold. Wet through and through. *Straight back to work.*'

'Ah.'

Jason, peering at the screen second to his left, said: 'Hey! Here we are – look at this!' The shaftless white arrowhead pricked its point at a red-traced, irregular ellipse on the chart, set over a criss-cross of different-coloured straightish lines, all with attendant numbers stuck on to them like ectoparasites, all equally incomprehensible. 'Davy's tow! He fell asleep, you see, right here in this chair. And the whole lot, the trawler, the miles of cable, the otter-boards, the net – they all went round in a circle! Davy's dream! Davy's tow!'

'Redmond,' said Robbie sharply, unbuckling me with his left

hand and, with his right at the small of my back, pushing me to my feet. 'I almost forgot too. You're wanted – right now, or before now. In the fish-room! Luke wants you, he's going through his baskets, through all his specimens like, the ones he's saved – and you're to help him measure, the whole ching-bang. And that's the point of you, aye? To help Luke?'

Luke had set up his scales in the usual place, on the steel shelf beside the main conveyor to the hold.

'Just in time!' he said, as I got into my oilskins. 'Right on time!'

There was an ominously long line of yellow, red and blue plastic baskets to his left. Noticing, I suppose, the hang-dog look which I could feel on my face, Luke, offensively happy, said, 'That's for the last three hauls! I waited – just for your sake – until the Force 12 had gone. What's it now? Force 8? 7? So you won't *fly*! Not even you could fly in a Force 7! But don't worry, it's OK, I've numbered my hauls and they're sorted by the colour of the baskets. That really pleases me, you know, big time, like my biscuit boxes. My red one . . .'

'Yeah. Yeah. I'm sorry.' I pulled on my sea-boots. 'Don't let's go through that again.'

'Redmond – cheer up!' (I pulled on my half-shredded blue gloves.) 'I'm going to show you the most extraordinary things, real things, not like the shit we talked the other night . . .'

191

'Ah.' I took the clipboard with its stack of Marine Lab record sheets, so many headings, so many columns . . .

'Aye – and did you know, the boys, they call you Worzel, Old Worzel? That's great! You've got a nickname. You know – after that scarecrow on the telly with white hair and whiskers and all crumpled up and he comes alive and moves about a bit. That's great! Magic! A nickname! So they like you!'

'Right . . .'

'Oh come on, just because Jason sent you up on watch. That really shocked Bryan, I can tell you, he held up his hand, gave you five fingers, five minutes. And then we all shouted, "Old Worzel's on the bridge!" or some such. Christ, Jason *moved*. So fast. And when he'd gone – God how we laughed!'

I sat on the up-ended fish-box, gripping the clipboard in my right hand, the stub of a pencil in my left, like an angry schoolboy, and I felt mean, but I couldn't express it, because the cold had got to my facial muscles. You're just like your cat Bertie, I thought (and had a moment of schoolboy homesickness) – because when he's stroppy, with his ears laid back, if I push them forward and hold them forward, he forgets how annoyed he ought to be, and he starts to purr, and eventually, overcome with ear-signal pleasure, he chirrups.

'Aye. Sorry. So look – this is great – dingle days!' chirruped Luke. 'Well, almost – I've sorted the main groups in each basket. So let's start with my favourites from the Polar basin, Polar sculpin, they can live up to 3 kilometres down, the cute wee things with horns on their heads that we always seemed to catch in pairs! Remember?'

'Eh?'

'Here – look!' (In his right hand he held out a couple of little fish.) 'But hey! You can't wear *gloves* for this! I'll need you to take measurements, do intricate things, and if we're *very* lucky we'll be here for hours, I hope so, this is our one big chance – science at last! Because Jason – he told me he's going flat out, due north, yes! To one day's steaming from the ice cap!'

'Oh, Jesus . . .' I took off my gloves, dropped them to the floor. And I looked at my hands, for more than a moment, holding them this way and that in the harsh overhead electric light, and I regarded them with deep satisfaction, and felt better, because they weren't girl's hands any more, or, at least, if they *were* female, they were the hands of the most frightening of sod-you fishwives – even on their backs they were so covered in puncture wounds from the redfish spines that they were almost young again; you couldn't see a single one of those age-spots . . . And the feeling was even good physically, too, because I couldn't feel the punctures one by one any more, my hands just burned, they felt very hot, the only part of me that felt warm . . .

'Redmond!' shouted Luke, right beside me. 'What the hell are you doing? Flapping your hands about? Please – look – *please* don't do that, you know, go off like that, it's spooky, your trances, whatever, you know.' (The two small fish, maybe 8 inches long, were, I was surprised to see, still in his right palm, in front of my nose.) 'I had a relative once, and I went to visit her, in an old people's home – and she went off just like you do! So sometimes I think – sometimes I think you really *are* Old Worzel!'

'Shit. Thanks . . .'

The two dead Polar sculpin nestled in my left hand. Their skin felt rough, their big heads had these knobs on top, not really horns, but tubercules, the buds of horns; they were brown, blotched with darker brown bands and yes, there was no doubt about it – they could have been the Miller's Thumbs I used to try to catch with my net in the childhood stream at the bottom of the Vicarage garden . . . I felt I was ten years old again, in shorts and black welly boots: you lifted a stone and a Miller's Thumb shot out, a rocket-trail of sediment behind it. And the little net on the end of its bamboo pole? Well, it was *always* in the wrong place . . . But I must not go off – what did he say? Go off! Jesus . . .

I laid one Polar sculpin on the scales, and the other, its husband or its wife, I placed gently beside it on the steel shelf.

The heavy steel door to our right slammed back and Robbie stepped over the sill. He was dressed, I was envious to see, in his equivalent of a dressing-gown: a white singlet, a pair of dark-blue tracksuit-bottoms, and white trainers. I thought: even Robbie's *away to his bed*; but there again, he deserves it, and come to that – how lucky you are that no one here expects *you* to wear a singlet ... Because Robbie has an absurdly muscled chest, and *biceps*. There's no flab and shame on him anywhere. In fact – to dissect Robbie: that would be a gift for any medical student: you would not have to cut through those thick layers of yellow fat. No, little Robbie is without price, an example of male structures at their very best, a rare reality, a one-to-one match for those diagrams of perfection in *Gray's Anatomy*.

Robbie up-ended another fish-box and perched between us.

'Luke,' said Robbie, clearly fascinated by the electronic scales, the Polar sculpins, the baskets of junk transformed into treasures, 'I just remembered, Luke – I heard you tell Redmond, you said you didn't know anything about Black butts, you mind that? Greenland halibut like, you didn't know where they went to breed. Well, I remembered, just now – and I think I *do* – I've been on the Hatton Bank, on a different boat like, no with Jason. We call it Manhattan – we tell the girls we're off to Manhattan! But Redmond, it's nae New York, it's west of the North Feni Ridge, north-west of the George Bligh Bank, north of the Rockall Plateau, aye – and I tell you, Luke, *that whole area should be closed to the new deep-sea fishery!* Aye, they should license the new fishery before it's too late. Make it like the Icelanders do, or the Faeroese, they've got it right, you know, they really have: I've been at the fishing in the Faeroe Box, too, that skipper had a licence – £120,000 a year and worth every penny! And you know why? *Because it's strict.* Strictly controlled. No messing. No free-for-all. No fockin Spanish fish-paedophiles with their illegal fine-mesh nets! Aye – and the *cod*, Luke, you shoulda seen them – bigger than me, and the heads on them! And the haddock – huge! – not one of the boys knew they could grow so big . . . And lots of Black scabbard fish, Black scabbards, rough brown skins, bristly all over, you know, and even more big Grenadiers – and we sold them all to France, pronto. And Luke, there was a different kind of Rabbit fish, even odder than the ones here, the kind that Sean would say were *freaky, man. You shoulda seen their noses . . .*'

'Aye!' shouted Luke, startling me. (Luke, I thought, may well blow up with excitement: *Boompf!*) *'But what about the Black butts?'*

'Aye, I'm forgetting, they're nae like here, in the Nor Nor East Atlantic – nae, here they've very small eggs as you can see for yourself, and guess what? Over Hatton Bank they're huge fish, the Black butts, and their eggs are big, really big, as big as grapes. Aye – if I do one good thing in my life, this is it. Luke, this is what I came to tell you, you must say to your boss in the lab in Aberdeen, whatever, the Government – Hatton Bank will be closed to Greenland halibut fishing, because *that* is where they breed, that's where the whole lot come from!'

And Robbie, suddenly shy, overcome (what was it? too much emotion? sudden plain speaking? had he offended against his personal code? I'd no idea) – Robbie, awkward, turned and went, as fast, as he might have said, as a fockin' ghost.

'Christ!' said Luke, shocked. 'Do you realize the significance of that? Have you any idea? Why is it only me? Why don't more Scottish office marine scientists get off their arses – excuse me – and go out on trawlers and *listen* to these boys?'

'That's obvious!' I said at once (trying to forget how sick and ill and abject-frightened I'd been . . . and if I *was* a government scientist would I come on a trawler in January again, or all-year-round as you'd have to? Or would I change my job? What if, say, there was a vacant post as a bed-tester and salesman in Aberdeen?). 'It's obvious . . . well, it's obvious . . . because there *are* only 6 million people in all of Scotland – so how could you afford more people than you? How many Scottish marine scientists do you think there are? Fifty? One hundred? And they have so many other things to

195

do!' (So: why couldn't I be a test-pilot for Dunlopillow?) 'Besides, get this country in perspective, Luke – do you realize that down in England, in my own county, unbelievably beautiful Oxfordshire, and Luke, so full of trees and so far away, yes, *in Oxfordshire alone*, there are 632,000 people!

'And Luke – all those certifiably brave, manic hairy Scottish warriors, the Scotii, Luke, the invaders from northern Ireland, they were from Orior, the O'Hanlon lands – and if you don't believe me, Luke, go check out Dunadd, the crowning place of the first Scottish kings: and there'll you'll find a trotting boar incised in the rock, and that trotting boar, Luke, that's the O'Hanlon coat of arms!'

'Aye. Big time, my arse – excuse me – but what the hell's that to do with anything, and anyway, didn't you tell me that every second sweet-shop round Lough Neagh is called Redmond O'Hanlon's sweet-shop? And that there are far more Redmond O'Hanlons in the New York Police Force than copepods in the North Atlantic?'

'Well no, not quite, but OK, *yes*, so what? *Fuck you!*'

'Aye,' said Luke, 'and here you are coming over *all grand*, all of a sudden, have you any idea how *pathetic* that is? Eh? Laying claim to Scotland? Jesus! *And you probably think that one or two of the boys are off the wall!*'

'OK, yes, it was a joke, sort of – but the wild pig, you know . . . Yes, you're right, Luke, *please*, forget that, Jesus, the crud that comes to the surface on this boat . . . yeah, no sleep, that wasn't me, you know . . .'

'Of course it was!' said Luke, happily, recovering from his rage at all the other Scottish Office marine scientists, wherever they might be. He tilted the (blue) basket immediately to his left. 'And here you are – my second extraordinary exhibit! Lumpsuckers!'

A layer of glisten-slimy grey-brown little fish looked up at me with their open black eyes, their big heads sparsely dotted with small black shiny growths (parasites? Sea-lice?) . . . And as far as a fish can be cuddly, I thought . . . They look so downturned-mouth sad, so big-eye worried . . . Yes, certainly, you'd want these little fish to be your friends . . . You'd want to comfort the lot of them . . .

'Hey Redmond! I can see – you *like* them! And quite right too, so do I, cute, eh? But also, much more important – they're fascinating, you know, *biologically*. How did they evolve like this?' He held one up and, cavalier with its dignity, squashed it towards me, belly-up: slightly aft of its throat was a ribbed and grooved roundel, a crater in its flesh. 'The sucker! Even C. M. Yonge in his New Naturalist volume in the late forties, you know, *The Sea Shore*, you must have read *that* – even he said the Lumpsucker or Sea-hen was the most remarkable fish you'd be likely to meet on the coast – partly because of its sucker. Everyone quotes Thomas Pennant – you know, a friend of yours probably, because he's eighteenth century, the guy Gilbert White wrote his letters to – anyway, I think that's right, but the point is Pennant bunged a Lumpsucker he'd just caught into a bucket of seawater, and later, when he took the fish by the tail to lift it out, the whole bucket full of water came too! The sucker's *that* strong!'

'Great! We should tell Sean! *Freeeeky!*'

'Aye! And guess what? The female makes her way up and ashore in April and lays up to 300,000 pink eggs between the mid-tide and low-water level, spread over a rock. And then? She fins it back out to sea, gone, buggered off, excuse me, she deserts and saves herself! And guess who stays and aerates the eggs? *Who* takes no food from April to November, his stomach distended with nothing but water? The male! Poor sod. So who's in guard position when the tide is out and here come the gulls and crows and rats? Who's not left his post (if he hasn't been pecked or gnawed to death) when the tide comes in and he does his main job, aerating the eggs with his fins, bringing home that critical extra oxygen? Eh? The male! He stays there when the tide sweeps in with those hungry big, big fish! That's the kind of father I'd like to be!'

'Jesus, Luke, *calm down*, it's OK – I'm sure you will be, if you

197

get the chance . . . I mean of course you will . . . You've got years and years to go . . .'

'But Pennant and Yonge – they didn't know the half of it! Even your Alister Hardy got a surprise when he caught Lumpfish way out in the North Sea. And the North Sea – it's a shallow pond! No, here's your evidence – *look at them all* – and from 700 to 1,000 metres down! They're *almost* deep-sea fish. They must be. Unless, and I hate this, unless the net caught them as it was coming up, and that's always a possibility, and you and I must admit that, because we're honest, and scientists, but it's no good for my figures, you know, no good at all, there's no accurate depth-reading for the capture of each individual fish, that's the trouble with commercial trawlers . . . But hey! Don't be so miserable, don't take things so *personally*, eh? Because there's one more great fact about them! The way they look – their camouflage – does that remind you of anything?'

'Yeah. *One of my aunts.*'

'Oh Jesus! Don't be ridiculous! It's obvious, isn't it? We all know they sometimes drift about in the open ocean feeding on comb jellies and jellyfish under floating mats of seaweed – so what protects them from their predators?'

'Give up!'

'Don't be an idiot – look at them!' He held the lumpfish, now right side up, six inches from my nose. 'It's obvious, isn't it? They look exactly like a pneumatocyst!'

'A what?'

'A *pneumatocyst* – a floating capsule of brown algae – perfect camouflage! And now – for the third and last of our little fish, don't move, wait here!'

Luke, his blue woolly hat stuck on top of his curly black hair, his now substantial black stubble shading his prematurely lined, lived-in face, making him look more decisive, obsessed, craggier than ever, disappeared into the laundry cubby-hole . . . And re-emerged, three brown-paper parcels under his right arm.

He laid them in a line, one, two, three, on the empty steel shelf to my right. They were books . . . 'Now, whatever you do,' he said, picking up volume three, 'don't laugh, because these books *really* mean something to me.' He was searching for a reference, turning the pages, in front of me, showing this treasure of his as if, in itself, it was the rarest of fishes: before my tired eyes passed black-and-white drawings of fish, one or two a page, diagrams of heads and fins, short texts full of numbers, maps . . . 'You'll think I've borrowed them from the library at the lab, but consider it – would any librarian in the world let a student take books like this *to sea*? At £123 the set? No way! Redmond, this is the greatest, the great co-operative work of scholarship, *Fishes of the North-eastern Atlantic and the Mediterranean* – only UNESCO has the resources you need! No commercial publisher could even *think* of an effort like this. First – it took *eight years* of cataloguing the available knowledge, you know, reports, specimens in museums, eight years from 1965 to 1973. So you understand the point, don't you?' Holding the precious volume with his left hand under its back, his right across its open insides, Luke turned his scrutiny from the book to me. 'You've got it, yes? Because it's all so new, this science of the seas! And sure, I know you now, and you're thinking it's just like the nineteenth century, all this mere cataloguing, but that makes it even more impressive! Big time! The *grind* of it – no glamour like molecular biology – no praise from anyone but your-self, and that's the secret, self-motivation, and a love of these animals simply for themselves, for how weird they are! Aye – and after the catalogue, we call it Clofnam, short for *Check-list of the fishes of the north-eastern Atlantic and of the Mediterranean* – only *then* could the real thing start . . . And these volumes came out from 1984 to 1986, *that* recent!' (Luke's eyes: so bright, so happy.) 'So how do you think I made them mine, on £7,000 a year? Eh?' His hands quick, jerky, he slid the open book flat to the steel shelf, pulled off his hat, marked the place with it, shut the book as far as it would go (two-thirds) and he said, 'Well, it was obvious, wasn't it? This was no luxury, I had to have these books to take to sea with me, so I thought, OK, I'll work it out, the money, if I don't go to the Moorings, you know, the dockside pub the marine-lab people use, in the evenings, or at lunch-time, or at all, if I drink no beer for eight weeks and limit myself to one proper meal a day, a big breakfast, then I could save £125. And I did! I bought them! They're mine!'

'Goaal!'

'Ayeeeee! And look – I protected them' (he held up volume three, the blue hat deep-fill-sandwiched inside); 'that very same day, at once, I cut up Manila envelopes from the lab, petty thieving, you'll say, but I thought that was OK, you know, justified, and several layers too, because I didn't want them stained with fish-guts and blood and engine-oil, so that was OK, wasn't it?'

'Of course it was!'

'Because Redmond, you understand, you must – when I'm old, older than you, very old, if I'm lucky, if I make it through, when I can't go to sea any more, I'll tell you what I'll do, I'll have a cottage by then, like I told you, with a fire, so *warm*, and a family, and we'll all gather round, and with my gutting knife I'll slit the Manila envelopes right off these three volumes, and underneath, you know what? The covers – they'll be as new, like the day I first had them! They'll be perfect, the covers, and somehow I know they'll remind me of everything, all my life – well, they're not covers technically, of course, there are no covers, no nonsense like that, no, they're the boards of the books themselves – and the *colours*, the only colours in the whole big deal are on the boards, and volume one, it's the delicate surface blue of the calmest of days in high summer, shading down to that dark blue when light gives up and you can't see in any more and the vast world of all those miles to go gets secret. Aye – and over it all is an ace, a really accurate line-drawing of a Common skate. And vol. two: the same idea, but in the sea-green of an algal bloom, with a drawing of a John Dory, the *Saint-Pierre* in French, *Pez de San Pedro* in Spanish – you *always* get given the French and Spanish names and, now and then, the common names in German or Russian, and I can tell you, as a fisheries inspector, that's marvellous, bloody marvellous, invaluable, as you'd say – but the John Dory, everyone knows it, but it's freaky in itself, the dorsal fin, the crazy long filaments on the finrays, what are they for? Defence? Antennae to detect the subtlest vibrations in the water around them? Who knows? Aye – we're still in the Middle Ages. The *Saint Peter fish*, can you get that? Just because it has this big black spot with a yellow surround on its flank, and aye – what's *that* for? – but it comforts all the Christian fishermen, because they're sure, all those Christian fishermen are *certain*, whether they admit it or not, they're certain that the black marks on each flank are the sacred thumb and forefinger prints of St Peter, burned into the species for ever, from that very moment when Peter the Fisherman lifted them from his nets!'

'Jesus!'

'Aye! *Jesus!* And volume three – guess what? All in shades of purple, the sea before a storm, certainly, but at other times, too, it goes purple and I've no idea why . . . but the point is . . . listen . . . the illustrator, *a woman*, Monika Jost, it's obvious, she's been building up to this, the finale, her third and last drawing, and she chooses – guess what? A deep-sea anglerfish! One of the very same deep-sea anglerfish that seem to obsess *you*, remember? But hey – she could have chosen to copy the drawing of *Halophryne mollis*, a female with *three* parasitic males attached, but no, she went for *Lynophryne brevibarbata*. And it's true, that's a female with barbels – you know, growths under the chin – that can be 15 per cent longer than her own body, downward extensions of her throat, thick and branched and twisted like the roots on a tree, and yes, she's tiny, 100 millimetres long, but if you saw her full size, I promise you, you'd throw up! Aye . . . I'm forgetting – the point is that this ace female artist, Monika Jost, she went for the one diagram where a deep-sea anglerfish is shown with only *one* parasitic male . . . so maybe you're right, I've been thinking about it, and I know, you'll deny everything, because for you that was your first time with no sleep for days and nights on end, but I remember what you said, because I've been through it, so often, with every trip on a trawler, so maybe you're right, maybe every woman really does want to settle down with just the one man . . .'

'Eh?'

'Aye! She loved it, like you say, the one male captured for ever, his head's absorbed inside her, only the rest of him hangs loose from her crotch, as it were, he's just a sperm bank, she's got him, he's hers, no doubt about it! And guess what? She's so excited about it, this Monika Jost, that for the first time she uses *colour*, she paints the attached headless male, his tissue and blood-vessels already fused with hers – she paints him in bright green!'

'Wow!'

'Aye, it's great, isn't it? And I'll tell my children all about it, one day, because she's right, of course, in biological terms, because our deep past is hermaphrodite, the penis is simply an enlarged clitoris, so the female is the basic, the ancient sex, and we're latecomers, parasites, if you like . . . And hey, do you remember saying that?'

'. . . Luke, please, lay off, it's so ghastly all this, you know, the terrible feeling that I'm losing my mind . . . OK, so what? Yes . . . But it's never happened to me before, or, at least, not so obviously, you know, bright-light obvious, right out there, in the open, for all to see . . .'

'Aye, that's it! That's the wipe-out shock of your first week or more of days and nights with no sleep. So you can't remember? Any of it? Can you?'

'No, that's right . . . No, I can't.' And I suddenly felt absurdly anxious (where had the fear come from?) . . . 'No, I can't. And I don't want to – it was like being drunk, you know, the worst kind, when you drink because you're unhappy, because something is stopping you doing the one thing you need and want to do, so the point and the value goes out of your life, and you keep drinking, to make it better, and then you say all kinds of violent things to anyone who loves you, awful hurtful things that the normal you is not even aware you could *think*, let alone say . . . But Luke, hang on, because I want you to know that I don't agree that alcohol reveals the subconscious, no, absolutely not, I think it's just the surface you, lashing out, *trying* to solve some problem, messing up, getting it all wrong . . . But Luke, it's not *that* bad normally, you know, I *have* been happy and fulfilled like you, sometimes, now and then, doing work I *really* want to do – and I can tell you, it's odd, isn't it? If you get drunk *then*, why! you *stay* happy and fulfilled, because you're all of a piece, all the way, all the way down to the depths! The abyssal depths!' And then something surfaced, and I tried to stop talking, but couldn't: 'You know the lines?' I said (not knowing them myself): ' "Mind, mind has mountains, cliffs of fall, sheer, frightful, no-man-fathomed" . . . So who the hell said that?'

Luke, in control of himself, as always, it seemed to me, re-opened his volume three, regained his blue woolly hat, re-rolled it on to his head and, still in absurd slow-motion, said, 'You're asking *me*?'

'Well . . .'

'No, come on, don't make such a big deal of it – you can train yourself to cope, just a little, and that's why I can remember *almost* all you said, and anyway, the boys go through this *every time*, it's their job, and they don't faff on about the subconscious! No – the only sign they give of the mental pain of all this is to get dead drunk the minute they go ashore. And, of course, no one, *no one* ashore understands or forgives them. And then they need at least thirty-six hours of graduated sleep – but their wives are already uptight, because they feel neglected, because for two or three weeks they've been without a husband, and they've been left all alone, and they've had to look after the children all by themselves, and not a day off, and their man's been out there enjoying himself, so they tell him all about the problems he's caused because he's been away, and then they damn well insist on taking him shopping . . . So, just occasionally, the trawlerman gets violent. And then *everyone* calls the police.'

'Uh . . . it's all so grim.'

'Of course it's not! Don't get me wrong – no one's to blame . . . How's the wife to know about sleep-deprivation? And come to that, I've got real mates in the police, there are two *grand* guys in my own lifeboat station at Aberdeen: and hey, Worzel, Redmond, I mean – excuse me – you know, well, imagine it: I'm walking back from the Moorings with a new girlfriend and she's tender, you know, so we're holding hands, and then *pow*! (or whatever you'd say, you know – drama, a *shock*!) this patrol-car mounts the pavement right in front of us and the policeman in the passenger-seat yells out the window: "You! Yes! You, sir! You're under arrest for your shit-bad dress-sense! We've had complaints! You upset the law-abiding public! So take that *horrible* hat off! Right now!" So I take my hat off, and my new girl does a runner, and the policeman jumps out of the patrol-car and pinions me and pushes me into the back seat and muscles in beside me and the police driver central-locks the doors and on goes the siren and the flashers and all the traffic down the docks road pulls aside and we swing into the lifeboat station at this *terrible* speed – and only then do I see it's Brian and Rob, the bastards! And they say: "Luke, why the hell didn't you get the shout?" And I say: "Boys, I switched my bleeper off – because *that was my first time with a new girl*." And Rob says (and Brian says, "Exactly!", all the time, because that's what he does whenever Rob gives you an opinion), "Oh Luke," says Rob, "why the fuck don't you get married like us and have kids? Eh? You're older than us, and yet here you are – you're *still pissing about after girls and missing shouts*!" '

'Great! But . . .'

'The point? Och aye, yes, that's right, how are they to know? Who could know? Even Rob and Brian – on that shout we got to a weekend yachtsman who'd capsized and got caught in the current and drifted way out, way out, and he was clinging to the upturned hull of his 14-foot dinghy, and he was lucky, because she was clinker-built, so he could hang on with his fingers, and you know what? You know what I remember from that one? The end-joints of all his fingers, and his thumbs, they were red and wrecked and bleeding – you could almost see the finger bones!' Luke paused, he laughed as some pleasurable new thought struck him. 'So hey – let's hope he wasn't an old-fashioned writer like you – a Worzel who had to use a pen!'

'Yeah, yeah, but Luke – your lifeboatmen, *what can't they know?*'

'Aye! About no sleep of course! You've lost it – you've lost the point! How are they to know, even Rob and Brian, how could they know? How are you to understand unless you've been through it? Does the judge in court allow for it? Of course not! He or she has no idea! And you can't blame them for that, because it's not something you can just *imagine* – the mind won't have it! You can't *imagine* it, because it's a physical and chemical disruption in the working of the brain itself! It's like real madness, schizophrenia, deep depression, whatever, and the whole point about that kind of change in the brain is that it *can't* be imagined. And no judge, OK, no one in their right mind, wants to go mad, even for two or three weeks!'

'Oh, shit, OK, if you say so . . . thanks . . .'

'Jesus! Stop *moping*. You're moping like a teenager! And look, Redmond, I've had enough of it – I thought you were tough, well, not physically, obviously, look at you! But mentally, yes, mentally tough, at least . . . But hey! You're not! . . . So come on . . .' He bent to his left and picked some trophy, or rather, he lifted, with both hands, with reverential care, some small piece of flesh, from the nearest red basket. 'Look at this!' he said, so loud, right in my ear, mankind and its problems suddenly and completely forgotten – and what a release, what an *escape* from tension-in-the-brain. 'This'll cheer you up! This would make *anyone* cheer up!'

In his right palm he held a 6-inch-long fat little brown glob of a fish: its small black eyes sat on top of its head, and such a big head, an upward-tilted mouth, a huge double chin; yes, a fat-old-man of a head, a glutton of an old man, dribbling a fork-load of spaghetti which had slipped from his lower lip and stuck to his protruding neck. 'What's this?' I said, flicking up the spaghetti-ends with my right forefinger, 'Spaghetti? Worms?'

'Barbels,' said Luke, calming down so instantly it seemed not right; it was a small betrayal of sorts, considered emotionally, man to man: Luke had re-entered his world of quiet scholarship, of gentle science, and left me all alone, outside. 'I'll be honest with you,' he said, so happy, so excited. 'When I first saw this in the hopper I thought it was a new species! And I went all hot and cold, you know, *dizzy*. But at least I had the sense just to lay it gently in the basket and try to forget about it and to get on with life – and when the haul was over and you'd gone to the galley and I was all alone in here, I felt calm enough to go to the shelf in the laundry-room (I'd named it, just for now, the *snotfish*!) and I got out volume three here, and I compared it . . . I knew it had to belong to the family *Liparididae*, the sea-snails, you know, their bodies gelatinous, jelly, full of water for their life at *ridiculous* depths, down to 7,000 metres. Anyway . . .' He placed the snotfish in front of me on the steel shelf. And beside it he laid volume three of *Fishes of the North-eastern Atlantic*, the book of books, protected in its multiple brown-paper covers, open at page 1276, the *Liparididae*. Luke's right index-finger hovered above the drawing of *Careproctus longipinnis*, Burke, 1912. ('Common Synonyms: none. Common names: none.') It would not be a good idea, I realized, to touch the pages of this sacred book, especially not with a fish-wet-slimy finger – if I do *that*, something told me, Luke will slit my throat. But hey – come on – in the illustration the sleek line of the downward-curving head, the level mouth, the swept-back barbels, the gaunt and muscled flanks: apart from its printed measurements, the picture bore no resemblance whatever to our beautiful fat little slob of a fish, a fish that had enjoyed life to the full, and drank, and slurped spaghetti . . . 'But Luke!' I said. 'I thought you had *balls*. It's obvious – this *is* a new species. And you – you've lost your nerve!'

'Oh, fuck you,' said Luke, but at half-power, unsure of himself.

206

'This *must* be it: because the map fits' (a cross-hatching, so thin, stretching from north of the Faeroes to Bear Island in the Arctic Circle). 'And you must remember, always remember, fish are described in museums from preserved specimens – fish in formalin or alcohol – whereas ours, this' (he stroked it, with affection), 'this has just come up from 1,000 metres plus, so fresh, and the colours are right, sure, but with the release of pressure its poor little stomach has blown up inside it, *poompf!* So give over, don't be silly . . .'

'Oh yeah? And the eyes on top of its head?'

'Look, it's OK,' said Luke, shutting volume three, picking up volumes one and two. 'You learn to allow for pressure-release, you know, you get sophisticated! . . . And besides,' he said, carrying the books, like chicks under his wing, those vital few yards back to the safety of the high-silled laundry-room shelf, 'the *Galathea*, the research ship, she trawled up a sea-snail from nearly 7,000 metres – and the brotulids, they look just like our snotfish, same shape, and there's one species that's the deepest-living fish, at abyssal or hadal depths all over the world – *Abyssobrotula galatheae*. But the present record-holder, as far as I know, was taken from the bottom of the Puerto Rico Trench – the absolute number-one deepest point in the whole Atlantic! Big time!'

'Hadal? What's that?'

'I've told you.' Luke was preoccupied again, grubbing about, head down, woolly hat almost beneath the rim of the first plastic basket. 'Abyssal – 4,000 to 6,000 metres. Hadal – below 6,000. Trenches! Canyons! Places you could drop Everest into and make no difference! Yes – places that you and me and no one else can begin to imagine! Right here! Right here on earth!'

'Yeah, well, that's as may be' (why did I say that?), 'but Luke, I don't believe you . . . about the snotfish . . .'

'That's as may be?' shouted Luke, who was usually so very mild, so absurdly tolerant. He straightened up, to his full height, which was not that high, but his hat helped, and besides, I was sorry, so that gave him an extra foot. Luke held a new fish right in front of my face – and, I thought, a conscious slither of a thought: to give me a surprise like this with a mere fish, after all the fish I've seen lately, in waking life, in my dreams, *search me*, so many fish, and this one is thick and eely and all blotched black with white rings around its muscly slime of a body . . . it's hooped with rings of white . . .

'No, no, Luke, I'm sorry, I only meant the snotfish . . . *Of course* it's a new species, and I'm going to get a camera to prove it!'

'Are you? I wish you would! I saw it all, your posh Nikons and that flash unit and all those lenses! So heavy! Aye . . . And you . . . you haven't touched them!'

'Of course not!' I said, determined not to take off my oilskins or sea-boots, trying to open the bulkhead door. 'Jesus! You forget who you're talking to? Look – I haven't been able to hold myself level, let alone a camera! So lay off, OK?'

In the cabin, I bashed my head on the bench-cupboard top, as I lifted it. I pitched backward into the space between the bunks. (And this is a nothing? A Force 9?) But at least, I realized, as I rolled myself up and forward on to my knees, I am now, officially, annoyed, I'm active, which is good, really good, because I am no longer in despair. I am *not* begging for help. And all I need is that camera which I bought specially, just for this, for four hundred whole pounds, and that's enough to make anyone anxious, a new Nikon FM2, all manual, no computer-nonsense to go wimpy on you the moment it gets wet, and the really sharp 50 mm Micro-knickers, just right for a snotfish. And, at last, falling about, as angry as a cat in a box, I managed to screw the camera base-plate to the flatbed-arm of the flash that I'd also bought specially – which was not the best, it has to be admitted, a Sunpak G4500 (so comforting, all these names), but it did look and feel like the real thing: a big black ribbed dick of a stand, with a head that promised massive and explosive power . . .

'OK!' yelled Luke, as I made it back through the bulkhead door, the absurdly oversized camera and flash suspended on its wide strap from my neck. 'Let's see! I'm prepared to waste time on this – it's worth it – so let's see if you can take photographs in a Force 8 gusting 9! Aye – so take your snotfish!'

Luke had it all prepared – the snotfish lay flat on a white plastic backdrop: the upturned base of my fishbox-seat. And neatly, so carefully positioned beneath the snotfish (which told me: whatever *these* are, they matter to Luke), were two deep-red prawns. And I'd never seen prawns like them, and hang on, get a grip, I thought, because of course you haven't, because I'm prepared to swear that these blood-red prawns have not been cooked – and yet they're dense to the eye, and red, dark red. But stop this, I thought, harder, because you'd better concentrate with this exquisite machine, this camera, so black, so beautiful, so accurate, so precisely tooled – and the fact is, you don't really know how to use it, do you? Not something as advanced as this, not under pressure. Because in your jungles the camera *had* to be simple: a heavy, green, insulated, anti-wet, anti-mould Nikonos, a primitive range-finder, *an underwater camera* with its greased seals, a 35 mm lens (one big chrome knob-screw to your left, for distance, one big black knob-screw to your right, for aperture). And what a friend, what a comfort it became, didn't it? – three or four months in – so much so that you'd take to sleeping with it in your right hand, a fetish, a miraculous object, a sorcerer's reminder that another world really did exist . . .

'Hey Redmond! You still there?'

'Uh?'

'Come on – take the snotfish, and the prawns . . .'

So I took the snotfish – the lens up close: until the fat little slob of a fish filled the frame (when I took a chance, full flash at f.32) . . . But the prawns were different. Focusing on them through the 55 mm Micro-Nikkor (a wide-angle microscope, or so it seemed to me), their complexity made me dizzy: eight, or maybe nine, antennae of different lengths projected from the front of their heads, from the top of their extended snouts, from their protruding upper and lower jaws. And their underslung modified front legs reached forward: pincers, grabbers, sharp-pointed scoops . . . And from the top prawn only, half-way down its body, from the base of its armoured jacket, two chitinous whippy-string wireless aerials, one to either flank, curved way back, exuberant whiskers, right out of frame, way back – and way off beyond its rear flippers . . . So did only the male or the female have them? So were they to receive signals of possible pleasure, vibrations, clicks, spasms of prawn-desire, transmitted in erotic pulses down in the blacked-out depths? Or had prawn number two simply lost its delicate receivers in the brutal chaos of a trawl? Yes, I thought, it's true, it's so exciting, but it's also *anxious-making*, this being introduced to an entire new world, and so directly . . .

'Redmond! Worzel! Come on! What's up? *Over here*. Please, stop it, I *hate* all this – your trances, you know? And besides, we may not have much time! Jason – for all I know, *he may have shot the net!*'

Luke (I hadn't noticed) was standing on the wet boards of the fish-room floor, to the right of the hopper. In his yellow sea-boots, holding a red specimen-basket by the rim beside him, to his left, he looked especially haggard, unshaven, intense, in scientific, I-must-get-my-doctorate mode: and at his feet he'd laid something big (it looked yard-long) and slimy (it glistened in the overhead lights) and it slid across the floor as the ship rolled, to port, to starboard . . .

I made my way round to him – hanging on to the edge of the conveyor to the hold, to the curve of the gutting table; I clambered over the hopper-conveyor; and I stood, beginning to slide, like the big slimy fish, port to starboard, starboard to port.

'That's right!' said Luke, impatient. 'I've just worked it out, a new photographic method, but you – you can have it, *gratis!*'

'Thanks!' I said, only vaguely annoyed.

'Look – it's brilliant! You, and the fish, the object, you slide across the deck *together*, in time with each other. So – all *you* have to do is bend over it, focus, and get the exposure absolutely spot-on. Right? Because I need these pictures, I really do. OK? So stop faffing, dithering, whatever, OK? That's *the real thing* you've got there, proper old-fashioned heavy kit – and yet . . . and yet, Redmond, to watch you with it, forgive me, but . . . *it looks as if you don't know how to use it!*'

'I don't! I don't! I bought it specially . . .'

'Oh, bollocks!' said Luke (and *bollocks*, for Luke, was a very strong swear-word indeed). 'What's the ASA? The film-speed on the slides?'

'200.'

'OK – so you're around six feet, aye, so you'll bend forward as you focus, so knock off a foot from the lens to the object, and another foot as you slide . . . So . . . Why not? Give it full power at f.32! But you've got to be *decisive*, aye, and *fast!*'

I stood over the yard of bulky slime – and (I could feel Luke's muscled right hand clamped on my left shoulder) we all slid together, the basket, Luke, me, and the yard-of-slime fish. And hey, I thought, as I focused, now *here's* a thing-and-a-half, and yes, that's right, *in extremis*, under pressure, in the rising heat-in-the-head of a delighted imagination, you bet, it's the clichés that jump first from the fur of the mind – and then, maybe, deeper down, if you're lucky, you think you *really* see the object that confronts you. And yes, it was one of those evanescent moments in which no one else seems to share, when for a time, you have no extraneous thoughts, no outer-world, a surgeon's moment, perhaps, when it's just you and the object . . . a sheen of violet light clinging to a dark-spotted skin of grey oil: the top fin stretching from the back of its thick neck to its tiny blossom of a tail, its ventral fin, half as long, a fringe of fan from its anus to its tail; its stomach distended, its eye half out of the socket; and two orange parasitic copepods stuck to its midriff, one above the other.

'Well done!' said Luke, as we all slid back to starboard. 'You got it!' And 'Hold this!' he said, pushing me against the stanchion beside the hopper (I held on). 'We can improve the technique!' (He tied the rope at the rim of the basket to the iron strut, at knee-level.) 'So I can *show* you the specimens! Because this one' (he grabbed the big slimy fish from the slush as it began to slide away to port) 'is *difficult*. The trawlermen call it a Jelly-cat, right enough, and so it is, but of course it's not a catfish, not at all, it's a Wolf-fish – and here's the problem: according to my UNESCO volumes, you know, Whitehead *et al.*, it might be the Jelly wolf-fish, *Anarhichas dendiculatus*, because it's certainly soft and jelly-like, look at it! But its body *and* dorsal fin are covered with these spots, so maybe it's *Anarhichas minor* . . . but it's not *Anarhichas lupus*, the ordinary Wolf-fish, because whatever this is, it's come up from around 1,000 metres . . . Anyway, aye, sorry. What do you care? That's my problem, not yours . . . but you, you've got to see *this* . . .' And Luke prised the jaws open – and I got such a shock that I forgot to take a picture. The Wolf-fish indeed had a front row of canine teeth like a wolf – but worse, splayed out, all order abandoned; and behind the canines were conical rippers; and, behind *them*, crushing molars at the sides, where they ought to be, but they were also erupting from the *roof* of the mouth . . .

I said: 'Oh Jesus!'

'Aye!' said Luke, flopping it back into the basket. 'Jesus, right enough!' He thrust both hands deep down in, into the slop of fish – searching for some small treasure, obviously. 'Jesus! Do you realize you keep saying that? And you call yourself an atheist . . .' In the basket, churned over by his hands, big fish sloshed against each other . . . 'And your vicar of a dad (Redmond, you're such a screw-up!) – your vicar of a dad would say that Jesus's dad – God, you know – your dad would say that the Wolf-fish was created millions of years before the same guy, God, got around to making a wolf, wouldn't he?'

'Eh? No. No – of course he wouldn't! The whole lot, Wolf-fish, wolves, you name it, they were all created, perfect, no changes, within a week. Exactly 4,004 years before Jesus himself was born.

Bishop Ussher's time-scale. From human generations documented in the Bible. *Boompf!* Although, it's true, sometimes my dad did think the holy idiot Teilhard de Chardin got it right – that God simply *started* the process of evolution and made sure it was running well, from omega to alpha, from algae to angels: to perfection!'

'Sorry,' said Luke, perhaps hearing the unwanted passion in my voice. He straightened up; with his right hand he hid something behind his back. 'Bollocks to all that, I was just making a point! And the point is this – life in the sea is so *very* old . . . mammals are not the only vertebrates which have several kinds of teeth for different needs!'

'OK, sure,' I said, still hanging on hard to the stanchion, not wanting to slide across the floorboards horizontally and dunk the camera through the slush. 'So say life began 3,500 million years ago, with those slimy raised mats of cyanobacteria, blue-green algae, you know, the stromatolites, mounds of gunge in the tidal waters of Australia and Zimbabwe – our bacterial ancestors, yes? And Luke, you're right, in a way, eternal life, you know, isn't it odd how we need that idea? Because this is the bit I can't deal with, Jesus or no Jesus: *in seven and a half billion years our earth will be burnt up by the expanding sun* . . . And everything we've achieved – art, architecture, science, books, music, all the great libraries of the world – all dead!'

Luke laughed. 'Bollocks! Worzel! You Old Worzel! By that time we'll be well gone to other galaxies, parallel universes, whatever – and we'll take our records with us! How absurd – so you *do* believe in eternal life!'

'Well, yes, I suppose so, put like that, yes I suppose I do . . . seven and a half billion years, but all the same . . .'

Luke whipped his right hand out from behind his back. 'This'll cure you!' He held a foot-long dart of a fish in front of my face. The fish and I were nose to nose, but the nose on the fish was a rapier. 'Get that! The Garfish! This is *really* fast!' He waggled the straight firm body. It was blue-green above, bright silver below.

213

'*So* unlike our deep-sea fish – and why? Because it's fast!' The rapier, I could see, was its jaws, the lower jaw slightly longer than the upper, the two together a dagger, a poniard, as surprising as the projecting jaws of a fast and elegant fish-eating crocodile that I'd hoped to see in Borneo, the gharial; yes, sure, but why had I thought of that? Of course, yes, Old English, *gar*, a spear, one of the few words I remembered from those wasted years of learning Anglo-Saxon: gar, gotcha, garred yer bastard! So much better than the poncy *spear* – except that *spere* was Old English too, wasn't it? In fact, why had I wasted years smoking so much dope: when I could have *really* learnt Anglo-Saxon and entered the world of *gar* and *spere* and farming and conquest and ship-burials and sex and warfare and *Beowulf*? Jason, Jesus, yes, Jason was right, I'd thrown it all away and now it was too late . . .

'Worzel!' yelled Luke. 'Wake up! The Garfish, remember?' He waved it about, manic. 'They swim *so* fast, shoals of them – skimming, in fact it's *such* a surface fish that it almost belongs in the air! They *spear* their prey. And if you're a small pelagic fish at the surface you can't escape, because these guys come after you, their tails whirring side to side in the water, the front of their bodies, their long beaks in the air, they *skitter* after you, a nightmare! And they can be a yard long! And their relatives – who are their relatives?'

'No idea!' I yelled, as, with his right hand, Luke dropped the fish lengthwise to the floor and, with his left, detached me from the stanchion.

'The Flying fish! We'll get its picture . . . Aye, *Flying* fish!'

And so we took its picture. And a portrait of a saithe (a giant: a yard long), the coalfish or coley, which Luke said had come up from 500 metres, maybe, and it was a member of the cod family and so common and so widely distributed (right into the shallows) and *so* good to eat, but Jason had no quota, so we couldn't land it – and out it went, down the scupper-chute, its coal-coloured back, its silver stomach shining in the incoming, the early morning light.

From his yellow basket (which they filled) Luke slopped two big fish out across the floor. They were long and thick: the first perhaps 6 feet, the head pink, the continuous rear dorsal fin pink, the body the palest brown with a random scatter of large black ink-blots, six to each side. The other was brown-backed, 4 feet long, beautiful . . . Or was it just the wash of pure Arctic light across their bodies, the horizontal light from the low starboard scupper-chute, light which I had certainly never seen before?

'Ling!' said Luke, as we began our photographic slide to port. 'The big one – plain ling, *Molva molva*, with a range down to 400 metres – and this one' (he nudged it with the tip of his yellow sea-boot), 'Blue ling, deeper, to 1,000 metres; and they're two more members of the cod family, *Gadidae* – they're half-neglected now. But I tell you: when the Emperor Charles V of France visited Henry VIII in London, guess what? The great royal turn-on for the banquet was salted ling! Aye, salted ling cost three times as much as haberdine, salted cod! Ling used to be *the best*!'

And yes, I thought, Luke really does like a little perfectly ordinary mainstream local English history with his fish which, for some reason, was a comfort . . . But why? Because, said that part of my brain that wished it was at home: an interest in the tiny time-span, the gossip of a hundred years in a single country, in a small expanse of land – it *excludes* the three and a half thousand million years that's passed since our single-cell ancestors first appeared on earth: our real history. It says *up yours* to the real geography that surrounds and appals us – the infinite but bounded space of our own universe that Einstein imagined or discovered; and all the parallel universes that perhaps make our own Big Bang no more than the pop of a shotgun on a Saturday afternoon. Yes – national history, that really is *such* an attractive mind-numbing displacement activity, as precious and necessary as planting a couple of snowdrop bulbs in the cottage-garden patchlet of soil that (in a nanosecond of micro-evolutionary time) really does seem to belong to you . . .

Luke, without assistance, I'm afraid, heaved both ling on to the stationary conveyor to the hold. 'To remind me,' he said. 'I'll gut them later. And I need their otoliths.' (So Jason had a quota? Or, more likely, they were not quota-fish? In any case, I thought, how stupid, how wasteful, this EU system: why can't we be rational – why can't we *all* be long-term clever, like the Icelanders? And hey! Get that – I'm *beginning* to be educated, so of course I have strong opinions!)

Luke, fast and focused, bent sharply over his blue basket. (Does he never give up? How come he got so all-in-one happy?) He extracted a football-sized something, solid, grey-brown. (What was it? A fish egg-ball in a hardish case? A sponge? The curved surface of the almost-football was streaked with thin shards of reflected light, needles of white shine on the dull mud-grey. No, I'd no idea. And so, instantly, I felt hopeless, finished inside . . . no, I was not even beginning to be educated . . .)

Luke held the ball (I could see it was surprisingly hard, there was no give in it) in both hands, in front of his chest, as if standing on the touchline, alert for a target, about to throw it to a player on the pitch. He said: 'Worzel – what's this?'

'*I don't know*. And Luke – sometimes, well – sometimes I think it's *all* pointless . . .'

'Aye, Worzel! You're sure this is a *sponge*, aren't you?'

'Well, yes. But . . .'

'It's not!' said Luke, triumphant. 'It's *duff*! And you know what – I looked it up once, in the Aberdeen University Library, the big Oxford English Dictionary, volumes for ever, you know, the so-called definitive dictionary – and guess what? You Oxford people – maybe just one of you wankers, *excuse me*, maybe just one of you dictionary people should've been sent to sea where so many of our words were made!' Luke, the football now held (no-throw) against his chest, stood (quite rightly) transfixed with outrage at these dictionary people. 'Yes! Duff! This is *it* – duff.' He looked at it, with affection. 'And no, it's *not* some nineteenth-century word for pudding as the Oxford wankers will tell you – dough, Yorkshire duff, as in *enough*. Spare us! Let's get out of the kitchen, right? *This is it*, duff. So ancient, in terms of our fishermen – *duff*. Something you really don't want in your catch. Duff. As in duff, a duffer, a duff catch, useless! Aye – it's coral.'

'Coral? Don't be silly!'

'Silly?' Luke looked me straight in the eye, mean as a good man can be. 'North Atlantic coral – they don't form reefs or atolls, no, the polyps make mounds on the continental shelves. They feed at night – their stinging tentacles unfold, their mouths open at night. Magic, eh?'

And Luke, with a teenager grin, as the *Norlantean* rolled to starboard, raised his arms above his head and pitched the duffball up and over the gutting table, between the starboard stanchions, and *bop*! No argument! *Zap!* Straight into the scupper-chute.

I yelled: 'Goaal!'

'Magic,' said Luke, pleased. 'But don't try that yourself.' He turned back to scrummage in his blue basket. 'Because those corals are full of *silica*, glass spikes that can damage your skin. It's their defence against grazing fish.' (Oh yeah? I thought, but it's true, which is another reason I don't like it – so you, Luke, you have hands like a leather-back turtle – whereas I . . . I probably *still* have hands like a girl . . . yes . . . one glance at them by the Khmer Rouge and I'd be taken away behind a bush and suffocated, with a knot-tight plastic bag . . .) Luke found the prize he was looking for and arranged it on the boards, dorsal side up: a starfish, but dark-red, swollen, chunky, a mega-muscled outsize disembodied hand of a starfish that, in your dreams, would grip you by the throat . . .

Luke said: 'It's a starfish. A deep-sea starfish. But I've not seen this one before, I don't know the species, so we need a photograph, a *detailed* photograph – so down you get' – he gave me a shove – 'that's it, on your knees.' (So we slid to port, on our knees.) 'As I was saying, there was an ex-trawlerman, you know, on the *Scotia*, the research ship, a lovely guy, one of the contract crew – all from Hull – and he used to collect the duff that came up in our

217

beam-trawls.' (Flash! f.32 – so I changed the aperture to 22, for the return run . . . close-up photography: why were the rules all different?) 'And one day I asked him what it was for, why he wanted it – and he said he was old now and he hated life at sea and he couldn't wait to retire and all he thought about was his allotment. He'd got *three*. But that bit of Hull was overrun with feral cats and they dug up his seeds. You know – the way cats sniff the ground and dig a hole with their right-front paw and then squat all rigid at forty-five degrees, and they hold their faces in the air and they think so hard they look like philosophers – and they do their business. And then one sniff later they cover it over – and rocket off as if *none of that was anything to do with them!*'

'Yeah! Luke! That's right!'

We slid back to the blue basket: he gathered up his starfish (gently, he liked this starfish) and, replacing it on the pile, he withdrew the fish that had mesmerized me some time ago – a day? A week? I'd no idea . . . but the image was as potent as an image gets, and here it was again, laid out right in front of me: thick and eely and all blotched black with white rings around its muscly slime of a body . . . it was hooped with rings of white . . . 'Esmark's eelpout!' said Luke, from above me. 'And no, Worzel – for this one you stand up!' (The effort of it, my knees, all my joints, they ached, they hurt, and Jesus, I thought, your only hope, if you survive this – your only hope is to take that cod liver oil and Omega-3 fish-fats, every day, bottles of it.) 'Anyway, as I was telling you, the cats dug up his beans, whatever, back in Hull, and he couldn't take it, the mess. So he'd mash up the duff with cat-food and he'd leave it out in bowls, on his allotments – and the cats ate it, and died. The spicules punctured their stomachs. So, like I said, apart from that he was a lovely guy, and we had this great argument – I told him it was cruel and he shouldn't do it. And you know what he said to me? "Eh, lad," he said, "thou's naught but a focking whipper-snapper!"'

And then the siren sounded.

'Bollocks!' said Luke, rigid. 'Esmark's eelpout! You haven't taken it!'

'I was listening to you!'

'Bollocks! OK – we'll have to do it later . . .' (He laid Esmark's eelpout in prime position, curled inside the top of the blue basket.) 'But this Jason – *I've never known anything like it* – the speed between hauls, the way he keeps it coming, the way he never sleeps! But we'll try for some science after the next haul . . . OK? Esmark's eelpout, the Blackmouth catshark! My doctorate! – And something I've saved up, *right from the very first haul*, I've kept it for you, it's still alive! A hagfish! Aye. The hagfish! The oldest and weirdest fish in the sea! *What a story* – aye, the hagfish, *that really is the story of stories . . .*'

'So come on, scumbag! Sperm whales! Copepods! Hagfish, *hagfish? Tell me about it!*'

'What? Now? With the siren sounded? You crazy? On deck – bring your camera! On deck!'

Out on deck, everything was transformed, etched, washed in the early morning Arctic light: and my own small world had changed: there was a swell, yes, but I could stand; in fact, *I could walk*. There seemed to be no wind: or maybe, I thought, my internal measuring standards of such things have altered for ever . . . The light was thin and white and pure and, somehow, directed upwards – and there, right above us, in this light I had never seen before, hung three gulls I had only half-imagined, Glaucous gulls, nonchalant gulls from the Arctic ice-cliffs, but their heavy barrel-bodies, their broad wings, their butch heads (they were looking down, straight at me, mildly interested, suspended in this extreme northern world of theirs, a hundred feet above us), seemed to be pink, a dull pink. So OK, I thought, they're teenagers, so what? It's just that the pure-white adults have more macho things to do, I expect, like hunt polar-bears.

'Luke! Glaucous gulls!'

'Ach,' said Luke, not even bothering to turn his head. 'Gulls. I've a minilog on the net.' And, preoccupied, unreachable, he made his way aft to join Bryan and Robbie and Allan Besant gathered at the stern.

Shocked, I said to a kittiwake, hanging in the air 6 feet above my head, 'That Luke – I'm sorry, he's just not in love with you, he doesn't care like I do, see? He didn't even notice the Glaucous gulls (those scary thugs up there, yes?) let alone *you*, you prettiest little gull, jeez, that Luke, *I'm sorry*, it's just that you're not his thing, it's OK, it's not your fault, it's him, you won't believe it, but Luke's love-in-life, his passion: it's *fish*.'

The kittiwake tilted her head down and right; she regarded me intensely with her soft, dark right eye: her bill was fresh yellow, her black legs and folded feet were suspended, dangling beneath her, so delicate; her pure white-feather wind-fluffed tummy looked so warm – 'And hey!' I said to her. 'You're my number-one beauty of the open sea, you tough little oceanic gull, you, I know all about you – you shear and hang and soar and *play* in those Force 12 winds that terrify us so . . .'

And the kittiwake, I swear, moved in closer and said: 'Luke? A passion for fish? Me too!'

'Hang on!' I said, emphatic. 'Stay there! Don't move! This lens, you see, it's useless, it's for close-ups of *fish*. So I must go below and change it – to your lens, the 200 zoom. But I *won't* change my oilskins or my boots. No. This is too important. And Jason won't know – he's on the bridge, as we call it. So *stay there*, because *I really* want your picture, for me, OK? To keep for ever . . .'

I went to the cabin (no problems) and changed the lens (the *pleasure of it*: the outer world had lost its hatred, its violence: I could think again).

And when I came back, yes, she was still there, but less responsive: 'Quick!' she seemed to say. 'Hurry up! You men, you're so slow, so indecisive! Because – look! It's not that I'm indifferent to you, it's just that, well, I have other concerns in my life, you understand, and I'm *so* hungry – and there's the cod-end, way back, just appeared . . .'

So I took her portrait – and one of a gannet waiting on the water, so very bright and white, lit by the low rays of the Arctic sun. And those pictures, I thought, with an absurd rush of pleasure, are the first and second best photographs I've ever taken (and oh yes? said the inner voice that countermands all our best emotions, and deserts us when we despair – so what makes you think you can take a good picture of anything at full aperture and one-sixtieth of a second on a rolling ship?). So (to prove I wasn't listening) I focused on Big Bryan at the stern: in his yellow oilskins, hood up over his red balaclava, his left hand on the lever that operated the power-block. And he was grinning, he thought it was funny, me trying to take his picture in this swell: even as he concentrated so hard, he'd noticed; it was true – Big Bryan noticed everything, which was another reason, I supposed, why he was the man you wanted on deck, should you decide to fall overboard . . . And then I turned the long lens on Robbie, beaky-faced, a Pict, in his worn red survival suit, but wearing a jaunty black baseball-cap which told me: OK, he knows about these things, so the Force 12 baby hurricane, the wee storm (as he'd probably call it) – it really is over, it's passed, *we're safe*. And next I took a photograph of Allan Besant, in his equally stained red survival suit, its black cowl up around his full cheeks, hatless, his hair cut short but for a bunch over the centre of his forehead, someone slightly apart from the rest of the crew (but why? . . . I'd no idea).

The cod-end swung round and up and over the hopper – Robbie untied the knot. A cascade of redfish dull-thundered down into the hidden steel cavern. Luke gave me a push (where'd he come from? Why couldn't *I* notice things?): 'Action! To the fish-room!'

And as we made our way below, we observed the purely symbolic psychological rules: Luke and I, like every trawlerman (and no, there was nothing practical about it) – we clambered out of our oilskins and we forced off our sea-boots on the shelter-deck: and we carried them with us the short distance down the companionway stairs, left along the thoroughly dirty corridor past the galley (it was nothing to do with cleanliness), through the bulkhead door of the fish-room – and put them on again at the bench to the left. And I was about to ask: Why the hell did we waste time doing that? When the answer came to me: of course: to maintain his sanity, to preserve the precious other-world of his domestic and sleeping time, a hunting male must make a barrier, even if it is invisible, a barrier between his two lives, his work and his rest, and he'll do so in some sharp symbolic way, especially if, physically, the two worlds are only yards apart.

Yes – and I got to the gutting table first (anxious) in order to take possession of the one and only wooden-handled gutting-knife (so comforting), and another question came to me from nowhere (which was in itself a pleasure, a reassurance – so maybe, one day, my brain really would be alive again?): why are all those seabirds up there, the Glaucous gulls (if only they were adult), the kittiwakes, the gannets, the terns (not that we'd seen any) – why are they all so white, so very white? And the nature of this little question was also a deep pleasure, because it was innocent, and external, and nothing whatever to do with the self, and, therefore, healthy, a matter of healing. And the answer came too – from something I'd read somewhere (but no, I couldn't remember the reference, so yes, my memory was still a partial spray-white-out, closed in with fear, confused) . . . Terns and gulls and, presumably, gannets (such social birds, all of them) – they have a very high percentage of orange and red oil-droplets in their eyes: they can see for miles right through the atmospheric haze that hangs over the ocean: from a vast distance they can detect a feeding frenzy of soaring and plunging white birds who've found a shoal of fish . . .

It's become a routine, I thought, it's almost a way of life, I'm sure I've done this for ever, this gutting-table business, *I know what to do* (oh yeah, said the inner voice, so how come you're so useless at it?). Robbie stood to my right, Luke to my left; Bryan, Jerry and Sean made their way down the ladder to the hold (yes, I thought, I must do that next – *what happens down there?*).

Allan Besant stepped up to the table, in control position – and he happened to butt his forehead against the end of the wooden handle of the steel, the knife-sharpener, which someone had replaced, not level in its tight slot between the overhead pipes, but at a downward slant. 'Fuck you!' he shouted, with eruptive violence. Grabbing the handle in his right hand, he hurled the steel, with a lightning backwards convulsion of his arm, across the fish-room where, like a bolt from a crossbow, it struck the plates to port with a horrible intensity, ricocheted half-way back towards him, bounced, with decreasing energy, almost to his feet, and, coming to rest, a pointer stern-to-bow, began to roll, like every loose and inarticulate thing, port to starboard, starboard to port . . .

Robbie and Luke, sorting redfish, kept their heads down. No one spoke. An hour or so later, Allan Besant, without a word, stepped off his box, walked across the rolling wet boards, retrieved the steel and replaced it, carefully, level, tucked up straight, in its usual place.

Luke, at once, abandoning his tray, his full section of the gutting table, hopped lightly off his own box, to his left, swung himself over the conveyor – yellow boots in the air, as if vaulting a gate – and, disappearing for a moment (I heard the corrugated-iron scrape of the hopper-door pulled open, and shut), he came back round the corner holding something in his right hand: light-brown, flattish, very wet. (So whatever it was, I thought, Luke, on one of his many private visits – the virgin, rich, ready hopper, it seemed to belong to Luke alone – he's stored that something in there, cached it.) With no apparent effort, he repeated his circus jump, one-handed, and he was there again, next to me, on his box, with a ridiculous grin on his face – and in the light of such enjoyment all tension in the fish-room burnt off like a morning fog . . .

Luke leant forward over the gutting table, he held out his prize with both hands, and he tilted it, in the beam of the overhead lights, to each of us in turn, to Allan, to Robbie, to me. And yes, even I knew that this something must be special, because otherwise Allan and Robbie would have looked polite, bored, and got on with their work – but, like me, they stared . . . It was an intense colony of small animals, I could see that, in shape like the honeycomb in a bee-hive, except that this was manic, the tunnels deep, needful, each exquisite little round hole (what? maybe 4 millimetres across, and so evenly spaced, their perfect circular walls perhaps half a millimetre thick) – every receding tunnel was filled, low down, by a withdrawn purple-white glisten-bright animal . . .

'What's this, Worzel?' said Luke, too loud – so that was OK; it was a social-bonding question, one for all of us.

Now, I thought, like a first-former, all of eleven (and biology, then, was already so exciting – in fact, the happiness of such a revelation was almost overwhelming; an instant release into the great testable world: so this is *real*? This is how the world *is*? So: *pow*! And I've been trying to regain that feeling ever since . . .) – I thought, well, so teacher Luke is asking me this question with such over-the-top pleasure, and I got it wrong last time, so yes, sponges are colonial animals, aren't they?

'It's a sponge!'

'No!' shouted Luke, with a little jump of *joie de vivre*; he *jumped*, on top of his box. 'No! Worzel – no! It's a mast!'

'A mast?' said Allan, eager, leaning forward. 'Get away! *Of course* it's not a sponge! Worzel! Old Worzel! But shite – the Marine Lab! *The Marine Lab, Aberdeen!* It's no a fucking mast!'

'Aye!' shouted Robbie. 'Yep! The Marine Lab – they canna take it at sea! They, like, they go to pieces!'

And Luke, far from being affronted, became super-charged with the energy that makes the rest of life worth the effort. 'It's a mast!' he yelled, his weathered face transformed, for a moment, into that of a young boy. 'It's a mast!'

He turned it over – and yes, there was no doubt about it: no holes, just a smooth curved surface, a quarter-cross-section of the outside of a massive mast.

'Aye,' said Robbie, without apology. 'Yep! That's right, sure enough – and imagine them wrecked *right up here* in a Force 12 like the last one. January – and in a *sailing ship*. No chance. No chance to keep her head into the lumps. No chance at all. Orkney men, I shouldna wonder. From Stromness. A whaler.'

'Aye, Christ!' said Allan, with excessive passion. 'What a *shite* way of life!'

Luke, ignoring Robbie and Allan (this was biology, not history), said: 'Worzel, Redmond!' (So there was more to come, Luke's interest was not exhausted, he hadn't finished.) 'How would you explain it? Because *these*' – the glisten-purple-white animals withdrawn into their holes, reflecting the overhead lights – 'are not *Teredo navalis*, the mollusc, the bivalve of shallow waters, the so-called ship-worm. No! Not at all!'

He tossed the piece of wood over the hopper-conveyor, in a faultless curve – straight into his stanchion-lashed blue basket. (How does he do that? I thought, my mind relaxing back into its usual wish-wash of trivia – why isn't he a professional bunger, lobber, whatever? There *must* be a post-prehistoric-hunting game that values Lukes who chuck things with their hands as well as the one that makes heroes of people who kick things with their feet? Hey – yes! Basketball!)

'No really, Redmond, *attend*, it's extraordinary – because these molluscs have come up from the deep sea!' And Luke, intent, was leaning forward over the gutting table as if the piece of mast was still in his hands – and his hands, with a life of their own, began to mime his words. Robbie and Allan, all work forgotten, leant forward, too, watching. 'And we now know,' said Luke, 'since the 1970s – that recent! – we now know that all across the ocean floors of the world there are *wood-boring* bivalves, waiting.' Luke's hands, as flat as could be, spread forward across the gutting table, laying out the great plains of the abyss of the watery earth and its population of specialized molluscs, waiting. 'Can you think of a less likely source of food? *Wood* – the deep ocean? It's as far from a source of wood as you can get! Of course, they'll attack masts like that' (he gave a violent nod towards his blue basket), 'the hulls of wooden shipwrecks – but come on – they evolved millions of years before we even stood upright, let alone made boats. So come on, Worzel! No one knows how or when – as yet – but what kept them going before men built ships and drowned themselves?'

Robbie and Allan, eyes bright, looked thoroughly entertained: after all, here was something unexpected: a tutorial given by a trawlerman, a fisheries inspector from the South Atlantic, now at their own fisheries lab, the Marine Lab, Aberdeen, where so many new techniques had been invented that had eased their lives and improved their catches and incomes – and for Chrissake he was a *lifeboatman*, too – and with him was this white-haired old Worzel, older than their fathers . . .

'Well, I can answer *that*,' I said, delighted – because I had this instant, multiple image of the great brown powerful river (the opposite shore a blur on the low horizon): the Orinoco, the Congo, the Amazon (and the island in the mouth of the Amazon, not that I'd seen it myself – it was the size of Switzerland): and all day long, mesmerizing, without a break (wherever you were), the remorseless brown river carried whole tree-trunks, branches, smashed-up rafts of white-weathered wood dislodged in a freak flood from the inner meander of some stream in the far interior – always, for ever, towards the ocean . . . 'Rivers!'

'Rivers?' said Luke.

Robbie smiled.

Allan Besant, for some reason, put his right hand up above his head on to the stop-start lever of the conveyor and, without activating anything, himself leant forward, to hear better . . . And I realized that we were having a four-man conversation . . . So it was not the deep-pounding rhythm of the engines, the mind-emptying thump of the diesels that had enclosed us. No, of course not, across all registers, it had been the appallingly more powerful sound-waves from the sea, the insane wind . . .

Luke, with a half-smile, repeated: 'Rivers?'

'Yes – I've seen it, an endless succession of broken trees, branches, mats of vegetation, on their way to the sea, above all in the Amazons and the Congo – but also from the fierce little rivers of Borneo!'

'Aye! *Yes* – that must be right!' Luke shouted. (And *so gratified*, I thought, yes: what a good teacher you'd make . . .) He lowered his voice to mere loud speech, became scholarship-serious: 'But the text-book explanation given, for example, in Tony Rice's grand little summary of it all in the official Natural History Museum booklet, *Deep Ocean*, it's this – he says that trees from coastal forests – *unlikely as it seems*, he admits, he says that these trees must fall into the sea, *sufficiently often* to make it worthwhile to be an abyssal wood-boring bivalve!'

'Aye!' yelled Robbie, so happy, cheering me on (and I thought: friendships, this is *friendship*, the most precious long-term emotional pleasure we can ever hope to experience . . .). 'Rivers! There you go, Worzel – the whole ching-bang!'

And Allan, newly friendly, pulled down the large overhead lever, which started the hopper-conveyor, and the small lever next to it, which set the gutting table in motion; and then, realizing that all our trays were still full, he pushed both levers back up, hard.

Whereupon, from the hold, as if they knew that up here in the partial light we'd been enjoying the life of the mind, knowledge – those *other* things beyond mere labour – and excluding them, down below, from the hard-won contents of Luke's brain: Bryan or Jerry or Sean sent the hammer-blow signal, steel-on-steel: Bang! Bang! Bang! – You lazy bastards! We're out of fish!

So we went back to work, in earnest, sorting redfish, and the world shrank once more to a blur between the hands, of red and silver and painful spines and the occasional other fish (Luke, from my left: 'Gut that one!') and steel edges and tubes and clanging drop-gates . . . And at last, for us, the haul was over . . . When Luke – so thin, young, wiry, so manic and committed – bent down, quick as a cat-strike, and came up with a yard-long fish of sorts (so where had he stored that? Aye, as he might have said, of course, *under* his stand-on fish-box . . .): a fish that, in its bulk, was all head, with a short and rounded snout tipped with horny plates, a large, underslung mouth – and a thin following body which tapered down to a real look-alike rat-tail, which was all the more convincing because its muscly last few inches were young-rat pink . . .

I thought: it's a rat-tail, a fish of the black depths, a grenadier – and hey, even I can now recognize a grenadier when I see one! – but this was different, it was elegant, in its way, yes, it was even graceful . . . 'It's a rat-tail! It's a grenadier!'

'Well done, Worzel!'

And Robbie yelled: 'Goaaal!'

And Allan Besant, less generous, said: 'Goal.'

'Aye,' said Luke, laying the fish gently in his tray on the empty and stationary gutting table. 'It's a Roundnose grenadier, *Coryphaenoides rupestris* (and don't they sound *great*, the scientific names? – and one day we'll find out what they mean, *I promise we will*), but right now, Worzel, would you mind? Could we photograph it, please, alongside the Roughhead, *Macrourus berglax*, you know, to compare the two? Would you mind?'

Robbie hosed down Allan – the *power* of that pump: an aureole of water droplets, an all-round overhead-neon-lit halo for Saint Allan Besant; and then, likewise, as Allan hosed Robbie in his oilskins, the water-cannon blasting, the neon-corona: the beatification of Saint Robbie. And they, I thought, the swine, the blessed, they're off to eat in the galley . . . what will it be? Haggis? Yes, God, *please* let it be haggis and clapshot. And (the rhythm of a solemn chant of the Wee-Free Fundamentalist Christians began to swell in my head, in the Gaelic, of course, but well translated: 'Oh Holy Mavis and the Tiny Tot/Let it be clapshot and haggis/Haggis and clapshot.') Jesus, I thought, yes, I've *earned* my haggis and my clapshot. Neeps and tatties. *The best.* Please. But now I have to photograph these fish . . . So I went straight (in full sea-dress, a protest) to the cabin (the *smells* from the galley) and got the

Micro-Nikkor lens, and, from the camera-and-flash hanging on its strap from its hook in the laundry-room ('Hey, I've arrived – this is *my* hook: *I belong here*'), repeating the little Nikon-mantra (on at 5.6, off at f.11), turned free the 200 zoom, transferred the Nikon base-cap (the *precision* of it, even in plastic, or whatever it was) from the micro to the zoom, stuck the zoom, for safe-keeping, into the right foot of Luke's pair of reserve sea-boots, labelled, at calf level, in heavy black marker-pen, LUKAS (so they were a special relic – from his time as a fisheries inspector on board Antarctic Spanish trawlers?) and clicked on the Micro-Nikkor, and why, I wondered vaguely, was such kit so comforting? So pleasing? Yes, it was a deep feeling, certainly, nothing at all to do with the actual object – so it was probably genetic, prehistoric. Yes, those males who *didn't* delight in the perfection of their kit, the delicious arc of the bow, the acme of balance in the arrow: well, they got naturally de-selected before they could breed, they got killed. And the female, she has other things to think about, mere kit is of no interest to her, she cares only for the end result, the successful male itself, so no wonder the girls don't read bow-and-arrow mags, or gun mags, or camera or Ferrari mags, or trawler mags – no, no, they've no time for that primary male testing-stage. ('Boys stuff!' they think. The insult of it! No – all they care about, rightly, is the end result: with the best kit or the worst kit, who cares? Can you bring home . . . the what? The haggis *and* the clapshot . . .)

I found myself standing (easily, at last) on the fish-room floor, to port of the hopper, and Luke, next to me, two fish in photo-position at his feet, was *shouting* at me. Why'd he do that?

'Redmond! This is *special*! You know why?'

'Eh?'

'Please – *don't do this* – you know, sometimes, excuse me, sometimes I think you've got Alzheimer's, excuse me, I'm sorry' (he touched my left arm), 'you know, a *real* Worzel, because sometimes I talk to you and you don't respond at all!'

'I don't?'

'No, I say something – and it's OK, I *know* you've had no sleep, but I'm *used* to trawlermen who've had no sleep, and they *always* react when you say something!'

'Ah.'

'Yes – so *forget* it – but this is *special*.' With his right yellow sea-boot (its inner steel toe-cap) he pushed the two lined-up fish closer together. 'You know why?'

'No, of course not.' And, even more testy: 'Of course not!'

'Well you *should*,' he said, fired up with this deep fascination in a world beyond himself. 'Because, remember? *Two-thirds* of the earth's surface is the surface of the sea – and 80 per cent of that sea is over a mile deep. And the deep-sea areas of the world are continuous – the deep basins of the Atlantic, the Pacific and Indian oceans, as the text books say, they all connect, connect! Imagine it! The vast power of those unimpeded currents – and there's no barrier between them and the great Southern ocean deeps either' (as we began our now slow slide to port, the fish at our feet, Luke's hand tightened manically on my left shoulder – ow! The strength of little Luke), 'and I know about *them* – at least, I've gone diving for specimens on their very edge, did I tell you?'

'Ow! Yes. Great! You did!'

'Yes? But of course within all those basins there are ocean holes and deep valleys and canyons that descend and descend – you know – unknown depths, and well, *those* are as cut off from one another as the tops of different mountains on land, but such places, they're local really, they're *rare* . . .'

'So how, how does speciation, Ernst Mayr's . . .'

'Come on, Worzel! For Chrissake – *take the picture!*'

'Can't.'

'Eh?'

'Can't. Can't move. You've got my shoulder!'

'Och aye! Ach – sorry!'

Luke released me: I stumbled to my right, recovered and bent forward until I had the two grenadiers in focus: the Roughhead (top) bigger, chunkier and, in comparison with the smooth pink-tailed projectile, the Roundhead, so scaly he looked dinosaur-armour-plated. Flash!

'Aye! But you were *shaking!*'

'Of course I'm shaking!' (And my other inner voice, an unwelcome, new, querulous, testy, old-man's voice, that, I'd noticed, seemed to have joined me out of Stromness and had tried to speak to me once or twice before, said: 'You'll be *bruised*, you know. All your joints *ache*, but your shoulder will *hurt*. So why don't you give up, *retire*? Yes, yes – you must find new interests before your family send you to the *very* comforting *It's-All-Over-Sunset-Totally-Fucked-Alzheimer's-Goodbye-Home* – of course you must, so how about gardening? Ambitions? Yes, yes, dear – and how are we today? Ambitions? Why – you could get an allotment, and even without poisoning cats, maybe, just maybe, *you could grow the perfect Brussels sprout* . . . And why not? *That's difficult!* There's nothing wrong with that!')

'Well, don't just stand there! *Take another exposure*. And then one more. Come on! *Bracket the exposures.*'

'Eh? Yes, yes, of course. Ambitions! The future!'

'What? Hey, Worzel! Aye. That's it. Well done! But there is *one* great barrier!'

We slid, slowly, back to starboard (even the sea was becoming friendly . . .).

'There is, across the deep seas of *all* the world's oceans, just the one great divide – and *where*, Worzel, where do you think that is?'

'No idea!'

'Right *here*! That's where – right off the UK! And no one in Britain knows or cares!' Luke, deeply offended by our ignorance, grasped the two precious grenadiers by their rat-tails and slung them into his yellow basket. 'The Roundnose, you see, technically he shouldn't be here – and why? Because this is Roughhead country! And why? Because between the two species-distributions, there's the one great barrier, a bloody great mountain-range, excuse me, a submerged mountain-range that links the continental shelf to the west of us, you know, Greenland, Iceland, the Faeroes, to the entirely different continental shelf that's us and Europe and the shallow North sea – a pond!'

The camera kit re-hung on its laundry-room hook, Luke hosed the fish-scales and fish-guts from my oilskins; I hosed Luke, from his chest-apron down to his boots: and from the scatter of water he yelled: 'Aye! It runs from south of the Faeroes towards Shetland and Orkney – slap across the Faeroe–Shetland Channel! The Wyville Thomson Ridge! But now – we must eat! Calm down! Whatever! But I'll tell you about it later, I promise I will . . .'

'Bollocks!' I shouted.

We arrived late in the galley, very late, but Bryan, Robbie and Allan Besant were still there: Bryan filled his usual far corner at the left-hand table, his back towards the galley; Robbie sat opposite him; and Allan Besant, to our immediate right, shoulders propped against the wall, hands behind his head, lolled straight out along the bench. All three looked up at us – all three very different faces seemed to say: hello, yes, but please, not now, you've walked in just as our *intense* discussion is nearing its climax.

Allan Besant, obviously the least engaged, said: 'Hi boys! There's pork chops and clapshot! And Jerry's made vegetable soup – and we all know, Jerry's a new boy, and he's a wanker from the sooth, *Edinburgh*, Edinburgh! But there's no denying it' (he shut his eyes), 'his soups, when Jerry *concentrates*, aye, the fact is, you could travel the world and no taste better' . . . (he opened his eyes) . . . 'So go get your warm chops – and then, take my advice, have the soup cold. Because that soup, boys, hot, warm, cold, fuckin' freezin', who cares? It's the best!'

We collected our white plates from the vertical wooden rack, our knives and forks from the screwed-down slatted box, our pork chops (one each) from the pan; and, grasping the ship's ladle, from the equally outsize bolted-on saucepan (next to its twin, one-eighth full of soup), we took an accompanying wack of clapshot: pure, warm, mashed-up happiness.

As Luke and I sat down in our usual places (me on the inside, next to the wall, Luke on the outside, next to the aisle, the two of us opposite Allan Besant), Bryan said, 'Hey Luke!' the volume notched up several stops: and we got the message, because it was as plain as a boom could be; and it said: You two, whatever you do, don't start *yacking* like fishwives, about fish, or anything else, because we three here, before you interrupted, we were having a *serious* discussion, and that's rare, that is, that's not a pleasure you get every day . . . And then a fresh small joy, a new thought, struck his sea-worn tired black-bearded face, and lightened it (by about 50 per cent, I decided, my head craned back against the bench-rest; and only a *boom* like that, yes, only volume that deep, reverberating around the steel plates of the enclosing claustrophobic dangerous galley, only a wave of sound like that could startle me off my clapshot . . .) and Bryan, the inner Old Man of the Sea, the outer First Mate, the young man with such a vigorous ultrasound, whale-communicating system, said: 'Luke! That's it! Now I come to think of it! *Of course* – you're the one to resolve this argument, this debate we're having, Robbie and Allan and me. You see it's like this – I was just saying: I've been reading Captain Sutherland's book about his life, you know, the man who taught us all, at the Nautical School in Stromness which, by the way, he built up himself, from nothing! And I admire him for that, of course, as we all do, but I also admire him because – in my opinion – he's written a good honest book and he admits he was an alcoholic and he takes no pains to hide that fact! So Luke – what do you think?'

'About what?'

Luke, I was reassured to see, had somehow managed to swallow half his clapshot but his pork chop, as yet, was untouched. So this clapshot-thing, no, it wasn't just *me* . . . I was sane, too . . .

'Aye, yes, I'm sorry.' Big Bryan looked concerned. '*You weren't here.* It's this – the *Longhope* disaster. The night those boys in the lifeboat were sent out to their certain death. They knew it. *Every last one of them.* They *knew* they'd no be returning. And yet they still went. Not a one refused to go. They all knew they were away to their drowning. And they went. They were no heroes! Ordinary men with jobs ashore! Aye – they were no in the Army or the Navy! *They were no even paid* – and someone sent them off to die, and that's a fact! And the long and the short of it, Luke – it's this: Captain Sutherland thinks that amounted to manslaughter, and the RNLI should have faced charges! So *you* – what do you think?'

'Ach. If there's a shout – you go. Simple.'

'But what if it's to certain death – like the *Longhope*? March 17, 1969 –'

'You go.'

'Captain Sutherland says . . .'

'Look – if you thought of yourself, *for one second*, instead of being *entirely* focused on the saving of other people's lives: you'd *never* go, would you? This Sutherland of yours – has he ever done it? As far as I remember, excuse me, he was in the *Merchant* Navy. He's no idea. We're not even in the *Royal* Navy. You can't think like that when it comes to *saving* lives. You can't weigh risks. No: we're *not* in the Royal Navy. You can't think like that! We're volunteers – you get a shout! Simple! You go! You always go . . .'

'Aye, me grandad,' said Robbie, in an entirely different tone of voice, reducing the unbearable tension (what a gift, I thought, *and why hadn't I thought of something?*). 'Me grandad,' said Robbie (and Luke, in a fury of some kind – dedication? disgust? – attacked his pork chop, *wop!* slice! off the bone! *pow!*), 'me grandad was an engineer on the Stromness lifeboat – and he had to go out and look for the *Longhope* people. Sutherland was really angry about all that, me grandad said, aye, Sutherland wrote to the RNLI, the papers, the Government in London, the whole ching-bang, *because all the Longhope people drowned.*' Robbie, in his white off-duty singlet, leant back, defensive, tense against the bench-support behind him; he crossed his absurdly muscled arms across his ridiculously over-developed chest and *ping!* I thought, that cheap singlet wasn't made to withstand such pressure – *zap! flack!* – they'll be strands of cotton shot like cartridge fluff, all over the galley . . . But, with a nanosecond to go, Robbie relaxed, leant forward towards Luke, and said, '*Sutherland's a good man*, a man who feels too much inside, you know, and that's why he's an ex-alcoholic like meself; and Sutherland said there must be decisions taken, sometimes, when you *don't* send a lifeboat out, when you're brave enough *not* to send all those volunteers to their certain death . . .'

'Aye!' boomed Bryan, excited, turning on Luke. 'Sutherland's right, he's a good man, it's obvious, right enough. Sometimes you *don't* get sentimental – you must think like a Viking. *Death happens.* Or rather, I should say: *sudden death happens.* You canna deny it, Luke. So sometimes you must let those people die who are going to die whatever you do – it's the sea, you've got to face it, so sometimes you must look death straight in the face and say: "OK, death – I see you, but no, not this time you're not, this time you're not going to have *one more man* than you've got already!" Eh? Luke? Is that right?'

Luke, the clapshot gone, the pork-chop bone picked brittle-clean, said: 'Bang! Up go the maroons, the flares! *Mayday Mayday!* And you get a shout! Ring-ring! And you're half-dead, in deep sleep, and no, it's not the alarm clock, it's four in the morning, no – this is the real thing! And you're warm in bed – and the desperate, the serious ones, they always seem to happen at four in the morning!'

'Aye, Luke, *wait*,' said Bryan, '*that's not it.* Look – a Liberian-registered ship grounds at Grim Ness, South Ronaldsay – the height of the spring flood-tide, an easterly-going tide of course, 10 knots or so, and against a wall of sea, as Sutherland calls it, a wall of sea built up in a four-day storm from the east, so there you have it, the worst local conditions, a fockin' maelstrom, call it what you like, but no 1960s lifeboat could possibly survive it, no chance, the lifeboats then, they weren't *designed* to turn turtle: no one could survive if the sea really played with you, flipped you over, end-for-

end . . . Aye, the *Longhope* lifeboat was lost on 17 March 1969 . . .
And Sutherland knew them all, the coxswain, Dan Kirkpatrick, a
man with fifty fockin' years of experience of the Pentland Firth;
the two Johnston boys, great hard-working lovely lads, you know,
fishermen in the Firth, booked in to study at the nautical school
that very next winter; and one of his favourite students, Eric
MacFadyen, who'd gone home for the weekend and stayed over
the Monday at his mother's request, as Sutherland says, to help out
on the farm, I shouldna wonder, whatever – and so he, too, Luke,
he got the *shout* as you call it . . . Well, Captain Sutherland hoped
that Dan would have seen sense and hove-to, in vast seas, right
enough, *but out of the tidal eruptions* . . . But no, that night he was a
lifeboatman, so he went as straight and as fast as he could through
Brough Sound *on that night, at that time*, with such a lifeboat, to try
to save the lives of those sailors on the Liberian-registered *Irene*,
and thereby – and as Sutherland says he *must* have known he would
– he drowned himself and his young crew . . .'

'Aye! Right!' shouted Luke, straight at Bryan. 'It's a shout! And
yes: *that's what we call it!* So what's wrong with that? There's men
out there – *they're drowning*. And excuse me, this Sutherland of
yours, he seems to forget – sometimes, *in fact more than sometimes* –
there's women and children too! So who the hell's going to take
the decision *not to go*? This Sutherland of yours, I've heard of him,
of course I have, I've read his letters in the RNLI archive, we all
do, and maybe, perhaps, his letters helped in the re-design of our
lifeboats, but I doubt it – because there's something wrong with
him: and why? Why's he jealous of us? Eh? What did he do in life?
Was he ever a lifeboatman? What did he *do* in life? Bum around
the Merchant Navy? Get bombed in the war, as everyone did? Hit
the bottle? Throw away the bottle? Run a college? So what? *Who
do these teachers think they are?'*

'Your father!' boomed Bryan, straight at Luke, equally fired up:
'Your *father*, that's who!' He paused, half turned away, looked
down at his empty plate on the table in front of him . . . we waited,

in a silence that obviously belonged to him and no one else . . . 'Or maybe . . . I suppose . . . yes, it's more likely, isn't it? . . . It's *you* who thinks *they're* your new father . . . Aye . . . Because here's this man who's *paid* to care for you – but you, you as a pupil, a student, of course you don't see it like that: no, because this is the new ideal father of your dreams who shares your interests and knows everything, and besides, he hasn't messed things up with your mother, *and that's a fact* . . . Aye, you can be pretty sure he hasn't even met your mother . . . And so you start to love him, just like you loved your real father when you were a real child . . .'

'Yes! Yes!' I said, too loud, crass, breaking in, carried away by all this emotion from men who'd seemed to me to be so heroically, so miraculously free of it. 'I've seen that often! It happened to me – *in loco parentis* indeed! And your tutor thinks that's *his* burden: to take over from your parents or your school or whatever, when you're so vulnerable, just emerged on your reed-stem over the parental pond, yes, late adolescence, drying your wings, you know, in your confusing new metamorphosis, when as yet you've no idea – you don't even know what the brand-new aerial predators look like – yes! In fact it's *your* burden, the pupil's burden, because it's impossible to resist – that moment when, unknown to you, your tutor displaces your father . . . Yes, I can think of at least two contemporaries of mine at university, students with me who, even now, *thirty-five years on*, still mimic, unconsciously, I'm sure, our tutor's way of *speaking* (let alone his wafty thought): the pauses, the breathy emphatic diction, the High Romantic Guff . . . And I can still remember that overwhelming excitement when I realized, in the here-and-now of a grey afternoon, that this tutor of mine really *did* imagine himself to be possessed of an intelligence, a searching genius that, with the almost-possible exception of Beethoven, *had never been surpassed* . . . Yes, what a privilege, but what a danger . . . Yes, you can find yourself enthralled for life by some kindly, well-meaning manic-depressive packed to the eyeballs with lithium. Not that there's anything wrong with that, of course –

you know, the manic depression and the lithium, it could happen to anyone . . . and it damn well does . . .'

Luke, Bryan, Robbie and Allan Besant looked at me, silent.

'Well, sorry, yes, you know – *I'm sure that only happens in the arts*: where it doesn't matter much, does it? The odd student suicide . . .'

Allan Besant came alive; he disconnected his head and shoulders from the imitation-wood panels of the wall, swung his legs right and down, and, alert, he was sitting erect, opposite me: 'Worzel! Worzel!' he said, putting both hands to his forehead and releasing them, into the air, a gesture repeated, fast, several times, a *very* effective signal, which meant what? Exactly? *Please – release me from this insanity*, perhaps, something like that . . . 'Worzel! Worzel!' he repeated, with a huge smile on his broad, open, healthy young face. 'Stop your vegetables! Stop your verbiage! Go on – fuck off back to your field of turnips!'

'Eh?'

'Yes, Worzel – no wonder you love your turnips and your potatoes so much! I've been watching you, you old scarecrow!'

'Uh?'

'Yes – keep out of this Worzel! Mr Gummidge! Because you're a country bumpkin from the far south, anyone can see that, and you've been on telly, and we all love you, but you're not supposed to speak, not really, and you shouldn't be at sea, that's for sure – *and you know fuck-all about any of this* . . .'

Robbie, ignoring Allan, ignoring me, said to Luke, fast and urgent: 'Yep. Well, one time, the head man in Kirkwall didna send out the Kirkwall lifeboat and the Stromness lifeboat went out instead.'

(And I was thinking: OK, yes, Allan Besant, so full of life, and I like him, *and it's a joke*, anyone can see that, and I remember Rosie-bud reading Worzel Gummidge to me, the very first book that was pure pleasure, no fear, and I hadn't yet been sent away to prep school, so I must have been six years old, yes, but all the same, he's *right* . . . And something hit my subconscious hard, in its

239

stomach, if it has a stomach; and I lost control of my face, as you do, and I must have looked lost, devastated, as you *suddenly do*, and there's nothing that will hide the fact. And I thought blankly, yes, these cliffs of fall, in the mind, these moments of inner vacuum and blank falling fear – they don't have to last long in reality to last for ever in the memory, do they? So how come it's always Robbie who rescues us? And I remembered something that Luke had told me in passing, a particularly convincing and horrible explanation for the mysterious disappearance of five or six trawlers, over the years, in perfect weather in the summer North Sea, the sea that's shallow as a pond – and you can see the same rising bubbles, now and then, *in any garden pond* – yes, the sudden release from the thick deposits on the shallow bed of the North Sea of trawler-sized bubbles of methane gas . . . The vacuum around you, the instant descent, the closing waters, the ripples outspreading, for a short distance, across the surface calm . . .)

'They went oot' (when Robbie really meant what he said, he said *oot*) 'because the Kirkwall lifeboat wouldna go oot. No, Luke – I tell a lie, *but it's a big wee story in Orkney*. The Kirkwall lifeboat went oot – its wipers wouldna work, so they came bloody back in – technical, the *wipers* wouldna work, so they turned back and came in . . . The Kirkwall lifeboat, they're still a joke, a joke like, me cousin was in it, and because of embarrassment, he left.'

Luke, fully attentive, said: 'He was embarrassed? He was *shamed* by it?'

'Yep. He was in the Kirkwall lifeboat – and he *left*. Because half of them all have no experience or nothing.'

'Aye, right!' said Luke, for some reason restored to himself, professional, reassured. 'That's easy, no sweat – it's all in the mind, as the Royal Marines, the Special Boat Service, as Dicko, an ex-SBS man, in our very own lab – as he'd tell you – all it takes is *training*. Townies, fantasists? Who cares? Training: practice, routine, repetition, a hundred times for each procedure, if you're very lucky, you know, until they're sick of it all and on the point of leaving from sheer fuck-you-in-the-head boredom – and they're *volunteers*, remember, they can leave any time – and after about six months or so they'll come and tell you, all worked up, they'll say: "This petty mindless routine is driving me nuts, nuts!" And then – one night – there's a *real* shout (and they turn up bolshy: they think it's another pointless practice) . . . But no, baby, big time, this really is it, their first time, and it helps no end, if it's a bit dramatic, you know, a storm in the dark, and the boat, she turns turtle and rights herself, and you get to the target, and it's bad, because half the crew of the sod-unseaworthy Russian merchantman have drowned already – and you have to do the whole biz you've trained for: rockets, lines, grapnels . . . And it's smack-violent and you're carried away off-board yourself, but *you're equipped*, you're on a line, *you're trained*; and your helmet protects your head as a wave chucks you skull-first against the side of the Russian ship; and you reel yourself in, as if nothing had happened; and you try again, and you get lucky – you've saved yourself, no problem; but now you find you're saving others *instinctively*; you're so well trained it feels like *instinct*. And then – guess what? Townies, fantasists? Who cares? They've got the point. They never complain about anything again – believe me: when you *save* someone for sure, *no argument*, there's nothing like it, I promise you: from that moment on, *they're in the service . . .*'

Well, myself, despite being full of clapshot, I very nearly got to my feet and saluted, but something saved me, kept me in my place – and Robbie, tough wiry Robbie, he just carried on as if Luke had said nothing of the remotest interest . . .

'The one Kirkwall captain was going to go over this shallow – he thought he'd get over it in the lifeboat – but there's no way he woulda done it . . . That's what the captain was gonna do.'

Bryan laughed – he remembered.

'Aye!' said Robbie, at Luke. 'But that's the main joke between the Kirkwall and the Stromness lifeboat. *That was it* – when they got the brand-new lifeboats . . . in Stromness and Kirkwall the same.'

'The Trent Class?'

'Yep. The Stromness lifeboat went doon sooth, two weeks, doing their training.'

'At Poole?'

'They did it, standard. But the Kirkwall boys were down there for weeks and weeks.'

'Aye. So bad?'

Robbie said: 'Yep.'

'Yeah well,' I said, butting in, just to show that I was thoroughly familiar with this Poole business. (And why? Because Luke had told me about his Poole training, but for the moment I'd forgotten that, and so now, in sleepless eagerness, I imagined that I myself knew all about these macho rites of passage, first-hand . . .) 'Yes, I'm well aware that Luke had no problems in Poole, none at all. He seems to enjoy RNLI super-discipline. And he's never missed a shout, as he calls it. He's always there. He's been out every time he could.'

Robbie said: 'Yep.'

Self-important, I held Robbie in my seen–it–all gaze and said, as if I was on a selection board: 'And so you think Luke's a fine seaman? Eh? Knows his stuff?'

'Yep. Aye. Bloody fine like.'

Bryan, his huge frame inflating further with suppressed laughter, a ridiculous grin on his massive face, mimicking my accent, said, 'Oh yes! *Awfully* so in fact, Captain Redmond. And if *I* was a skipper, sir, and Deckhand Luke Bullough applied to join my crew, I can say, without reservation, old bean: I'd take him. *He's a damn good chap.* He'd be a simply splendid addition *to the team.*'

And they all laughed outright, the bastards, and I went hot in the face, and turned to my plate, but I'd already cleaned it up, like a dog, so I put my head in my hands, and closed my eyes.

I heard Allan Besant say: 'Worzel!' And I heard his sharp snort of a laugh. (I looked at him.) 'The questions you ask! Right out of order! But I know what you're thinking, and I'll tell you! You're right!' He put his elbows on the narrow table, into *my* space, way over the half-way mark, and he got very close, trying to look into my eyes (*I don't like that*, no, I don't – so I concentrated on him below the neck: he was wearing a dazzling white-clean T-shirt with an inscription, but only the capital letter B was visible in the open-V of his dark-blue, expensive-looking fleece-jacket, complete with toggles). 'Worzel – I know you want *the truth*, anyone can see that, and it's a pain in the arse, because whose truth? But I'll tell you, my truth, and it's this, so listen up, Worzel! Lifeboatmen? *They're all mad.* Because who'd want to go out on a lifeboat? For free – *for no money?* What's healthy about that? Thank Aunt Fanny they do it, sure, but *listen, Worzel*' (maybe I'd tried to look away at Luke, 12 inches to my immediate right, for comfort), 'it's like the VC. *I've read about it.* Those guys who won the Victoria Cross – unless they're from the best men in the British Army, *the Gurkhas*, men from an entirely different culture, like the Shelties at sea, Shetlanders to you – all those men who go for acts of impossible bravery, the ones we hear about, because 99 per cent of them of course get killed, and there's no story in that, is there? – there's just 1 per cent who succeed and really do wipe out a machine-gun nest single-handed – and guess what? They were depressives like your tutor: *they wanted to die*, that's why they were brave! They didn't care if they lived or died. Sure – they got the VC, so that keeps them going a little longer – the adulation in the mess, as it were, even Colonel Jason Schofield respects you for a time . . . But Worzel, what happens next? They get discharged, they're back ashore, or rather, they're back in civilian life – and then? Can you guess? Of course you can: *a huge percentage* of those men with a VC, I forget the exact figures, but it's way over half – they failed that one time when they really meant it, when they charged that machine-gun nest or rescued a wounded colleague under intense sniper-fire, whatever, you know . . . But next time, in civilian life, they slit their own throats *so neatly*; they jump off a cliff or under a train and no mistake; they put the shotgun barrel right in, right in tightly against the roof of the mouth . . . *And it's just the same, in my opinion, with lifeboatmen*, with heroes, like Luke here . . . No, I don't trust heroes, not at all . . . *I don't believe in them . . .*'

I looked straight at him, outraged, and with the uncensored angst of a teenager I said: 'That's sick! That is! Sick . . .'

'Oh, is it?' said Allan Besant, immediately turning on Bryan. 'So maybe Old Worzel here has a touch of the lifeboatman too – you know, death or glory, all that shite, and he hasn't got the energy, but all the same, here he is and you have to admit there's something not quite right about it: because here's Worzel . . .' From his elbow-propped hand under his chin, he unfurled his right fist, palm up, fingers and thumb out-stretched towards me: the exhibit. 'And what's he doing here at his age, fifty, or what-the-fuck, and he knows *nothing*, anyone can see that, and he's come out in this piece of Jason-Schofield-scrap-metal in the worst shit-weather an idiot could imagine – *you can all see that* – and yet no one says a thing? And why? Bryan – have you *ever* heard of this happening to any other boat? Why the fuck should we have to look after a Worzel? Is it because he's paying Jason £50 a day for his keep, and Jason's sharing it with us, so we're supposed to look after him? Well, frankly, I've other things to do, but there again, Worzel's hardly spoken to me, so maybe that's why I'm angry with him, and he's *paying* to suffer all this shite! For the privilege! Whereas you, Bryan, I know, there's no denying it, you yerself, you appear to be a good man, everyone thinks so, but for me, it's like this, I can't help it, it's the truth as I see it: there's something warped, there's something wrong with Luke, lifeboatmen, with anyone who's ever won a medal – and as for Worzel, well, search me, I give up!'

Big Bryan gave me a quick, kind, fatherly glance . . . (And hadn't he strapped me into that First Mate's chair, his chair, on the bridge, when I couldn't stand up, when I'd felt worse than at the onset of cerebral malaria? And hadn't he guided me there with real sympathy, without the faintest trace of the professional derision to which he was fully entitled, *without even a smile?*)

Agitated, Bryan said to Allan Besant: 'But Redmond's here to write about you, to tell the truth about our way of life, you understand, Jason told me, and besides, he's done his apprenticeship, and that's not easy, at his age, he's apprenticed to Luke, at the lab in Aberdeen – so he's not just a writer, he's a *scientist*. He's here to help us.'

'Is he hell? So how come he asked me, "Is this a Force 12? Is this *really* a hurricane? You sure? You ever been in a Force 14? *Is there a Force 14?*" Old Worzel here' (he outspread his right hand, palm up, in my direction, again), 'old Worzel – fact is, he's disappointed with our fuck-horrible see-you-every-January hurricane. Oh yes – he wants that total boring pointless all-out ocean shite that drowns everyone pronto – he wanted to *come here and give up and die!* Why's he so interested in manic depressives? Bi-polar disorder, my arse. Why? Because he's one himself. That's why! I know what he's after, you can't fool me . . . To write about us? Shite! He might, he might not. Who can tell? And anyway, as it is, he could just as surely have gone overboard and drowned, or banged his head open, or stuck his gutting knife into his wrist' (my friend, my ally, Uncle Luke, he began to laugh; yes, he did, making no noise, shaking the bench beside me, looking away, hard, at Bryan) '– or, *Jesus wept!*, into his throat! Because, Bryan, you were below, but you should've seen him pitching about, trying to gut a Black butt, a Black butt! When we had that weather! Stand clear, boys – because Worzel's knife, *there's no telling where it's going next!* So I ask you, Bryan, *First Mate*, and you, Robbie Stanger, one of Jason's favourites, as we all know, why do we have a Worzel on board who could go get himself killed so easily and stop the fishing and halve our earnings? And why did we all have to go to nautical college for so long? *I'll tell you* – to stop us dying at sea the first week out, that's why! And Worzel – not that I've anything against him personally, even though he's hardly fucking bothered to speak to me ("Besant?" he says. "So are you related to Annie Besant, the playwright?" Well yes, as it happens, probably, *but fuck that for a laugh!*) – and Bryan, *you*

245

know what I mean, innocents at sea, on a *trawler* of all things. Jesus wept! It shouldn't be allowed!'

Luke, I felt, was no longer so amused . . . And as for Robbie – he turned sharp right on his bench to confront Allan Besant across the alley-way between the tables. Robbie's biceps, his triceps, his pectorals were so taut, and his singlet, I was sure, stretched further with other groups of muscles whose names I couldn't raise from my dimming memory of the illustrations in *Gray's Anatomy* (those extracted cardboard plates we used to place alongside the corpse in question): but *pow!* I thought, comforting myself, maybe they *weren't* illustrated: because only trawlermen develop them – and who's ever got lucky enough to dissect a trawlerman in his prime? No, that's right – you can't just drop in to your local hospital: you'd have to search the bottom of the sea . . .

Robbie, so intense, said to Allan: 'It's no allowed – and you, you mind that right enough!' (And Jesus, I thought, this Robbie, my new friend, my Jason-appointed protector, it seems he's biologically ready to *fight* for me, my inconsequence, our friendship; I'm sure that's not required, as it were, not right at all . . .) 'Redmond here – he's a scientist! He's from the Marine Laboratory, Aberdeen. He's Assistant to Luke Bullough! And Luke's here to help us oot, whatever *you* may think, and Luke gave Jason a copy of one of his papers in *Fisheries Research*, and Jason says its *really* bloody interesting like, and he's lent it to me.' (Luke looked startled, and, a second or two later, as proud as he should.) 'And it's on commercial deep-water trawling at sub-zero temperatures in the Faeroe–Shetland Channel. Yep! Something like that – *and you should read it.* And anyway, Jason told me to look after Worzel, Redmond rather: so he's *my* responsibility, *my job.* He's *not* your worry. So what's it to do with you? Eh? He's a scientist. So you, Allan, well: *you can go fock your auntie!*'

Bryan, I noticed, in his turn, like Luke, began to laugh, internally, as it were, obviously trying so hard to control it, as if he were in church, and failing . . . What was it? I hadn't seen all this since school . . . and yes, maybe that was it, on a trawler, so *very* close to everyone, the fire-hose shut-tight pressure not to offend, the need to get along, to control yourself . . . But Big Bryan, the alpha male, he began to shake in earnest with silent laughter: he turned his head away to inspect the imitation-wood plastic panels to his right, a foot from his eyes . . . and his back, the back of his massively muscled upper body in its supposed-to-be-loose, outsize, black woolly sweater – it stretched tight, it earthquaked with deep tremors of a soundless hilarity . . .

Allan Besant, stung in some way, snapped at Robbie: 'Aunties? It's *you* who's got aunties!'

Robbie, on his seat, edging towards Allan Besant, said: 'You! *You lay off me aunties!*'

Big Bryan broke up; he came apart; and his mega-bass full-out laugh was deep-down reassuring: it was something so elemental, so powerful that, had it come at the right time, it might have removed, for half a second or more, all fear of the wind and waves and the depths out there . . . 'Aunties!' (A deep seizure, a phlegm-block in the foghorn.) *'Aunties!'*

Big Bryan, facing forward, his big head in his big hands, massaged his eyes with his palms, as if he was very tired, and with his fingers he was wiping away – what? Yes: tears! . . . Big Bryan had been *crying with laughter* . . . 'Redmond!' he choked, and tried again: 'Redmond! . . . Robbie here . . . you won't know, but our Robbie . . .' Bryan mastered himself; he turned to address me, his big hands, bizarrely, still pressed to either side of his bearded face: 'Our Robbie . . . he's got *ten* uncles: Ronnie! Tony! Jeremy! Bobby! Billy! Colin! And *oh shite*, forgive me, I've forgotten, and I'm only telling you their names, the names of his uncles, because they dinna matter, *because he's also got six aunties*, and I'll no be telling you *their* names, because they do matter, that's for sure, *because his aunties* . . .' Big Bryan's hands released his head; it was all too much to hold in; and his infrasound of a happy laugh, an all-in laugh – it travelled, on that longest of wave-lengths, leisurely

247

through the rusty double-hull of the *Norlantean*, and it fanned out across the surface-to-upper depths of the ocean: where it lifted the spirits of several bored and lonely Minke whales; and a group of friendly Pilot whales; and one whole iffy pod of Killer whales . . . 'No! *I'll no be telling you the names of his aunties!* Because his aunties, I've seen them all – and they're goers, they're real lookers, believe me! You'd never know' (another pulse of the very happiest infra-sound). 'Aye! Yes! You'd never know – not one of them – *you'd never know they were aunties!* And I can tell you straight, Redmond, because I'm *married*, and I tell you, Redmond, *I'm happy with it*, I'm very happy, and that's a fact – so I can say, without offence, I can say without offence to anyone, and there's no reason why I shouldn't come right out and say it: because Robbie here, he has six slim sexy aunties, believe me! *And he could start a strip-club!*'

There was a short, shocked silence. And then Robbie, delighted, said: '*You big dirty bastard!*'

Allan Besant, still aggrieved, immune to aunties, said, 'Scientist? Worzel a scientist? *Scientist, my arse!* You should hear him talking to Luke! He knows no more science than I do. In fact, Worzel' (from 18 inches away across the table – he gave me a big, kind, friendly, condescending grin: and I thought: am I *really* this old?), 'what are the different regional names of the saithe?'

Now, I said to myself, hang on, calm down, even *you* know that the various dialect names of the saithe have nothing whatever to do with science, but all the same, I've got the answers, *so up yours*, Allan Besant . . .

Bryan (who'd stopped shaking) and Luke (mild again, his relaxed self) and Robbie (no longer quite so protectively murderous) looked at me, too, exactly as anyone in any classroom in the world (if they're lucky enough to *have* a classroom) always looks at Teacher's potential victim . . .

I said: 'Coalfish! Coley!' And, naturally enough, I expected tumultuous applause . . .

'Is that all? Worzel – is that the best you can do?'

'Yes!' I was pleased with myself, very pleased. Here was an absurd question – *and I'd got it right.* 'Those are the names. What an easy, what a silly question! Go on – try me again, ask me something *difficult.*'

Allan Besant, acerbic, said: 'Coalfish, coley?' And then, like Bryan, only with a bitter-teacher edge, he mimicked my English accent: 'How *awfully* unimpressive, old chap. No, Worzel, no . . .' And he gave me, this time, a genuine big grin, his young eyes alight: he was enjoying himself. And the two deep vertical furrows which ran upwards from the bridge of his nose between his eyebrows, for an inch or so (converging) into his otherwise flawless forehead (and which told you, without the trace of a conscious thought: 'This young man – *he's suffered*') – these furrows, for a moment, they disappeared, as if they didn't live there at all. Allan Besant, for this here and this now, he was happy.

'No, Worzel! You've failed! In fact – *coalfish, coley* – that won't even get you an honourable discharge, *old chap!* No – you see, I too, *I know some science, Worzel,* and OK, so it's my party piece, as you'd say, and Bryan and Robbie have heard it all before, but they like me really, you know, so they won't interrupt and fuck me up and put me off – because they know, science, knowledge, it takes *concentration.*' And he gave me another grin, a last kind of a goodbye smile, and he looked up at the low ceiling, and, with the index finger of his right hand, he checked off the outspread fingers of his left – and the index pointer-finger itself, so close to my nose, was almost hypnotic as it touched and flicked – partly because, as yet, just above the main joint, ringed with the raised red workings of cells intent on healing a communal wound: it was marked with the clear imprint of *Homo sapiens sapiens'* front teeth: it had got itself bitten when Allan Besant, reasonably enough, was sitting on the prone chest of Gillespie, the Big Fellah, and bravely attempting, *with that very finger,* to poke out Gillespie's eyes . . .

'Saithe, coalfish, coley. Poor old ignorant Mr Worzel . . .' he intoned, face up, staring at the asbestos ceiling-tiles and pretending to be, what? A magician? No – of course, he was a quiz-show host on the telly, or a megawinner, yes, Allan Besant was taking the grand-slam title . . . 'Baddock! bannock – no, sorry, *I withdraw that*: blackjack! Names from eastern Scotland.'

Allan Besant glowed, full of youth in its twenties, packed with unbidden energy and delight: 'And then we have' (a flick of opposing index fingers) 'the coalmie, a name for the full-grown fish, from the Moray Firth. And the comb – and that's a fish in its fifth year, in Banffshire, and if it's made it to fifty, it's called a *Worzel!*' (Big Bryan clapped.) 'And then there's *real names*, the names the young fish were born with, and they'd tell you so, too, they'd *answer* to those names, because that's right, *those are their actual names*, their Orkney names: cuth or cooth. But our local village idiot, Sean Taylor, of Castletown, Thurso – well, he comes from Caithness so no one can understand a fucking word he says, whatever it is, but if you ring up the Thurso public librarian and you ask him, politely, what the fuck the horrible prehistoric natives of Caithness call a saithe, he'll grunt at you and he'll say: 'CUDDIE.' So there you go – and in Angus, the small fish, it's called a dargie. And yes, on the Moray Firth, and I'm not making this up, I promise you – the young stages, the small fish just like Robbie and Luke: they're *geeks!*' Big Bryan clapped again, caught out (because he should've known *not* to join in) – and he looked so pleased with everything, and he clapped with such force (the trapped-air explosions, the shotgun blasts between his cupped outsize palms), and he laughed, and he carried on clapping, letting off his personal hand-to-hand firecrackers for, well, *for more than several seconds too long* . . .

'But decent fish in their second year, in the real language, the Orkney language, the names they were born with – they're called peltag or piltack – and Worzel, if you don't believe me, you try it, OK? Promise me? When you're next fucking about, fatman, in a rowing boat, or sitting on a fat rock: you try it! OK? Promise me? You raise your voice – in an inviting sort of way – and you cup your hands round your mouth, and you call, straight into the water: 'Peltag! Piltack!' And they *know* their own names when they hear them called correctly – and they'll come to you, they'll swim straight towards you . . . And then, unless you're a right little shite, a real peltag- or piltack-teaser, you'll bung in, pellet by pellet, one half of a stale loaf of bread – just to show that we're friends really, you know, all the fish and all of us, we understand each other!'

There was a silence – Bryan and Robbie looked away, and then at their empty plates . . . Because, I thought, on the instant, Allan Besant *was not supposed to be a deep-down emotional softie*, a man who could even imagine the feelings of young fish . . . No, Allan Besant was meant to be tough, tough right down and through, and yet here he was, a grown man who'd sat on a rock, all alone, more than once, and called to fish, and he'd fed them pellets of bread and scraps of food that he'd saved deliberately, and that's what this tough guy liked to do, on his own, when no one was looking, and it had all come out by mistake. And well, Bryan and Robbie, instinctively, they felt for him, they were embarrassed, for the future, *on his behalf* . . .

Allan Besant came to himself, and reasserted himself, and his body tensed and he raised his voice: 'And in eastern fucking Scotland, for Chrissake, the small saithe are called pirrie or poddlie or prinkle which just shows you, doesn't it? Because that's where Jerry comes from – and he can't make up his mind about anything, either, so that makes sense. Whereas in Banffshire, boys, they at least *try* to say what they mean, so a saithe in its second year is called a queeth – and in Orkney and Shetland which, by the way, Worzel, and you don't seem to understand this: *they have fuck-all to do with horrible Scotland* – in Orkney and Shetland, a no-religion, *a no-bullshit zone*, as I think you noticed yourself, a place where people know they'll have to die, and face the fact . . . Aye, there the fry of the saithe have their own real names, the names they were bloody well born with, and no mistake: sellag or sillack. And in Shetland, where, it's obvious, isn't it? because that *must* be the place where the number-one name really came from: from the crazy Shelties who dinna *say* anything much: great guys, aye! But Worzel, in *your* language, or any other, come to that: *they don't speak*. Aye? So the fucking delicious fish they send south or chuck overboard or use for bait in the creels, because they willna eat it themselves, they despise it, it's unfit for a real man, guess what they call it? Guess what they call it − when you can get those big fuckers drunk enough to speak at all? No? No idea? Well, I'll tell you − they call it a *said*, a *seid*. And why? Because that big giant motherfucker Sheltie, who can lift eight sacks of salmon feed on his shoulders, no problem, you know what? Rumour has it that *he said something*, so he's not a real man, he's a poof, he's almost a woman, you know, because he *spoke* last month, and everyone got to hear of it and it's all over Yell, the very worst of their islands, and so now he's like that fish that's taboo, the one that no genuine male will eat: the he *said*, or he *seid*.'

(OK − so it took more than a moment to get the point − but then we all clapped, and Robbie yelled: 'Goaaal!')

Allan Besant turned to Bryan, the only real could-be Sheltie present. 'And do you know what they call a Worzel-saithe, in the Firth of Clyde, an overgrown and ancient saithe? No? You don't? Well − it's a stenloch, a stone in the loch, whatever, something that gets in everyone's way . . . And the Yanks? That's where we should all go, where we ought to be − *right out of all this shite* − because they're sensible, they don't give a shit, whatever the damn thing is, they call it a pollock! And if you really love it − you call it a clare pollock! And what could be better than that?'

Allan Besant, exhausted, took his elbows off the table and leant back against the bench-rest. It was obvious that the show was over − and it was such a polished theatrical piece that we clapped again, all four of us, without a thought and with no reserve. Allan Besant beamed transitory happiness at each of us, in turn, as if taking a bow to all four quarters of the theatre. I thought: *What a guy!* And Luke said: 'Aye, magic! So what's its scientific name?'

We stopped clapping, and watched.

'Its *scientific* fucking name?' said Allan Besant, getting to his feet, reverting instantly to the resentment that seemed to suffuse him. 'Who cares?'

'Ach,' said Luke, affronted, in his turn. 'If you don't know the scientific name, even on this trivial level, excuse me, then you can't call yourself a scientist, can you? And besides' (he looked at me, for support – which was touching – and so: 'Absolutely!' I interjected, and nodded, with vigour), 'the scientific names, they're beautiful, they sound so good, don't they?' (I nodded further, as if, well, to me, you know, these names were not just musical, but full of meaning, and besides, *I knew them all.*) 'The saithe, *Pollachius virens* (Linnaeus).'

'Fuck that!' said Allan, half out of the door. 'Who cares? And get this – people like you, full of shite, and they all live in Angus, you know what they call it there?'

'No,' said Luke simply, taken aback.

'Rock halibut! Lies – fucking lies!'

'Wait! Wait!' boomed Big Bryan. 'Allan – what's up? That was star-turn stuff! And no mistake!' His bass voice, not even raised much – with no effort it filled the galley, and, in its mesh of deep waves, it seemed to hold Allan in the doorway. 'So – halibut? What's the scientific name for White halibut in Shetland?'

Allan swung right round. He put his large muscled hands, one to each top corner of the door jamb, above his head, and he leant in towards us. 'Fuck you, Bryan! Mister Blameless-Silence! You think I can do that with anything else? You think that was easy? You mad as Worzel all of a sudden? Jeesus – I *learnt* that. Took me weeks! The women love it! But that's it – finish – that kind of thing, science, it *hurts* you know, *it hurts the brain!* So fuck off!'

'Hey no! Wait!' said Bryan, with extra volume, throwing some internal switch to mega-bass. 'You've got me wrong!'

'Oh yes?'

'Aye! The scientific name for White halibut in Shetland? In the only no-bullshit zone on earth? The name? It's DA FISH, that's what, DA FISH! And that's a fact!'

We laughed. Allan laughed, and his hands unclenched off the door jambs, and he said, formulaic, happy, in the full Orkney lilt: 'I'm away to ma bed.'

Luke moved sideways and up, as if something had gripped him at the back of the neck, as you might pick up a cat, and, stumbling slightly, in the space between the tables, he steadied himself with his left hand against the back of our bench and said, in a voice not quite his own: 'I'm sorry. So sorry! I must go. I have to work!' And – but the echo or the joke or whatever his brave self meant it to be, it wilted and died in the warm fug, by the door, as he said, so obviously racked with guilt: 'I'm away to ma fish-room!'

Poor Luke, I thought, it must have hit him in that instant – yes, because he'd forgotten himself, listening to Allan Besant, he'd begun to live out of himself, free of anxiety, out of time, in real pleasure, the clamps off the head, such a relief, just as if he *was* in a theatre . . . free of his doctorate. And what is it about doctorates? Why such suffering? Even for a Luke? The otherwise most courageous man you might ever hope to meet? Well, obviously, for a start, it's an absurd privilege, a great (and expensive, so expensive – other people's taxes), a great gift to *you* (which you know, which makes the pressure worse): a real chance to discover something entirely unexpected about the way the world works – and the examples of doctoral students' work changing the way we see ourselves and the universe, they're too very many to mention: so how's about Jocelyn Bell Burnell's discovery of pulsars, pulsating radio stars, in 1967? An impoverished doctoral student, analysing signals from a new radio telescope, a Cambridge effort, a telescope four-plus acres in area, but that's not the point, no, only *she* was intense and engaged enough to notice an extraordinary radio source: and she was *young enough* not to dismiss it as *local interference* (because it was too freaky to fit any then-current theoretical model); and for a time the jokey explanation of her elders, who plainly thought it was a technical fault of some kind in this new telescope – it was this: the signal was a message sent by the other life out there that we lonely people so yearn to find. And the older establishment-astronomers named this regular pulse, this signal every one-point-something seconds, LGM – Little Green Men. But yes – like so many fresh-thinking, young, committed doctoral students before and since, *she was right*: she went ahead, unfazed, and found other sources, and *pow!* It was a new type of star. A tiny star, a neutron star, and they're no more than 10 miles across, but so massive, and they and their magnetic field spin like crazy, and don't ask me how, but they produce this signal . . . Yes. See? So why shouldn't Luke discover something equally remarkable about life in the unknown deep-sea? Why not?

But the golden chance, the great opportunity to spend three or more years pursuing some obsessive interest, the intensity of it, you don't know it at the time, of course, because you're all of twenty-two years old, *but here it is*, your real life, and it gives you the foundation for the whole of the rest of your *intellectual life* . . . So there you go, you must make your own real choice of interest for a doctorate as deeply as you possibly can – something that connects at once with the half-forgotten entrancements of your childhood, something that *really* excites you, the more secret the better, because this is your last chance to *play*. For instance: take your very first sight of a smooth newt in a pond; you, the child, captivated by the mysteries of this life before you, so unlike your own; the smooth

256

or common newt, suspended in this pond, so unexpected, its delicate hands and feet so out-stretched; and it swims, its paddling hands and feet, its zig-zag tail, so ancient, so like the tiniest of dinosaurs straight up to the surface; and it takes a breath of air, and you see its orange underside and it flits back to safety, and it regains its floating composure, a steady control over its emotions . . . But hang on a minute – its sex life, like us, there's no composure about it, oh no: my friend, Tim Halliday, now so old, like me, but when he was a doctoral student some thirty years ago, well, his doctoral thesis was on *The Sex Life of the Newt*: and you may laugh – but *he* discovered that the sequence went: *whip, fan, flash and sniff.* I remember that, because no one could forget such a thing – and he was a tidy boy, so in the mating season he'd go out with his net and capture a male and a female smooth newt from some farm-pond near Oxford, and he'd bring them back in his collecting jar and release them into newt-sex heaven: his newt-club in his lab, a gravel-bottomed, well-aerated, just-the-right temperature, pond-planted designer-tank-for-newts: a red-light, after-dinner prairie bed, a secluded Masters-and-Johnson, a Kinsey all-permitted sex-club for newts . . .

I heard, from a very long way away, from far out, from the wildly anxious surface of the deep sea, way out beyond the snug little illusory comfort of the *Norlantean*'s double-hull – I heard *a shout*, as Luke would call it . . . 'Redmond!' It was Robbie's voice . . . a shout! But I hadn't been trained, and *training*, again and again, as Luke said, that was everything; *but this was an emergency*, and it was *Robbie* out there, asking *me*, of all people, to rescue him . . . And he was right of course, because only Robbie knew me well enough to realize that I was the fattest old fuck ever to go to sea, so I was *insulated*, I had my own survival suit, an excessive covering of subcutaneous all-over yellow fat, like all mammals in the sea, so, sure, I must jump in, and I must fat-swim, and I must *rescue* that little Robbie, so thin as he was, who for some reason had decided to become a close friend of mine . . . So I jumped off the gunwale of the *Norlantean*, from the stern-deck, and my legs kicked out like a frog and my hands paddled as hard as they could, like a newt, rising for air to the surface, and when I got there, a hero already, I yelled: 'Robbie! It's OK! Your troubles are over! It's me! Redmond! *So don't worry!* Because it's me! And I'm here! And I'm coming! I'm coming as fast as I can! I'm coming to rescue you!'

And *I got there* (*such* a flailing of limbs – and the sea was so salty and my mouth went dry), and Robbie, drowning, desperate, he grabbed me with both hands, so hard, on the ridges of my shoulders; and he transferred his right hand to the hair on the back of my head and he pulled my face out of the water . . . or, as it now seemed, out of my shallow bowl of soup . . . 'Redmond!' he said, right into my left ear. 'So you'd rescue me like? Aye – *I'm sure you would!* Don't get me wrong – I appreciate that! I really do!'

And Big Bryan, way out in his corner, he was convulsed with laughter: Boom! Boom! 'So here comes Worzel!' he yelled, delighted. 'Here comes Worzel! Gurgle gurgle! So don't you worry about a thing, Robbie! Because here comes Gurgle Worzel, gurgle gurgle!'

Jesus – how *very* bad: so I must have been shouting in my sleep . . . But how come I'd been asleep at all? Because it didn't feel *at all like waking* – and anyway, how dare they play a trick like that on me? Because I'd been talking, *so rationally*, hadn't I? I'd been talking, I'd been giving my all to Luke and Robbie and Bryan and they'd been spellbound, as they should be, and they'd said nothing, as they ought . . . Yes: *I'd been talking*: and they were playing some trawler-game with me . . . Or were they? Hadn't I been swimming, and so well, in the sea?

Robbie said, as if Allan Besant had but left that second (perhaps he had): 'Redmond, you mustna mind Allan. He's not like us, he's not like you and me – because he came into a lot of money like, *a lot*, from some relative he'd never met, I shouldna wonder.'

'Oh boys, Jesus, excuse me, but it's *so* frightening, this life of yours . . .'

'Aye. Anyway, he was no prepared for it, if you know what I mean, and mebbe we'd all do the same, how can you tell? So he stopped work at the fishing, aye, and he was a joiner, too, you know – one of the best in all Orkney, but there again, there's no much work for a joiner in Orkney!'

'No – you don't understand, it's so *very* frightening, you know, because I thought I was talking to you, to you, Robbie,' and I looked to my right at Bryan, who'd stopped laughing, I could hear, and who came blearily into focus, 'and to you, Bryan; and to Luke . . .' But Luke had atomized, he was no longer there . . . And I felt that deep fear that can take possession of you without warning; that fear that seems to arrive in the back of your skull like the talons of a Monkey eagle – and OK, if you haven't been unfortunate enough to have seen one of them in action, then the sudden cold intrusion of acute anxiety into your mind at three o'clock on an ordinary grey afternoon – and just in case you think you can ignore *that*, well, your stomach starts to hurt, and then it burns, and it's playing host to a Forest cobra – and no, you realize pronto, this one is different, because this one, no, *you can't sleep it off* . . . But, even so, it was some seconds before it occurred to me that I might be going mad . . . And then I said, too desperate, too loud: 'Robbie! Bryan! It's so frightening – *because I thought I was talking to you!*'

'Oh *that*,' said Bryan, at once looking bored, 'we all get *that*.'

'Aye!' said Robbie. 'Dinna you worry. You're no different.'

Bryan, relaxing, settling back into his corner said: 'Aye, near midway on a trip, we all get *that*: we all think we've said things to each other and, you know, *such good things*, sometimes, because as you speak you'll no be getting any interruptions so you can *concentrate*, and say what you really mean, but no, you ask around and *no*, you were asleep like you, Redmond, just now, your head on your plate, at the galley table, that's normal that is, that's the usual – but I've known people fall asleep standing up, or drop their heads on

259

the *gutting table*, for Chrissake, or keel over quietly into the ice in the hold – and when you shake them awake they'll deny it and say they were *talking to you*! Aye, but I've noticed, once in your bunk, somehow you know it's dreams, and that's a fact, so it's important, it's important to get to your bed and to lie down, even if you've only got the fifteen minutes, and then, once you're in ya bed, there again, they're *dreams* – but when you're knackered right out and you fall asleep at your job or in the galley here: after a week or two of no-sleep, that's right: *you think you're talking* . . . So don't you worry . . . *You think we weren't frightened?* The first time it happened? When you haven't the nerve to tell anyone? Because they're all older than you and serious men and you'll be thinking: "If I tell *them* about this they'll know I'm a nutter and they'll kick me off the boat when we land in Stromness and I'll never get another job for the rest of my life." Aye – but one time you *do* tell them, right here in the galley, like as not, *because you can't stand it a moment longer*, and you've become afraid of *everything* – and they *laugh*, all of them, and you realize there's nothing special about *you*, you've no need to worry, and that's great, that is, and so you become a trawlerman . . .

'But I tell you, Redmond, *you're* weird, you really are, because you'll talk to anyone about anything, I've watched it happen: you've no sense of measure, what's the word? *Restraint*, that's it: you've no sense of restraint. So it's important, this, if you want the truth of things, because it's way under half of would-be trawlermen who last more than the first few trips – even, as I say, even if they've been trained in Captain Sutherland's nautical school in Stromness – and why? The sea? The weather in January? No, *that can't be it*, because they sign on at all times of year, no: it's the no-sleep, it's the *fright*, it's the terror, even, if you will (and who can tell how scared another man *really* is?), the way they can't adjust to live with madness, even mild madness, for a week or two, three weeks at the most. *That's* why they'll do anything to try and find a job ashore . . . They don't like that Viking place, you know, open ships, no shelter, no sleep – the place that made Viking culture and myths and the world-tree, Yggdrasill! The witchcraft and trolls and the little Orkney and Shetland people in their burial mounds, like Robbie, *the only bullshit that I really like . . .*'

Robbie said: '*But Redmond, listen to me, your friend, Robbie . . .*'

Bryan's big Viking bass drowned him out in easy waves of deep sound: 'You'll get used to it, no your next trip, mebbe no your next twenty, but after that, aye, then you'll know when you're no talking, you'll know when you're *dreaming*.'

Robbie leant right across the table, intense, and he said, in a powerful whisper, 6 inches from my left ear, 'Bryan *talking*, aye, he can and he does, but dinna listen no more, because he only talks, like, when there's extra food to be had – he's big and he burns it up and he needs it, aye! He's like a dog – a St Bernard, yep – that's our Bryan, he's big and fluffy, and he gets hungry and out comes his tongue . . . But Redmond, listen to me, all that guff, aye, it's waking-sleep, that's what we call it, but who cares? No, listen to your real friend, me, Robbie – you mustna mind Allan, it's *nothing* to do with you, but I saw, you got hurt inside, real bad like, and you lowered your head, *so slowly*, right into your plate, and you went to sleep: *to shut everything out.*

'So Allan Besant like,' said Robbie, sitting back, raising his voice, 'he came into this money, *lots of money*. And what does he do? Aye! He bought a house, cars. More than one car.' (Big Bryan, I noticed to my surprise, now looked so relaxed that he seemed to have lost his high-tensile giant status altogether. Big Bryan looked almost *floppy*. Yes, Big Bryan *did* look like a St Bernard lying massively in its warm corner, secure in the knowledge that another meal was on the way . . .) 'And he got married. And then, well, mebbe we'd all do the same, who can tell? He had all this money, so he was allowed to be just himself like, no restraints, as Captain Sutherland was forever telling us, every man needs *restraints*, and he hadna got them any more, no discipline – or as I'd put it meself, he'd got clean away from the fucking bother of mad skippers or anyone else, if you know what I mean, because Redmond, apart from Jason, you know – and I hate that, yep, that's the only one thing that's not right between you and me, you as a writer, and this your one chance, and you're trying to get it as much like it is as it *really* is, I can see *that*, yep, *you're busting your old balls to try and tell the truth!* Aye – we can all see that – it's so obvious, and it's questions, questions! And one in five of them, that's what we decided, mebbe one in five of them makes sense, and it sets us thinking – and when you're not around we discuss it, of course we do! And Jason and Bryan here' (we both glanced, on the instant, at Bryan – *and he was asleep*, so peaceful, massively wedged into his corner, his head upright, resting against the base of the bracket that supported the small platform for the video-machine, the screen – lovers and gangsters, inaudible – above him: his face had lost the anxious creases of a First Mate: asleep, but for his newly grown, his absurdly potent beard, I could imagine Big Bryan as a little boy . . .), 'Jason and Bryan think that writers, now and then, they *do* tell the real truth, you know, not like newspaper-truth (but Allan, well, he's a great guy – and I'll tell you – but he's sure that *no one ever tells the truth*). So Jason and Bryan like, they think that if you *do* write the book, and we all agreed, on the bridge like, that that was a chance of one in a hundred, like the fishing, because you're old and you don't have the life in you, and *oh shite*' . . . Robbie looked at me, *so* friendly, so apologetic . . . 'I shouldna said that, I shouldna said that in a hundred years . . . Anyway, if you do manage it like, and you tell the truth, and you've come out at the worst time of year, there's no denying that: then – we can give the book to our wives, women, our girls, whatever, that's the point, that's why Jason had you aboard, you know, aye, he wasna fooled by no shite about the Marine Lab in Aberdeen . . . So we can give the book, if you ever do it, whatever, to our women, you know, the one we really fancy, OK, fuck it, the one we *love*! Shite! Yep! But that's the way it is: you give this book to *the woman you love* – and she'll take it all in, and slowly, you know, for *weeks*, as she reads it, in silence, you

262

know, she says not a word, and you have to put up with that – when she's reading it, if she loves you enough to read it at all, if she loves you enough to bother to read a single fucking word of it – eh? Well, as Jason says, it's up to you, Redmond, isn't it? *Are we wasting our time with you?* Are you really just an Old Worzel? Eh? Or are you the whole ching-bang? Or even a peedie bit of a ching-bang? Can you get our women, *the ones we fucking love*, to understand what happens out here? Can you? Because we canna tell them ourselves, that's for sure, because they wouldna believe it – and no matter what, every last one of them seems to think that we *want* to be out here, that we *want* to be with the boys, whatever, or that we love the sea (we love the fucking sea!). So maybe your book, even if it's a piece'a shite, maybe she'll read it and understand a peedie bit and love us, and aye, maybe she'll let us sleep straight out for two days and nights when we get home – and *then* we'll have sex!'

'But Allan Besant,' I said, 'you know – you said I was not to be so wounded by, you know – by Allan Besant!'

'Yep! Yep! He's a great guy, but *you* need to understand about *him*. Or you'll take it personally, you will, because you're that kind of a Worzel. And you need protecting. But I tell you: all the times I've been to sea you ken the skippers, apart from Jason, they rip you off, they use you to get their money, so they make their money. You get a good percentage, most times, but it's no what the amount they're getting – they're getting a real good wage for you working for them, plus, like, as I said, all me pals ashore, in me car I'll run them here, I'll run them there, I'll be a real good friend to them, and because I'm a trawlerman, they think I'm rich, they'll ask me for money, and it's as if they're sure I've no earned it in the first place – and there's precious few amongst them, builders, farmers, butchers, there's precious few amongst them that will ever return that money – it's only yer mates at sea who ever remember a loan. Aye! I get stabbed in the back like . . . Yep – you give your friends money, even to help them over the night or something, small amounts, but even so you never see it again – because you're *rich*, you're a trawlerman! Aye, Redmond, sometimes it seems that all me life I've been used and abused, lots of times – and the women, well, mebbe it's my fault, not theirs, but they're the worst. Every woman I've ever bin with, apart from Angela, me first, and she was sensible, older than me, and we had a boy, my son, you could say, and he, well he's the light of my life! And you know what? I even *like* Angela's new man, aye, there's nothing wrong with him! But apart from that, as I say, every woman I've been with, the four I've been engaged to, every last one of them – she's done it to me.'

'Done what?'

'Gone with another fellah when I was at sea! You stupid? That's what happens – *the same for every trawlerman.*'

'But why? They can't wait?'

'Yep! I tell you – they can marry you for your car, that's what! Because they think you're rich. And they dinna mean any of it – one of them, I'll no name names, but when I was at sea she were brakkin the bed with the Stromness gravedigger! And I come home and mend the bed – and when we parted her dad blamed me for all of it, *because I was away at sea!*'

'But Allan Besant? You were telling me about Allan Besant . . . you said I shouldn't feel so bad . . .'

'Aye! Well – *he* got married, too, but then, you see, he was *really* rich, and it went to his head as it would to any of us, I'm sure of that, with the possible – no, forgive me, the *certain* exception of Bryan – aye! So then Allan Besant resumed his old ways, and dinna get me wrong, he's a grand guy, and it's only when he's drunk that you have to watch yourself – his eyes – you dinna know what he's thinking! And *that's* scary, it really is! So, as I say, he took lots of girlfriends, so he had to sell the house, and even the cars, and eventually he was out of money, he'd lost it all, so he had to go back to sea, to sign on with Jason, *so no wonder he's not like the rest of us . . .*'

'But heroes, the Victoria Cross – what was that about?'

'Aye, well, yep – I'll no name names, but that's what I *had* to tell you, to cheer you up, you old Worzel, I was forgetting, but aye, *that's what it was*: that's what I *had* to tell you, fast, because I need my sleep, you mind that – I'm away to ma bed – because I saw how cut-about, how wounded you were, and it wasna your fault – it was nothing to do with you!'

'Yes? You sure? Robbie?'

'Aye – dinna you worry – and I'll no name names, and it happens *all the time*, all the time with trawlermen, but Allan – and how do we know we wouldna do the same? You can only judge people like that, and that's what I think, that's my opinion – you can only judge if you're 100 per cent sure you wouldna do the same! Aye – so Allan, he's almost out of money, and he's living with his great best friend from childhood, who's a trawlerman *and a lifeboatman*. And this friend has a *very* beautiful wife and, fact is, in my experience, *all* best friends fancy each other's wives, just like they share most of their other interests – or they wouldna be best friends! Right? So – probably before he meant it – when his best friend's away at the fishing, or, more likely, when he's *called away at night on a shout* (women *really* hate that! They're insulted, like), Allan finds himself with his best friend's wife: and who's to judge? Who knows? Eh? Redmond? What if – and I know them well – what if the lifeboatman's bleeper went off when he was makkin love to his wife? Eh? And he answered the call and got to the launch? Eh? If you were a woman how'd *you* feel? Because those bleepers, you know, *you can turn them off* . . . So she's *very* angry, like, and *she goes to the lodger's room*. Aye! But it all came out; as *everything* does on Orkney; and this was a mess, such a mess: and she tries to kill herself several times, she slits her wrists; but Allan saves her, and it seems he really loves her now, and he cares, he lives with her – but who knows? It's no easy, life at sea. *It all depends on the woman at home.* But the point for you, Redmond, the reason I've stayed away from ma bed, it's this – *dinna mind what Allan says about life or lifeboatmen* . . . OK?'

And Robbie, nimble, a little Pict, so athletic, even now, in the middle of the night, or the black dawn, or whatever it was, got to his small feet, and disappeared.

And I myself, I thought, trying to stand up (and oh god, of course, once again, I have cramp down my left thigh, and my ankles – *where the hell are they?* They've gone absent without leave *again*: they've gone walkies to somewhere more interesting . . .) *'I must get to my bunk,'* I said to myself. But as I couldn't move, I sat there, massaging my legs . . .

Big Bryan, surprisingly, woke up. (And the worst part of myself said to itself: was he ever asleep?) Big Bryan, sleep free and succinct, said: 'Aye, Redmond, I was having a *dream*, you know, about Allan Besant – and I can tell you, in my dream, on his next boat out, he was completely changed, a different man. It's odd how it takes us, isn't it? Because, on his next boat out, he had to be the *best*, but the best at *everything* – so he was gutting so fast he left half the guts in; and in the hold, right there with the ice all round him, he'd only wear a T-shirt; oh yes, as you writers say, *he was punishing himself,* or not, or he'd gone mad, or not . . . But you know what I think? I think that all that time, with all that money (*so he really could*), Allan Besant, like Luke perhaps, but then I dinna know Luke, *Allan Besant was looking for the ideal woman* – aye, and such a focking *big* mistake, an outsize mistake, the ideal woman! I've seen it so often, all the young deckhands, the deckies, but never on *that* scale, never the same search *backed with so much money* – no, never the ideal bullshit pursued to ruin like that, if you excuse me. Because of course it's bullshit! The ideal anything is *always* bullshit! And if you go after it, in religion or politics or love or what the fuck – the *result*, it's always the same: you destroy yourself; and, *far more important*, you shit on the lives of everyone around you. Isn't that right? People like you – they're meant to know about such things, aren't they? The Ideal Woman! Such bullshit! If only these young guys would realize – but it's not *my* place to tell them, so I don't – but if only they'd realize that all you have to do is find someone, *anyone*, that you like to talk to, to get drunk with, *to be with*: that's all: it's so simple: that's it!'

'Yes! Yes!'

'Aye,' said Bryan, 'I'm glad you agree – and that's a fact!' He leant towards me, half off his bench. 'But . . . aye, dinna get me wrong . . . those pork chops? You and Luke – I couldna help but notice . . . You had the one each? So would you object, as it were – would you *object* if I took those unwanted second chops from the both of you? Just asking you, mind . . .'

'Please do!' I said, with absurd emphasis, because it was such an unexpected pleasure, such a kick to be able to do *anything* for Big Bryan. 'Help yourself! Eat all you can – you deserve it.'

'Thank you,' said Bryan, formal. 'I appreciate it.' And he re-inhabited his muscles, he moved himself, tight and massive, to the stove.

And hey – he brought me, round the partition, he brought me a *huge* bowl (OK: so all the bowls were huge), a bowl of Jerry's vegetable soup, and he set it gently in front of me, and he produced a spoon from his trouser pocket and he said (I took the spoon): 'You're an odd one you are, and no mistake. But you'll do, I suppose.' And without a word, true companions, we began to eat. And even I, an old man with very few taste buds and a very limited experience of soups that had not come (their contents freshly and specially annihilated for your exquisite pleasure, as the labels always say) from a tin or a packet – even I could tell that this soup was the kind of soup that you'd get given (the super-sexy waitresses all fanning you, gently, with their little fluffy golden centre-spread wings) in paradise, if only such a thing existed . . .

'So Bryan,' I said, after ten or so unbelieving slurped mouthfuls of small-boy delight (and it's a soup!), 'how come you're a trawler-man? Is that what you wanted – as a boy?'

Bryan, happy as he ate, I could see, would have been yet happier if, for this one half-hour, say, he'd been allowed to eat in peace. And I understood, of course I did, because I myself, when it comes to a meal you need, or something special: a small piece of a fillet of a hunted roe-deer that you're now roasting in the entrance to the family cave, say – well, you want to take it off to a darkish safe corner, don't you? You want to eat it, to enjoy it, mouthful by bolted mouthful, *in complete privacy*, like a dog.

Bryan, resigned to this questions-business, the tiresome Worzel-factor (and after all, I just *knew* he was thinking: it's only for the one trip, the one landing – otherwise we would, we really would, we'd *have* to do something to stop it); Bryan said, in slow bursts, between huge, slow mouthfuls: 'Aye, Orkney. I was brought up in Orkney, Stromness. And I'd set my sights, you might say, on the Merchant Navy. Aye! The big ships! The really big, the *beautiful* ships!' A long, a chewing, a contemplative pause, and then: 'So I did my O levels in navigation and seamanship – you can do O levels like that, you know, in Orkney and Shetland.' He looked at his warm and welcoming, his friendly plate – and not once at me. 'And I did well, because I enjoyed it, because it's in the blood, and so I went to Captain Sutherland's *great*, in my opinion, nautical school, Stromness.'

'And after that?'

Bryan took his time, so very calm, so at-ease-with-himself, the only man on board who really was all-of-a-piece, right through, and besides, there was half a chop to go, and still warm. And the clapshot, too, of course, the mashed turnip and potato and lashings of butter and a little salt and pepper, but that wasn't so important, not at all . . . And he said: 'Why the fuck don't you eat your soup?'

So I did.

And when I'd finished (how did something so comparatively simple, you know, *food* – how did *that* make one feel such a different person? So happy and so confident all of a sudden?) I said: 'And after that?'

'After that?' he said, well settled. 'After that – I discovered that the British Merchant Navy, the fleet that no long ago was the best

268

and the biggest, by far, in the whole fucking world, and that's a fact
– guess what? It had ceased to exist! That's what! *There were no jobs!*
So I went to the creels, the lobster-pots, the crab-pots, and I have
to say I loved that – but it's no much of a job for a young man who
wants to be away to sea, to the deep sea, is it? So I took a chance,
Redmond, and I joined a trawler – and my mother never forgave
me, that's what I suspect, because it's no like the Merchant Navy.
No. Not at all. She's right. Because it's fucking dangerous and crazy
for half the year – and for the whole year it's no secure and you
don't get a salary and you have to take your chance – but you know
what? I'm happy with it!'

'You *are*? Because you'll be a skipper one day?'

'*Fuck no*, Worzel! And *sorry*, but how would *you* say that politely?
Eh? *Absolutely not*. Yes that's it: absolutely not, *old bean*.' Big Bryan's
red-tired eyes went bright, and twinkly. Yes, I could see, he liked
that, the *old bean* . . .

'To be a skipper? No – hell on earth, that's what *that* is. And if
you don't believe in eternal life – aye, and most skippers *do* – but I
don't, really don't: then why spend your one chance of life here,
at sea, *and on earth ashore* (because you'll no forget your debts, even
ashore): why spend the one chance of life you've got *in hell*? Why?
No – *never* be a skipper. That's what I think. *Let someone else worry.*'

'So what do you mean – *you're happy with it?*'

'Worzel – I thought you were supposed to be a writer, you
know, someone who *thinks* about these things, the stuff the rest of
us don't have time for, *emotions*, all that, guts and offal really, isn't
it? But I agree, and Jason says so too – you're a dead man without
your own guts and offal . . . Yes, that's what we said to each other
about you, and don't get me wrong, because Jason and I and
Robbie – we're pleased you're aboard, we really are, though one
of the boys isn't, really not, but Jason said, in the galley, right here,
only a few days out, when you were still throwing up and before
we knew that you'd actually join in, and try and *help*, when we all
assumed you'd just stay in your bunk or simply ponce about with

a notebook or whatever and *observe* us, like in a fucking zoo, Jason says, "Boys!" he says. "Look at it like this, Luke's a prize, a worker, the best you'll see, and boys – we have him for nothing and he guts as fast as any of you and, compared to him, you're *fucking ignorant peasants*, aren't you? When it comes to fish – and, *fact* is, we're all supposed to know about fish – that Luke knows the lot! But Redmond, yes, he's old and for now he's sick, but he's paying us £50 a day and he *doesn't have to do that*, so he knows he's no good, and that's something to respect in a man, and besides – he's official, he's an Honorary Member of our Marine Lab in Aberdeen and he's Luke's assistant, so if he gets drowned or injured, as he surely will, that's not our problem, *we're not liable*, no, that's for his boss, that's for the lab in Aberdeen!" And then Jason says – and I can't remember if Luke's there or no, but aye, he *can't've* been – Jason says, "Besides, boys!" he says. "Whatever the fuck, that's what, to have a Redmond aboard, I've never heard of it happening to any other skipper, ever. So just enjoy it while it lasts, whatever he does, because you'll never go to sea again with anything as weird as this – I can promise you!"

'And Allan says: "Thank God for that!" And we all laugh. And Jason says: 'Besides, he's not *normal*, is he? Because he's *already* been banned from every bar and hotel in Stromness!' And Allan says: "Thank God for that!" And then we *really* laugh – even Dougie laughs!

'And in fact, Redmond, I can tell you, I'm thirty-three, and I've been at sea a *very* long time, and I can tell you, as honest as I sit here, with you aboard, not one of us – and even old Dougie got talking – not one of us, no, *we've never had such laughs!*'

'Oh yes?' I said, *very* huffy.

'Aye! But Allan – you shouldna let him upset you, because he doesna mean it . . . And he has problems of his own, you know, and I really like him, and he said, "*Thank God for that!*"' (And Bryan laughed again: Boom! Boom!)

'Yeah – *you just told me!*'

'So look at it this way – he must like you, or he'd no have given you a nickname, aye! *Worzel!* Just right! Because you'll no be giving nicknames to people you don't think about – and if you don't believe me, consider this: in Orkney we call the Shetlanders *Shelties*. But what do the Shetlanders call us? Answer: they *don't*, because we're to the south of them so they'll no be giving us a thought!'

'So what did you mean? Happy? You said you were *happy* with life on a trawler . . .'

'Happy?' said Bryan, and he laughed, a kindly run-of-the-mill laugh, not a caught-out helpless boom like a bittern in a marsh. 'Happy? Can't you see? Of course I'm happy! Because that's what I was *saying*. You a writer who knows about these things – emotions – or a dumbo, or what? I'm happy because *I have a woman at home that I love and trust*. I have three children, two of hers, a gift to me, as it were, and one of ours – and I love her, and I like to think that she loves me, but Redmond, *Mister Writer-Man*, I'll tell you for nothing: you take that love for granted, and you, *as a whole man*, you're finished! And that's a fact! Because you'll get divorced – and after that, Worzel, all your memories, the places in your mind where you used to go, when the weather comes, you understand me, the places that you used to visit to get away and get happy, those safe places – *and they never fail you*, because they're only there in your own mind – well, you get divorced, and I've talked to lots of my mates, friends, colleagues, whatever you'd say, you know, trawlermen who *had* to get divorced, because she'd deceived them when they were at the fishing, and that's right, you think you're OK, you'll tough it out, and like as not you have this *new* young woman, so sexy – but guess what? Next time, next year, January, like this, *when the weather comes* – you find yourself trying to get back to those places, those memories that made you happy, but you can't! You can't get there! No! That's what they say! And myself – I can imagine it – the *worst* thing in a man's life, really: because what could be worse than that? You drown? Simple. You get cancer? Sure. But this – *at least half of it*: you *must* have done it

271

to yourself! And aye, you're away at the fishing, and you're on your own out here really, and no one cares back home, apart from your new young wife (and who knows what *she's* up to?) – aye, so you go where you always used to go to get your comfort and be a man, to your happiest memories, and – guess what? You can't get there! Not at all! There's a black knot that you can't untie, no one could. Because, how can I put it to you, Worzel, an old man who knows sod all? I know! Aye! Of course! Aye – it's like the trawl-doors, the otter-boards (what did Robbie say you called them? Search me. I've forgotten – and anyway, it wasn't *funny*, not like the car tyres, the rock-hoppers . . .); it's like they're crossed, they're locked, *they've been flipped right across and over each other by the cold deep-sea*, the currents up here that flow so fast and cold beneath the warm surface North Atlantic drift that keeps us all alive! So – your old love, it's gone cold, and your memories have frozen under pressure, with it, and you, *you'll never get them back*: they're miles down, and cold and gone, but you, Worzel, of course, you're doing your best, but from that moment, really, you know yourself, you're half-a-man, you're waiting, that's all, *you're waiting for death.*'

'You hadn't told me about your wife,' I said, glum, not sure if he had or not. 'You never told me!'

'Of course I did!' said Bryan, bouncy. 'But don't you worry, Worzel. It's obvious – you've got this thing called Alzheimer's. It happens to everyone over fifty! But don't you worry, old Worzel, because that's great, that is, it means you can ask any old person a question, and it's private, it really *is* confidential, because you can be as sure as the Merry Dancers, the Northern Lights, you can be sure that the ancient in question won't remember a damn thing of the question in the morning . . . And nowadays, of course, on Orkney, things are different, there's food and healthcare and such, so we have quite a few old people like you, and we all agree, in the Flattie and the Royal and the bars like – you need to catch them, you must hook them (if you want the *real* truth that they'll forget in forty-eight hours) just as Alzheimer's is *beginning*, like with you: because if you wait too long, and their memory's now down from forty-eight hours to twenty-four to eight to half an hour, to half a minute, you've had it! You might just as well go ask your question late at night of an incoming mermaid on the shore, or one of the little people, like Robbie, squatting on a burial mound – or the other Robbie, Robbie Mowat, beaten to bits, because I was no there to protect him, lying on the cobbles outside the Royal Hotel!'

'So you're happy – because you're in love? But, *far more important*, you're happy because you somehow know that *she's in love with you?*'

'Aye! I told you! And hey, Worzel – there's this thing called the *Mission to Seamen*: and they *must* run Old People's Homes, and now you've been on the *Norlantean*, K508 (*remember your registration number*), I'll bet you'd qualify!'

'Thanks,' I said, glummer still.

'But Redmond, there *is* something I'd like to ask you, to talk to you about . . .' And Bryan's voice lost its volume, it deserted its big hold on life so drastically, in fact, that it became almost a whisper, or as much of a whisper as a voice like that could reach: 'Redmond, joking apart, I do have one worry . . .'

And in order to catch the words I edged myself surreptitiously along the bench-seat, to my right, across Luke's habitual place, to its end, at the narrow passage-way down the galley, between the tables – and to cross *that*, the crudest common-sense told me, would be to stop Bryan talking altogether, to disrupt the pathways in his brain, to send him, obscurely outraged, to his bunk.

'You do?'

'Aye – it's simple, but it's difficult to deal with, to know what to do – it's this: I *really* love my wife, you know, I *adore* her, or whatever the right word would be, she keeps me going when I'm away at sea, *the thought of her*, all of her, you know what I mean, it fills my head, *so I can do any job*: any boring old job that goes on for ever, like stacking in the hold, well, that's simple, I just take it slow,

273

and I remember every detail, every moment of our life together, all the private moments, and don't get me wrong – don't be a male jerk – I don't just mean the sex, though that's *great*, no, it's odd, isn't it? It's not the memories of sex that keep me going, no, I find all that *difficult* to remember, as it happens, so maybe I'm not normal, perhaps there's something wrong with me? And maybe, you, you know, as a wise old man, maybe you'd do me the kindness of *telling* me, if you think that that's the case . . .'

Stupefied, unprepared, out of my depth (Big Bryan – *he was talking so quietly*), I couldn't think of a thing to say, not for the moment, and the truth is, well, I wanted to *cry* . . . But you must *not* do that, and besides, my mother used to beat me, with the flat of her hairbrush, every time I did . . .

'No – when I'm down there in the hold (and aye – you've *got* to come down there, too, next haul, or you'll never be able to tell yourself that you've even been a junior apprentice, a baby-trawlerman – oh no!) – when I'm down there, stacking, for hours and hours, and it's so cold you canna feel your hands, it's times like that when I start at the beginning, right at the beginning of our life together, from when I first met her, and *of course* I think of her body and all the sex, but it's odd, it's not really that at all, not at all, no, it's her *face*, and her laugh, and the life that's in her, as you'd say yourself, and the things she says to me and even now, you know, years later, she *surprises* me, and I laugh!'

'Aye!' I said, my face in my hands. 'Bryan, you . . .'

'Yes!' said Bryan. 'I knew you'd understand, but you *don't*, really, *not at all*. No – you see, whenever I get home – and I go straight home, I can't be doing with all this drinking the boys do first: *I tell her*, it all comes out, I can't help it, I know I shouldn't, *but I can't help it*: I make a right fool of myself, every time, and first, *I'm so glad she's still alive*, and second, aye, and it *is* second, but it's the kind of second that anywhere else would be a first, if you catch my meaning, well, I let her know, and no mistake, and that's a fact, and I can't help it: every time I tell her, and every time I think I *mustna* do this ever again because it's no manly and she canna like it, and I tell her how much I fucking love her, and how I've been thinking of her at the power-block or at the net at the stern-ramp or bored shitless at night-watch in the wheelhouse or stacking, like I say, in the hold . . . And then I take the kids in my arms, and I stink of fish, of course I do, *I really smell*, but they dinna seem to mind, and mebbe they really love me, *mebbe they do* . . . but who can tell? How do you know when you're away all the time? And my wife, and I'm her *second* husband, you know, so maybe she really *did* choose me and mean it, what do you think? She says, every time, "Bryan," she says, "you big soft stupid love-bag, *go to sleep. Bryan, stop it*: you're going to your bed, *right now*, and you're to sleep for a day and a night and a day – and I'll be there, too, for some of the time, but you'll be none the wiser, but Bryan: when you wake up, after a day and a night and a day" (*that's* what she says! Every time), "then it'll be *our* bed again, and we'll have fun, and we'll get up and go out and *we'll do things together . . .*" '

'Jesus! But isn't that happiness, *real happiness*, the most any man could *ever* expect?'

'No! It's not! At least – it might be. But how do you make sure it goes on *for ever*? *As a man* – how the hell do you do that? And it was Allan Besant, or someone, no, mebbe it wasn't him, but someone told me, around six months ago, to look up a word, in a dictionary from *your* town, as it happens, yes – in the focking Oxford dictionary, and the word was *uxorious*, and whoever it was, he told me to look it up, in passing like, *because that word was me* – and this *horrible* word, a really nasty little bit of stinking dogshit, this word, it means: to be *excessively fond of your wife*. So my question to you, from Oxford, my question to you is this: is it possible? What if I love her too much, or rather, what if I let her know I love her too much? And it's a fact, but I can't help it, I told you, when I'm at sea, I'll go anywhere, do anything, it doesn't bother me, however bad it gets – and I'm sorry Worzel, I know how you feel, and I'm sorry to disappoint you, but the truth is it *can* get a very little worse,

OK, let's be honest, a fuck-sight worse than the Force 12 we've had this January – and all the time, in a hurricane, aye, sure, a junior hurricane, I'll be going through, in my mind, the beginning of our life together. And you know what? I've done no more than the first three months – and it comes to me, I realize, the hurricane's gone, the storm's over, and everyone's panicked, and I've hardly noticed – and now it's calm. So how do I tell *her* that? Or should I? Is that *uxorious*? This word, Worzel, you, as a writer, uxorious, this *foul word*: do you think, you as a writer, do you think that when I get home and like the rest of us I've had no sleep and so *I say things*: and I tell her (every time, and it's got *worse* over the years), I tell her how much I love her, and I really mean it, so I'm almost in tears, OK, I tell a lie, *I'm always in tears*. I'm so pleased to see her, and the *babies*, well, the children, they're getting big now – *uxorious*: so do you think they secretly hate it? Eh? Now you know the truth – do *you* think I'm uxorious? Do you? Is that why they send me to bed straight away and no mistake?'

'No! You've got it all wrong – uxorious, my arse!' And then, deeply disturbed, all the same, I said: 'You big fucking furry Viking!' which helped me, but not him, to get things in perspective. 'No, no – with your job, you can't be uxorious, that's a word that describes bust-up depressive frightened little husbands who've enclosed themselves in the home, just like the males attached to female deep-sea angler-fish – and believe me, baby' (I'd called Big Bryan *baby*?), 'I know all about that: but you, *you're not a case in point*, far from it. As far as you're concerned, with this one love of yours, I can tell you, there's no such thing as *excessive* love: as far as I can remember, which is not very far, no, there's no case in the entire literary history of the world – the history of the emotions – there's not a single case in which a woman, faced with a genuine, outsize hero, a real alpha male, thinks: "This man loves me too much!" Excessive love – for them – there's no such thing . . . She sends you off to sleep because she loves you, she really loves you, and so she can imagine this hell, let's be honest, this hard and sleepless hell you go through every time you're at sea – and in what other job could you find routine conditions like this? Eh? Not even in the SAS!'

Bryan got to his feet, jerky, like an automaton, a robot – as if he'd received a signal, a small electric shock. It was obvious that I'd been no help at all – and that this deep problem, this male problem of his, which had at first seemed so laughable: no, it was real, and he'd probably carry it with him, secretly, for the rest of his life; a jagged spiky fragment of ice from the hold – in a domesticity that should have been as warm and constant as happiness can get . . . And the little piece of ice-spikes, refusing to melt, would say to him: 'If you think of your wife for the greater part of each working day and night at sea; if you adore her like you do; and, worst of all: if you can't help but *tell her so* every time you get back ashore sleepless, half-mad, semi-hysterical, like a woman in distress – then you'll lose her. She can't love that kind of a man . . . Nobody could . . . And you realize what that means, don't you? Oh yes! You'll lose your children too! And all because you're a trawlerman . . .

Back in the cabin, making my slow, delicious way to the bunk (hang on to every upright: take it easy: you'll get there: paradise awaits), I realized that Luke's blue sleeping-bag, dim in the light from the door, the passage-way, was occupied: there was a small and thin, a most insubstantial something slotted into three-quarters of the length of that blue tube – it could only be Luke himself. For once – Luke had gone to his bunk before me!

So, of course, forgetting that Luke, like Sean, and unlike me, had probably had no rest for forty hours, I felt superior, so superior – and a thoroughly irritating and untrue saying of my childhood came back to me: 'Early to bed, early to rise, makes a man healthy, wealthy and wise!' Yes, that's right, Rosie-bud used to say that to me when I was little, and I'd watched *The Lone Ranger* on the very first of televisions, and she couldn't get me to bed – *I didn't want to sleep?* Could I ever recapture *that* piece of childhood? No! Never! That bit, well, that really had gone, and here, right here, was my snuggly green nylon parachute-silk soft womb-lining sleeping-bag . . . So I got into it, in at the lips, an effort, because the base of the top bunk, with its felt-tip portrait of the leering trawlerman, it was *so* tight-down on my space, but eventually I worked myself in and

278

down to a line, a dead-line of that flat-out unconscious which the Bantu of the Congo call dead-for-a-time, as opposed to that worst of states, dead-for-ever.

But the dead-for-a-time would not come: although the *Norlantean* out there (even I could tell), she'd relaxed, she knew she could cope with this Force 8 gusting 9 or thereabouts, her rhythms were regular, predictable. Yes, I thought, I feel secure at last, as if I was wrapped about in the amniotic fluid of a *reasonable* uterus, safe in the womb of some prehistoric mother who was doing nothing more unusual than, say, run for her life from a sabre-tooth tiger: swing/slosh/swing/port to starboard, starboard to port . . . Or, more accurate, perhaps she was in the Congo forest and climbing up, with deliberation, but as fast as she could, to get to those thin, those topmost branches, swing, dip, rise, reach and lurch, left, right, up, quick — with nothing worse than an ordinary leopard clawing at the bark behind her . . .

I felt inexplicably energized and chirpy and so, yes, I thought, I really must have had an instant sleep head-down on the galley table, but no, there was no doubt about it, I really had *not* had enough sleep to reach that most advanced stage in our emotional evolution, that moment when we become fully social, fully sympathetic to the needs of other people . . . And Luke, it was obvious, he was *pretending* to be asleep, his exaggerated, regular breathing, his pathetic attempt at a snore — it was insulting, he was an amateur actor . . .

'Luke!' I said, good and loud. 'Knock it off! Because you don't fool me — you're pretending to sleep!'

'No!' said Luke (a thrash of legs in the blue tube). 'No! I'm *not* pretending! I want to sleep. *I want to sleep so badly.* But I can't, I just can't!' (His voice faded, he sounded more miserable than I'd ever heard him.) 'No, I can't — because I've been lying here, I'm worrying, Redmond, I am so *fucked up* and not even a big shaggy joke of well-meaning friendship like you can help me. No. Because I am so alone. I'm in a panic. A work-panic. And once it happens and it gets going you can't stop it – and you, how could *you* ever understand? It's horrible, you know, my doctorate – *the deadline!* It's out there waiting for me, in the near future, and so of course it poisons the present – and when I feel like this, well, I tell you, each smack of a wave on the hull, you know what it says to me? There goes another batch of seconds, time going away from you, time that you should be spending on your doctorate – and in Fittie, in Aberdeen, you know, in my cottage, it's worse, far worse, because there I am at my little desk, and the sea's outside, but I can still hear the traffic on the road, you know, the road along the coast, and I can take *that*, more or less: no, it's the high-pitched scream, you know, the *wheeeee!* The female scream of mopeds flat-out, the 50cc or 100cc motorbikes . . . The banshee wail! Yes – and every time I hear that female scream I think, Luke, *forget it,* this doctorate, because *you'll never meet the deadline,* there is *so much* data to process, so give up right now, go on: do the rational thing – kill yourself! *Drown yourself.'*

'Come on, Luke – listen to me, I *can* comfort you, you're forgetting, I did a doctorate too, and I'm sure I felt worse than you do, but I've scrubbed all that from my memory, so it must've been bad, because I can remember just about *everything* else in my life – so, well, hey, Luke, if you're *serious,* and if your university can *see* you're serious, *committed,* half mad with the excitement of it all: then, *pow!* They give you *extensions.* Yes – up to a maximum of seven years for students who really *do* seem to be on to something, students like you, Luke, and guess what? *My doctorate took me seven years!'*

'*Seven years?* Worzel? Please! *No!'*

'OK, Luke, forget it!' (His curly head was now way out of its protective-casing Caddis-fly-larva pond-safe sleeping-bag – and here it comes! Yes! An arm! He'd propped his head on his left arm. *I* had his attention: so he was lost to healing sleep.) 'There's something I've been thinking about – there's a bargain I want to strike with you, man to man.'

'There is?'

'Yes, Luke, *there is*. Because your knowledge, you see, it's *already* so very precious, so valuable; so, on the whole, I *don't* think you ought to drown yourself, or, at least (I don't want to intrude) *not yet*. Because you promised – oh yes you did! *You really did* – you promised to tell me about the Wyville Thomson Ridge, you bastard! And Sperm whales! And copepods! Oh yes you did! *You got me all interested* – and then you ponced off, and said you'd tell me later, and you went silent!'

'I *didn't* ponce off! We had work to do – and besides, I'm human, you know, I get *exhausted* . . . and aye, fuck you! Excuse me . . . But *teaching*: that's the most exhausting thing there is . . .'

'OK! Maybe – but I'm old enough to be your fucking legitimate father, well-married, Luke, and I tell you – you promised me! So *here*, look, here's the bargain (because I can sense it, you're not going to tell me for free) – I'll enlighten you, I'll let you into the secret of a powerful Congo sex-charm that's never been known to fail . . . and in return you'll tell me about the history of the Wyville Thomson ridge . . . And then, *if I'm satisfied*, I'll solve your entire sexual-selection problem for you: I'll tell you *exactly* who you need to marry, the one woman you must seek out and capture and settle down with, for ever. The one woman who'll give you children and stay with you, always. And, for that, you'll fucking well go right ahead and tell me about the deep-sea dives of Sperm whales, as you promised!'

'Nuts!' said Luke, with doctorate-forgetting enthusiasm. 'A sex-charm! Bollocks!'

'No, no – no bollocks. Bollocks don't come into it, *not until much later*. You see, *imagine* it, you're a young woman in a northern Congo village (the only bit I really do know a little about), and you've fallen (goodbye to good sense), you've fallen sleep-wipingly in love with a young man in your village – you know *all* about him, his feats as a warrior, a hunter, his muscles, his sweat, his rhythm as he plays the Great Drum, and besides, he's so strong he's cleared almost twice as much of a forest-plot for a five-year plantation as his nearest rival in your affections, and besides, because he's such an alpha male, and all the other young women are after him (and how!), he's no time *to settle down*, as you call it, and why should he? Or, at least, *not yet*. But you – you have other ideas – but it takes foresight, patience, determination, real planning (which, biologically speaking, in fact makes you his ideal mate): and so what do you do? Well, it costs. Because there *are* only five iron knives in this village – and to borrow one of them for a night, *in secret*, that's three chickens. And *you*, of course not: *you* can't afford three chickens; so you have to tell your mum and dad, and they think you're crazy, because that young man, well, he's already a young Big Man, and you're aiming too high, but all the same – maybe! So they part with three whole chickens (and how that hurts!) and you get your piece of iron, the enabler, the knife, you get it, in secret – for one night! And what do you do? Well – your dad, he takes you, once it's really dark, to the fetish-house, where you take a scraping of clay from the inside of the upturned skull of your grandad, or great-grandad – or, let's face it, if you're of a lower lineage, your ancestral skulls filled with clay (they'll be hidden in your own family hut) . . . Anyway, with that magic piece of iron you take a scoop of forefather clay. And you smear it into a tiny pot, kept for the purpose; and then your dad, relieved (he really does not like this kind of thing, and besides, he's lost three chickens), he goes to his bed, and 'Daughters!' he sighs to himself, and turns over on his palm-leaves, and tries to forget everything. And you – feverish (how you love and want that boy!) – very slowly you scrape the hairs on your armpits; and with your fingers you squeeze the sweat off the knife and knead it into the clay; and when you're satisfied there's no more moisture to be had you do the same with your pubic hairs. And then Luke – this is the important bit! What next? Can you guess? No? OK – and remember, you *really* want this young man, you want him so *very* badly, so what do you do next? Eh? No idea? Well – I'll tell you: you scrape the skin, the gunge between your toes and the calluses along the ball and heel of the flat of your feet – very carefully, and you shred the scrape and the peelings into the clay and you hope, fervently, that you haven't been and gone and washed too thoroughly in the river lately, that you haven't already washed the magic away . . .'

Luke said: 'So what? *You're mad.*'

'Mad? Is that what you think? Well thank you, Uncle Luke, Mr Bullough – but no, as it happens. And don't interrupt – because all her intimate pheromones, her sex-smells, chemicals, subconscious molecules of sexual desire, they're now embedded in that tiny pot of clay . . . And she leaves it out to dry in the fierce sun on the baked mud away from the forest trees . . . And then she rubs it away into a fine powder, in batches, folded tight in leaves. And her mother – it's almost always the mother – she finds a way to drop that powder into the young man's palm-wine. And if she misses the first time, and some boy nonentity drinks it, and *he* falls in love, well, bad luck, mistakes happen, but eventually (she's got at least ten little leaf-packets) the mother (she loves her daughter) – she gets it *just right*. And the young alpha male drinks his palm-wine, the hooks of passion. And a day or two later the mother *tells* that young man what she's done: and then, for her daughter, *poompf!* There's such love – such *love-making!*'

'Bollocks! Suggestion! That's all that is – suggestion!'

'Oh yes? You sure? Then – consider this – *why* do you think I thought that so very interesting in the first place? The moment that Nzé told me about it in the Congo? Eh? Because I remembered a perfectly rational, a *Western* experiment conducted at Berkeley or some such – the researchers took over a local cinema for a week, and they told their psychology students that they'd all been working too hard, they needed a break – so hey! They were going to watch classic films for a week, to teach them about relationships (and yes, you can be sure of it – the poor suckers had to write *essays* on these films, but there again – what a privilege!) . . . Aye, as you'd say, but there was another agenda – the researcher, their teacher, he or she

283

pre-sprayed fifty or so random seats in that cinema with a massive dose of female pheromones (gathered from hundreds of female armpits) when the fifty or so male students were to watch a film – yes, and you know? It worked – 100 per cent! Yes, the boys all sat ("Sure – I think I'll clock it from here, the far left front-seat. Why not?") *in those sprayed seats*. They were given half an hour to choose. It worked! 100 per cent! And likewise, two or three days later, with the girls, in the seats sprayed with male pheromones!'

'So what? You're off the wall!'

'Oh no, Luke, not in the least, because it seems I had a sleep at the galley table, so I *remember* the point of all this!'

'You do?' Luke sounded anxious.

'Yes, I really do! And it's this – good and strong!'

'Aye?'

'Aye – *really rotten fish*, you know yourself, it smells *exactly* like very old, *very old*, much used socks, socks that, through no fault of their own, you've walked in every day, for hundreds of miles . . . *They smell of rotten fish.* And our noses, even mine (which hardly works), they're so good, so primitive, *so sensitive* at detecting the tiniest amounts of pre-conscious or conscious molecules of interesting smells in the air . . . But they *can't* tell the difference between rotten fish and rotting feet. So there you go, Luke, when you get ashore, you can't help it, you're carrying a mimic of the human sex-pheromone in your skin and in your hair, in your clothes, all over you, the rotten-fish pong, the unwashed-foot-pong, and you, like every trawlerman – you're a nasal sex-bomb delivered direct to the most primitive part of her brain!'

Luke was silent for a moment – and that was *very* gratifying, because his head was still propped on his left arm, and he was attentive, yes, *he was certainly not asleep.* And when *that* happened, when young Uncle Luke was silent for a time after something that *I'd* said, OK – so this took place, I flattered myself, around one occasion in a hundred: it meant that *I'd* thrown *him*: that it was *me* who'd made *him* think.

'Aye, mebbe,' said Luke, reflective and slow (delicious!). 'Mebbe, just mebbe, you're *right* – because I forgot to tell you, about a recent so-called superstition I've come across. It's this: it's bad luck to wash before you come ashore . . . So how's that?'

'Gooaaal!'

And Luke shouted: 'Gooaaal!'

And that's called *male friendship* . . .

'OK – so you liked that, Luke, you costive arsehole. So you – now you *tell me* about the Wyville Thomson Ridge?'

'The Wyville Thomson Ridge?' said Luke, suddenly grudging, resentful. 'What's sexy about the Wyville Thomson Ridge?'

'Everything, Luke! Because when you reach my age you've done it all, or you think you have, and sometimes, just sometimes, there's nothing sexy even about the *thought* of sex, and in a way that's a gift to you; because knowledge, that *stays* sexy, learning things, about the way the great world really is: that's sexy! In fact, as D. H. Lawrence said (and I know, that does *not* seem likely, but all the same, I'm sure it was him) – he said that there comes a point in a man's life when he loses his *obsessive* interest in sex: and *pow!* What a release! You are *unshackled from a madman*. You can think! You can *enjoy* the life of the mind, unfettered. Yes – you can *wallow* in the discovery of the vast and complex history of our species, our genes, since life began, three-and-a-half-thousand million years ago!'

'Eh?'

'OK, Luke, I hear you, maybe he did not say that, but if he'd known, he *would* have done! So come on Luke, and, by the way, you must *stop* this intellectual prick-teasing, you really must! So – the Wyville Thomson Ridge? Yes? Now?'

Luke, bolshy, said: 'Well, I'm a little disappointed with you, Redmond' (Luke said that? Luke, I thought, he *must* become a Professor), 'because I've already told you about the Wyville Thomson Ridge. The great mountain range just off our northern coast, beneath the surface of the sea – the one and only barrier in the continuity of the deep oceans of the planet!'

'Yes, yes – but how was it discovered? You said that was one hell of a story and you promised, you promised to tell me!'

'OK, then, I will – but I warn you, Redmond, I warned you, I really did, I warned you: your question-time is almost over, because I can feel it coming on right enough . . . I've had a lot less sleep than you . . . Less sleep, in fact, than anyone except Jason . . . And my brain, for sure, big time! It's about to shut down, you know: and then I won't *want* to speak, *I won't be able to speak . . .*'

'But – Wyville Thomson?'

'Aye – he was a great man (even though he didn't believe in Darwin, in evolution by natural selection), Chief Scientist aboard the pioneering research ship *Challenger*, on her three-year marine biology voyage around the globe – 1873–76; 68,000 miles; around 4,500 new species discovered . . . All that's *really* famous . . . But very few people know, or even care, they don't bother to find out – they don't know that the whole future science of oceanography began right here, in UK waters! Just as geology began with UK rocks! And modern biology began with the voyage of the *Beagle* and Darwin writing his multiple doctorates about it, forgive me! In his house in Kent, in the UK!'

'Goaaal!' I yelled, but Luke did not respond. Crestfallen (Oarfish-flame-crest-flattened), I realized, horribly, that our days and nights of insane and wonderful play, a play of thoughts, perhaps . . . perhaps they really were almost over . . .

'Aye – Wyville Thomson. Well, there he was, in the research ship *Lightning* or *Porcupine*, I forget which, but on one of those summer expeditions, probably around 1868, and he took a series of temperatures (*not soundings*, you understand, *you must remember that*) right down from the surface to as far as they could reach in different stations in the Faeroe–Shetland channel. And guess what? As you'd say or I'd say, I forget which, and it doesn't matter, because I'm used to it – but you, you'll *panic*, tomorrow or the next day . . . Aye, at around 200 fathoms, as they said then, the temperatures were roughly equal at the south-west and north-east ends of the channel; but from 250 fathoms to 640 fathoms, in the north-east, they got readings of 34 degrees down to 30; whereas to the south-west, and so very close, the corresponding temperatures were 47 and 42 degrees Fahrenheit. But hang on – there were sod all, excuse me, other temperature readings from the oceans to compare those with in 1868 – no, nay, no, it was only after all his experience of checking thousands of thermometer readings across the oceans of the world, as Chief Scientific Officer (or whatever they called it then), as the Number One Oceanographer on *Challenger* that Wyville Thomson, re-checking those UK temperatures, *so near to home* (it had obviously *nagged* at him, even in the distant tropics, or my Antarctic, come to that), it was only *then* that he had the balls to predict that there was a real physical underwater mountain-range across the Faeroe–Shetland Channel . . .

'But it's great, it really is – one of those scientific stories where the right credit was given, almost at once, to the right person . . . The Hydrographer of the Admiralty (the things we owe the navy – remember the *Beagle*?), he sent the survey-ship HMS *Knight Errant* to check it out. And Thomson himself, who was paralysed from a stroke, was yet allowed to believe that he was directing operations, from Stornoway in the Outer Hebrides . . . And he lived just long enough to know that the soundings proved the weirdest thing: he was right! Here – and only here – a real break occurred in the deep sea. And he died, knowing that this vast unseen mountain would be called the Wyville Thomson Ridge!'

'Goaaal!' I yelled; but again, Luke did not respond.

'Aye – but he was dead before HMS *Triton* came back in 1882. And that's a small pity, because what the hell? He'd *done* it, hadn't he? *A great life*, despite being an anti-Darwinian twit? Don't you think? Anyway, the boys on board *Triton*, even with their primitive collecting gear, they caught around 220 species and varieties from the cold area, the deep, unsalty current from the Arctic ice-melt to the north; and around the same number from the warm North

Atlantic Drift to the south – and only fifty or so were common to both! So there you are: Ernst Mayr, as always, is *right*, and *he's* the man who reminded everyone in the twentieth century, stuck in their genetic labs, bean-bag genetics, genetic drift, bullshit! No – out there in the real world, for one species to break into several, you needed *a physical break*: geographical, spatial isolation: a climate change: a new desert, a new forest, a lowered lake-level that split into a thousand pounds before it rose again; a new rift valley opening up; a new great river course that divided populations of, say, chimpanzees . . . Or, *here we go* . . .' (Luke was now lying on his back in the semi-dark, as the *Norlantean* continued, but *so* gently, to go through her six degrees of freedom: a pitch, a roll, a sway, a heave, a surge, a yaw: and yes, that should be happiness, I thought, but I'd blown it, hadn't I? Luke, it was obvious, he was now in his *last* manic phase, and so were the rest of the crew, and from tomorrow or whenever, yes, he was right, I thought, yes, he's right, this Luke, because he's been through it all his working life, and so, from tomorrow, *no one will talk to me*. The talking phase of no-sleep is over – and you, you, Redmond, how come you *wasted*, how come you blew away *such* an opportunity by talking so much yourself? *So many* questions unasked? And all because *you couldn't stop talking yourself*? Yes, I thought, well, I've learnt, for the rest of my life I'll keep my mouth *shut*: I'll be a strong silent idiot male . . .) 'Aye . . . here we go . . . *Craaak!* A terrible cracking – as the block of land divides and the islands and continents are forced across the surface of the earth as new sea-floor is made at mid-ocean ridges and swallowed again in the deep ocean trenches. Even real geology only happens at sea! And *that* – that was only formulated by Dan McKenzie at Cambridge (and independently by Jason Morgan at Princeton) *in 1967*! But hey! Sorry! It wasn't really a *craaak*! Plate tectonics – and we know about it in such detail, we've got it mapped – ach, it happened as slowly as your fingernails grow . . . And aye, no one man or woman would have known about it, even if *Homo sapiens sapiens*, as you say, had been around at the time. But there again, Redmond! I'll bet – you still don't know about it, do you?'

'No!'

'I thought not! Because hey! *It's still going on* . . . Even as we speak . . . And I'll bet you don't know that England and Scotland really *are* different, do you?'

'What? Well . . .'

'No – because they both came north from round about the present-day Antarctic, but by different routes, because they were parts of different plates. And England nudged up against Scotland – and the buffer-zone, that, the soft rolling hills of the borders, that's the uplifted mud of the ancient floor of a shallow sea!'

'Great!'

'So the land and the people – they really are different!'

'The people? Come on, Luke – bullshit! The people? You romantic! People? There were no people – *they hadn't yet evolved!*'

'Aye,' said Luke, ignoring me, 'and do you remember all that bullshit nineteenth-century geology we were taught at school? The Old Red Sandstone rocks for example? So Great Britain (as we used to call it) must once have been a hot desert? And how it made no sense? So *any* schoolmaster, *every* geography schoolmaster might and should have had the simple idea: *Great Britain has moved*. But they didn't of course – but imagine! As you'd say – if they had: wouldn't *that* have made boring old geology interesting? OK, so it wasn't *that* boring, because it gave us *time* – thousands of millions of years. But imagine! If only it had also given us movement in geographical space! *Then* it would have been exciting, and made sense, and Ernst Mayr's *so right*: even to understand the emergence, the diversity of life, you need *geographical* change, spatial change, don't you? Because the Old Red Sandstone – *that was laid down when England was where the Sahara is now!*'

'Ernst Mayr?'

'Aye! And guess what? We're still moving, us, the UK – we're still going north: the land, you and me, *the whole ching-bang*, as

289

Robbie would say! Aye – so one day the Arctic really *will* be land, a continent, and Edinburgh will be at the North Pole . . . And Shetland, aye – Shetland will be well on the way towards New Zealand . . . But by then, of course, New Zealand will have moved . . .'

'Ernst Mayr? Hey Luke – *he* stayed with us too, you know (and yeah, yeah, only because of the *TLS*) but I think the old boy came because he knew he'd need a rest somewhere: he was over here from Harvard to be fêted by the Royal Society and given its gold medal for lifetime achievement in zoology, something like that, and he realized from my letters (he wrote such *wonderful* reviews for me at the *TLS*); he must have realized that I knew sod all about anything, but I sounded a friendly sort of a guy, so he thought that he could hide out with us, to recover from the flight, I suppose, and to take it easy before all the official prize-giving . . . So I went to Blackwell's bookshop and I bought *all* his books – and jeeez, Luke, like you with your UNESCO fish volumes, that was one hell of a sacrifice, because they're big books, and I've never been rich, you know, in fact I spend my life in debt, but I don't want to think about *that*: but yes, again like you, those books, like your UNESCO volumes, they're now so precious . . . Because he signed them all for me, he inscribed them, each one, and guess what? As we collectors say – I've *tipped* in his letters to me in all five volumes, I've stuck in his amazing long letters!'

I looked across at Luke (well of course I did), because in the normal or abnormal routine of things in this new life of mine on board this trawler, a way of life that had gone on for ever and would never cease, one of the constant pleasures had been Luke's sudden never-failing young-boy interest in the pioneering books of biology – and the heroes who had managed to write them . . . But now, no, now I wasn't even sure if Luke was listening . . . He was lying on his back staring at his plywood-ceiling, the base of the bunk above his head . . . And please, I thought, please don't let him start tinkering with that imaginary drawing of his, not again . . .

So with added emphasis I said to myself: this is Ernst Mayr, for Chrissake: this is Ernst Mayr I'm talking about – the guy who's given us so much pleasure, so much new ordered insight into the natural world . . . And if you don't believe me, Luke, *I wanted to say*, consider the concepts, the words that you use in your professional life every working day: they're all his: sympatric, allopatric, peripatric, founder population, sibling species . . . *But that was it*, that was all I could remember . . . The rest was a blank: a dark space of forgetfulness, with just a faint echo of the distant laugh of a hyena about to start the night-time hunt of the pack, a female, an alpha female, because all hyena-packs, as Hans Kruuk had told me long ago in Oxford (and he discovered it, and that's a fact, as Big Bryan would say), all hyena-packs are led by a dominant female, which is perhaps why they're so successful, so deadly at night: and in the morning the altogether more stupid lions arrive to finish off the remains of the hyena-kills, and the annoyed hyenas hang around the edges (lions are *big*) and make a lot of noise, and insult the lions, and trade gossip (*yack! yack!*) – so that's why all the previous male naturalists assumed that it was the hyenas who were always the scavengers . . . But Jeesus, where was I? Ernst Mayr! Yes – so I said out loud:

'Luke, Ernst Mayr! I didn't know it fully at the time, of course, and yeah, you're right, I had *not* read his books, but I *did* know about his Number One Contribution to the history of mid-twentieth-century biology . . . a genius like W. D. Hamilton, but in a very different way . . . as you knew yourself, of course . . . But the point is that the old boy, then in his eighties, I suppose, now in his nineties and *still* producing magnificent insights (see? Luke? If you want to live long, it's simple – get *consumed* with an interest . . .) – well, it was winter, and maybe our cottage isn't that warm, so he sat in the armchair of honour, in the big room, and instinctively (and this has not happened before or since) Belinda and I sat at his feet, like small kids, and Belinda had made this risotto (so *advanced*, then), and we ate it from plates on our knees, and we drank lots of wine, and she'd made a Queen's pudding, too – and we sat at the feet of a truly great man (as I now know), but there he was in a ragged old green sweater ("I always *relax* in this") with huge holes at the elbows; and on his feet (he said his feet were cold) he wore the last pair of Belinda's hippy calf-length heavy-wool Afghan socks (and *I* was never allowed even to try them on); and they had these lovely goatskin soles . . . And you know what? He talked and talked! Such stories! And we listened entranced, spellbound, whatever, and I was thinking at the time: "You, Ernst, you are the loveliest old grandad that anyone could ever wish for" – and I wanted to put my arms round him and give him *such* a hug and say straight out: "You – you're the fucking most wonderful old man I've ever met!" But I didn't, of course, *but I should have*: and you know? Even now I regret that I didn't have a recorder, a tape-machine, yes? But Belinda says, *don't be silly*, and besides, that's so unworthy, so tacky, and how could you think of using a thing like that? But all the same – *imagine* – he talked about the entire course of his extraordinary life, as if it really *was* to his grandchildren, and the intellectual value of it, *pow!*

'But I do remember most of it – OK, a tiny part of it – how he was fourteen or so, and he'd seen this extraordinary rare duck on his local lake, and no one believed him (least of all his family), so he wrote to the greatest field-biologist in the Germany of his day. And guess what? I warn you Luke, this is hair-on-the-back-of-the-neck time, or a funny feeling at the back-of-the-knees, or a tingling on the underside of the first joints on all your toes . . . Yes: the Grand Old Man replied, pronto! Because he was obviously a *grand teacher*, too, and he was old enough to recognize really great talent when he read it, once in a lifetime, even in a fourteen-year-old . . . Yes – Ernst, at fourteen, he was already recognized. And the duck, sure, it *was* there (which old Ernst obviously *still* thought was the point, seventy years on): but of course the duck didn't really matter

– no, it was the knowledge, the conversation, the reading, the conviction, the focus of this *fourteen-year-old*: *that's* what beguiled the great professor. So he says to this provincial boy: "Look here, Ernst, you won't understand, but I'm *very* busy, and I have to get the train back to Berlin (or was it Heidelberg?) *tonight* . . . So *please*, tell your parents (and of course his parents didn't believe a word of it) I think you taking your A levels (as it were), that really is a waste of your time . . . No, I want you to come and study *seriously*, as you do already, of course, but in *my* department, *my* research unit, in two months' time, October first, OK?" And so the young Ernst was on his way . . . to a continued, seamless, deep-interest happiness . . . And then what? Can you guess? What happened next? Rothschild? You know that great story?'

No – it was no use; and something had already told me: an absence of grunts, and snorts of outrage, and repressed snuffles of laughter, friendly or derisive: no, it had all gone away – there was nothing now but the usual deep thump of the engines (and even they seemed thoroughly at peace: no rising roar, no scream as the screws lifted almost clear of the hurricane-sea: no, they were doing their job, calm, content, day-to-day . . . the engines, the Blackstones, seventy-years-old-and-more, way-past-retirement, they themselves were happy, planting winter broadbeans in their allotment, pottering on with life . . .

But no – it was pointless – there was nothing I could do – because at last I looked across again at Luke (and come on – that was a great story, wasn't it?), and it was precisely as I'd feared: Luke was asleep. Luke was so asleep, in fact, so still, so lost, so gone – Luke might well be dead . . .

For the next haul I followed Big Bryan and Allan Besant down through the trap-door to the fish-room, down the unexpectedly long and steep ladder, way down into the forward hold, as agreed – because Dougie, in the galley, he'd said, in front of everyone: 'If you've no worked in the hold, Redmond, you're no a trawlerman

293

– because that's hard, that is. Aye – it's a peedie thing compared to the work of an engineer in the engine-room, right enough, but I tell ye: it's hard in the hold . . .'

But my first impression, as I reached the last rung of the ladder (the base was frozen into a mound of ice-pebbles), my first thought, as I stumbled across the pile of ice, was: *'It's so cold in here!'* Which I must have said out loud, because Allan Besant laughed and Big Bryan replied: 'Cold? Ach no! Just you wait – it's hot in here, it's roastin' hot!'

And so it proved to be – once the redfish began to tumble remorselessly down the wide-diameter tube from above, way above, from the end of the forward conveyor: and you lobbed them into the white-plastic fish-boxes (which you took from a ten-foot-high stack to starboard of the mound of ice, which, surely, had once been a mountain). And Allan shovelled in the ice, and I carried the box (so heavy) to Bryan who, without a word, took it (as if it was a box of feathers) and stacked it – a hard shove, right in, at the top of the line of boxes, his big arms outstretched, two and a half feet above his head; or, with less effort, as he built up the next wall of boxes, he'd bend easily, his back still flexible, intact, despite the weight he carried in front of him – whereas I, doing no more than carry a full fish-box from the packer Allan to the stacker Bryan: I felt it, that terrible warning at the vertebrae at the base of the spine, that dull nasty something at the pelvis, the sacro–iliac joint. ('No, we do *not* like this,' said the muscles and the vertebrae: 'No, you really *are* a jerk – and we, we're going to sort you out! Because – before you went to *Congo*, you *prepared*, as you should, as the SAS told you, and you really *did* go to the gym three times a week for two years to prepare your back to carry those 70 lb loads . . . But for *this*, you wanker – what did you do? Did you train us? No! Did you hell! Because you, you pitiful bozo, no: you'd decided that there *were* no wild places in the UK! So what did you do to prepare? Nothing! You drank and you slept . . . you couldn't even get your fat self to run round your local wood! Yes

. . . we'll get you for this: four months or so flat out to rest us, on your back, unable to walk; yes — that's about right as a prison sentence goes . . .'

Bryan said nothing, Allan said nothing, and me? Well, I was far too hot and exhausted and sweat-slimed even to *think* of the effort of speech . . . So was this the final stage of sleep-deprivation as observed by Luke (probably backed up by hundreds of studies in what's-the-point-of-sleep labs)? No, I thought, really not, this is called simple all-out pressurized physical labour when no one can speak . . . That's all. And, oh god, my old back, *how it hurts* . . . So I repeated the mantra that I'd found a *great* help in jungles (but when I was more or less fit, and when I was *young*, too), the incantation (on-and-on) that eventually saw you through those eight- or ten-hour so-called *walks*, those demi-runs that went on way beyond your idea of time, with the Iban or the Yanomami or the northern Congo pygmies: 'This will all be over one day . . . This will all be over one day . . .'

And, at last, it was: and Allan Besant, without a word, but so kindly now, so caring, so gentle (and *no*, Redmond, do *not* say anything — and above all: get a grip, be a man, do not burst into even silent tears of gratitude or exhaustion or any other fucking thing: yes, your muscles are shaking, you're shaking-weak all over) and Allan, well, *he's coming up the ladder right behind you,* and somehow or other he has his right hand at the base of your spine, so you can't pitch back way down into the ice: and jeeez, that's right, even the muscles in my legs are shaking, and they won't do what I say, but what's that? Yes. Allan Besant must have his left hand on the ankle of my left sea-boot, and now my right — one, two, yes, the next rungs up . . . So why's he being so kind to *me*? . . . OK — so maybe, as Matt Ridley thinks, there is no mystery about it: maybe, most of the time, most of us, we're *not* selfish, we're altruistic, we can't help it . . .

And, at the top of the ladder, at first on all-fours in the fish-room, and then (the sea out there — it must be flat-calm), when I managed

295

to stand up . . . Allan Besant (dressed in his yellow oilskin trousers and waistcoat, a one-piece with braces over a thick, red-cloth fleece-jacket), his hands still in their blue gloves . . . he took my own right blue-gloved hand and shook it, and smiled, and gave me a wink, and raised his blue-gloved right index-finger to his lips (not a word!) and, without bothering to change on the bench, he swung open the heavy bulwark-door to the galley, stepped over the sill, and disappeared.

'Hey Redmond!' came a familiar shout – and yes, it was Luke, and he was standing way over there by his baskets, to port of the corrugated-iron door to the hopper, and oh no, he looked so eager . . . 'Come on! Just in time! What took you so long? Bryan – he was out and gone: *way before* you and Allan!'

'Oh god!'

'No – *come* on: get your camera: it's on its hook in the laundry there – I took the liberty of changing the film and slotting on your Micro-Nikkor!'

'You did? So why the fuck didn't you go ahead and take the pictures?'

'Eh? What? How do you mean?' said Luke, looking, even at that distance, I could see, semi-poleaxed with some kind of shock-to-the-head . . . 'Do that? I could *never* do that: the grip, the photographer, *he's the man who owns the cameras* – that's *his* job! You must *never*, you must *never* take another man's job!'

Oh Jesus, I thought, all this really is beyond me; but at least my legs seem to have stopped shaking. (But my back, how it hurts all over, but that's a good sign isn't it? No *specific injury*, the kind that no one else can *see*, no injury that you know has split you in half; and this huge thing that you take for granted, your back – so very boring, so very physical to your GP, your doctor – but when *that* goes you're not even half-a-man, you're a nobody, no work, no pleasure, no walkies, and, certainly, *no sex*.)

'Redmond! For Chrissakes!' yelled Luke, agitated, both hands clamped on the rim of a blue basket, way over there. 'Get the fucking camera! *Excuse me!* But please – please! *No trances!* I can't take it any more! Come on! Now! The camera! *We've all the left-overs to photograph* – and the Esmark's eel-pout that you forgot to photograph. And why? *Because you were in a fucking trance!* And Jason – Jason's shot the net again already! So we've no much time – because this, you, you – *Worzel, this is the Arctic Circle,* a great rich fishing-ground that's *so expensive* to get to! And there *you* are – in a Worzel-trance!'

Stung, well, buffalo-kicked, I suppose, I grabbed the big camera-and-flash from its hook among the oilskins and, in no time at all, like a real trawlerman (OK – so it was calm out there – and yet so very far north – yes, the fish-room floor of the *Norlantean,* the beautiful shiny wooden floorboards of the fish-room were almost as stable as the floorboards of the bedroom of a terraced granite house in Fittie, in Aberdeen, where the best sex in the world took place . . . Woof-woof! All that lovely together-sweating . . . Until, that is, you got a call from that bleeper-under-the-bed . . .).

'Redmond! Worzel! What's up? Stop it! Whatever it is – stop it! Because you're *still* doing it! And you know what? If you were a dog, if you were Malky Moar's dog – I'd think you'd got rabbits on the brain!'

'Woof-woof! You know?'

'No – I don't. So now, please, and we have to be fast, because this is great redfish country, and the net'll be full before we know it: look – all these odds and sods, the important ones, you're lucky, because I've already measured and weighed and sexed them: so all I need is your pictures, OK?'

'OK!'

And it really was easy, at last – no slipping, no sliding, no panic at the impossibility of everything . . .

'Esmark's eel-pout!'

So I took two photographs – and Luke tossed Esmark's eel-pout on to the gutting table, for later transferral down the exit chute, food for the kittiwakes . . .

'The Blackmouth catshark!'

Lying at my feet, maybe a yard long, its brown mottled back shiny in the overhead lights: yes, there was no doubt about it: the so-called Blackmouth catshark was a *dogfish*.

I said, my energy seemingly recovered (perhaps all that sweat-exercise had done me good): 'It's no a catshark – it's a dogfish! Woof-woof!'

'Worzel! Grow up!' said Luke, still a little severe. 'Dogfish *are* catsharks. But here – look' (he held it up), 'this one is rare, a real deepwater catfish, down to a kilometre and more – and see?' He opened its mouth: yes! It was black inside, and so many teeth . . . Luke cast it up and on to the table.

'And *this*' (a grab at the basket, a fish at my feet), 'this is the spurdog, the Common dogfish – from the first haul.'

The real dogfish – something I recognized, and how! The great meticulous pleasure of those A-level dissections, T. H. Huxley's biology course, as it still was then – it all came back to me; and to Luke I said: 'On Old Olympus Towering Tops a Finn and German Pick Some Hops.'

'Eh?'

'It's a mnemonic – you know, an aid to memory: the cranial nerves of the dogfish: occipital, trigeminal . . . oh shite, well, Luke, there you go: at least I remember the mnemonic . . .'

'Aye. So what?' (Up and across went the dogfish-and-memories.)

'Look – I may not even *use* these photographs in my doctorate, but I need to have them, all the same, just in case.' And, one to each hand, he laid a couple of small squid on the floor: 'The Short-finned squid! The European flying squid!'

I took their pictures – and Luke lobbed them on to the table. 'Hey Luke – come on!' I said. 'What's happened? Don't be so aggressive all of a sudden . . . What's up? You call it a European *flying* squid . . . And yet you won't tell me about it?'

'Oh – Worzel, let's just get this job done!'

'No,' I said. 'Certainly not. No! That's not right. The bargain was: you'd *tell* me about things!' And, indignant, for the first time I drew myself up to my full height (well, I couldn't do that before, could I? Not with the floor chucking you all about the place), and, like a Dowager-Duchess, I repeated: 'Certainly not!' And, thanking Luke's absurd ideas of job demarcation (learnt at his Antarctic station, surely?), because, after all, it was obvious, he knew far more about this poncy camera-kit of mine and could take far better pictures than I *ever* would – I said, tucking my camera into my ample Dowager-Duchess oilskin jacket: 'No info! No pictures!'

'Oh for Chrissake!' said Luke, *almost* mean. 'I told you – it can happen to us any time now. And it's sudden and *total* – you can't speak.'

Slightly alarmed, I meant to say, man to man, in words as commanding as Big Bryan's: Luke – the European flying squid! Tell me about it now – *or else*! But instead I heard myself say (and meanwhile Luke had slapped a couple of small flatfish at my feet), 'Oh *please*, Luke – it won't hurt you – *please* tell me about the European flying squid!'

'OK! You win!' said Luke, disgusted, backing off, sitting on the edge of his blue plastic basket, drawing his right hand across his forehead and then, for some reason, snatching off his blue woolly hat (anger!) and stuffing it (right hand to the small of his back, forward, down, and into the pocket of his jeans beneath the oilskin apron-and-trousers) . . . 'Squid – well they're not my thing, nothing personal, you understand, they're about as interesting as marine biology gets, and that means they're *far more interesting* than most animals on land – but, can't you see? It's *impossible* to know every-thing about life in the oceans! I'd like to, I *try*, I really do – but sometimes I can't take it any more, you know, because it's *all* so exciting, *so unexpected*, you couldn't invent it for yourself! No! Never! Sometimes it gets *overwhelming*, you know, like the biggest lump in the worst storm you ever saw! Aye – and I feel myself drowning . . . Because I can't know it all! I'm reading for my doctorate, for Chrissake, that's all – and yet you, you seem to think I should know everything!'

'Oh Jesus, Luke! I'm so sorry, don't be silly, yes, but maybe I do, I did, you know, yes, you're crazy, but I'm sorry – forgive me, no, it *wasn't like that* –' And, guilty, I took the huge camera-and-flash out from under my oilskin jacket.

'OK! So!' said Luke, not moving but, disconcertingly, shutting his eyes tight. 'Squid! There are two great and weird things that you need to know about squid! One: you remember your Darwin and *The Origin* and how he talked us through, step by step, the probable evolution of the mammalian eye? Because that was *his* big test! Because religious people said: "Up yours!" Excuse me. But they did – they said, "OK, just you explain to us how the human eye evolved!" Because what use could a wonky blurry half-formed eye possibly be to anyone? No! God made it – perfect, fully formed! Well, no, as it happens, because he didn't. No – for humans, proto-angels, whatever we were, you'd know! Pre-angels, wingless angels, *so special*, each of us, and yet we still have to shit at least once a day: and the odd Worzel-angel – *that one throws up*!' Luke, happiness re-approaching, opened his eyes and looked at me, and almost laughed: but no, he shut them tighter than ever (which wiped the furrows on his forehead down to his eyebrows and away off his face, his brow was stretched clear – and, even as he concentrated so hard, he looked ten years younger, back to his early twenties).

'No – fact is – get this! *God prefers squid!* Our own god-given perfect eyes – they're nothing of the sort! What a lie! Like all religion . . . No: *God likes squid best. Their* eyes evolved entirely independently of the vertebrates' and sure, they developed in much the same way, convergent evolution, but their eyes are *so* superior: because their retinal cells face towards the incoming rays of light and they have their ganglion-cells, their receiver-cells, *behind* them; whereas with us, God was having a sleep, he messed up, big time! Because our ganglion-cells are *in front* of the light-sensitive cells –

they *really* foul up the light-rays forming the image . . . Aye, compared to a squid, we're practically blind!'

'Jeesus!'

'Please, Worzel, *please* – stop saying that, because it's so *lazy* of you, and *I hate it!*'

'Ah.'

'Aye – and the second thing about squid? Is that what you want?' Luke, perched on the surprisingly rigid rim of his blue basket, a hand on each knee, eyes tight-shut, said: 'Is that what you want?'

And 'Yes!' I said, standing there, limp, I'm afraid, and: I don't understand it, I thought, but I *did*. And I wouldn't put my best friend through this, whatever it is; but there again, I thought, isn't Luke now one of my best friends? And the inner voice, in Luke's clear tones, said to me: 'Grow up! There you go again – talking like a teenager!'

'So – squid. Number Two (*and that's your lot*). Aye: the nerve fibres of molluscs – squid are molluscs – they never evolved the myelin-coating, the axon-sheaths, the electrical insulation that we have around our own nerve-fibres, which are from around one-fiftieth to one-thousandth of a millimetre thick: no, but who cares? Because the rate at which nerve fibres conduct impulses increases with their thickness – and guess what? The squids, between their brains and their mantles they've evolved nerve fibres that are one half of a millimetre thick! So *pow!* They're *fast*: jet-propulsion from their mantle-funnels! Plus an ink-blast to fool their predators! And – it really is almost instant – how's about their all-in spectacular camouflage colour changes?'

Luke, the lesson over (could teaching *really* be that painful? Yes, I supposed, it could, and, anyway, it obviously *was*), Luke opened his eyes; he got to his feet, and, as if nothing untoward had happened, he gripped my shoulder, hard, in the usual way – the photographic routine, even though the floor was juddering with nothing more than the thump of the engines, and: 'Go on!' he said.

'Full flash! Two exposures each – f.32 and f.22, bracket them! Witch! Long rough dab!'

Click-flash! Flash-click! Twice. *So satisfying.* Just as if you were actually achieving something . . .

And 'OK!' I said, as he threw the flatfish, one after the other, backwristed, as if he was spinning a couple of frisbees into flight – and they landed, perfectly, in the exit-chute. 'OK! So why was that last squid called a European *flying* squid? Who ever heard of flying *squid*? Flying *fish*, yes. Flying *squid*, no. So it's some kind of historical misnomer? Some charming mistake?'

Luke, who, a moment before, had seemed to be back in possession of a peaceful sense of self (perhaps he thought the lesson had gone well? Well, it had, it *really* had) – Luke, disturbed again, chucking, with unnecessary violence, two very strange little fish to the floor in front of my boots, said: 'Misnomer? Charm?'

'Well, you know . . .'

'No! I don't – flying squid, they fly! It's only academics like you, marine biologists who never leave the lab – it's only people like you who sneer at the stories of men who go to sea, the reports of trawlermen way out in mid-ocean: yes, it's people like you, it's people like you who make our lives a misery, trawlermen like me; and you treat us like peasants; and you don't even bother to read my scientific papers or, if you do, you pretend you haven't!'

'Eh? Luke?' (Well – I was *very* flattered; me: a marine biologist? But the rest of it . . .)

'Oh Jesus!' said Luke, grabbing my left arm (*quick as a squid*, I thought, pleased with myself). 'Aye. Yes. Aye. Don't you *mind* that . . . I'm sorry. I warned you, Worzel . . . But I'm forgetting myself – for a moment there I think I thought you were this terrible bitter senior guy in the university, in the department; you know, you know the type, we all do, he was passed over for promotion . . .' Luke brightened, he smiled, he let go of my arm. 'But there again – don't you *ever* use words like *misnomer* again or, worst of all, *magisterial* or, even worse than that: *first-class mind!*'

'Aieee! No!'

'Goaaal!' shouted Luke, the real or imagined bitterness of this outer or inner academic temporarily flung out of his mind and overboard. 'Aye! Flying squids – they fly! *Pow!* There're several species – they've wide fins and extra-broad membranes on their arms and they leave the water with such power they can fly for sixty yards or more – and we've well-documented accounts (yes! from merchant seamen!): these squids have struck ships a good twenty feet above the waterline!'

'And so,' I said, seizing my chance in all this euphoria, but still tentative . . . '*Giant* squid? Sperm-whales?'

'Ach! All right!' said Luke, with a happy grin, like old times. 'But first – take these little beauties, OK?'

The top one, furthest from me, was brown-backed, silvery-stomached, with a long fringe of rear fin top and bottom, a whisker, a barbel, beneath its chin – and two long trailing feathery filaments stretching from its gills to beyond its anus: so what were they for? For feeling about the pitch-black mud?

'The Greater forebeard – cod family,' said Luke. 'But *this one*' (he bent down and stroked it, he ran his right index-finger along its slim flank, tracing its lateral line), 'this one I *really* like.'

And by now, with all my training, I told myself, even I can see why: it was a *very* beautiful streamlined little fish, its back mottled light brown, its flanks a light red, its underside – well, its underside was *pink*. So it was a girl-fish, a fish off to its first adult dance, a proper ball . . .

'You know why?'

'Yeah – it's a young girl; she's off to a dance.'

'What? Spare us! No, well maybe – who knows? No, no – this is a rockling, a deep-sea rockling, a Bigeye rockling. And I like them now, Worzel – because I can see they're *your* kind of fish.'

'They are?'

'Aye!' He picked it up. 'See? The front dorsal fin – it's like a line of hairs, isn't it?' (It was.) 'And the fish lies flat-out half-asleep on the sea-bed, taking it easy, you know?'

'Ah.'

'And the only part of it that moves are these hairs, modified fin-rays, and they vibrate constantly – and they waft a current of water along this groove around and beneath them, see?' (Maybe there *was* a groove there; but you'd need a hand-lens or squid-eyes . . .) 'And you've guessed, haven't you?' (No, I hadn't.) 'Of course – the sides of this groove are lined with exactly the same kind of taste-buds you find on a tongue! So the rockling can lie very still in its bunk day and night, tasting the water around it for a passing prawn or crab or bristleworm – and it need only stir for a meal when it really feels the need!'

'Great!'

'Aye,' said Luke, pushing the two little fish aside with his boot, turning back to his basket, 'I thought you'd like that!' He straightened up, a big, heavy, grey skate, held at the base of the tail, in each hand. 'Aye, I know, Sperm whales . . . and I remember! It was a bargain! In return you – you were going to find me the perfect wife, or some such . . . aye! You know what? You – you're crazy, barking!'

'Thanks . . . But I *do* have the perfect wife for you. In fact, Luke, I can tell you *exactly* where to look for her – the only place you'll have a chance; and it's *very* specific: yes, your one possibility of *real* happiness, lasting happiness, happiness for *life*. And, by the way, it's *not* a joke, I'm serious – and I don't think you should laugh . . .'

'I wasn't laughing,' said Luke, with a laugh, plainly interested, despite himself, laying another pair of skates out on the floor. 'Sperm whales, aye! But these skates, they're Arctic skates, adapted to the furthest north, *Raja hyperborea* – and they're interesting too. You know their behaviour? *No one has a clue.* And if you don't believe me, get this, big time! The very last haul, when you were in the hold – around 150 skates came up in the net, but all Arctic skate, and all the same age, *and all male*! So what the hell's going on?'

'A regiment. A club. An old-boys reunion . . .'

'Och aye. Your usual bullshit – but where are the females? Are they all together too? And what about the young? The different stages, eh? *Where are they?*'

'No idea!'

'Aye – and neither has anyone else! Now I want a *series* of pictures of these skates, to prove they're all the same sex and the same age – I took a random sample from the 150: six. And I know that doesn't sound much, but it was the best I could do. Because Jason has no quota for skate; they were in the way; 150 big skate! The boys had no choice – even though skate-wings are a feast for a king, God, Darwin, whoever, *they're so good to eat*, and such lovely animals, and yet out they all went, dead of course, because *nothing* survives the sudden decrease in pressure from such depths . . . Aye . . . It's a waste, *a terrible waste* . . . If only we were governed by Icelanders! Then we could control and manage the seas that belong to us, for 200 miles offshore: aye, and do away with this quota-nonsense, and we'd conserve our own fish-stocks and find out *everything* about the life-cycle of these skates, and protect the females and young (once we know where their nurseries are) – and gradually our own trawlermen would get as rich as the Icelanders and there'd be *lots* of fish for the rest of us to eat, for always – and everyone would be happy!'

'Yes! Yes!'

'So you – what the hell are *you* doing?'

'Eh?'

'Why aren't you taking their pictures?'

'Luke – lay off!' I said, peeved, swinging the heavy camera-kit into position, stooping down. 'I'm a man – *I'm a bloke* – so hasn't your biology taught you anything? I really *cannot* concentrate on two equally interesting things at once! No – if I'm listening to you talking so well about skates, how the hell am I supposed to photograph them?'

'But you *wanted* me to tell you everything!'

'Yes — of course I did. So fuck off! It's so complicated, isn't it? Except no, so *don't* fuck off, it's actually simple, so *very* simple . . .'

Luke, nonplussed, as he well might be, stood beside me, silent. And through the lens which always, so completely, excludes the rest of the external world: Luke, the *Norlantean*, the nearby galaxies, empty space . . . (Hey! So no wonder so many cameras are sold! And yes! No wonder people like me then forget to use them — so the average number of exposures taken per camera per year is twelve). But oh Jeesus, and Luke says I must *not say that*, this skate, this skate that fills the frame: it's on its back, yes, but it's so fleshy, flabby, thick, glistening, spotted with brown, and the underside of this individual skate here is covered with green spots that look like mould, and angry red spots that look like terrible on-coming acne; and at the base, the start of its tail, just behind the thick globular head, there's a puffed-out couple of swellings (its guts?) and then, again, to either side, two thin sticky-out things like a bat's ears, which protrude beyond two more fleshy elliptical sacs, which give way, yes, still on either side, to two semi- or fully erect (who could tell — except a womanly skate?) to *two* penises, their stems smooth and thick, the glands of each protuberant, eager, and, apparently, circumcised.

'Luke!' (Yes — I may have yelled at him, a foot away.) 'Luke! They're like me — they're circumcised! . . . Well — *very* young middle-class vicars' sons in the 1940s, you know, they lined you up on the wooden vicarage-kitchen table, you and the cocker-spaniel puppies — and they docked the tails of the puppies and (*much* less important) the foreskin of the baby . . . And it was *always* done by a spinster-aunt . . .' And: 'Sorry — so sorry!' I said, not to Luke, but to the Arctic skate, because I really did feel that, man to man, I'd intruded, unforgivably, on its deep-sea privacy.

'Oh Jesus,' said Luke, standing there, unmoving (yes — he said *Jesus*). 'If we ever *do* get home, you know what? Aye — I'll sleep, as always, more or less without a break for three days and nights, to recover from this trip — and then? You know what? Aye! I'll sleep for *another* four days and nights to recover – can you guess? From what? Aye! *From you!'*

'Ah, sure, why not?' Which, I thought, was macho-nonchalant of me, because, I'm afraid, I *really* wanted to tell him about a visit to the new London Aquarium with my family where all was all it should be in an ordered world (the sharks! the sea-horses – so small, so intricate!). Yes – until we got to the big shallow pool full of skates or rays (OK – so they were *very* shallow-water species, but all the same . . .) And this is where everyone gathered: and they bent over the low side of the big pool – and why? Well, it hurts to say this, Luke, but the rays or skates, they swam up to every visitor, as desperate for friendship as any pussy-cat, and they had a good look at you – and then they raised their heads right out of the water, and you know what they wanted? Bizarre but true; as instructed by the multiple official notices: you were to wet your fingers in the pool and, very gently, stroke them at the back of their heads. And oh, Luke, shite, they went all trembly, all wibbly-wobbly down their tails, and they hung there in the water, wanting *more of it.* And of course I didn't say anything to my wife or young daughter or young son: no, you don't, do you? Not after a shock like that . . . (To fall in love with a skate?) But as we left there was a young man beside us with his girlfriend; and he was obviously a soldier on leave (the cropped hair, the non-gym-fit, slim body, the way he moved, packed with assault-course, marathon-energy); and he said to her: 'So what the fuck do we eat now? Because I promise you – *I'm never touching fish again!'* And *she* said, because women are so much tougher than men, she said: 'They weren't fish, asshole – they were skates!' But I didn't say anything to Luke because for a thought as awful, as disruptive as that, the internal censor, in and out of fever and coma as it still was – it said: 'Redmond! Fatso! *Silence!'*

'Go on – take the *dorsal* surface of this one!' (The next along.) 'And then I want two photographs, at different exposures, of *all six*, ventral and dorsal – OK?' (OK. So we photographed skate number two.) 'Got it? Thirty-six exposures for this – it's very important – as far as I know there's nothing in the literature about Arctic skate living in all-male or all-female groups: why should they? It's weird, smashin'; a discovery! Aye: so maybe *three* exposures per side? f.32, 22 – and 16, to make sure, OK?' (OK.)

'And I took the liberty,' said Luke, 'when *you* took so long to come up from the hold – what happened down there? You faint or something? Anyway – I went to our cabin and, excuse me – I *liberated* another film.' (Luke laughed, he thought that was funny.) 'Aye! From your camera-case – and I've got it in my pocket! But hey! Worzel – even your camera-case: the mess in there! There are socks, *even in there*, socks round lenses, or just stuffed in – and the *crud*, filters, useless ancient films, batteries, bits of paper: Jeesus! I half expected a fucking mouse, excuse me!' And Luke, he went right ahead and did his whole helpless laugh business, both hands across the stomach, a bending forward, a doubling-up, and then, a spin on his own axis, a whirling dervish howl of all-out laughter: 'Aye! I half expected a fucking mouse! Aye! A fucking *mouse*! To jump right out at me!'

'Yeah, yeah!' I said, ruffled, at first, but then I thought: 'Young Luke, Uncle Luke – he hasn't laughed like that since early times on this trawler, long ago, I can't remember when!'

'It's weird – magic! A discovery! Your behaviour, you know, it's as odd as these skates! Socks! Socks everywhere! And the mess – even in your *camera case*! Why socks, eh? Aye . . . I know! . . . Aye! . . . Socks! Of course! I know – you, Worzel, *you think that socks are sexy* – all that fucking bullshit, excuse me! All that nonsense about feet and rotten fish and mumbo-jumbo spells in the Congo! You – you *really* think socks are sexy!'

And Luke, thoroughly offensive, did his all-out-laugh thing, all over again.

And I tried to think of a reply, but I couldn't, because something spoke to me from the subconscious (no big deal!) *except that that's not right*: because the subconscious *can't* speak, can it? No – it's

308

much older than speech, and in fact I *heard* nothing. No: I *saw* two images, so very present. Yes: that girl in Boha, a village in the northern Congo, scraping her feet with a small worn–away knife; and an even more powerful picture: Luke, in his trawler clothes, the blue woolly hat, the blue T-shirt, the blue jeans he wore under his oilskins; yes – he was coming ashore *anywhere*: Lerwick, Stromness, Scrabster, Peterhead. And twenty or thirty young women were waiting there to welcome him home. And they stretched out their multiple arms, just like the tentacles on a Giant squid, but the most benign, the most gentle, squid that ever was: a squid desperate for love, for a lifetime of the very deepest happiness.

So I said nothing substantial, nothing that *mattered*, in reply, just: 'Giant squid? Sperm whales?' (And we were still only on skate number three.)

'Aye! Sperm whales!' said Luke, still jovial, happy, enjoying life again. 'Well, the fact is, I thought I knew all about it, as you do, before you try and remember the details, but I never wrote it down, I took no notes on this great paper I read, because, really, I shouldn't have been reading it in the first place, not in the library of the Marine Lab, Aberdeen, where I was supposed to be *focused*, you know, working on my doctorate – and this had nothing whatever to do with my doctorate. But it was *brilliant*, an extraordinary piece of work, yet for now I can't even remember the reference . . . (Go on! Take that one! Don't stop! No, no – please! *Three* exposures – each time!) Aye – but this guy had dissected *lots* of Sperm whales; and that's no easy, even when they're stranded and dead, washed up on some beach (the stench!) and even more difficult on board a Norwegian whaler, whatever, because the boys need to render the great corpse as quick as they can. Still, he did it! He discovered that the right nostril (or was it the left? Sorry – no idea!), aye: he discovered that this nostril loops and curves and folds back on itself for miles, as it were, right through the giant spermaceti organ, the sac in its head full of oil. And somehow or other, I forget exactly

309

how, the whale can close this nostril and *really* heat up the air in it, and the heat liquefies the oil in the sac, whatever, changes its properties, which regulates the animal's buoyancy; and equally, it can open the nostril and drop the temperature and solidify the oil . . . Now that account may not be exactly right . . . But the point is: the Sperm whale, with its weird swollen head, its spermaceti organ (and it's a *mammal*, like us, for Chrissake!), and there's nothing like it on earth, no, nothing at all – aye, it can control its own buoyancy so efficiently that it can dive down to at least *two kilometres*: no effort, no sweat. And what does it do down there? And don't forget – despite the spermaceti organ it still has space in its head for *the world's largest brain* – what does it do two kilometres down? Well, we don't know, of course, but it has an incredibly complex social life, and lots of them go down, all together, and yet they keep in touch and they surface together, as one, in the same place on the surface from which they dived – so how's that? Aye, but I'm forgetting – when they're down there we know, from their stomach-contents, from whalers (and all that, by the way, it should fucking well be stopped!), aye, we know that they eat all kinds of squid and fish – but, most exciting of all: they eat Giant squid, *Architeuthis*. They've *seen* Giant squid! Or, rather, they've electronically imaged Giant squid with the acoustic system they also keep in that huge head of theirs, aye, a system so advanced that no one can begin to work it out: so one theory has it that they can deliver a massive pulse, a blast of volts that can stun even a Giant squid. And believe me, that's quite something, because no Giant squid, you know, and I *am* sure of this, no Giant squid actually *wants* to get eaten . . . And after all, *they're the largest invertebrates ever to have lived on this planet*: they can be at least twenty metres long, they can weigh half a tonne, and their eyes! Their eyes – they're a foot across!'

Luke sat down again, on the edge of his blue basket.

'Great!' I said (but I was still only on skate number four). 'That's ace! Yes – that pays off all your intellectual debts!'

'Excuse me?'

'Yes – it does. So now, in return, as promised, I'm going to tell you exactly how you can be happy for life!'

'Sure.'

'Yes! I'm serious! Only – there's just one thing. You see, Luke, you don't know this, why should you? But I really am the sole inventor of an entirely new photographic technique.'

'You are?' Luke, almost immediately, lost his look of pleased exhaustion, the gratified yet resentful look of all good teachers who've had enough. 'You are?'

'Yes – I really am. I'm its father, its originator, and it's been extraordinarily successful.'

'It has?' Luke's face regained all its young energy. He raised both eyebrows in enquiry: the three-and-a-half transverse furrows reappeared on his forehead (and perhaps there was another one, higher up, but it was lost beneath the flop-over fringe of annoyingly abundant, black, tousled hair). Luke (his body *always* seemed to respond directly to an idea): Luke stood up. 'It has?'

'Yes – a discovery!'

'Aye?'

'Yes!'

With both hands I eased the weight of the camera-and-flash off my neck; I lifted the strap over my head, and I placed it, a close-up lasso, perfectly, over the potent black curly dense kitchen-mop of hair which belonged to Luke.

'Whassup?'

Luke's sticky-out ears stuck out a little further, twitched, and pointed forward – a dangerous sign, which I recognized, all too well, from Bertie, my cat. Luke, at any moment, might strike.

'Now – *don't you be silly*. It's true, it's simple, there's no point getting all iffy about it – it *is* a new method, an unheard-of technique among great photographers, as yet. And it's this: you give the horrible camera to whoever's nearest you: you get *someone else* to take the fucking pictures!'

And I assumed Luke's place, on the edge of his blue basket, and it was surprisingly comfortable, like a shooting-stick.

'You – you bastard!'

'No, no – no need for that – and besides, how can I repay you for the story of the Sperm whale if I have to take *pictures*? Eh? How can I tell you about this woman you're going to find? The perfect, the ideal, the dreamt-of woman! The *only* one who'll make you happy! The love of your life who, as yet, you have not even imagined – or, rather, not specifically, not practically, *not in real life* . . .'

Luke, I'm afraid, said: 'Shite!'

'No, not at all.'

And then: 'So how the fuck *do* you take a picture with this thing? Why won't it work?'

'No really, Luke – please don't *fret*. How could you know? Only real professionals are familiar with these things . . .'

'Aar fuck.'

'Yes, quite . . . So all you have to do is remember it's the incomparable Nikon system. You have to half-wind the wind-on lever: you *cock* it!'

'So it gets you in the eye?'

'Yes. It *pokes* you in the eye; to speak technically.'

'Ach,' said Luke, getting the hang of such trivia at once. 'Aye! But this *lens*, Redmond – it's great! As *you'd* say; aye, it's smashin', magic, sweet as a nut! Hey, yes!' (Flash!) 'Big style! The *clarity* of it! Jeesus – and it *costs*! I'll bet!'

'Yes – the lens, it ruined me, big style! But Luke – this woman of yours . . .' The slightly springy edge of this blue basket was *so* comfortable. (Flash! Flash!) And then it occurred to me, in a minor way, that of course Luke was a man too, albeit a young one: so perhaps *he* wouldn't be able to concentrate on two equally impor-tant tasks at once, either? (Flash!) Still – too bad – if he really thought that these skates, his doctorate, his interests, his research – if he really thought that that was more important than finding the perfect woman and happiness for life then: sod him. 'But hang on!'

said an inner voice. (So this was *not* the subconscious – maybe it was reason?) 'What would the ideal woman – who adores him – what would *she* think of it? Yes, *of course*, she'd want her Luke to *get* his doctorate, to be a successful alpha male, rated highly by his male peers, in whatever life he chose (the choice itself wouldn't matter to her) . . .' Still, I'd *got* to *tell* him, hadn't I? Even if he wasn't listening . . .

'So, Luke,' I said, 'I've thought about it, long and hard!' (And then I ruined the *ex cathedra* effect, because, without meaning to, I said: 'Woof-woof!') 'This perfect woman, this lovely voluptuous creature of yours . . . It's obvious! She has to be *special*, and I don't mean romantically special, no banality, no, I mean specialized: a particular background, a special childhood, a specific career. A lifeboatwoman. No – because you tell me there *are* only two in the entire service.'

Flash! 'Redmond – I can't *believe* this lens! Leica – aye, no one can match those optics; but there again, they've a *pitiful* choice of specialist lenses; so perhaps it's true what they say: Leica, a rich man's toy! Whereas this . . .'

'So you – you really *do* love the extreme north, or extreme south, come to that, but there again, there *are* no indigenous peoples of the Antarctic continent – so: the far north? An Eskimo girl perhaps, an Inuit? But I don't know, because I've never met one. So let's be rational; and *no*, Luke, no Aberdeen oil-company accountants, no lazy-bullshit picking up anything that happens to come to your spider-web, your dance-club, no! Luke – you've got to get out there in the big world and *hunt for her*, because she's rare! She's special! Yes – so she *has* to be a woman born and raised in the far north, within sight of the sea, that rarest of women who will *never* ask you to take her to London, even for a weekend. And she *has* to be able to understand your altruism, your *very* odd compulsion to risk your own life at four in the morning to save the lives of people you don't even know and will never meet again! Yes – so what's the nearest profession to that?'

313

Flash! Click. No flash. Luke said, as if it was *my* fault: 'The flash – it keeps missing. I'm losing film here!'

'You have to *wait* after the flash! That is one powerful emission of light you've got there! So you wait – until it's ready again; when the little button on the back of the head of that big black prong lights up – and you can try once more, give it another go. You know the feeling?'

'Ach, Worzel. You're so *crude*.'

'And accurate.'

'Aye, well – but I'm *not* listening to you. I want you to know that.' *Flash!*

'See – it worked! And this will work too, Luke – because this woman will have her *own* bleeper under the bed, right beside yours. And there'll be times when *she* has to leave *you* in the middle of love-making. So that's fair, isn't it?'

'No, it's not,' said Luke, who was not supposed to be listening, head-down over the grey dorsal surface of Arctic skate number five. 'Not at all! And anyway – grow up! Stop trying to be funny!'

Stung, I said, a little louder perhaps: 'I am *not* trying to be funny . . . And if I was, well, fuck *you*, Luke: I'd be *funny*! No – I'm serious . . . So this delicious warm soft fantasy woman of yours, she's *so* loving and forgiving, and she lives in Shetland, right?'

'Right!' A pause. Flash! 'Got it!'

'But what does she *do*? That's the point. What is her work?'

Luke pretended to be focused on *his* work, on the ventral surface of skate number five. No flash. No reply. He was listening.

'What work would give her a bleeper and call her out in the middle of the night – perhaps to some offshore island, some out-skerry, to save someone's life? Eh?'

Flash! No reply. Not even a grunt of recognition that this great central question of his life had finally been formulated . . . A discovery!

'OK, Luke – so if you're not going to talk to me, if you think

314

it's fine to indulge in self-satisfying *passive aggression* at a time like this: fair enough! But I won't forget your refusal to engage in sexual reality at this point. No! But I'll tell you anyway! Yes! She'll be a district nurse!'

'Eh?' Luke stood up straight. He left skate number six un-attended. 'A district nurse?'

'Yes – on Shetland. You'll never catch a female doctor, a GP. No, the odds are absurd, the statistics are all against it – but a district nurse? There *must* be a statistically significant number of district nurses of breeding age who might fall in love with you . . . Yes, Luke! You'll have to go to Shetland – hunting: a focused, com-mitted, single-minded ruthless hunt for a district nurse . . .'

Luke, photography forgotten, came and sat beside me, perched on the rim of the adjacent red plastic basket (the *triumph of it!*). And we sat there, on our baskets, hands on knees, like two old men on a park bench.

'Yes, Luke – imagine it! Just imagine – peeling off that blue-and-white stiff starched uniform! And underneath it's all so soft and warm!'

'No! No!' Luke tensed up: he took his hands off his knees and straightened his spine and put both hands to the back of his neck. 'No! How wrong you are! How crude! No – it's not a *uniform* or a *type* of girl, a blonde or a brunette or a black-haired woman with small breasts or big breasts or with this or that and whatever! No! No! No!'

Taken aback, I edged away from this onslaught and, very nearly, fell off my basket, to starboard.

'No! It's none of that superficial yuck that you and your kind seem to like. No! I *really* want a woman to live with for ever, aye, *just the one*. And, as you say, Ally won't do.' (Had I said that? No. Certainly not. At least – I don't think I had . . .) 'No, sure she'll leave me; aye, you're *right*, I'll give you that: because, just like you said, well, she *did* tell me that in two months' time she's leaving Aberdeen (no more dances!) for a great promotion in the company;

she's got a new job in the London offices. But you, Redmond, *you seem to think it's all a joke . . .*'

'Of course it's not a joke! For Chrissake, Luke . . .'

'Aye, well, I *really* want this woman, *as you seem to have guessed,* perhaps because you're so old; and I'm getting desperate, it's true, but I want a woman whose *personality* I can fall in love with, I want to be in love with *who she is,* the real her . . . Aye – all this *crap* of yours: nurses in uniform, blondes, whatever, where *does* that come from? Eh? Can you *imagine* how offensive that is to a woman?'

'Yes – now you mention it, Luke, yes, I can. I'm sorry. Whatever it was – I take it all back,' I said, feeling, rightly, rebuked; and just, very slightly, ashamed.

'Ach – no: I want to fall in love with the whole, the *real her*' (at this happy thought Luke's hands returned to his knees and he leant a few degrees forward, relaxed). 'And in return, if I'm *very lucky,* she'll love me, for myself, as it were – and she won't tell me lies and, above all, she won't wear lies on her face: make-up!'

I thought: so that's a great relief – because that means I'm not the only nutcase in this fish-room . . . Make-up? What's wrong with make-up?

'Because I'll want her *exactly as she really is:* no bullshit! No pretence – I'll want *her,* for *herself,* no argument; and especially, aye, *I'll want all those little things that she imagines are her faults* – or big things, come to that, I don't care, just as long as she stays with me for ever, and I *really* want children, but say she can't have children, for some reason, I'll still love her to bits as long as she stays with me for ever. Aye! No lies – exactly as it is when you *go out on a shout* in a flying gale, a Force 10! Aye – and then I'll respect her, and love her, I'll love her to bits until I die – and maybe, you know, just maybe, we *will* have children, lots of children, but there again, who can tell?'

'Luke – you've *got* to go to Shetland for a month or two! Hunting!'

'Aye! So if it's a district nurse and we'll be together always then

I can add to my fantasy, can't I? You know – the Viking cottage, as it were, all that, I can add to it, can't I?'

'Of course! Why not?'

'Because by then I'll be earning good money, and so will she, so maybe, just maybe, in the honeymoon period, you know, which I'm sure will last for *years*, because I'll love her to bits . . . we might buy a sailing-boat? What do you think? Eight metres or so? And I'll name it after her, of course. And that's all a secret dream, really secret, a silly fantasy that I've had for twenty years . . . And we'll explore the coast of Shetland from the sea, just the two of us, and then, when she's used to it, we'll sail to Norway together, just us, and we'll nose around the islands and push up the fjords between Bergen and Stavanger; and then we'll return to our cottage! Aye – and we'll have *children*. And another thing: I know – this will seem ridiculous to you, I know it will; but I want a *garden*; because I want to grow vegetables; and I *want to plant trees*. Aye, I hear you, as you'd say . . . But you're wrong, because even on Unst, between 60 and 65 degrees north, I forget exactly, *but it's on the same latitude as southern Greenland*, it's the most northerly of all the islands of the British Isles, the far north of Shetland – aye! – and the most beautiful, believe me, the most beautiful place on earth, excuse me, because even *there* you can grow trees!'

'Bullshit! There *are* no trees in Shetland – everyone knows that!'

'You're wrong!' Luke became so agitated, passionate about – what?

Trees? It was *trees* now, was it? And for a moment I thought he might get to his feet and *ruin everything* (the old men; the *conversation*; peace; the park-bench). But, just, he stayed where he was, on his red-plastic-basket rim; and yes, I thought, the *bounce* in these up-and-down (and sideways) plastic seats: *wow!* So active-kind, so move-you-about-comfortable at the base of the back; and maybe, with a twist or two, you can *visit* the site of that low-down back-pain and *shift it*? To the right? Oh Jesus! No! So: to the left? Yes! That's better; that really is *so much better*, such a relief . . .

'You're *wrong*, Worzel – aye, because, as it happens, I *have* been to Shetland! And aye, as it also happens, I fucking well was *not* looking for a district nurse!'

'You weren't? Really not? Then more fool you! That's all I have to say – because you *should*, and fast, Luke, *fast*: because you're ageing! Now – now is your *last chance*.'

'Jesus! Will you lay off? Will you lay off for just a moment – and listen?'

(Luke said *Jesus*, didn't he? So I'd got him – yes: Luke was coming apart; so Luke *would* take my advice; wouldn't he? Yes – whatever happened, I'd make *so sure* that this absurd wayward hero of a young lifeboatman was *happy*! And as for that: there's no other way, everyone knows – *all you need is the right woman* . . .)

Luke, aggrieved, but not (I was *so* pleased!) moving from his basket, said: 'Because – the great Dr Saxby, a guy you'd really like – och aye, you *really* would, because he lived in the nineteenth century, and now he's *dead*! Aye, Dr Saxby *was* the island doctor, the man who wrote *The Birds of Shetland*; well, to be *accurate*, as you say, his brother (a vicar! How's that?) – he put it all together from Saxby's papers after his death and published it in 1874 . . . Still, where was I? Aye! Trees! *So Dr Saxby loved trees too*: and he built a big *walled* garden beside his little house near Baltasound on Unst and he planted sycamores (I *think* it was sycamores) – and guess what? They grew! The most northerly wood in the British Isles! But now his house, the scene of all that nineteenth-century northern science – it's a ruin . . . But if you climb over a broken iron-gate – you can go and *enjoy* this little wood: spooky, magic! A magic place! And all those poor migrant little birds, the robins and blackbirds and God knows what else who *have* to get out of Scandinavia where they breed so well in summer (the insects! the blackfly!) but which in winter becomes one impossible bird-hell of snow and ice – aye! The lucky ones, of all those thousands (millions, perhaps?): the lucky ones of all those thousands of little land-birds blown off course in the wrong Arctic wind (so that almost all of them ditch exhausted into the sea and drown, pronto, and feed our fish) – aye, *the very few lucky ones all get to go to Dr Saxby's wood*: and they *can't believe it*, they're safe, they're in a wood, they survive!'

'Goaaal!' I shouted, automatic, formulaic – but all the same, it *was* a great story, wasn't it? And then huffy, feeling left out (hadn't Luke agreed to tell me *everything*?), I said: 'Luke – you *never* told me you'd stayed on Shetland!'

'Aye: *because my mum paid*. That's why I never told you. And another thing: I really want to own a dog. A collie. One of those magic dogs: they're *so* intelligent; you wouldn't believe it! Aye: a big fluffy female collie – their eyes! They look at you all the time . . . And when you say, "Sit!", they sit . . .'

'Yeah, yeah. But *Shetland*? You *never* told me you'd stayed on *Shetland* . . .'

'Aye, well. I did. And I can't tell you everything, can I?'

'Oh yes you can – and you *should*. You told me about Signy Island – but *Shetland*?'

'Aye, OK, well, no wonder I didn't tell you, *because my mum paid*. But the fact is – it was two months, in the slack period for us, in Aberdeen, at the university, at the Marine Lab; and, as you know, a graduate working on his doctorate is allowed no more than two weeks off a year, and, for some reason, *especially not* mature students . . . But I think my supervisor (a great guy!) and my mum (she's *lovely*: you'd really like her) – I think they *must* have got together, because, it's true, I *was* having terrible trouble *starting* my doctorate! Aye – I already had *lots* of data from trawlers, from the sea; and from the landings, from the fish-market at Scrabster, where people like Jason come into harbour at three in the morning; and the lumpers arrive and do the unloading from the hold on to the boat's hoist down there; and the boxes are swung up and ashore under the trawler's lights; and the crew pull them into the great shed on these horrible unstable three-wheel market-trolleys . . . Aye, and the merchants arrive around six in the morning, and it's all *so tense* . . . And when everyone's ready the auction begins –

hundreds and hundreds of boxes, if you've been successful, all spread out, and the auctioneer and the merchants step from box to box, row on row, and the sale is done . . .'

'Luke! Shetland! I *really* want to hear about Shetland!'

'Aye, well, okay – but you see, despite my earnings, my savings from my years in the South Atlantic, on Signy Island, and as a Fisheries Inspector in the Falklands: fact is, I was out of money. And in Aberdeen, well, you know, the distractions! The Moorings, the pub in the docks, full of all your friends, every night! And the clubs – the dances! Aye, so as I think I told you, my mum and my supervisor may have had a word on the phone – and the choice was a cottage in Penan, the *prettiest* little east-coast Scottish tourist village where they made scenes for a film called *Local Hero*. Or, more expensive (because it's *so* far away), a place way up north, on Unst. Well – that was it, wasn't it? The obvious place to send someone into isolation to begin real work on his doctorate . . . So I took my little white van from the lab, the one I use for all the kit, for sampling species in Scrabster market – and I had my thesis-notes and computer in one case, and my clothes in another, and my boots and anything else I thought I might need in the back – but *no*, even then I made an effort: *I thought about what I might need*: I did *not* bung everything in like you do: socks, papers, books that are one hundred years out of date, piles of crud . . . No! . . . I couldn't stand that!'

'Yes, yes! Great! But where did you *go*?'

'Aye!' Luke, uneasy, looked hard away to port. (To port, there was nothing to see: just the rusty brown-circled rivets, the rusty brown-orange-edged plates; but hey, I thought, it must be dawn *out there*; because the weak pure white Arctic light is coming in *here*, horizontally, through the starboard scupper – and it's making the *loveliest* patterns with the stains of rust on the iron, and across the old, bubbled white paint; and yes, *watch it*, I thought, both ways, because *that*, I suppose, is *exactly* how otherwise perfectly reasonable people decide to become painters, artists . . .) 'Aye!' said

Luke, turning his head, concentrating, now staring straight in front of him – at the gutting table (littered with a miscellany of his lovingly documented but now discarded fish). 'For me – it's *not* a good story, which is why I've never told you, despite something: well, to be honest, it was absolutely the best time I've had in my life since Signy Island: since the South Orkney Islands, the Antarctic!'

'Yes?' I said, easing forward slightly, trying to move the pain in my back without standing up from the rim of my blue plastic basket – because, it was obvious, I must *not* move, I must *not* disrupt things in any way, no, not at all . . . 'But Shetland?'

'Aye! I took the *St Clair*, the ferry (a *big* ship!), from the pier in Aberdeen – right out of the harbour-mouth, past Fittie, and you can *see my place* as you leave the coast . . .'

'So what was wrong – why wasn't it a good story?'

'Eh? Because I wasn't paying, of course! All my life, until this fucking doctorate, excuse me, *I've paid my way, and more.* But now, it's so shaming, I *can't*: and the lifeboats, you see, I'm a volunteer, and I wouldn't change that for anything – but *I don't get paid.*'

'Luke – come off it – no graduate students get paid! But you're going to *finish* your doctorate: and *everyone* will want to employ you! And, in a year or two, you can pay your mum back, all of it, with interest!'

'Aye. If she lives long enough.'

'Ah. Well. Sorry. Forgive me . . .'

'Aye. It's *bad*. But look – now I've told you . . . I'll tell you *all* about it: because the place I stayed, the place she paid for, well, it was *bound* to make me feel guilty . . . *Because it was the most beautiful cottage in the whole world!*'

'It was?'

'Aye! It was! It really was!' Luke looked at me, full on, such a grin, *such* a set of perfect frontal-upper-jaw white teeth. (So how old was he? Really? Thirty? Thirty-five?) No – *come on* – but all the same – how'd he managed that? Yes, of course, I thought, all

321

his active working life, *of course* – Luke had eaten nothing but the very freshest fish . . .) 'Aye! But there again, right enough,' he said, 'I don't *bullshit* like you! No, nay, never – so maybe it was only *the most magical cottage in the whole of Europe*: aye! And *everything about it*: sweet as a nut!'

'Yes? *Really?* So for Chrissake – *where is it?*'

'OK, OK – I hear you – so I haven't seen cottages in Europe, so I don't know; but I'm *sure* of it, OK? Because you couldn't imagine a better place, however hard you tried! But maybe, Worzel, just maybe, you're so old, and you've been around and you're worn out, old as the Blackstones, the engines, as the boys say, excuse me – so maybe you have seen better cottages in Europe: but I don't believe it! So, I tell you what: how's about this? It is *absolutely the most smashing cottage in the whole of the UK*, the *entire* British Isles! So how's that?'

'Luke, for Chrissake – where the fuck is it?'

Luke – so fired up by the thought of this *cottage*, a mere place (and no, it really did seem that no woman was involved in the memory) – Luke, all black-topped and curly and looking so young said: 'Hannigarth, Uyeasound, Unst, Shetland. Aye – that's all you need to remember: and *anyone*, even you, can go there! You can *hire* this place, rent it! And you *should*, Worzel – because it will change your life!'

'But,' I said, immediately sullen at the thought, despite all the excitement, 'I don't want to change my life! No! Not in the very smallest, not in the tiniest – not in one single fucking harvest-mouse of any particular! No – *I don't.*'

'Worzel!' said Luke, still horribly buoyant and revitalized by the thought of this *dot on a map*. 'Worzel!' And then, from nowhere, with an all-over, genuine, right-through-body laugh (which was almost as wounding as Jason's, and less explicable) he spluttered, through those perfect teeth which, in my opinion, he had no right to own: 'Mr McGregor! His wheelbarrow! A watering-can! Peter Rabbit!'

322

'What the fuck?'

'Eh? *That* – that is' (he imitated my accent) 'to say things like that, old chap, *that is not nice* –'

'Up yours!'

'Aye – but joking apart, and *smashing* jokes too' (Luke was still rocking slightly) 'you *should* go there . . . To Hannigarth. Everyone should . . . Just once in a lifetime . . . And it's easy, so easy . . . The Shetland Tourist Board – *they* know all about it! Although no one else does . . . Mary Ouroussoff, she lives near Gloucester somewhere . . . That's it! Weird, isn't it? Magic – whatever? Something that happens just the once in a man's life . . . Is that right? You'd know! Ach – the point is, *as you'd say*, it was only a cottage, a converted croft: no woman, no romance; no, just a place – *but what a place!* Aye: it's the nearest that you or I will ever get to paradise . . . You know – the bullshit that you *pretend* you don't believe in; and which I *really* don't!'

'Oh, Luke: for Chrissake!'

'There you go! Aye – but it's true.' Luke looked away again, to port, a quick little convulsive movement of the head. 'I've been thinking what I could give you – to thank you, you know, for your companionship on this trip, one of my many trawlers: *but the truth is, I've never had a time quite like this one*, because, I'll be honest, normally it's just a routine number of stations, hauls, whatever you'd call it: a record of depths, of everything that comes aboard, the temperatures from my mini-log on the net . . . all that . . . but I've never had someone else with me before, you know, someone from the outside world, as it were, a companion who's made it all so different and *completely fucked up my head* . . . Jesus! I'll need *to sleep!* But I thought, all the same – maybe, one day, we could have a joint venture to search for the *females* of the Arctic skate; or the *very young* Greenland halibut, the Black butts – and Robbie: I'll bet he's right! Aye – or better still, I thought, we could explore the Rockall Trough – lots of trawlers work there; or the Porcupine Seabight or, best of all, the *Porcupine Abyssal Plain* – and *those* areas,

323

seabed and waters that are only a few hundred metres deeper than here (although, aye! the Porcupine Abyssal Plain *is* a little different, because there, I think, if I remember correctly, the seabed is around four and a half kilometres down): but the point is *this*: those areas, on our doorstep, so to speak, just off our coasts – *those areas are almost totally unknown* . . . So is that *wild* – or what?'

'Wild!'

'Aye, but I can't guarantee any of that, not until I've *finished* my doctorate: if I ever can, or do! So instead I thought I'd tell you about this secret place, Hannigarth! Because you *can* go there, anytime; and you can take your family; your wife; and your children, too! So, you see, I have to pay you in *knowledge*; because I can't do *presents*; because I have no money!'

'Luke! Luke! Don't be silly! Of course you'll find a wife – you really *will* marry a *district nurse* . . . And *yes*, sure as hell you'll have children!' Which didn't sound exactly right; and anyway, I thought – Luke is still facing away; but if he says just *one* more kind word to me like that: well, I've had no sleep, have I? (Or *rather*, said the inner voice – yes, you've had some good sleeps *lately*; but not, of course, the ten-hours-plus you're used to . . .) Luke, I said to myself, *stop it*, please, Luke, *stop it*: because I've had no sleep; and that's *not* my thing; and if you thank me for anything ever again: I'll burst into tears . . . And how would you handle that?

Luke, coming to himself, I supposed, was now staring straight ahead, at the long conveyor whose stainless-steel sides led from the gutting table to the hold (and the top two inches of its port side shone in the horizontal light from the scupper to starboard) . . . 'Hannigarth looks out across sheep-grazings down to the sea, to the great bay in front of you, and there's a *real* Viking cottage down there on the upper shore of the beach: you can still see the walls, and the cow-shaped (it's wide in the middle) entrance to the beast-house. And – I can't describe it, but I tell you, it's all in my head, even now – the headlands, the cliffs away to the right (where there's a *huge* deep raven's nest at the side of a gulley – aye: the ravens have been there for thousands of years, too, it's not just us). And under a grass-overhang on the foreshore you'll find the nest of a Shetland wren; and there's Arctic terns and *their* children on the beach; and as you walk north to the little cemetery where so many drowned seamen have their memorial stones, the adult terns, the parents, they dive-bomb you – *tirrick-tirrick*! And there's a pair of Arctic skuas that breed there, too, and you should see the way *they* fly! Bastards – because they wait sitting on the beach and they watch until they see a plunge-diving tern come up with a sand-eel, you know, and then *pow!* They're off up into the wind – and you should see them! The swept-back wings, the wedge-tails with a pair of feathery pincers out the back . . . So what are *they* for? Aerodynamics, I'll bet. That little extra something that helps you as you come curling down and get right on the tail of an Arctic tern . . . An Arctic tern – the best long-distance flyers in the world . . . The one bird that migrates each year from the Arctic to the Antarctic; and yet those two Arctic skuas, nine times out of ten, as I watched, they outflew the Arctic terns, and the tern dropped its sand-eel into the water and the skua picked it up and glided back to its nest, to feed *its* children!'

'Luke, I'm sorry, but I can see: it's time you started breeding . . .'

'And there are otters down there too of course, and minke and pilot and killer whales – they all come into the bay. But I tell you what worried me: birds, as you know, they're not my thing – I like fish, I really do! But all the same, I got *really* fond of these Red-throated divers – which they call the Rain-goose in Shetland, because they make this cry that sends shivers down your spine – wild! Really wild! And just before it rains! But there again: it's always just-before-it-rains up there – unless it's raining . . . Anyway – you'd know – so *why*, when they've been feeding in the bay down there, why, when they fly back in the evening right over Hannigarth to their children in a nest beside a lochan, why do they call *wack!* on every down-beat of their wings, and *wack!* on every upbeat? Isn't that an insane waste of energy – big time?'

'Search me, Luke – because I've never heard it. But look – are you *sure* that anyone can go to this special place of yours? Eh?'

'Of course! You just *book* it. My mum did it for me – because really, she thought, Unst is almost off the end of the earth . . . So it was obvious: that *had* to be the perfect place for me to start on my doctorate, my thesis – so far from any social life, distractions, dances – because even then the *first* deadline was getting close!'

'So who owns it?'

'I told you – Mary Ourousoff; and they say she's one hell of a character: she's an interior designer, you know, and that's another reason I felt so guilty up there – furthest north, *and yet you're so comfortable*; well, aye: it's *fucking luxury*, excuse me . . . A converted croft, but so well done. Preserved, somehow . . . And her husband, well, I never met either of them, of course; he's a White Russian, I suppose, but he's a *real* inventor, unlike you, you wanker . . .' (Luke, reminded of the offence of it, the camera business, took the big black apparatus off his neck and laid it gently, it has to be said, on the floor in front of him – which was OK, because the floor was now only a little wet and salty and besides, young Luke was my friend . . . And there again: he was offering me this place, Hannigarth – and that was in Shetland, for Chrissake . . .) 'Aye, Mr Ourousoff, they say he's a *real* inventor, not like you; no, he's designed all kinds of things: real *agricultural bits of kit*, apple-pickers, all kinds of new machines . . .'

'Great!'

'Anyway, Hannigarth – it's magic! Pure magic! So *that's* what I'm giving you: the chance to go to this paradise! Aye – and when you get there, you'll meet Dougal, who crofts the land; you'll see his sheep and his collie, of course, she's called Meg, but also his chickens, and the movable hen-house that he made himself; and I only mention the hen-house-on-wheels, you know, because he's *very* proud of it; and, in my opinion, as you'd say, he has every right to be: because, believe me, it's one hell of a piece of carpentry, sweet as a nut!'

'So what happened, Luke? Did you do any work? Any *writing*, I mean?'

'And you'll also meet his wife, Angela, who grew up in Hanni-garth when it really *was* a croft . . . She's come back to Unst; and she brought Dougal with her, from the south, from Scotland. And they've two lovely perky little girls . . . And that's how it goes. I tell you: Unst is *something else*, smashing! So everyone born there tries to get back home, eventually . . . Angela, she teaches physics in the island school . . . But OK – the real point, it's *this*: they're musicians! *Grand musicians!* Dougal plays the guitar; and Angela – she plays the fiddle, the *real* Shetland fiddle, a technique, you know, passed down from generation to generation – and you'll no hear better, and they play together in a band, a group aye, they play at all the dances in the community halls, and they're *so* good: magic! And you wouldn't believe it: the dances! So many nights of dances! The drinking! The friendship! The social life! Right up there on Unst! I tell you, *it wears you out* . . . Smashing! Wild! Aye – so much better than Aberdeen! *And when I got home to Fittie I passed out for a week . . .*'

'Luke!'

'Aye, I know – and *please* don't tell my mum, my folks . . . Still, it *was* some time ago . . . But all the same . . .'

'So, the actual *writing* of the doctorate? As opposed to the fun, the excitement, of lifeboats, of trawlers? Yes, Luke, you're hooked on the adrenalin-rush, that's *your* problem; so – *did you get any writing done?*'

'Aye – I did! So sod you! Excuse me! Yes – I did . . . Three chapters. Well, very short chapters . . . and I did those in no time, in two weeks. Aye – I did those in the two weeks before I got to know Dougal – before he told me about the community halls, the dances! And after that . . . Grand! Big time! And I met all his relatives by marriage; and just about everyone else on the island.

327

But all the same . . . as it happens . . . I don't think I ever saw a district nurse.'

'Of course not. District nurses – *you have to hunt for them.*'

'But for the thesis, you know, to be honest, I really *did* try – when I first got there, ach, with the curlew calling, and Golden plover actually *breeding* all over the place, and I was all alone and there was nothing else to do, so it was *easy*. I moved the smaller of the two kitchen tables under the window of the ground-floor big bedroom. And that looks straight out to this wild sea. And I found exactly the right chair and I got to work.

'But there's a low-walled enclosure immediately outside, once a nursery for young vegetables, I suspect; and in the far left-hand corner of this small enclosure there's an upturned white fibre-glass dinghy. And as you try to concentrate on your work (statistics! I *hate* statistics!) and you look out the window – a baby rabbit will pop out from under this dinghy; he'll check out the world, he'll wiffle his nostrils, you know, and he'll start right in on the serious business of eating grass . . . And you get back to work and do some calculation and write down some boring figure – and then you look up: and there's another baby rabbit, ears flat, peering out from under the upturned boat. Aye! There's a whole family: a doe, a big buck, and *lots* of children . . . And guess what? They're all that smashing soft brown, you know, as rabbits should be – but every last one of them has this little vertical white stripe – a flash! That's it: a flash! – right in the middle of their foreheads, just above their eyes; up a bit and just between their big soft brown eyes . . .

'I tell you, in those two weeks, I got *so* fond of my rabbits . . . And you, Worzel, you'd *love* those rabbits – aye, just right for you, you white-haired old Mr McGregor, you.' (Luke rocked with laughter.) 'Aye! You could push a wheelbarrow about up there! And manhandle a watering-can! But you, *you don't fool me*, you're an old softee, you've lost it – so you could never shoot those rabbits!'

I said: 'Cold iron!' And touched the stanchion to my right.

Luke, the laughter instantly frozen inside him, said: 'Jesus! Aye! What was I thinking?' And 'Cold iron! Cold iron!' (And he touched the stanchion to his right.)

And I said: 'You superstitious git!'

eep-beeeep-beeeeeep went the siren.

'Shite!' said Luke, springing up so violently that he knocked over his seat, the red basket – it was empty. 'Come on! We must clear all this!' With both hands, left, right – one skate, two, up and over to the exit-chute, three skates, four ... And when the skates had frisbee'd away towards the light he began to throw the discarded fish on the gutting table after them. 'Robbie – he'll *kill* me if he comes in and finds his table in a mess like this!' ... Luke could move so *very* fast; whereas I had collected the camera, sure, and put it round my neck, and I was doing well, easing my stiffened back this way and that (Ow! Yes, there's no doubt about it, my back *hurts*; so I must be *old*) and I had very nearly succeeded in the great, present and still almost possible achievement of standing up straight.

'Worzel – come on! What *are* you doing? Quick! We really *do* need to clear this place up before the boys arrive – hey! And what's in *your* basket? The blue basket – is there anything left? Have we missed something? Go on, dumbo, *Mr McGregor* – tip it up!' Luke laughed; yes, I thought, annoyed, Luke's temporarily frozen capacity for laughter has thawed out fast – in fact, I wouldn't be at all surprised if young Uncle Luke is about to pretend that he's never touched cold iron in a little spasm of fear in all his life, no, not *once* . . .

'Go on! Tip it up!'

So I did.

And out came one male Arctic skate and something that looked like a haddock and something else . . .

I said: 'One male Arctic skate and something that looks like a haddock and . . .'

Luke, now scrabbling about, gloves on, in a tray at the far side of the gutting table ('I'm going to have to hose the whole area!'), jumped up on a fish-box and attempted to peer over the table, across the hopper-conveyor and down at my bit of floor – but he wasn't tall enough.

'Aye, McGregor – if it looks like a haddock – guess what? It's a haddock! Ach, I'd forgotten – I *did* keep a haddock, because it came up from deep water, at around 800 metres – and their normal range is from 80 to 200, but it's not that interesting, is it? Not after all the different species we've caught since – so bung it, will you? Just chuck it down the chute. And the skate too . . .'

'But, Luke! There's this *other* thing . . .'

'Oh come on! Bung them!'

So I grasped the big haddock at the base of the tail and slung it towards the chute, the scupper – where it went, sort of, only not quite; so I heard it bounce a bit, just the once or twice, across the floor, towards, I think, the side-wall of the laundry. Encouraged by such damn-near accuracy I took the skate by its right wing, copying the frisbee-master, Luke (although, it has to be said, I'd never actually thrown a frisbee). And, with my right hand, and arm, just like Luke: yes, for the best effect you kind of bend your right arm, at chest-level, way over to your extreme left as far as it will go, which you'll find, surprisingly, is behind your back, roughly in the lower-middle of your left scapula. And then, with all your upper-body strength, you uncurl your hand and wrist and arm and send the frisbee rotating, uplifted, into the air, a flying saucer, its path steady (because it's spinning) and laser-accurate . . . Except that it wasn't quite like that, not really – because the skate, spinning, it's true, *exactly* as it should, clockwise, its tail hard-curled to the right, its undercarriage, its two enormous dicks, bent flat to their right against the wings: it took off, not towards the exit-chute, but in a low curving fly-past over Luke's curly head and, rising still, slapped, hard, against the upper steel-plates beyond the laundry and – a distinct, wet, multiple zappy slosh – it hit the top of the closed bulwark-door to the galley and dropped to the boards. *Wow!* I thought, if *only* that door had been open and young Sean had been in the passage out there, all unsuspecting, and besides, maybe I *should* have taken more interest in sports at school . . .

Luke, upset, said: 'Mr McGregor – that was *not* funny!'

'I didn't mean it to go that way!'

'Och aye. *Of course not.*'

'But Luke! There's something else here!'

'Och aye?'

'Yes.'

'So what is it?'

'Well, search me, Luke, I don't know, how could I? I've no real experience of these things . . . But I'd say the bloke in question was *big*, way over six feet, maybe nearer seven . . .'

'Eh?'

'Yes. Because it looks to me . . .' (I took a closer look) '. . . Yes. *Certainly*. A bit has fallen off a drowned sailor. In fact, Luke – it seems to have got clean away.'

'What has?'

'No. That's fine. *That's fine by me.* I don't care. I can take it. If you're not interested – if you'd rather wash the dishes over there, be a new man, all that, well – I'm a tolerant sort of a guy, so that's fine by me.'

'You what?'

'No – don't bother. Why *should* you be interested? It's just that

I'm not used to this kind of thing . . . But after *all* I've seen on this trawler . . . OK: I am now quite prepared to accept that *this probably happens all the time . . .'*

Luke, reluctantly, pausing to scrape off fish-scales from the trays as he came, began to make his way towards me round the table. 'What does? For fuck's sake?' (And not even an *excuse me* . . .)

'*This* does – look! Look at this! On the floor here! It's *obvious*: some poor big drowned bloke – he's lost his penis. *It's taken itself off* – it's broken free; and now it's doing *exactly* what it wanted to do all along; so, naturally, it's got just a little excited; in fact, it's semi-erect, right on the floor here, *right in front of me*; but it's still *remarkably* bendy and Luke – it's squirming about the place . . .'

Luke, interested at last, vaulted over the hopper-conveyor, and took a look. 'Jesus! You silly bastard! You *silly* bastard! It's a hagfish!'

'OK – fine – if that's your pet name for it. Not bad. But I have a friend who calls his *moldeewarp* and that's Anglo-Saxon for a mole, because it will only come to life in the dark, in a tunnel.'

'*It's a hagfish!*'

'Sure – suppose it is: not bad, not bad at all! Because it's not so young or pretty any more, is it? It's old, obviously; and at that age it's *learnt*, hasn't it? Yes – it's learnt – you must only search for an *appropriate* mate; and for this one here that means a truly lovely cuddly old hag . . .'

Luke lost his cool. Right at me he shouted: '*Myxine glutinosa!*' And, in case I hadn't heard: '*Myxine glutinosa!*' He flicked his short supple body down and picked the thing up. 'And stop it, Worzel! My head! *Stop pissing me about!*'

'OK,' I said, extraordinarily calm. '*So don't call me Mister McGregor.*'

'Worzel – *you're a schoolboy!* How could the things we're called, names, labels, whatever – how could any of that possibly matter when you look at *this*?' He held the hagfish six inches in front of my face. So (as short-sighted as Mr McGregor) I took off my glasses and grasped them by the right ear-piece between my teeth (a salty taste). He said: 'The very oldest, the most interesting fish in the sea!'

Light brown, a foot long, three-quarters of an inch thick, muscular, cylindrical, it appeared to have no fins – unless that narrow keel of wrinkled flesh snaking down the centre of its underside and vertically folded into hundreds of little flaps – unless *that* was a fin? And what *were* those white pimples – two lines of them, one to either side of the fin, the central fringe of flesh? There were two regular rows of tiny white raised roundels – as if the animal had been double-slashed with a razor all the way along the underneath of its bendy shaft of a body, and the twin slits stitched, and it now bore the scars: the entry and exit holes of a fine needle . . .

'Luke – I've never seen anything like it!'

'Of course not! It's a hagfish!' He waggled it; he curved it about in front of my face; and I thought: OK, so that's OK, because it *must* be dead – or it would *bite him*. And come to that: where *is* its mouth?

'Where's its mouth?'

'Here!' said Luke, pinching the hagfish behind the head with the thumb and index finger of his right-hand – as you would hold a dangerous snake. 'Here!' He rotated the head, underside-up: set back between a pair of downward-and-backward-pointing tusks, like those on a walrus, was a tight-shut puckered hole, flanked, on either side, by two nasty-looking swellings.

'Don't be silly! That's its *anus* – and it's got a couple of nasty eruptive haemorrhoids . . .'

'It's the *mouth*, you hinny!'

'Hinny?'

'Aye, dumbo!' said Luke, inserting the tip of the little finger of his left hand into the upturned mouth that was obviously an anus: 'A hinny – the offspring of a female donkey and a male horse: *that's* you! Because look, feel *this*: stick your finger in here – is that *sharp* or what?'

'Sharp!' (As sharp, to either side, as the edge on the little special wooden-handled gutting-knife.) 'OK, so you win! But tell me – which end are its eyes?' (Removing my little finger, resolving never to let a mouth like that anywhere near me ever again, I flicked a tuft of four small horns on its head.) 'And what are these?'

'Barbels, feelers. And its eyes, as we say, are much reduced – in fact, as far as we know, they're not functional.'

Luke (still holding the hagfish in his right hand) restored the blue basket to its usual place, but bottom-up; and he sat on it.

So, with the red basket, I followed suit, and there we were again, two old men on a park bench – except that now, it seemed to me, there was nothing peaceful about either of us: because, well, there *is* nothing restful about the presence or the thought of a hagfish . . .

'And you wouldn't really *want* functional eyes – but there again, its sense of *smell* is *so* acute, *how it can smell things out! –* and maybe you wouldn't want that either, maybe you wouldn't want sight *or* smell?'

'Eh? Why not? We *all* want sight and smell.'

'Maybe,' said Luke, reflective on his basket. 'But maybe, just maybe, even *you* wouldn't want to see and smell *too* well – *not when you're forcing your way head-first up the arse of some poor drowned sailor.* What do you think? Ach – and you'll be chewing and cutting and rasping, with your primitive horny teeth, teeth on your tongue and palate. And that *must* be an effort, because you're such a survivor, such a very ancient form of a fish that you have no jaws – you haven't even evolved a pair of jaws! But you're rasping, you're eating your way, as fast as you can (because there's competition, there's always competition, because hagfish *swarm*), you're racing to get to that paradise for hagfish, a liver, anyone's liver.

'But Jesus, Redmond, what am I saying? It's true, that *does* happen to a drowned corpse – and the amphipods, like fat shrimps, thousands of them, they pick you clean from the outside . . . but really they scavenge dead fish and crustacea on the seafloor, they live in burrows in the mud and they come out and scavenge – so why are we talking about my mates, trawlermen? It's *your* influence,

335

aye, I've got crude, I've been infected, I've got really *crude*, just like you . . .'

'Oh thanks, Luke, thanks a lot for that – but what are these?' I said, running a finger-nail down the row of spots on its flank. 'Decoration?'

'Some decoration! No – you wouldn't want to do that if this was alive and in the water! *Really not* – and if you did you'd be in trouble big time! Aye! Big style! *Big trouble!*'

'Wow!'

'Aye – it's *so* complex for such a primitive animal, but sweet and perfect, sweet as a nut! You, say you're a predator, a shark, and you see this hagfish, a mouthful: it doesn't even have the first-line defence, scales. So in you go! But that's a mistake, a bad mistake! Because these spots, as you call them – there'll be around 150 in all – they're pores, glands. This hagfish, just like that – *zap!*' (He tossed his head.) '*Zap!* And it's produced *five gallons* of slime . . . mucus – and this mucus is *disgusting*, sure, but worse than that, it's *deadly*. You, the shark, have this truly horrible stuff, five gallons of it, all round your head – so you shake your head, and lash about, and then you start to panic, you struggle to get it off, to get free, but it's in your mouth and eyes and gills and the harder you struggle the tighter it closes in; you die by strangling, suffocation.'

'Jesus!' I said, backing off a bit.

'There's a great guy, working for his doctorate – aye! – at the University of British Columbia in Vancouver, much younger than me, and he keeps lots of pet hagfish and he milks them. Douglas Fudge. Smashing! He's only in the second year of his thesis and yet he's worked it all out – the pores hold tiny packets of dry mucins, and fibres coiled up in thread cells.

'You threaten a hagfish – it squeezes all its glands at once; five grams of slime-powder and dry thread hit the sea; and they hydrate, they swell faster than any other substance we know. And sure, you'll say – you've strangled your big shark, more or less instantly, but now you're in trouble yourself, aren't you? You're going to suffocate in your own slime . . . Well, no, because you have another talent (and as far as I'm aware you're the only animal on earth that can do this). Feeling unwashed? Bothered by your own coat of slime? (As we all are, at times.) OK – you tie yourself in a knot and squirm the knot tight down your body and wipe yourself clean. But your enemies, your predators, the people out there who really bug you – not one of *them* can do that . . .'

'I should hope not!'

'Aye! So they get strangled!'

'But Luke – all that sounds very highly evolved, doesn't it? And yet you said they were *the oldest fish in the sea*; and I admit, they certainly *look* like it, but what did you mean?'

'Not much! Only that their family tree has no branches . . . but *tree*: that's no good at all! Not as an image! Family *tree* – pathetic! *That*'s one reason why people don't realize the age, the *stretch* of time that life's had in the oceans . . . This hagfish that I'm holding – this *real piece of life* – its family line is unbranched; it's straight; it goes *directly* back to its fossil ancestors, the first jawless fishes – and *their* fossils, the impressions of *their* bodies, their record begins in rocks that we can date as 510 million years old. So – in the ocean – you can hardly talk about family *trees*, can you? And besides, the very first signs of the tiniest scraggiest vegetation only appeared on the *land* 425 million years ago. And the life in your jungles, as compared to the life in my oceans – forget it! Your jungles began *yesterday* . . . no, it's the sea that's old!'

'Great!'

'But hey! Worzel! What's that? That noise!'

We listened. Yes – Luke, who still had ears that worked, was right: even I could hear it: a succession of high-energy, manic, heavy hammer-blows; a sound that seemed to be reaching us from above the stern-ramp, at the end of the net-room; a series of fast deep blows from the stern of the working-deck that carried all the way down and forward and through the open bulwark-door to our fish-room to make the peaceful air around our baskets, our old men's talk, everything good about life: yes, to make it all jagged and ripped apart . . .

'Oh God!' shouted Luke, dropping the hagfish to the floor, jumping up. 'No wonder the haul's taken so long! No wonder there's sod all coming down the hopper . . . Aye! Come on! Quick!' Luke vaulted the hopper-conveyor (and I climbed over, trying to keep up). 'Aye! There's something very wrong up there! A disaster! I've heard that only once before in all my years at sea!' We were already in the passage past the galley. 'The trawl-doors! The trawl-doors are *locked*!'

Up on deck (the great circle of sea and sky; the kittiwakes; the Glaucous gulls; all of them unconcerned) – up on deck (the light so pure and thin and clear) everyone except Dougie stood at the stern-rail, Bryan at the power-block controls, the crisis obviously over, something resolved.

As we joined them, Robbie said: 'Jason here – he was out of that wheelhouse door like a fockin' ghost!'

And Jason, not at all his usual confident self, shaken, almost pale, said: 'That's it, Redmond! Finish! And no – don't blame yourself, you did *not* bring us bad luck. The doors flipped right over each other. They *locked*, as we call it. They locked well beneath the thermocline, at around a kilometre down. It's nobody's fault. No – you must understand – the contrary current, the really deep southerly flowing current in the Norwegian basin, the ice-melt from the Arctic, that can be *fierce*. It can be calm like this up here, perfect. And yet wild, fast, rough as hell down there. And you never know. So don't blame yourself, it's not really a matter of *luck*, all that bullshit. And besides, the catch, it's not good, but it's not *that* bad: because we've got 883 boxes of redfish and 249 of Black butts – and Bryan, what else?'

Bryan, in his opera-bass, half-sang: 'One hundred and sixty-one of Argies; four boxes of Blue ling; one box of Grenadiers!'

And *wow!* I thought, *how it all matters*: at every stage they know how many boxes . . .

338

'There you go!' said Jason, cheering himself up. 'Perhaps 75 grand, if we're lucky – but we'll have a sweepstake on it!'

Allan and Jerry disappeared down the port ladder to the net-deck, on their way, I supposed, to the galley. Sean, a few yards from us, was standing holding the rail, uncharacteristically silent, preoccupied, and he seemed to be gazing astern (at what?).

Robbie, looking very small and Pictish beside tall Jason, said: 'Aye, the skipper here' (an upwards nod), 'he saved the warps and the doors right enough – but there's one peedie problem, Redmond, the fockin' net: it's ripped to bits.' In his right hand Robbie already held a yellow plastic net-mending needle (which is not really a needle as we know it: because it's one inch wide, ten inches long, and, in addition, it is loaded with cord in a complex fashion known only to trawlermen). For emphasis, Robbie waved the needle about: 'And guess who?' (A flick towards the vast expanse of the clear Arctic sky . . .) 'Guess who will have to mend it, right enough?' (A flick towards the deck, as if the net was already in position.) 'Robbie!' (Tapping his chest.) '*That*'s who! Aye! It's me that'll have to fockin' mend it, all the way home . . .'

Sean caught the magic word and, in his yellow oilskin trousers, his red oilskin jacket, he spun round, his face squashed up with his very biggest lop-sided grin, and he danced about, where he was, a jig, yes, it was a jig, and he sang a little chant all of his own: 'Home! Home! Home! I'm going to see my nan!'